THE ANCIENT SCIENCE OF

MANTRAS

THE ANCIENT SCIENCE OF MANTRAS

Wisdom of the sages

OM SWAMI

Published in India by Jaico Publishing House

Worldwide publishing rights: Black Lotus Press

ISBN: 978-93-86348-71-5

www.omswami.com

Om Sri Matre Namah

saṃkalpo vāva manaso bhūyānyadā vai saṃkalpatate'tha manasyatyathaṃ vācamīrayati tāmu nāmnīrayati nāmni mantrā ekaṃ bhavanti mantreṣu karmāṇi.

Will is greater than the Mind. For when wills, one reflects, then he utters Speech, then he utters it in Name. In the Name mantras become one; and in the mantras, the sacrifices become one. (Chandogya Upanishad. 7.4.1)

Contents

PREFACE

Words can turn our world upside down. They can build it or raze it to the ground.

Everything we do and feel in our lives is dependent on the maze of words that constantly surrounds us. Words of encouragement, when spoken to a child, at the right time, can be a lifelong inspiration, propelling her to be a better individual as she grows older. Some words of recognition uttered to a fellow worker can instill confidence in him and prod him to go the extra mile. At the same time, the damage done by unkind words filled with animosity can haunt you for a lifetime. Hurtful words can destroy a lifelong relationship within moments as if nothing had ever existed between two people.

Forget about spoken words, even our own thoughts, when they play as conversations in our heads, completely change the way we feel about ourselves and others. Our mind is under a constant siege of words, both positive and negative. The compelling hold of words, their immense potential, ability to influence our lives, were not lost to the seekers of truth. The sages of yore recognized the hidden power held in the nucleus of a word. The birth of the ancient science of mantras was no accident.

For, it recognized our intricate connection with words. They are our link to the world within and without. It's the energy of the sound that bonds us, with the universal energy around us. Every living entity responds to words spoken with love.

Even when you call out to a dog with love, it knows and it wags its tail. When you scold in anger, it cowers in fear.

The universe too is a body, a living body, made up of billions of entities. Each planet is a cell in the universal body. However tiny it may be, every entity matters, for if you start to take away one grain at a time from a heap of sand, one day it will cease to be the heap. The presence of a grain is the existence of the heap.

In other words, the energy of the mantras is aimed at calling upon the universal energy, a way of drawing its attention towards us. Mantra yoga is a path to strengthen your bond with the universal energy around you, so you may realize your own potential and use the kinetic energy latent in you that can be used for creative pursuits designed to attain the highest goal.

The science of mantra believes that if you can use the right words to train your mind, to sharpen its focus and to channelize the divinity in the universe, you can rise above every negative tendency that holds you back and go past the shackles of your limited conscious mind. You can cut through life's myriad problems like how a sharp sword cuts through grass. Above all, you can attain liberation, moksha, nirvana.

INTRODUCTION

In the past, I've always shied away from speaking much on the science of mantras. Mostly because awakening a mantra is a very personal affair. Invoking a mantra to attain a desirable outcome is entirely dependent on the training, mindset and calibre of the adept. No doubt that mantra yoga is a scientific framework comprising of methods, techniques and immense benefits operating on a cause-and-effect principle, much of that, however, depends on the temperament, determination and quality of the practitioner honing it into an art as well.

Like any other stream of science, like any other art, the sonic science of mantras, too, can be examined, explored, practiced and mastered. Its precise methods and promised rewards have reassured me repeatedly over the last two and a half decades.

I have met seekers from all walks of life who are willing to put in the effort to benefit from what is arguably the most ancient science in the world.

The first question they ask me is whether a guru is necessary, if yes, where to find a good guru. The answer is, yes, it's absolutely critical to have a preceptor guide you and, there's no set way of finding a good guru. Having said that, the absence of a guru does not mean that you can't succeed on this path. Ultimately, individual effort is the key. While *diksha* (initiation) makes it easy and it can be transformational, it is not a substitute for individual practice.

I've written this book for serious aspirants based on the assumption that you don't have a guru who can impart to you the knowledge and secrets of invoking and awakening a mantra and the benefits you can expect from its correct practice. By following the steps enumerated for various sadhanas in this book, you can awaken your inner guru, The Guru.

This text alone will act as your guide in the absence of an enlightened master. If you patiently build a strong theoretical foundation as explained in this book and diligently follow the process, you will succeed —with or without a guru. Even if you have nothing else but this book, an intense longing, unrelenting discipline and time to pour into your *sadhana* (spiritual practice), you will unlock a whole new world of consciousness and mystical excellence. It's like going from a GPRS/Edge mobile data network to a much faster 4G network. You don't see any changes in the sky, but suddenly you can tap into a frequency offering you much higher bandwidth and speed. Prolonged and sincere practice of mantras offers you that spiritual upgrade from a draggy GPRS to a complete 4G network. It's like setting up your personal cellular network, complete with your own satellites hovering in the space.

The most ancient tradition of mantra yoga has been passed on orally from a guru to a disciple. It's been forbidden to publicly expound on this science. For, we don't know to what purpose the recipient may use it. It's like selling nuclear weapons without knowing who's buying them and for what. I've broken away from the norm and bared all the essentials and fundamentals of the super science of mantras in this book.

You need to know why I've taken this risk after sitting on it for years. Firstly, even though I've compared the power of mantras to a nuclear weapon, the truth is that besides an intense effort, it takes certain inner purity and strength, to invoke a mantra. Someone with malefic intentions can't benefit from mantras in the long term, let alone use them to harm others. In other words, a spiritual terrorist can't reap the rewards of mantra science. Secondly, this powerful and ancient system of knowledge is fast disappearing. I hope this book inspires at least a handful to take it up again and use it for their own as well as the world's welfare.

Like one sun is enough to support billions of life-forms, one *mantrin* (an adept in the science of mantras) is enough to cause ripples in the universal consciousness. I know this is a tall claim, but then again, I hope, your own experimentation with mantras will lead you to a similar conclusion. Thirdly, good gurus are extremely rare. They don't appear on TV, they don't get caught up in building infrastructure or a following and you can't lure them with anything – other than extraordinary devotion maybe. More importantly, they may not even possess the right knowledge to guide you. Not every guru is an expert meditator or a specialist of mantra and tantra or yoga. Some are just great human beings doing a lot of selfless work for the society. Some are intellectual powerhouses. Some are protectors of sects and custodians of religions. With this work, I've tried to remove the dependency on human gurus. If you are serious and sincere, everything is in here to get you started and guide you right through to the end.

Books on mantras have been written before this one and will be scripted after this one. I can't say with certainty how much in those books is the truth. I'm not sure what qualifications those writers possessed, whether they were adepts, exalted souls or mere theoreticians. They must have had noble intentions, I presume, to put in the effort. At the end of the day though, it's immaterial what all's been written or whether that holds true in this day and age, too. But I can promise you one thing: I've written this book based on my truth. It's founded on years of practical knowledge and insight, painstakingly gained through my continuous and tiring practice and play with the sonic science of mantras.

The *sadhanas* (spiritual practices) I share in this book have been personally validated by me. They worked for me when I fulfilled the conditions required for each *sadhana* and followed the scriptural injunctions. Will they work for you too? You must find out for yourself. I can only say that if you do what I did with the mindset that I possessed, you'll get what I got. And what exactly did I get, you ask? In brief: plenty of wealth–material and spiritual, a lot of positivity, the courage to walk the path of truth and above all, immense peace and bliss.

Lastly, I've written the kind of book I wish I could have drawn upon when I first started experimenting with mantras roughly 26 years ago. I hope you benefit from this work and pass on the rich rewards of its practice to the rest of the world.

WHO IS THIS BOOK FOR?

This book isn't for everyone. Before we get on with what all mantras can do and how to go about awakening a mantra, I feel it's critical, and my duty, to make it clear who may not benefit from this book. This way, you won't waste your time and resources on an unrewarding pursuit.

It's no secret today that you can use the power of sound to heal yourself and others. There's enough data and research to show how music and musical training can alter the physical structure of our brain, even an adult's fully-formed brain. Certain sounds can make us cry, make us laugh, melt us or evoke other inexplicable emotions. I haven't written this book to cover those aspects of sound, though.

The book you hold in your hands expounds on the ancient and traditional path of mantra yoga. The spiritual basis of this book is different from its scientific basis. On the path of mantra yoga, faith and devotion, in the deity of the mantra, plays a vital role. In fact, it's the key to awakening the mantra.

Do you believe that God exists? And do you believe that God can have a form? If you don't believe that God exists or that He (or She) can have a form, let me tell you at the outset that mantra yoga is not for you. You will not stand to gain much by walking the path of mantra yoga or by reading this book.

Simply using some sound in your meditation does not mean

that you are practicing mantra yoga. If you don't believe that the guardian deity of a mantra can protect you or help you on the journey of your life, if you feel that tapping into universal energy to expand your consciousness has no reasonable basis, then this book is not for you. If you wish to just meditate on a sound like "Om" or any other sound, you are unlikely to benefit by the chanting of the mantra. You will gain a lot more by mastering the art of meditation in that case.

Mantra *sadhana* places great emphasis on adhering to the framework of mantra yoga. And that invariably entails faith in your god, guru, mantra, lineage and initiation. These are not mere words or titles but the keepers and champions of a time-worn tradition.

This is a book for believers and for those who wish to benefit from the power of the mystical hymns and syllables written in the most ancient language of our world —Sanskrit. Every word in Sanskrit can be sung and assigned to a rhythm. Every Vedic scripture is in fact a poem and Ved Vyasa, the first practicioner of kundalini on earth, the great sage who compiled many texts, including the division of the four primary Vedas, was called the greatest poet of Sanatana Dharma (commonly known as the Hindu religion). You just have to read some scriptures of the Sanatana Dharma to get a glimpse of how ancient and advanced this knowledge is.

I reiterate: if you don't believe in Vedic scriptures and similar other exegetical texts, you will not benefit from this book. A *sadhaka* (aspirant) on the path of mantra yoga cannot succeed without reverence and devotion. This has been my unfailing experience, too. Real devotion makes you humble, it melts you, transforms you.

If you have longed to be one with God by chanting the holy names, or if you have wondered about the ancient science of mantras, but couldn't find a guru to guide you, you have the right book in your hands. By the time you finish reading this book, you'll know all there is to know about mantra yoga — certainly enough to get you started.

BOOK ONE

THE FOUNDATION

MANTRA YOGA

- The Origin of Mantras
- What is Mantra Sadhana?
- Do Mantras Work?
- Four Aspects of Mantra Sadhana

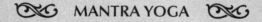

THE ORIGIN OF MANTRAS

It might seem far-fetched and may even challenge human intelligence but there are indeed more than two billion earth-like planets with life-forms in our universe. Many earths have existed and perished before our planet even came into existence a few billion years ago and many will be razed to dust in times to come.

Shiva had just returned to Devi, from his abode, Kailasha, after an intense meditation and solitude lasting eighty thousand human years. The Mahayogi had never taken anyone to Kailasha at the time, not even Devi. Even the tiniest interference in his meditation could send ripples in the cosmic consciousness causing chaos in the entire creation.

Two billion light years away from Shiva's Kailasha, and three hundred trillion years ago, on a beautiful planet abound with tall trees, dense forests inhabited by two, four and eight-legged creatures, there lived Devi, the empress, with her eternal consort Shiva. All life-forms lived in perfect harmony for their brains were wired differently. The gravitational force of the planet was less than one-tenth of our current one. As a result, feelings of happiness lasted ten times longer. Less food gave them sufficient nutrition and satisfaction. The concept of money did not exist. There was no trade nor bargain. There was no need for all that, as they could manifest whatever they so desired. Seasons came and went on time. Light was the primary vehicle of travel.

The element of fire did not exist back then. There was heat from their sun, there was light, but no fire to disrupt the inner or outer harmony.

Chintamani griha, the palace of Devi, was unlike anything else in the whole of creation, a glimpse of glory of the empress. Magnificent arched roofs carved most exquisitely rested on pillars that ran a few hundred feet high. Those pillars, studded with rare jewels, gems and stones, would reflect light from the sun to light up the entire palace. Towards sunset, which occurred once every seventy-two hours, the light would dim automatically. Some gems would retain light and some heat which was exuded softly throughout the night which also lasted seventy-two hours.

The mellifluous sounds of Devi's anklets, the tinkling of her bangles could be heard at her slightest movement. Duality of light and dark, sound and silence, hot and cold added to the color of life and its beauty. Such duality was external phenomena though. In the minds of its inhabitants, there was no notion of sadness, jealousy, possessiveness or envy. Even for Shiva, it was a welcome change from the austere environment of Kailasha where he would be tired from intense meditation.

Here, Nityas, companion energies of the Devi, prepared the finest food, fragrant and divine, well transcending the six tastes known to humans today. Gandharvas sang most beautiful ragas and played instruments imperceptible in today's world. One of Shiva's favorite was a large drum the size of a big lake. One beat at the edge of that drum would produce drone, a bass ripple, for the next eight hours.

Today at Shiva's arrival, there was much joy, excitement and bliss in the air. Devi washed Shiva's feet, Nityas bathed him, yoginis anointed him with the rarest unguents, yakshinis prepared the fragrant pool of water where Shiva sported and Devi pressed his tired limbs. Nothing about Shiva's smile, his shapely yogic body and his intoxicating voice gave away the austerities he had practiced in the last eighty thousand years.

One million years passed in great bliss at *Chintamani griha.*

"I must leave for Kailasha," Shiva said to Devi one night, soon after an evening of bliss and union, of celestial music and festivities. The long drapes of their palatial room were swaying with the gentle breeze. Various stones in pillars were emitting soft light in different colors.

"Why, Lord?" she murmured. "Your creation is so beautiful. Everything is perfect. Forgive me for asking, but why do you go to Kailasha?"

Shiva laughed at Devi's innocence. "To carry out my task of transformation, which some call destruction, I go to Kailasha to sit in one-pointed concentration. This is not the only planet in the creation, Bhadre." He took her outside and said, pointing to the dazzling vast universe, "See all those stars. Some of those planets have life-forms just like ours and on many of them people don't have an empress like you. They are not graced with my physical energy for so long. Some have a different composition and their elements are different, giving birth to various kinds of life-forms. As a result, there's more grief and suffering on those planets.

"I understand grief," Devi said. "I experience it every time you leave for your solitude. But, what is suffering?"

"When due to ignorance, you can't get over your grief, your sorrow," Shiva said, "it is suffering."

Devi struggled to understand the concept of suffering, she was *sumangali* and *sukhakari*, an embodiment of auspiciousness and happiness. Above all, she was *nitya-yauvana*, eternally youthful, well endowed, the splendid empress who lived in perfect harmony and had no insecurities. No doubt, her heart would sink every time Shiva left for Kailasha but it would last less than a fraction of a moment in that flawless creation and she could feel Shiva still always a part of her.

"Can I *see* suffering?" Devi asked innocently.

"Suffering can only be experienced. You can see people who are sad, unhappy, but you may not experience suffering, for suffering is individual karma."

"What is sadness and unhappiness, Nath? I want to see those too."

The wind stopped blowing, the twinkling stones turned grey and stopped emitting light.

"Oh Bhadre," Shiva lamented losing his equanimity for a moment. "What have you just said? In my presence, you expressed a desire that is going to have eternal repercussions." Shiva looked at a far-off point in the universe. He was suddenly withdrawn and introspective.

Unaware of the feelings of fear or grief, Devi did not understand what the Mahayogi meant. But, Shiva knew what was coming ahead, and that the creation had to enter into the second stage. A stage where Devi in the form of energy, or movement, would play an integral role in creation, sustenance and destruction. The Mahayogi agreed to take Devi on an excursion where she could see other life-forms ailing from various emotions and afflictions, so she could *see* suffering.

Holding her delicate, pink hand in his slender and fair one, Shiva took her across many universes. In a journey that lasted ten thousand human years, Devi saw people quarreling, fighting, diseased, dying, stressed, killing themselves and others, crying and wailing. She saw the whole gamut of sorrows, emotions, their karma but she still didn't understand why they were at unrest, or what suffering was.

"You'll have to be a part of their world, that creation, Devi," Shiva reasoned, "to understand their plight."

"I'm ready to do anything, Mahadev," She said, "for, I wish to know why you have to spend time in solitude where there's no one to take care of you."

"You will be my witness at the time of my first act of complete annihilation and subsequently be born to Daksha Prajapati in a creation that will be made up of five elements, to experience suffering, separation and sadness," Shiva declared.

Devi still unbeknownst to the feeling of sadness or anxiety, didn't know what it meant. What she did know, though, was that Shiva never spoke carelessly. And that in due course, it would all unfold.

For the first time, three hundred and eleven trillion years ago to be precise, he took his consort to Kailasha. Twenty eight times more he would take her there, but this was the first time ever.

Shiva plunged in deep dhyana on Kailasha while Devi watched him patiently with contentment. She had not known the feelings of lack, discontent or aggression. She did not miss the comforts of *Chintamani griha*. The snowy mountains or the icy cave meant nothing. Like the blowing wind is not careworn about its destination, like rain that falls cares not where it lands, Devi just existed in the present moment. Moment by moment, six hundred thousand years passed at the end of which, Shiva rose from his seat.

"The time has come, Varanane," he spoke somberly.

Devi saw a slight but momentary smile on Shiva's pink lips. In his all-knowing long eyes, she saw a blinding flash and then utter darkness before they returned to being normal. His forehead showed a hue of soft red. The sun dimmed as if shrunk and in the middle of the day, it became twilight. For the first time, she experienced an unknown feeling in her heart. She could not express it but it was anxiety, a sort of paranoia. Of what, she knew not at this stage.

"I can't explain, Nath," she said, "but I'm feeling something I've never felt before."

Without answering, Shiva held her in his yogi's arms. Billions of new planets were birthed in that moment of embrace. Devi's anxiety didn't die down though.

"You are about to see what no one has ever seen before, O Devi," he spoke solemnly. "And you'll be the only one to see it every time, once every eleven trillion years that I do this. Till now, you've been my own creation. Now, you'll merge in me. Bound by dharma, henceforth, you'll be born separately and will have to win me back every time. Some elements will re-manifest and some new will form in the new creation. I'll create the element of fire. You'll need it to end your life in a future incarnation. Many worlds will need it for sustenance."

Devi felt a churning in her stomach. She broke out in sweat.

Her heart raced. She had never experienced or known any of these emotions ever before.

"What is happening, Lord?" she asked with trembling lips. It was fear she felt but she knew not what it was.

Shiva, the detached yogi, separated her from the embrace and touched Devi on her radiant forehead granting her divine vision to behold his real form. The Mahakala undid his damaru tied to the trident. In two giant strides, he stood far away from Devi, fifteen light years away. Devi felt as if Shiva was still close.

Dimi-dimi-dum-dum-tadik-dimi-dimi-tadik-dum-dum, he began playing his damaru at a slow tempo. With every strike, at a great distance, Devi would hear sounds of rumbling, roaring and loud explosions. These were not the gurgling skies, thunders or lightening, she knew. These explosions were crumbling planets like one kicks at a sand castle. Before any of the life-forms could take shelter, the planets were shrinking and disappearing like bursting balloons.

Shiva's body began to expand beyond proportions anyone could fathom. Countless planets went right into his growing form as he continued to grow. He became the Universal body. Trillions of planets settled on his body like pollen in a valley of flowers. Devi trembled. She had no knowledge that her *tapasvin* Shiva was not just *Maharetas*, the greatest seed, but the universe itself. The damaru was playing at a faster pace now. Many planets with all their life-forms, oceans, rivers and trees, were being sucked right into him. She saw her own planet along with her palace, nityas, yoginis and yakshinis merging into Shiva. One million human years passed and there was no end to Shiva's *vistara*, expansion or his *samhara*, dissolution. Raising his right hand up in the air, vigorously playing damaru, he lifted his left leg.

Shiva, the Nataraja, was performing his cosmic dance, *Mahatandava*.

Devi found herself being pulled towards Shiva's gigantic form. She was no more than the size of a grain of sand in front of the Mount Everest. Before she knew it, she merged right into Shiva.

From Shiva's body, she saw the dissolution of the entire universe that went on for four million years more. Shiva stayed in his form of Nataraja, the sovereign dancer, the universal body for ages. Over the next few million human years, countless planets released from his body like arrows from a bow. Transformed, new planets. Creation was taking place again. All this while, Devi lived in Shiva bearing witness to what all had transpired.

maheśvara-mahākalpa-mahātāṇḍava-sākṣiṇī

Devi, Shiva's own feminine and kinetic aspect was the only witness of *mahatandava*. For, sound is kinetic energy. Sound cannot be static. The vigorous play of *damaru* created many sounds that lay scattered in the universe for eons. Seventy million different sounds manifested that covered the entire spectrum of all mantras to be ever created.

At the end of the first cycle of dissolution, the new creation took sixteen billion years before the first lifeform appeared. At the end of nearly eleven trillion years from Shiva's Mahatandava, earth was created in the universe. This was when Devi was born to Daksha Prajapati and Queen Prasuti and married Shiva, she remembered what all she had been through and how long she had waited.

Born from the union of Daksha and Prasuti, made up of the five elements of earth, water, fire, air and ether, Devi was now well aware of suffering, sadness, sorrow and all the other emotions.

"O Virupaksha, the ruler of all energies," Devi humbly addressed Shiva, recalling the time when all she knew was bliss in her abode, "when I lived in *Chintamani griha*, I did not know jealousy, envy or any of the negative emotions. I did not know what was suffering. But now I do, and it is very painful."

Shiva kept his yogic gaze fixed and lowered it a bit more to indicate that Devi could continue talking, his gentle smile on his chiseled face as if carved by the perfect sculptor.

"I have you," she continued. "I see you and I only feel bliss. But, what about the rest of the creation? I saw infinite planets shooting out of you and billions of such planets have life-forms. Why do they have to go through suffering?"

"The various elements are in play, Gaure," The Mahayogi spoke like rainclouds gathering in the sky. "There's no suffering, only ignorance. What people call suffering is merely their perspective born out of ignorance."

"It may well be, Nath, but it's extremely painful. It makes everything feel worthless. It causes fear and anxiety. People don't know they are ignorant. What can they do?"

"They must remain connected to the source, the universal energy," Shiva replied. "For, the source has all the wisdom anyone ever seeks."

"And, how can they do that?"

"The easiest would be to pick any sound my damaru created. Everything in its current form originated from those sounds."

"But, no one heard it other than me," Devi contended. "I was too spellbound watching the cosmic dance of dissolution and there's no way I can ever recall all the sounds your damaru made."

"You'll have to wait till the next tandava then," Shiva said playfully.

"O Mahadeva," Devi said clasping Shiva's feet, "never in a million years do I ever wish to see the tandava again. It created primal fear in me."

"That was the Mahatandava, Varanane," Shiva corrected. "I do that at mahapralaya, the great dissolution. The Tandava, I do out of love."

Devi's eyes lit up. "When will you do that, Lord?"

On his abode, next to the beautiful lake, surrounded by complete silence, outside his cave where Shiva's trident was plonked, he untied his damaru. Devi felt no fear. Shiva was *saumya*, pleasant and *shanta*, calm.

Out of compassion for all living beings across the universes, Bholenath, merrily raised his damaru and began playing it. As he danced to its heady rhythm, millions of sounds spread in the sky like stars in space. Every time the string of the damaru swooshed through the air, it created a sound. Many other sounds of different frequencies were produced when the beads at the end of the string would strike the damaru heads. Shiva's moving hands and feet, they all created sounds. His swaying matted locks, the sound of rudraksha beads around his wrists, the slithering cobra around his neck ... every movement gave birth to a sound. And each sound was a mantra representing the feminine, masculine or neutral aspect of creation. From his kundala, ear-loops, originated the seed syllables of kundalini.

The sages of yore meditating on *nirguana-brahma*, the formless, were quick to perceive these sounds. It is why, on the path of mantra yoga, Shiva is the only creator of mantras. All the sages are merely the seers. They did not create or discover mantras, much less invent them. They only saw what was already there and hence, they are called *drashta*, seers. All of this took place 900 million light years away, at Shiva's original abode of Kailasha.

A few million years after the mantras had been seen, the sages at Shiva's abode traveled to earth following him. Some of those seers, most notably Kashypa, Vashishta, Parasurama, Dattatreya, Atri and Gautama decided to stay back on earth to pass on the mantras to the flourishing but suffering race we know as humans today. The original seers intelligently captured the sounds into 14 categories.

1. a i u ṇ
2. ṛ ḷ k
3. e o ṅ
4. ai au c
5. ha ya va ra ṭ
6. la ṇ
7. ña ma ṅa ṇa na m
8. jha bha ñ
9. gha ḍha dha ṣ
10. ja ba ga ḍa da ś

11. kha pha cha ṭha tha ca ṭa ta v
12. ka pa y
13. śa ṣa sa r
14. ha l

These 57 letters came to be known as *Maheshvara Sutra* and formed the basis of the most ancient spoken language in the world: Sanskrit. Each letter belonged to one of the five elements (earth, water, fire, wind or space). On the path of mantra yoga, when an aspirant selects a mantra for *siddhi*, ideally he should consider matching the element of the mantra with his own. This is called *kula-akula vichar* and is covered in the chapter, 'Selecting the Right Mantra'.

The importance of the sounds emanating from Shiva's *damaru* was not limited to the creation of the first language but a lot more.

The 14 categories gave birth to 14 essential *tattvas* (elements) in the whole of creation.

They were the five core elements of *prithvi* (earth), *jala* (water), *tej* (fire), *vayu* (air) and *akash* (ether).

Three modes of material nature: *sattva* (goodness), *rajas* (passion) and *tamas* (ignorance).

Chatusha-antahkarana (four aspects of mind) *of manas* (mind), *buddhi* (intellect), *citta* (fluctuations of mind/consciousness) and *ahamkara* (ego).

Masculine energy (Shiva) and feminine energy (Shakti).

There are 28 spokes around Shiva's cosmic form of Nataraja (the dancer). Shiva was given the epithet of Nataraja when he did the tandava. These 28 spokes represent the continuous cycle of creation and destruction in the form of the lunar calendar. The 14 categories of *Maheshvara Sutra* represent the 14 dates of the lunar calendar, the 15th date being Shiva himself (new moon or full moon) and the 16th or *shodashi* became the Devi at the cusp of each *paksha* (moon phase).

Together, these 28 dates created one of the most important aspects of human existence: a woman's menstrual cycle.

All existence is simply an arrangement of silence and sound. Or simply, sound at different frequencies, for silence, too, is a type of sound.

Science believes that there are two types of energies: potential and kinetic. Mantra science says the same thing but takes it a step further. In mantra yoga, while kinetic energy is an aspect of potential energy, the movement in energy causes sound. When this sonic aspect of energy is harnessed or channelized, it becomes the creative energy. This potent creative energy can be used to aid creation, destruction or sustenance of your world, dreams, goals and desires.

Mantra yoga is about going to the source of all sounds, the first voice, the originator, so you may connect with the universe at a different level altogether, a level beyond comprehension to an average mind.

Vedas have called it *Nada-Brahman* or *Shabda-Brahman*. The highest, eternal and only true reality of sound. I present it to you in its entirety based on my years and years of devoted practice.

MANTRA SADHANA

There is a certain tribe in Africa and it's said that their happiness quotient is very high. In that community, whenever a woman discovers she's pregnant, she's assigned a certain tree. The woman then picks out a song or lullaby of her choice for her unborn child, and what follows over the next decade is quite remarkable. That tree is her happy tree and the song she chooses is her happiness song.

Throughout her pregnancy, she sits by that tree and sings that song to the child growing in her womb. While bathing, sitting, standing, cooking, and going to bed, she caresses her belly, softly singing to her baby. When she's finally undergoing labor pains, the same song is sung to her by other women in her tribe. The birth of the child into the world is yet again celebrated with that song.

Soon the mother is humming the same song as she nurses and puts the baby to sleep. During every festival, every celebration, every joyous occasion, that song becomes the song of the child. Gradually, the child associates that song with every happy incident in his life. After all, so many happy memories from long before he was born spring from that song. And this is where things get interesting.

Now, whenever the child, who may be a young man by now, is depressed or facing challenges in life, he just sings his song. The sound of that song evokes positivity and strength because that's his happy song. Subconsciously, his mind swells with beautiful memories and a lot of happiness because this song was uttered on countless happy moments from the beginning of his life. That song is now inseparable from him.

This is mantra *sadhana* in a nutshell. The basic principle of mantra sadhana is to practice the utterance of a sound with such intensity, fervor and determination, that your whole being starts to reverberate with that sound. You become that sound. It becomes your sound, your mantra. The one you not only connect with, but that transports you to another dimension of consciousness.

This sound or mantra usually gets passed on to you traditionally and orally in a guru-disciple relationship. For, when it comes to mantra yoga, we believe that we can benefit from the austerities that various masters of the mantra practiced before us. Have we not reaped the fruits of trees planted by our preceding generations? Have we not inherited the rewards of wealth accumulated by our forefathers? Mantra yoga believes that the same holds true for sonic energy too — that what was uttered before me can be inherited or claimed by me.

There are different mantras to accomplish various outcomes in life. Some want to progress materially, others spiritually, some both. Before you arrive at the conclusion that you can just chant a mantra and win the lottery, let me tell you that that's not at all how mantras work. Mantra science is not a substitute for right karma or action. Mantra *sadhana* can help you experience deep states of *samadhi* if you so wish or it can help you learn anything faster. It can help you become more decisive and responsible in life.

In a nutshell, when you become one with a mantra, you no longer remain the individual you, the tiny you. Instead, your entire being is elevated to a different, higher level of consciousness. I say it without the slightest exaggeration. All other things being equal (that is, you work hard and sincerely), the path of mantra *sadhana* has the power to make you the master of your destiny.

DO MANTRAS WORK?

I had just finished my midnight *yajna* in a remote temple in the pitch dark night. The little temple housed a small Devi idol and just outside was a square fire pit three feet wide and three feet deep. I had been attempting to awaken a certain mantra of Devi for many years without any success. But this time was different, for I had a bit more hope. Hope, I may add, is the number one trait a true seeker must possess. I had hope not because of any great confidence in my own abilities but because of a prediction made by a wandering sadhu that I would come to this very temple to do a *sadhana* and attain the desired outcome.

Just six months earlier, in March 2009, a year before I had renounced, I was in my SUV with my driver on a beaten path when I saw a small temple beautifully studded on top of a quiet mountain, like a prized jewel on some precious crown. I felt irresistibly drawn to it. It was a rundown temple, barely visited even by the locals.

Without expecting anything out of the ordinary, other than a few minutes of peace and quiet, I walked to the temple from where I had asked my driver to park the car. Climbing an L-shaped staircase, I reached a platform that had a small temple of a Devi. It was a small room no more than five feet by five feet. The height was perhaps not even four feet in addition to the small triangular dome it hosted on top. Two or three people could barely squeeze in there. It had a small grill door, which was unlocked. A rusted plaque on the door read 'Jai Jwalamalini Devi'.

Jwalamalini Devi is one of the 15 companion energies of Mother Divine. In the *shakta* (those who pray to the Goddess) tradition of *Sri Vidya*, Her awakening is necessary for anyone wishing for a full vision of Mother Goddess. Other than bestowing unearthly intuitive awareness, awakening of Jwalamalini gives the seeker control over the *manipura chakra* (solar plexus) and the fire element that allows him to weather extreme conditions like cold and lack of food with much greater ease than ordinarily possible for an individual.

On the outside, the temple had a small, neatly tiled path for circumabulation.

Exactly in front of the idol, some three feet away from the door, was the unusual fire pit. Normally, square fire pits are all too common but in this case, the angle of the fire pit pointed at the Devi. So, if you sat in front of the pit, you would be sitting at one angle with the opposite pointing towards the Devi. In other words, this was a rhombus. It immediately got my attention because only a tantra adept would construct a fire pit of such dimensions and style to perform a specific *sadhana*.

Some six feet to the right of the pit was a giant peepul tree with a large periphery covering the pit, going past the temple and leaning majestically to one edge of the compound. A gentle but firm breeze was blowing. Some fallen leaves were prancing about on the floor and the rest on the tree were fluttering most melodiously, almost rhythmically.

It was at once divine. Being all alone, in front of a small Devi idol, on top of a mountain, next to a peepul tree, on a sunny day, I couldn't have asked for anything more.

After sitting there for a little while, I paid my obeisances again and went close to the staircase where I'd left my shoes.

"You have one brother and one sister," a voice startled me from behind.

I turned around. There sat an ascetic clad in bright ochre. In this confined place, I certainly hadn't seen him sitting there when I'd entered. Nothing about his appearance gave away his spiritual status. His eyes looked particularly bright on his very dark face that sported a yellow *tilak* on his forehead and in the middle of the yellow *tilak* was a smaller red one. Normally, those who pray to Rama wore such *tilak*. It wasn't the *tilak* of a tantric or a *devi upasaka*.

Rather than wearing my shoes, I walked to him and offered my respects.

"You are right," I said humbly.

"You've lived in a foreign land for many years. You have come back to live in Bharatvarsha forever," he continued, "and your sister has a son."

I nodded.

"You want to be alone, you want to do *sadhana*. You want nothing less than God himself."

I kept quiet. Hoping for something more than this accurate rundown of the life I had lived so far.

"Six months from now, you'll come here and do a *sadhana*. Here," he said giving me a scribble, "chant this mantra before beginning your day. The fruit is ripe."

I accepted his gift with a slight bow.

He went on to give me three precautions I must follow in my *sadhana* and told me that success was imminent. I didn't doubt him but I didn't believe him fully either. I didn't think I would choose this place for any *sadhana*. I always fancied even remoter and more secluded spots to immerse myself in meditation. But the ascetic said that this place was actually ideal.

I tried to talk to him bit more about *sadhana* as nothing excites a *sadhak* more than meeting another genuine practitioner. But, he said he knew nothing about *sadhanas* as such and that all his life he simply chanted the mantra given to him by his guru and that he lived the life of an itinerant. He told me that he had already stayed at this place for three days and that he would be leaving that very day.

I offered him a ride but he declined. I tried to give him money but he wouldn't take any. I had nothing else to offer at the time. My mother, a deeply religious woman, had always told me to never visit a saint empty-handed. After much pleading, he accepted my offering and I felt that my visit to this temple was complete. I took his blessings, put on my shoes and walked to my car.

While walking back, on one of the boughs of a lean tree, I saw the hide of an animal hanging. I went closer to examine it. Once again, while coming up, I hadn't noticed it at all. Then again, I'd always had the habit of looking down while walking. The animal hide looked a bit old. It could have been used as a seat for a tantric *sadhana*. It's not unusual for an adept to leave behind his seat, rosary and other implements after a specific *sadhana* is complete. In fact, at the end of many *sadhanas*, it is mandatory that you do not use the same rosary, seat, *puja dravya* (ingredients used for worship) ever again.

Sandeep, my driver, was asleep in the car. He had been driving for hours on windy, unpaved roads. I didn't want to wake him up from his deep sleep. So, I went back to the temple. Below the staircase, on the ground level, were a small room and an adjoining hut. Everything was locked. Tall grass outside the room indicated a sort of abandon, and it was right at the edge of the mountain. Just outside the room, a careless step, a mere sway of a couple of feet and one would end up in the gorge. The view was breathtakingly beautiful.

I sat there for a little bit more, before walking back to the car, hoping for Sandeep to be awake.

"Did you see anyone around, Sandeep?" I asked.

"No sirji," he said, rubbing his eyes.

"No one spoke to you?"

"Sorry sir, I fell asleep as soon as you walked out of the car; I was very tired. "

That was six months before this day. The day I was midway through to my sadhana at that very place, exactly as he'd predicted. A barrage of events in those six months made me visit this particular temple to awaken the mantra of one of the lesser forms of energy, a *yakshini*. In terms of energy hierarchy, *yakshinis* are third in command. They are beautiful, youthful, enigmatic celestial feminine forms that can guide and assist an aspirant in the absence of a guru in a human body. I needed clear directions regarding the future course of my spiritual journey and this *sadhana* was the doorway. Six months ago, I hadn't thought of this *sadhana* but when I did get it, I couldn't think of a better place to do it. This place was most ideally suited.

Observing complete silence except for chanting my daily *stuti*, subsisting on a small glass of cow's milk and one fruit in a span of twenty-four hours, my routine was quite hectic. I would wake up in the morning at about 2.30 am and bathe just outside my room. From 3 am to 9 am, I chanted the mantra in front of an *akhand jyoti* (a lamp that remains lit throughout the *sadhana*). Just after finishing, I would step out and offer my obeisance to the temple deity and the sun. Meanwhile, a villager nearby would leave a bottle of milk outside my room based on a pre-arrangement. I would have my only glass of milk and then rest for 90 minutes. From 11 am to 2 pm, I would meditate on the deity. From 2 pm to 5 pm was my rest period. At 5 pm, I would have the only fruit of the day and sometimes I would even skip that.

From 6 pm to 9 pm, I would again meditate on the mantra followed by rest for an hour. At 10 pm, I would step out and take a bath once again. By 10.30 pm, I would be upstairs, just outside the temple, ready to do my *yajna* that would finish by around 12.30 am. It would generally be 1 am by the time I gathered my ingredients, firewood and put them all back in my room. From 1 am to 2.30 am, I would wind down by lying down on my back and breathing deeply (but normally). It would allow me to gain much more rest from my short sleep, so I could start my day afresh for an intense session of six hours.

Ideally, a *sadhak* should sleep on his or her right side, in a slightly crouched position as this allows you to maintain a degree of awareness in your sleep and regulate your body temperature better, but at that time, I wasn't used to sleeping on hard surfaces, so I couldn't rest in that position at all. My bedding was a seat of *kusa* grass and a blanket on top. On that hard surface, I couldn't lie on my stomach or on my side, so I did the best I could — I slept on my back.

Presently, I had just finished my *yajna* and came back into my room. I tended to the lamp to ensure the wick was alright and it had enough oil to last till I resumed my meditation at 3 am. Everything seemed in order. I stepped out to wash my hands and feet before lying down.

As soon as I went back to my room, I realized I had just passed a rope, barely one feet away from the main door. I was somewhat intrigued because there was no rope in the room. So, I stepped out again and saw a beautiful snake. As I flashed my light at it, it turned towards me; it was fluorescent green.

I was both dismayed and happy. Dismayed because just two days ago, right in the middle of my *sadhana*, I had the vision of a black snake, but this one wasn't black. I was happy because at least it was a snake. Depending on the level of your spiritual attainment, the visions one gets during the *sadhana* are flashes that generally shouldn't be ignored. The snake continued to move towards me. I turned my flashlight the other way and saw a scorpion scurry past my feet. All of this was happening just outside my door.

"*Har Har Mahadev*," I said mentally. "Thank you, Lord."

I flashed in the direction of the snake again and once again it began moving towards me. It was no more than an arm's length from where I stood. I wanted to eulogize Shiva but I had vowed to speak only once to chant my daily *stuti* to Goddess. I began whispering a hymn to Shiva, barely moving my lips, almost reciting in my mind.

The snake became still and then it turned. I wasn't even half done with the hymn when it began moving in the opposite direction. I sat down looking at it. It slithered about so softly without even disturbing the blades of grass below its body. The snake was completely out of my sight by the time I finished my hymn.

I came back into my room and looked at the clock. It was 2 am. I had been out for over an hour. There was no time to sleep. I opened my notepad and scribbled a hymn to Devi. Soon, it was 2.30 am, time to begin my morning routine.

The next afternoon, I was feeling particularly energetic and chose not to nap at 2 pm. Instead, I sat with my eyes closed and mentally sang glories of Devi. I had barely finished chanting when I heard some noise behind the gunnybags containing firewood of my *yajna*. I had four bags in my room full of firewood that would last me 30 days.

I opened my eyes and saw the tail of a snake, a black one. It was moving into my room, close to the wall, as its long tail was disappearing behind the bags. I was overjoyed for it was exactly how I had seen in my vision. I got up to take a closer look at the snake but sensing my presence it turned and began slithering out. Only when it turned I realized it was at least six feet long, taller than me. It was extremely agile and thick. I went after it but it swiftly slunk through the grass and into the gorge.

One of the most remarkable things that happen to a *sadhak* is that you are no longer afraid of anything, really. When your intentions are noble, nature guides you and protects you at every step. I'm not suggesting that you walk into the jaws of death or go lift snakes to see if Mother Divine protects you, but something inside does change in you forever.

A sort of fearlessness, a kind of oneness with everything around you. This happens naturally to every genuine *sadhak* of mantras.

Some two weeks later when my *sadhana* was about to conclude, my deity indeed did come to me in my dream, to give me unambiguously clear instructions on my next steps to the Divine Mother. This was not a real-life vision as I had desperately hoped for but the instructions in my dream were as clear as if happening in broad daylight. I was told that five months after the completion of this *sadhana*, I would don ochre robes, renounce the material world and go on to be formally initiated and then pursue intense meditation in the extreme quietude of the Himalayan caves. Those who have read my memoir, *If Truth Be Told*, would know this and how the sequence of events turned out to be.

Let me gently remind you though that this was not my first *sadhana*. It was more like the 45th. Even these experiences were not exactly new to me; far more beautiful ones had happened in the many *sadhanas* I had performed all my life. And that was why my faith and belief in the science and art of mantras was unshakable.

Throughout my life, I've immensely benefited from the power of mantras, right from when I was an 11-year-old, who practiced astrology; as a student, whose mind was set on studying abroad; to a young man working towards material wealth; and finally to the renunciant who wanted to see God. They have aided in my spiritual, material and intellectual progress at every step of the way. You too can use them to further your pursuit of dharma, *artha*, kama or *moksha*. Using them for petty gains, though, is like trading a rare and precious pearl for an ordinary stone. How do you want to use mantras to further your cause is your individual decision and I leave that to you. The true and lasting reward for a *mantrin* (a seeker) is to merge his spiritual consciousness into the universal consciousness while living.

The sonic and ancient science of mantras bestows nirvana upon the practitioner while in this very body. You become a *jivan mukta*, free from the bondage this world is, just as stated in the scriptures.

THREE MANDATORY REQUISITES

- **Devotion and Faith (Bhakti)**
- **Initiation (*Deeksha*)**
- **Daily Duties (*Nitya Karma*)**

DEVOTION AND FAITH

I once heard a beautiful story by Swami Rama. His guru had adopted him when he was a five-year-old boy. At the time of initiation, Swami Rama's guru promised him that he would experience samadhi in 12 years. The young Swami Rama held on to that promise with great hope and expectation.

Gradually, 19 years passed in which he assiduously served his guru, but Swami Rama was still deprived of any experience of samadhi. He was 24 years old now. Upset and hurt, he confronted his guru saying that he had already given 19 years and nothing divine had transpired. His guru urged him to practice a bit more, saying that he wasn't ready yet, but Swami would have none of it.

"I'm going to drown myself in the Ganges," he retaliated.

"Oh, in that case," the guru joked, "make sure you jump with a big rock tied to you so that you are able to carry your resolve even if you change your mind once in water."

"Fine!" And, Swami Rama stormed away. Barely had he reached the door of the cave, his guru called him back.

"Come, sit here," he gestured. "Calm down and repeat after me."

The guru whispered a mantra and Swami Rama repeated the mantra after him. A moment later, he touched him on his forehead and Swami Rama felt himself completely immersed in bliss, when he came out of that experience.

"It was beautiful," Swami Rama said. "But now I'm even more confused."

"I told you, you were not ready."

"Was it the result of my 19 years of sadhana," Swami asked, "or, what is your touch? If it was my sadhana, then why did you have to touch me and if it was your touch, why on earth did you have me wait 19 years?"

The guru smiled. "You silly boy," he said, "it was neither my touch nor your sadhana."

"Then?"

"It was divine grace."

There are 16 critical factors that will ensure your success on the path of mantra yoga. Throughout this book, I'll expound every one of the 16 factors in appropriate sections. All 16 requisites, however, depend on the singular most important element — grace. Without divine grace, it is impossible to attain *siddhi* (success).

The amount of grace you receive on the path of mantra yoga is directly proportional to how sincerely you fulfill the 16 conditions. They are:

1. *Bhakti* (devotion)
2. *Shudhi* (purification)
3. *Asana* (seat)
4. *Panchang Sevan* (five types of food)
5. *Achara* (conduct)
6. *Dharana* (concentration)
7. *Divyadesh* Sevan (self-identification)
8. *Prana Kriya* (breath regulation)
9. *Mudra* (hand locks)
10. *Tarpana* (libations)
11. *Havan* (fire offerings)
12. *Bali* (sacrifice)
13. *Yaag* (contemplation and inner worship)
14. *Japa* (chanting)
15. *Dhyana* (meditation) and 16. *Samadhi* (absorption)

I have covered the most important of these throughout this book. You can gain a brief overview of the 16 aspects above in the appendix of this book.

It may sound a lot but for the sincere practitioner, who continues to practice step-by-step, it all comes together naturally.

In this chapter, I'll focus on the first one, bhakti. It's first for a reason. Bhakti is the most important condition to succeed in mantra yoga.

Every educated practitioner asks me one question: why do I need devotion if mantras form a scientific framework? It's a question even I've asked myself at one time. Before I answer this question, I have to ask you whether you believe that Vedic scriptures are true and not a work of fiction. If you have come to believe that our scriptures are mere mythological texts, then mantra yoga will disappoint you completely. Mantra requires that you invest your faith in a deity. Every mantra has a deity. If you don't believe in the existence of God or that God can have a form, then you would be better off practicing pure meditation and not bother with the sonic science of mantras.

If you feel good by just chanting a mantra, by all means, you can continue doing that. If, however, you wish to experience all that mantra siddhi can bring you, it is imperative that the entire system of mantras is followed in its entirety. Walking this path invariably begins with some faith in the truth of Vedic scriptures, existence of God and the possibility that God or energy can manifest in a physical form.

Over the last few centuries, many scholars have led us to believe that Indian religious texts, which form a bulk of Indian history and culture, are figments of someone's imagination; that, those are works of mythology. Miraculous stories in many books of other religions are classified as history, whereas any reference to a miracle in Vedic texts is simply labeled and discarded as mythology.

Ramesh Menon, whose literary renderings of our many scriptures I've so fondly enjoyed, most eloquently puts forward thought-provoking passages in his introduction to retelling of *Shiva Purana*:

The length and breadth of India is strewn with temples that have a startling commonality of themes. Increasingly, I do not believe that the Puranas, the books that describe these themes, are merely fictions of men of old. Rather, they seem to describe a human history more primal than the one of a few thousand years to which we habitually think of ourselves as belonging. In the Puranas, we see reflections of a cosmic history, when this Earth was open to the universe.

It is difficult to accept that the greatest glory of ancient India was the drainage system of Mohenjo-Daro and Harappa. We know, from modern cosmology, that the universe is much older, vaster and more complex than we imagined a hundred years ago. We know our own history is less than a speck against universal horizons of space and time. It is absurd that we pass any judgement whatsoever on a universe in which we are such infants: that we dare say 'This is so and this not in the cosmos'. Surely, our human history is an infinitesimal part of the history of the universe, not vice versa; and our ignorance is far more profound than our knowledge.

The characters in the Purana are 'cosmic' in dimension, even the lesser ones; as is the sweep of time, space and spirit we encounter here. We can easily dismiss it all as the exaggerated fantasies of nameless writers of the dim past. Or else, we begin to suspect there is more to learn here than we dreamt: that human history is fundamentally different from what we have been taught.

In the Purana, we find this description of time, which is hardly the invention of brutish man scrabbling to create the spoke and the ploughshare:

The basic unit of life is the nimesha, the instant. Fifteen nimeshas make one kastha, thirty kasthas one kaala, thirty kaalas one muhurta and thirty muhurtas one day. Thirty days is a maasa, a month, which is one day of the gods and ancestors; six maasas make an ayana, two ayanas a year. One human year is a day and a night for the celestials, uttarayana being the day and dakshinayana the night. Three hundred and sixty-five human years make a divine one.

Four are the yugas in the land of Bharata: the krita, treta, dwapara and kali. The pristine krita lasts 4,800 divine years, the less perfect treta 3,600 years, the half-corrupt dwapara 2,400 and the almost entirely evil kali, 1,200.

A chaturyuga, one cycle of four ages, is 12,000 godly years long, 12,000 x 365 human years. Seventy-one chaturyugas make a manvantara, fourteen manvantaras a kalpa. A kalpa, of 1000 chaturyugas, 12 million divine years, is one day of Brahma, the Creator.

8,000 years of Brahma make one Brahma yuga; 1,000 Brahma yugas make a savana. Each Brahma lives for 3,003 savanas.

A day of Brahma's has 14 Indras, his life 54,000 Indras.

One day of Vishnu is the lifetime of Brahma.

One day of Siva is the lifetime of Vishnu...

Can it be that our past was more than what we think? Was it, in its way, inconceivably superior to the present? By the Puranic calendar, we live today at the outset of a kali yuga. Thus, Rama lived in the world more than 800,000 years ago and Krishna, some 4,000 at least.

The entities we worship as gods were once our ancestors. They roamed our planet like you and I move about now. There is an eternal, intricate and definitive link between our ancestors and us. They live in us. We carry their genes. It is, therefore, reasonable to conclude that if they attained the status of "God", we too have the same potential. All that is required is to put that potential energy in motion, to turn it into creative energy, so you may elevate yourself.

Potential is not the same as reality though. Everyone can become Buddha, but not everyone does. Anyone can score 10,000 runs in cricket, but not every cricketer does. In a car race, where only Ferraris compete, not all of them will not cross the finish line at the same time. We all have the potential to be divine, but that doesn't mean we are already divine. We have to reach that level of divinity. It demands that we put aside our ego, which is never an easy task. To reach any level above where we are, we must first have to accept with humility that we require help from someone who's already there; that we haven't yet figured out everything; that we need the beneficence of someone more superior than us. Receiving that benediction is grace and to be a worthy recipient of grace requires bhakti.

Bhakti is not the only hurdle for an educated mind that yearns for logic and rationality. Mantra yoga requires that you be devoted to a form, for a mantra is the verbal or sonic representation; it's the sound form of a deity. Every deity has a mantra. If I need to call you, I ought to give you some name. I don't know your name, I must assign you some noun even if I don't spell it out. I may loudly say, "Excuse me!" Or, if you can see me, I may gesture to indicate that I'm addressing you. Either way, I must find a way to express myself.

While there is no right or wrong way of praying or worshiping, when it comes to mantra yoga, a practitioner must direct and invest his faith in a form. It's one of the fundamental requirements even if praying to a form appears counterintuitive in the beginning.

Swami Vivekananda was once visiting a king who told him that he didn't believe in idol worship.

"It's illogical, primitive and baseless," the king said. "How can you love a stone? It's not like the stone is actually God."

Vivekananda kept quiet and a little while later, when he was just about to depart, he pointed at a big portrait on the wall.

"Whose picture is this?" Vivekananda asked the king.

"This is my great grandfather's," he replied with pride. "His valour is known throughout the length and breadth of the country."

"Can you please have this picture taken down for a minute?"

The king was intrigued. Nevertheless, he did as asked.

"Now, spit on it," Vivekananda instructed.

"Swamiji," the king cried, "Had it been anyone else, I would have thrown him in jail for uttering such words. This is my great grandfather's portrait. How can I even think of spitting? Visitors and workers bow before it."

"Why?" Vivekananda countered calmly. "What's the problem? It's just a picture. How can you love a picture? It's not like the picture is really the person."

The king got Swami Vivekananda's message loud and clear.

Idol worship does not mean that you only worship the idol, it simply means you have assigned a form to the one you pray to. It can bestow immense inner strength. Imagine, you have a pen friend. For years, you exchange letters with your friend and he always makes you feel important, loved and cared for. You feel that your friend understands you, listens to you and even helps you in need. His care will naturally evoke feelings in your heart. One day you would want to know what this noble person looks like. You would want to meet him in person and express your gratitude.

Idol worship is something like that. It's a devotee's sentiment. A *bhakta* says: the Lord who's been taking care of me must look this beautiful, adorned with the best *vastra* and *alamkara* — this is simply a devotee's way of expressing his gratitude.

If you don't believe that God has a form or just don't like idol worship, you could simply pray to the universe, the formless God. It's just as beautiful, for, ultimately, all rivers merge into the ocean. Therefore, it doesn't matter what your method of praying is, if you do so with moral, mental and physical purity, it will not go unheard. But, if you want to walk the path of mantra yoga, a belief in a deity is absolutely required. You don't have to pray to an idol, but you must believe that God can assume a form and the form you believe in is your deity.

A *mantrin* believes that in the vast universe, there is a divine entity that can assume a form and that form can bestow upon me *siddhis* or protection. The firm belief that the divine form is my savior and can help me navigate through the choppy ocean of life to reach the shore is the foundation of bhakti. To be totally in love with God (or your deity) and to exercise complete self-surrender towards your object of worship is bhakti.

Mantras are not merely phonetic sounds. If this is the view we wish to take then we must negate their origin as it's written in scriptures. Therefore, by definition, we must also denounce the injunctions or requirements as stated in various texts elucidating the science of mantras. And, if we are brushing them aside as works of fiction, clearly, we fail to accept the framework of mantras in its entirety. Partial acceptance won't lead to complete success.

Somewhere along the line you have to make up your mind about which camp you are in. You can't travel in two boats at the same time. If you firmly believe that God cannot have a form or you are unsure about God's existance, but still want to practice mantra yoga, then all that's left is *Pranav Sadhana* —meditating on 'Om', which allows you to meditate on the formless. And that meditation is not a part of mantra yoga but *dhyana yoga* (you can read in detail about meditation in my book *A Million Thoughts*).

Goswami Tulasidas, Ramakrishna Paramhamsa and Narsingh Mehta spent their entire lives immersed in bhakti.

There are three stages of progression on the path of bhakti.

1. Vaidhi Bhakti (Preceptive): Vaidh means enjoined by rules or precept. This is the first stage where you do something just because it's written in the scriptures or just because you have been instructed by your guru to do so. In this stage, you may pray to a form of God or the deity of your mantra, but you don't necessarily feel anything. You express your devotion but you don't feel it inside you. It's okay. Keep going. It's the first step. If you stay on course and persist, you'll soon reach the second stage.

2. Ragatmika Bhakti (Passionate): Raga means to have feelings or passion, especially love and affection. It also means vehement desire and intense longing. In this stage of bhakti, you begin to develop strong feelings for God. Your desperation to see your deity, to be one with God, increases manifold. You look upon God as your brother, mother, father, sister, husband, wife, son, daughter, lover, beloved, as everything. All your relations begin and end with or in God. Very few, less than one percent of the aspirants even reach the second stage, let alone cross it. You become increasingly disconnected from the physical world as your longing turns into despair. Have hope though; soon you will reach the third stage.

3. Para Bhakti (Supreme): In *Bhagavad Gita*, Krishna says that the one who attains my *para* bhakti most certainly merges in me. In this stage of bhakti, you no longer feel disconnected with the world around you because you see God in everything around you. The longing is still there but it takes the form of divine union and wisdom. You realize that there's nothing or no one out there who is not a part of God. Therefore, you come to the natural conclusion that there's nothing to run away from or run to. It's all God, everywhere. Every particle, every entity, every object, every being, is the God you seek.

Narad Panchratra, an important text on Vaishnav Bhakti, states most beautifully:

vedasāraṃ kṛṣṇamataṃ mamāpi nahi kalpanā ||
antarvahiryadi hariryeṣāṃ puṃsāṃ mahātmanām ||
svapne jāgaraṇe śaśvattpasteṣāṃ ca niṣphalam ||
sa eva viṣṇutulyo hi tadaṃśo bhārate mune || (1.2.31-32)

The one who is immersed in the bhakti of the Lord, while sleeping and while awake, in his inner and outer world, for such a person, practicing any austerities will not yield any results. Why? Because O noble sage, austerities are practiced with a view to attain something (even salvation) whereas this *bhakta* has nothing left to realize. He's become Vishnu himself. He can purify the whole existence with a mere cast of his glance.

Even if you don't believe that God can assume a form or are

skeptical about it, but you still want to explore the science of mantras, give yourself the benefit of doubt. Go through this text patiently and embark on the journey to unlock your immense potential in the ancient manner; the one that's been used by sages over countless yugas.

INITIATION

Initiation is not just the spiritual link between you and your guru, it goes way beyond that. It's your access to all the siddhas and awakened energies in the lineage that you are initiated into. It's not like those siddhas will manifest and talk to you in person (although sometimes you do get visions and guidance during such visions), but you are protected and guided in ways words can't explain. If you as an aspirant are sincere, you won't be disappointed. This has been my personal experience too and of many others who have walked the path sincerely.

Initiation is not just a privilege; it's a kind of training as well. Various levels of initiation are milestones to indicate your spiritual progress within the lineage. A good teacher will train you over a period, gradually increasing the bar to build your skill level. An ignorant teacher will either overwhelm you with what you still have to do or can't do, or, he will dishearten you by exposing you to a level of difficulty far ahead of your reach at the moment. A good teacher, however, will give you the vision, the goal you can attain, but will structure your practice in a way that you move one step at a time.

The nature of initiation given to you varies vastly based on the tradition, lineage and the guru's own attainment.

There are three ways of initiating a disciple:

Shakti

It's called *shakti diksha* or by the more commonly known name of *shaktipata*. When imparting *diksha* in this manner, the guru touches the disciple (usually on the forehead) giving the first step towards the awakening of the primordial energy — the kundalini.

Just because a guru received initiation by way of *shaktipata* does not infuse him with enough energy to pass it on. A disciple must nurture the newly received *shakti* by way of meditation or individual practices on the path to truly awaken this energy. Only a guru who has actually done *sadhana* himself is truly able to pass on the energy on a sustainable basis.

It is important to mention this point here because *shaktipata* is one of the most abused form of *dikshas*. I meet hundreds of gullible seekers who have gone in search of a guru and believed someone to be their guru — a guru who often told them that he got initiated by some divine manifestation and so on. They tell me that they received *shaktipata* from their guru but nothing has changed inside them. It's because the guru himself was empty to begin with. Nevertheless, a good guru's touch can trigger profound feelings and a strong desire to do *sadhana*.

One touch of Ramakrishna was enough to put the seed of transformation in the young Narendra, who from Naren went on to become Swami Vivekananda.

Shambhavi

When a guru is happy and decides to initiate a disciple by merely casting a glance at him or touching him, it is *shambhavi* initiation. When *shambhavi* is given by way of looking at a disciple, it's called *drishtipat*. The primary difference between *shambhavi* and *shaktipat* is the origin of initiation. In *shaktipat*, the basis is the transfer of *kriya* (active) energy, whereas in *shambhavi*, the fundamental essence is the transfer of thought energy. *Shaktipata* says: if I could act like my guru, I would start becoming him. Shambhavi says: if I could think like my guru, I would naturally start acting like him.

In the eastern tradition, *shambhavi* has been practiced since time immemorial. A true guru's glance can evoke irreversible feelings of devotion, reverence and transformation. This was what Buddha's glance had done to Angulimala.

Maantri

When a guru decides to transform the disciple by imparting a mantra, it is called *maantri diksha*. Maantri diksha is one of the most common forms of *diksha* and a guru can initiate a disciple only into a mantra he's been initiated into by another guru in a human form or into a mantra the guru has awakened himself. When a guru initiates the disciple into a mantra he hasn't himself chanted enough or awakened, that mantra remains empty. The disciple does not benefit from such a mantra without putting an intense effort himself.

Mantras are usually transmitted orally. This has been the tradition from the beginning of time. A guru whispers a mantra into a disciple's ears.

In this book, I've taken a deviation from this norm hoping it'll benefit some of you, primarily because, it's extremely hard to find good gurus in this day and age; gurus, who have been *tapasvis* themselves. Most of them are good for the masses but not for sincere *sadhaks* who are few and far in between. I have given you every detail of the *sadhana* so that even if you don't have a guru in human form, at least you should be able to awaken the guru within you.

Different initiations are meant for different people. An adept examines the temperament of a disciple and initiates accordingly. The path of tantra has seven types of initiations, which intricately involves mantra yoga as well. The seven levels of tantric initiations and three forms of Vedic initiations are outside the scope of this work. I'm briefly mentioning this here so you know that even when you are not initiated using *shaktipata*, *shambhavi* or *maantri*, your guru may still have used a legitimate form of initiation.

There is no doubt that a guru plays an important role in the path of *sadhana.* As far as a disciple and the tenets of mantra yoga are concerned, a guru is at par with God, that adept, *siddha* is at the same level as what's sought, *sadhya.* Having said that, I feel that sometimes individual growth is hindered because we give way too much importance to a guru.

Yes, importance should be given, service should be done. I'm not prohibiting you from doing that. All I am saying is that if you want to awaken a mantra, it's something you have to do yourself even if you are initiated into an awakened mantra. If I were to just hand you the gold medal I won in the Olympics, it won't bring to you the same rewards and respect that winning one yourself will.

It's entirely possible that someone finds joy in serving and connecting with their guru and feels the need to do no more. That's perfectly fine if you are happy with that. I believe that you are reading this because you want to know how to awaken a mantra, how to walk the path of mantra yoga. Keeping that in view, my personal experience says that while having a guru can immensely help you, there's no reason to lose heart if you don't have one.

I can only share my own experience with you. I'd met with so many saints but I couldn't find the kind of guru I was looking for. Simply put, I was looking for a guru who had practiced various aspects of sadhana and not just read them in theory; someone who had verified the truth first hand, if there was any. I was not interested in charismatic orators or famous gurus. To me, the number of disciples of a guru had never been an indicator of that guru's true worth. I wanted to know if the guru had actually walked the path. It could be my own ignorance that I couldn't even find a guru; it could easily be that I was looking for a perfect guru when I wasn't the perfect disciple myself. Whatever it was, it was a disheartening and painful learning experience.

Dismayed and desolate, one day I decided to pray to sage Gautama. Gautama was a great ascetic who wrote monumental works on *nayaya* and tantra. I chose to pray to him because that was my *gotra* (lineage of a rishi one is born into). I thought, my family tree had started with him tens of thousands of years ago; he's in my DNA; he ought to help me in my path because I didn't want any *siddhi* or material attainments, I just wanted the truth.

In line with the injunctions of *Atharva Veda*, a scripture I was quite familiar with, I constructed a mantra of Gautama rishi even though I wasn't qualified in any way to create my own mantra. Nevertheless, I did what I thought was needed, out of grave despair. Making that mantra mine, I prayed fervently. Day and night at every opportunity I chanted that mantra. In every prayer, I asked him to guide me regarding the next step. This was a 40-day *sankalpa* (vow) I had taken to call out to him.

On the 36th day of my *anushthana*, I woke up to a beautiful dream at around 3am. He gave me my first mantra of Ganapati and asked me to first do my Ganapati *sadhana*. He then guided me to the next *sadhana* of a *devi*. He told me that I would get the next mantra during the Ganapati *sadhana*, and that he had done his job. He was a tall and a beautiful sage. His snow-white beard was almost touching his navel. Clad in a white dhoti, with an *angavastram* on the top half of his body, he was wearing a *yagyopavita*. Three lines of ash marked his forehead. He wore his hair in a topknot. A rudraksha chain adorned his long neck. He was barefoot. It's a dream I would never forget.

Though this was only a dream, not a real vision, it catapulted my zeal to seek the truth. Without divulging too much, I can tell you with absolute sincerity— for I only speak the truth— that on the path of *sadhana* there was no looking back for me. Whatever I did thereafter was mostly based on the guidance I received during various *sadhanas*. Even going to my own guru, a Naga sadhu, was based on the instruction I'd received during a *devi sadhana*. I was asked to surrender to a guru in human form. I was asked to live like a disciple before embarking on the most important *sadhana* of my life. I did what I was asked to. Though Naga Baba didn't teach me any *sadhana*, he did initiate me into a mantra and he was a top *sadhaka* himself in his hay days. Much of my success I gained after meeting him, I completely owe it to him.

Various scriptures state the following precepts on initiation:

1. A guru should examine his disciple over a period of one year, six months or three months, before initiating him.
2. A disciple must also examine his guru over the same period and should take on the guru only after checking and testing him. If the guru does not possess the qualities a disciple seeks, he should not accept mentorship from such a guru.
3. Initiation into a mantra can be done in the months of *Vishakh*, *Shravan*, *Ashvin*, *Kartik*, *Maagh*, *Falguna* and *Margashirsha*. All months of *adhimasa* or *malamasa* are to be avoided at all costs. Initiation in *Kartik*, *Margashirsha* and *Maagh* bear the most results, followed by *Falgun* and *Ashvin*. *Shravan* is most suitable for initiation into the mantras of Shiva. *Vishakh* is right for any form of initiation.
4. Those desiring liberation should be initiated in *krishna paksha* and those wanting material progress should take initiation in *shukla paksha*. *Poornima*, Fifth, Second, *Saptami*, *Tryodashi* and *Dashmi tithis* are good for any form of initiation.
5. *Ashwini*, *Rohini*, *Svati*, *Hasta*, *Vishakha*, *Jyestha*, *Utrasharda*, *Utrabhadrapada*, *Ultra Falguni* and *Poosha nakshtra* (asterism) are perfect for any mantra *diksha*. *Shravana*, *Adra*, *Dhanistha* and *Shatabhisha* are great for tantric initiation.
6. Among the zodiac, Aries, Cancer, Libra, Scorpio, Capricorn and Aquarius are good signs for initiation.
7. On certain holy days (Vijaya Dashmi, Guru Poornima, Holi, Diwali, etc.) no consideration is required and the disciple can be initiated anytime.
8. Ultimately, what matters the most is when your guru wants to initiate you. The word of the guru is final.

Initiation is the vital link between your individual energy and the universal energy.

yathā deve tathā mantre yathā mantre tathā gurau
yathā gurau tathā svātmanyevaṃ bhaktikramaḥ priye.

O Devi, Shiva says, there's no difference between mantras and deities. Mantra is God. Just like there is no difference between a mantra and a guru. Guru is mantra. As there is no difference between Guru and me. Guru is me.
The devoted disciple knows this much.
(Tantraraj Tantram, 1.30)

FOUR ASPECTS OF MANTRA SADHANA

- **Guru (Siddha)**
- **Aspirant (*Sadhaka*)**
- **Resources (*Sadhan*)**
- **Goal (*Sadhya*)**

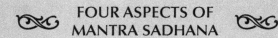

The journey of mantra *sadhana* has four key aspects. While success on the path depends on the sum, quality and consistency of efforts you put in, the truth is the other three elements do play an important role. To understand mantra *sadhana* in its entirety, its four aspects must be understood. This is where mantra yoga is different from the path of meditation.

In meditation, you can succeed without a guru. You don't need to meditate on a form, you don't need to have any faith or devotion in a deity or God and you can still meditate and enjoy the quietude that springs forth from mediation. When it comes to mantra yoga, however, belief in a form is a prerequisite.

In the following four chapters, I'll cover the four important aspects of mantra yoga. Absence of any one of the four puts the whole practice on shaky ground. It is worthwhile to understand the fundamentals of *sadhana* before delving into the actual practice.

Siddha (Guru)

Do you know the difference between the light of the sun versus that of the moon? The sun's presence annihilates any darkness whereas the moon dissipates it without eliminating it completely. The moon is soothing while the sun, seething. Like the moon, a guru allows you to exist the way you are, accepting you the way you are, ever exuding the gentle rays, the full light of love, care, wisdom and guidance.

The guru-disciple relationship is like no other, for it's free of the usual give-and-take exchanges. It's one of the most intimate and purest relationships because there are no secrets and there's no hidden agenda. It's a bond, a covenant, capable of rapid, profound, and irreversible transformation.

There are two types of gurus: *shiksha* guru and *deeksha* guru. *Shiksha* guru is the one who imparts knowledge. In Eastern culture, all teachers would be *shiksha* gurus. They make our lives worthwhile by dispelling our ignorance. My focus here, however, is the guru of the other type: *diksha* guru. *Diksha* guru is the one who initiates you on the path of self-discovery. This is the form of guru whose virtues are extoled in the scriptures. This is the guru who has been placed at par with God in Vedic texts.

In my vocation, I regularly meet seekers who have fallen prey to fake gurus. There are fake disciples too — those who get initiated but don't follow the teachings in its entirety. And then there are those who follow ardently and practice sincerely and yet their doubts and negative tendencies remain. They don't experience an iota of transformation.

Finding a guru is often the case of love at first sight. Sometimes, you just know that this person is your guru — that unmistakable, instant pull to a guru's ideology is experienced by many. And that's where the problem lies. Just feeling good in the presence of a guru or feeling psychologically empowered because you are in the presence of an enlightened master is not enough on the path of mantra *sadhana*.

If you wish to discover your truth by walking the path of mantra *sadhana*, you must examine the stature of your guru. Has your guru ever done *sadhana* himself? Has he invoked any mantras? For merely chanting a mantra in the name of *sadhana* is not going to yield any results.

For example, if you wished to learn piano, you would quite naturally approach someone who's been playing piano for a long time. A person could be a world-class drummer but he's unlikely to be the best person to teach you piano.

Similarly, if you want to master mantra yoga, you must get initiated from an adept.

Before you take anyone as your guru, for your own good, reflect on the four categories of false gurus listed below. I must reiterate that the views below are strictly in the context of mantra yoga. The types of gurus below could be great people doing great work. It's not my prerogative to judge. I'm simply stating that from the perspective of the science of mantra, for only a certain class of adepts can impart this ancient knowledge to you.

1. The Crusading Guru

The crusading guru is on some grand global mission. This is not a false guru, merely a famed one but he is certainly in no position to help you realize your truth. The crusading guru is too engrossed in worldly affairs and material pursuits. He may be doing great social service but he's also busy raising funds and building centers, ashrams and other infrastructure. Such a guru may introduce you to the basics of meditation or even touch briefly upon mantra science, but not much beyond that.

If you wish to participate in a social cause or the cause of the crusading guru, you may find a certain direction or purpose in your life in following that guru. This may even be good for you and the world at large. But there's a price to pay. And the price is that you'll never know the real science behind mantras. Unfortunately, our world today is full of charlatans parading as gurus, complete with charm and charisma, who are initiating others into mantras without ever mastering them first.

On the path of mantra yoga, any mantra imparted by the crusading guru will have little to no impact on your spiritual progress. No matter how good an orator that guru is or how well he can expound on the scriptures, if you want success in mantra you must seek guidance from a practitioner of this sacred science.

2. The Cryptic Guru

The cryptic guru is even more common than the crusading guru. With the cryptic guru, you rarely get a straight answer to any question. This guru will claim to know everything about everything, but all your questions will be answered in a manner that you end up even more confused by the end of it.

Your master must make sense to you; he must practice what he preaches; his teachings must be acceptable to you (not out of a sense of duty or pressure). Never take someone as your guru who curbs your questions or makes you feel stupid. In the presence of a genuine master, you feel important, loved and peaceful. Everything feels right, life feels worthwhile. This is how you know that you are in the close vicinity of a real master.

On a sunny Sunday, after a discourse, many members of the audience approached the preacher to clear their doubts or to just greet him.

"Thank you, Father," one of them said, "I had my doubts at first but now, I stand convinced you are even smarter than Einstein."

The preacher beamed with pride and thanked him for the compliment. Over the next few days as he reflected on the remark, he felt increasingly baffled. *What did the man mean?* he thought. He went through his notes to see what had he said that was so profound that someone deemed him smarter than Einstein. When no answer came forth, he decided it was best to ask the seeker.

The next Sunday he saw the same person in the audience. He asked him if he remembered his last week's comment.

"Absolutely, I do," he said.

"Exactly what did you mean when you said that I am smarter than Einstein?"

Well, Reverend," the man replied, "they say, Einstein was so smart that only ten people in the entire world could understand him. But sir, no one can understand you."

If your master is too cryptic, he doesn't know what he's talking about. Truth is always simple, lies are complicated. If you examine the lives of the greatest sages, the realized ones, you'll discover that they preached in a way that even a child could grasp their simple teachings. Such simplicity only comes from experience, from genuineness, from truth. When they don't make sense to you, chances are, they are not talking sense at all. It doesn't mean you must agree or disagree with the master, but, at least, their words should be within the purview of your comprehension.

3. The Eager Guru

The eager guru is, well, too eager, to take you into his fold. If ever a guru tells you to take initiation from him, ignore him like a bad dream for the simple reason that no true guru would violate the basic requirement of initiation, that is, a disciple must approach a master with a request for initiation.

The eager guru is more interested in building his following and spreading his fame. He'll promise you the world and deliver practically nothing. When a guru is too eager, usually there's something he wants from you. It's not always money. Sometimes, it's just your devotion or acknowledgement. The eager guru will never tell you your flaws because he doesn't want to alienate you in anyway.

If you see the signs of indulgence, restlessness or excessive talking in the person, you are most likely in the presence of an eager guru. Get out of there as fast as you can.

4. The Fake Guru

The fake guru always banks on your fears. If you are holding this book in your hands, chances are you are educated enough to not to fall for such gurus. Having said that, I meet so many people who have been ripped off by fake gurus.

The fake guru is only focused on furthering his cause without caring for your wellbeing. You never feel important or valued in the presence of such a guru. You will be used till they can extract the maximum out of you. If you find yourself caught up in the web of such a guru then god help you.

Leaving a fake guru isn't always easy though because they are master manipulators. Just when you gather the courage and strength to make the move, they'll tell you something nice; they may even bait you, so that you hold on for a little longer believing things have changed. Nothing has changed though. The tides will rise once again.

Be careful before you take on someone as your guru. As the famous saying of the Nath sect goes: *Guru banayo jani ke, pani piyo chani ke* (Take a guru after examining and drink water after filtering).

There are gurus who use tricks, sleight of hands, to produce ash, chains, shivlingams and what not. I don't have to tell you which category they fit in. The most important thing is to study your potential guru thoroughly before you choose to be initiated.

Above all, when it comes to mantra yoga, it's very simple: choose a guru who understands and practices this science. Only such an adept, only a practitioner, can truly guide you on the path when you face practical challenges; someone who hasn't been there, done that, can't tell you what to expect and how to go about it beyond a bookish explanation.

At any rate, I've written this book and the *sadhanas* herein assuming that you don't have a guru in human form. If you diligently follow the steps, there's no reason why you won't succeed.

When you tread the path with sincerity and honesty, nature is left with no option but to manifest a genuine master in your life. If you feel guilty, angry, resentful or restless in a master's presence, it can only mean one of the two things: a) The guru is fake or, b) You are not ready for him. Above all, make absolutely no attempts to deliberately feel reverence for any master. Surrender or acceptance can't be forced — either you feel it or you don't or maybe you feel it intermittently. Either way, it's fine. If adoration doesn't come from within, give yourself time or get yourself a new guru. Faith need not be blind.

A true guru inspires you to walk your path with resoluteness and conviction. He invokes incredible feelings of strength, divinity, love, acceptance and fullness in the deepest recess of your heart. Above all, a true guru is an embodiment of truth and compassion.

Sadhaka (Aspirant)

A man was in search of a perfect guru. For years, he traveled the length and breadth of India. Anytime anyone told him that some *siddha* was visiting his village or that some great sage lived in such and such place, he would immediately drop everything and go there. But each time he returned disappointed.

Some gurus, he thought, were downright insane and some he found too devoted to scriptures. One or two he liked were all about bhakti and some he found too cryptic. He found greedy gurus, fake gurus, even cruel ones, but he never found the kind of perfect guru he was looking for.

A few years passed by and even his family members started praying for him because this dejected man lost interest in everything.

"Is there no perfect guru for me?" he would often say.

Twelve years went by like this and one day, he heard that an adept sat in *dhyana* just on the outskirts of his village. With hope and excitement, he rushed to the spot. Sure enough, he found his perfect guru. His family was happy that finally he had found what he was looking for.

"But," they asked him, "how do you know he's the perfect guru?"

"Oh, there was never any doubt," he replied, " as soon as I met him, he told me that I was his perfect disciple."

When a guru simply declares his disciple perfect, without finding out areas of improvement, the spiritual growth stops right that moment. The whole point of having a guru is so that we may no longer remain oblivious to what we need to work on.

The second most important aspect of *mantra sadhana* is the *sadhaka*, that is, you. Without a musician, there's no music; without you, there's no sadhana. A guru can guide you, help you, direct you, but ultimately, it is you who have to sit through the gruelling hours of *sadhana*. And, it'll be you (and the world, if you use your new energy to help others) who will reap the rewards of that effort.

Before I share with you the various types of *sadhakas*, let me tell you what the scriptures regard as signs of a good disciple:

caturbhirādyaiḥ saṃyuktaḥ śraddhāvān susthirāśayaḥ ||
alubdhaḥ sthirgātraśca prekṣakārī jitendriyaḥ ||
āstiko dṛḍhabhaktiśca gurau mantre sadaivate ||
evaṃvidho bhavecchiṣyastivataro duḥkhakṛdguroḥ ||
gurūcyamāne vacane dadyādittham vacaḥ sadā ||
prasīda nātha! deveti tatheti ca kṛtādaram ||
praṇamyopaviśet pārśve tathā gacchedanujñayā ||
mukhāvalokī seveta kuryādādiṣṭmādarāt ||
asatyaṃ na vadedagre na bahu pralepadapi ||
kāmaṃ krodhaṃ tathā lobhaṃ prahasanaṃ stutim ||
(Tantraraj Tantram, 1.23-27)

In addition to the four signs (humble, neat, soft-spoken, content), a good disciple is full of faith and has a degree of stability. A disciple should not be greedy or full of doubt.
He should address and approach his master with humility.
He needs to have faith in God and unwavering devotion for his guru, mantra and deity. A good disciple refrains from speaking too much or telling lies in front of his guru. He should not engage in any material transactions with his guru. Above all, he should have the desire to serve his guru.

These are too many 'shoulds' if you ask me. Perhaps, if a person had all these qualities, he wouldn't need to seek anything or anyone. Having said that, we won't get there unless we try. The whole purpose of *sadhana* is to transform you from within, to cast off your old skin. To be free of the shortcomings that led you in search of a guru in the first place.

In fact, there are only two types of conversations that are permissible in a guru-disciple relationship. In the first type, the guru asks a question and the disciple answers. And in the second, the disciple asks a question and the guru may choose to answer. There is no room for argument or *utar-pratiutara* debate.

That naturally leads to the question: Does that mean a disciple should be a meek cow and never challenge his guru? Of course, you can challenge your guru. But such a challenge should be to resolve the burning queries in your mind; a question should be asked out of curiosity and not with the intention to win a debate or prove a point. If that's the feeling you harbor, then why take on that person as your guru. If you feel that you already know more than your guru, then why enter into the sacred bond of guru-disciple relationship.

And, if you feel that you now know more than your guru, just thank him for the blessings and move on. If, however, you feel that you made a wrong choice in selecting your guru, feel free to move on still. My personal recommendation would be to not pollute your mind and voice by speaking ill of your guru, just move on if your faith has shifted. A guru should not speak ill of his disciples, and a disciple of the guru. In a spiritual relationship, there's no room for ill will or ill speech. If your guru's actions are not in line with your own moral and spiritual precepts, there's little sense in continuing with such a guru.

Broadly speaking, there are three types of *sadhakas* or disciples.

The Hopper

The hopper is the restless type. This type of a disciple is impatient and too eager. He believes that if his guru or his current belief system has no answers for his questions, perhaps another one would. He is in search of a panacea, some solution that will give him peace. The trouble, however, is that the hopper is merely jumping from one belief system to another without focusing on his own *sadhana*. He has not sat down to identify the problem or to ask the right questions. He's like a window shopper. He is hopping because he is restless. He'll jump from one guru to another. Here today, there tomorrow, and somewhere else the day after. All his attempts to turn inward or practice devotion prove futile because he lacks the resolve and often morality too.

The hopper wants an easy fix for his deep-rooted problems. When he comes under the fold of a new guru, he feels good, relieved and consoled. This is the beliefmoon — honeymoon-like stage of a belief when all looks attractive and rosy. It fades away quickly before he finds himself in the same old boat, almost as if reality woke him up abruptly after a short dream. His restive tendencies and desires overpower him and out he goes again in search of another solution. The hopper has little chance of experiencing bliss, realization being out of question altogether, until he makes some amendments in his way of living, thinking, conduct and belief. Dry speech, tall ego, unbound anger and a lustful mind are the signs of a hopper. He wants to change without letting go.

The Prisoner

The prisoner-type is more stable than the hopper. His stability varies based on his internal state and external circumstances. Such stability is not necessarily because the prisoner is a better believer but because he couldn't be bothered with any cognitive pursuits, intellectual quests or spiritual conquests. This type of a believer is called a prisoner because he is a captive of someone else's belief system. Often the prisoner will leave everything to his guru. Rather than doing *sadhana*, the prisoner believes that just because he or she has received initiation from an adept, all will work out on its own. It's a common and grave mistake.

Even outside the path of *sadhana*, on the path of bhakti too (which requires complete surrender), one must not forego his own efforts. Any path that discourages you from taking responsibility for your own life and actions is no different than a prison. In a prison, you are dependent on the jailer and guards to feed you and look after you. A disciple of this category is very unlikely to realize his truth because he has given up on action.

The Discoverer

The discoverer is a rare type of disciple, for this type of belief requires a perfect balance between effort and surrender, determination and devotion. The discoverer finds the right master and settles there. He understands that beyond blessings and guidance from his guru, he is responsible for walking the path himself.

He gets past the hollow arguments and dry polemics. With his own efforts and guru's grace, his beliefs transform into wisdom. Belief is a product of intellect. As long as one says, "I believe", it means they have not discovered their own truth yet. The freedom of a pet is restricted to the whim of the owner. The expression upon realization automatically changes from "I believe" to "I know".

Anything secondhand cannot be knowledge; it is merely information. When we use that information, and arrive at a conclusion based on our own experience, it is knowledge.

If you are the patient, it's you who needs to take the medicine to get well. You may have the best doctor in the world but it's the patient who needs to undergo the procedure and make lifestyle changes. You, the patient, and not the doctor, needs to be on prescription if you want the benefit.

If a disciple is not committed to the path of *sadhana*, even having God as his guru won't amount to much. The *sadhak* who's patient, vigilant and diligent on the path is sure to attain *siddhi*, with or without a guru.

Sadhan (Resources)

I was staying in a cave in Badrinath, at an altitude of 12,000 feet, when one day a young boy, no more than 23 approached me.

"Can I meditate in that cave?" He asked me pointing to a cave that was a few hundred meters away from mine. I told him that that cave was not fit for a *sadhak* as it would get flooded whenever it rained, which was almost every day.

"Your groceries, cooking stove, bedding, everything will be soaked."

"I don't care because I'll have no bedding or utensils or anything like that."

"Oh," I exclaimed impromptu, "I didn't realize you only wanted to sit there for a day."

"Of course not!" he said animatedly, "I plan to stay there until I attain samadhi. Even if takes me six years like it took Buddha."

"And how do you plan to feed yourself or take care of the necessities?"

"God will take care," he said raising his hands in the air.

I chuckled and wished him good luck because he seemed to have made up his mind and I discovered long time ago that there's absolutely no sense in offering unsolicited advice. He told me that he would start meditating the same afternoon. I offered him a blanket but he said he was wearing a thick jacket and thermalware so he didn't need a blanket. I told him that in case he needed any help, he could come to me.

"That cave is not fit for sleeping in my view," I warned him again.

"I won't be sleeping at all," he replied, "I'll just meditate."

That evening when I sat in meditation, I was very concerned for him. I was wondering if he had eaten properly, if he was warm enough, for the floor of that cave was certainly wet. I contemplated breaking my meditation midway and walking up to his cave but bound by the rules of *sadhana*, I chose to wait. The next day, I rushed to his cave with two packets of biscuits and a blanket. But, he was nowhere to be seen. A month later, he visited me again and said that he only sat in the cave for some 20 minutes and then went back.

"The floor was not just damp, it was wet. My behind was frozen in no time," he said.

"What now?"

"I'll look for another cave that's more suitable."

"What about your living arrangements there?" I repeated the same question I'd asked him the first time and he gave me the same answer:

"God will take care."

His answer reminded me of a simple and beautiful anecdote.

Once upon a time, a man in search of livelihood on his way to another town had to pass through a jungle. He lost his way in the woods. Roaming helplessly, he came across an old banyan tree. Its roots hung low and it canopied a wide area. He saw a fox sitting under the tree. At first he got scared and thereafter relieved because he noticed that it was a lame, old fox, unable to hunt.

The man sat down in a shady corner. What he witnessed a while later amazed him: he observed that birds who sat on the tree occasionally dropped pieces of meat and the fox ate them. That was how it survived. It dawned on the man that there was no need for him to run around; he too, like the fox, could just take up a corner somewhere and God would provide for him too.

He managed to navigate his way out of the forest and parked himself under a tree, outside the first village he came across. He vowed to surrender to God and only live off what was offered to him. Days went by and no one offered him anything. He was starving, at the verge of collapsing. His faith shook, and he wondered how could God be so partial, how could He provide for the fox and not him.

While he was engrossed in his own world, he saw a *sanyasin*, a mystic, pass by. In his frail condition he called out to the mystic and narrated his story. He asked the *sanyasin* the same question that bothered him. The monk chuckled, and said, "Who told you to take on the role of the fox? Are you disabled? You should be the bird, working for yourself as well as providing for those who depend on you."

So often I meet aspirants who want to renounce and do *sadhana*; be the fox in the story.

You can't do proper *sadhana* in an ashram because social interactions, which are distractions for an aspirant, are inevitable in ashram-like environments. And if you want to go away in solitude, which you'll need to eventually, you'll need to put in some basic arrangements, which often requires money.

It comes as a big shock to the new aspirants that God will not take care of them, that they can't just walk away and do *sadhana.* The answer is, you can just walk away and do *sadhana* but that does not erase the need to handle the practical aspects of life. If you are willing to interact with people, in a country like India, there are countless generous people who will support you and fund your endeavor, but it comes at a cost. The cost is, you can't be in pure solitude if you still have to stay in touch with people to fulfill your needs.

It's a lot more practical to simplify your life, cut down on your needs, forego your desires for material acquisitions and support yourself with your limited means. When I went for my first main *sadhana* after renunciation, I needed money to buy a wooden plank, a tarp, some utensils and a couple of blankets. Even the guy who agreed to put a tarp under the rock to prevent water from falling on my head, put stones on three sides to cover me at night and put a small door in my cave, charged me Rs. 15,000.

It sounds so anticlimactic, so out of place, but sooner or later if you walk the path of *sadhana*, you'll realize that at least in this day and age, you have to have access to resources. Even Ramakrishna Paramhamsa used to get his salary from the Dakshineshwar Kali temple where he worked as the priest. Even Ramana Maharishi had a patron who took care of his daily meal while he meditated for six months in the Shiva temple. You too may find a patron, but the point I'm making is that pursuit of a divine goal does not mean you won't have any practical challenges.

On the path of mantra yoga, if you are doing sadhana that requires ingredients for puja, for *yajna*, you'll have to procure them from somewhere at some cost.

My personal view is that if you can take care of your basics, you can spend much more quality time on your *sadhana*. At least, this is the path I took. I let go of the wealth I had no use for on my journey, but a stipend of Rs. 15,000 per month from the company I'd once founded helped me to travel, stay, make arrangements and remain in isolation and devote all my time to *sadhana*. And a few years later when my books started generating some income, enough to pay my bills, I asked that the stipend be stopped. That money could go for some other cause.

In other words, I'm not suggesting that you stash money somewhere or start hoarding. I'm only saying that you are going to encounter the question about resources on the path of true *sadhana*. We are not living in the times of Buddha or Mahavira. If you want perfect solitude, you'll have to make your own arrangements.

It is not possible to practice *sadhana* without support. By resources, I do not mean that you require substantial financial capital. In the initial stages, you can start *sadhana* sitting at home. As you progress, your circumstances should allow you to do almost like a 'sadhana getaway' for a week, ten days or a month once or twice a year minimum. Your routine during that getaway will be intensive meditation.

Further, with continued advancement, you will need a quieter place for intensive practices of silence and solitude. You are not going to see serious results without intense practice.

I know many aspirants feel that my practical talk on resources and money is so not-spiritual. But, my job is to tell you the truth as I see it, and offer you the guidance many aspirants tell me they wish they had earlier. Even if it brings down the fascination by a few notches and makes you feel I don't understand the ways of the Divine, or this book doesn't sound like a spiritual classic, or this is not how a saint or a realized person talks, it's fine. Because, truth is more important to me than any of the above.

Besides, I'm not saying anything new, Krishna too, said the same:

adhiṣṭhānaṁ tathā kartā karaṇaṁ ca pṛthag-vidham
vividhāś ca pṛthak ceṣṭā daivaṁ caivātra pañcamam
(Bhagavad Gita, 18.14)

There are five elements in play for anything to take effect. They are, our approach towards our goal, our mindset and strength, resources, our efforts and fifth, destiny.

If you are serious about walking the path of *sadhana*, I hope you won't be the young saint waiting on the outskirts of a village for someone to come and feed you. Instead, you'll be a Vivekananda who worked tirelessly on myriad social issues than talk gloriously about elusive concepts of spirituality.

Sadhya (The Goal)

There's a story that my guru, a Naga saint and a tantric adept, had told me once. There was a devotee of Hanuman who used to pray everyday and yet his life was still full of troubles. Sometimes he would feel frustrated thinking that God in the form of Hanuman was not listening to him. For, naturally like many devotees out there, he had the mistaken view that praying meant fixing your life's problems. This went on for a decade when one day he decided to try something different.

"Hanuman is no good," he said to himself. "After all, he's a devotee himself of Lord Rama. I need someone more potent. I should go for Krishna. He seems to help his devotees a lot more. After all, look at the crowd that goes to Vrindavan and comes back happy. Yes, Krishna it is. I'm upset with you Hanuman, I wasted 10 years of my life on you."

With this, he went to the market and brought a beautiful idol of Krishna. He lifted the idol of Hanuman from his home and put it in the attic, just above the altar. Adorning his altar with Krishna, he lit incense and lamp. Soon, he noticed that the smoke from incense was traveling upwards, towards the attic.

"Hmm... " he thought, "Hanuman is still partaking of my offerings. This is not done."

He got a chair, climbed on it and once again reaching out to his attic, got hold of the Hanuman idol. He took two pieces of cotton and tried to stuff them in the idol's nose.

"You are not getting anything I offer," he said angrily.

The next moment, a live form of Hanuman manifested before

him — the glorious Hanuman with his mace resting on his shoulder, his body glowing with devotion to his Lord Rama. The devotee, however, trembled with fear, thinking Hanuman would now turn him into ashes any moment.

"Jai Shri Ram," Hanuman bellowed. "I'm pleased with you. Have no fear."

"Pleased?" the devotee asked gathering courage. "All these years you never showed any sign of being pleased with me and now when I was about to stuff your nose with cotton, preventing you from enjoying the offering, you show up. It doesn't make sense."

"All those years," Hanuman said, "you treated me like an idol. You thought I was just a stone idol. But, today, for the first time you felt that I was real, that I existed. You didn't just assume that I was partaking of your offerings, you actually believed it in your bones. It proved your faith. I had to come."

The ultimate goal of any *sadhana* is to attain *sadhya* (that which is sought). Upon attainment, you inherit the attributes of your *sadhya*. That brings about a magnificent expansion of consciousness in you, changing you completely, transforming you from a caterpillar stuck in a cocoon to a full, beautiful butterfly, flitting about on fragrant flowers.

Attainment of *sadhya*, however, depends a lot on the quality of your effort and purity of your faith. The path of mantra yoga, as some philosophers and secularists have you believe as simply the chanting of some letters and syllables to help you connect with the universe, is not true. At least, this is not what various exegetical texts on mantras state and this has not been my personal experience either.

Mantra yoga requires that you invest your faith in the deity of the mantra, so you may invoke that deity to guide you, nurture you, protect you, help you and be there for you. A deity who, unlike people in the temporary and conditional relationships of the material world, will stand by you at all times. Once again, it does not mean that problems will disappear from your life. It only means the changes in you give you immense strength to deal with the challenges differently. It means that you are guided to act differently by a mere change in your perspective. Because everything changes when you change your perspective.

In other words, nature or your deity may not stop the rain for you because others may be fervently praying for it, but it can give you an umbrella so that you don't get drenched.

This bond with your deity does not develop overnight. It takes time. The one who seeks refuge in his deity is called *sarnagati*. *Lakshmi Tantra* enumerates most beautifully the six key attributes of true devotee, a *sarnagati*.

māmekaṃ śaraṇaṃ prāpya māmevānte samaśnute ||
ṣaḍaṅgaṃ tamupāyaṃ ca śṛṇu me padmasaṃbhave ||
ānukūlyasya saṃkalpaḥ prātikūlyasya varjanam ||
rakṣiṣytīti viśvāso goptrtavavaraṇaṃ tathā ||
ātmanikṣepa kārpaṇye ṣaḍvidhā śaraṇāgatiḥ ||
evaṃ māṃ śaraṇaṃ prāpya vītaśokabhayakalamaḥ ||
nirārambho nirāśīṣca nirmamo nirahaṃkṛtiḥ ||
māmeva śaraṇaṃ prāpye taret saṃsāra sāgaram ||
satkarmaniratāḥ śuddhāḥ sāṃkhyayogavidastathā ||
nārhanti śaraṇasthasya kalāṃ koṭitamīmapi ||
(Lakshmi Tantra. 17.59-63)

Lord Vishnu tells Sri that there are six components of becoming a *sarnagati*. They are:

1. A firm resolve to perform only those actions that please me. (Actions in line with the scriptural injunctions.)
2. Refraining from performing any act that displeases me. (Following the word of the scriptures and your guru).
3. Unrelenting faith that I'm your sole savior and your protector.
4. Self-surrender.
5. Humility.
6. Benevolence (*anukula acaret*).

The path of mantra yoga is accepting that there is a higher force I can draw energy from. It is living a life that is morally, physically and emotionally pure. It requires that you do not hurt, harm or injure others (these acts displease the deity); that you have undying faith in your God. Since you believe that you seek something from someone (or some energy operating at a higher frequency than you), that you exercise a degree of self-surrender with the belief that you can't control everything in life and even if you could, controlling is tiring. Sometimes, you just have to let life flow.

Fifth is humility, for a tree laden with fruits bends naturally. The more substance you have in you, the humbler you will be naturally. And, it goes without saying that the purer your *sadhana*, the more you are filled with substance. In other words, the more you empty yourself, the more the Lord fills you. And finally, benevolent conduct. Literally, it's been written as *anukula acaret*. That is, act in a manner that befits you.

On the path of mantra yoga, some want occult powers, others, Samadhi, and many others may just want a better way of living. Almost anything is possible with the right practice. For a yogi, the goal could be achieving yogic trance. For the *mantrin*, the goal could be to invoke the latent power of the mantra. For the worldly, it could just be acquisition of material wealth. For the ill, it could be to regain his physical health. Whatever your goal is, it is important to have one goal at a time and carry out the practices accordingly. The course of action can only be charted if you know the destination.

Your *sadhana* is to attain your *sadhya*. The rules, discipline, framework and philosophy are only a means to an end. Once done, you are ready to define your own rules because when you are delivered, you are free. Free of everything.

It is important to follow the rules initially. Just like when you are driving on the highway, for your own safety and that of the others, you follow traffic rules. But once home, you no longer walk in lanes or put on the indicator before turning. Rules on the spiritual path are there to assist you, just like the lane markings are there to guide you while you drive. If you turn your discipline into a ritual, losing sight of the ultimate, your path will become a conglomerate of dry practices devoid of bliss and joy.

Initially, to benefit from mantra yoga, it must be accepted and practiced in its entirety. To truly benefit from the part and understand it, we cannot ignore the whole.

TENETS OF DISCIPLESHIP

The bond between a guru and a disciple is one of the most divine and beautiful relationships. It doesn't have the usual give and take approach of worldly relations. A guru is someone with whom you can share all your challenges and sorrows without being judged. Having said that, being a disciple doesn't mean that you start your progress automatically. While initiation and guidance play a big role, ultimately a disciple's conduct, actions and speech must have a degree of purity. Various scriptures, including *Narada Panchratra*, give guidelines on becoming an ideal disciple. Here are some of them in brief:

A disciple's ultimate duty is to serve his master with reverence and humility. Service does not mean that the disciple has to live with the master and take care of his needs. To diligently follow a guru's instructions is to serve him. As with anything that grants you power, it saddles you with great responsibilities as well. The relationship of a guru and disciple has some set boundaries. Just as an employee must adhere to company policies, a disciple must perform his duties in line with the tradition. It strengthens his bond with his master and the lineage he now belongs to. Per *Narada Panchratra*, a disciple should do the following:

1. A disciple should not disclose his guru mantra or the mantra he's initiated into to anyone else.

2. He must keep pooja *vidhi* to himself and not disclose it, unless instructed by the guru.
3. He should protect the chastity of his mantra and the scripture like he cares for his own body.
4. He should respect his elders and his guru.
5. He should be willing to serve his guru.
6. If he gets any flowers from a shrine, he should touch them to his forehead. Those flowers should not be thrown in a bin. He can immerse it in running water or he can wait till they are dry and then burn them or put them at the root of a tree.
7. He should try to see the divine in everyone, notably, in the sun, the moon, cow, peepul tree, fire, a Brahmin who practices vedas, and in his own guru.
8. During travels, in the mornings as well as in the evenings, he should pray to God and chant his guru mantra.
9. If he gets a vision or witnesses a miracle in the waking or sleeping state, he should first share it with his guru.
10. A disciple who serves his guru to the best of his abilities and follows the precepts above is sure to attain *siddhi* on the path of mantra yoga.

These may seem simple to practice but often slip out of the mind of even the most devoted disciples. As you progress on the path, greater precision and mindfulness are required in imbibing these principles in your heart and mind. Following these tenets shows the readiness of a *sadhaka* on the path of mantra yoga. You may wonder why. If you go through the above guidelines again, you'll discover that inherently they encourage an aspirant to stay away from any attention, ego, misconduct and delusion.

All too frequently aspirants start to walk the path and soon get distracted by their experiences. Soon, they will start sharing with others the path of their *sadhana*, their mantras, temporary attainments and so on. Some even start bragging about their guru and so on. All these are serious and great impediments on the path.

The moment a disciple gets distracted, the quality of sadhana is sure to be affected. In a nutshell, a disciple should take his time before accepting anyone as his guru but once done, he should try his best to follow the path. Discipleship comes with its own rewards. Our history is replete with stories where disciples attained the highest wisdom just by serving their gurus sincerely.

Giri was a disciple of the great master and scholar Shankracharya. Some 1200 years ago, the young and brilliant Shankracharya revived Sanatan Dharma with insightful commentaries on the vedas, upanishads, samhitas and more. He composed some of the greatest hymns chanted by hundreds of millions of people even today. Out of the disciples who were close to him, the most ignorant was Giri. Unlike Shankracharya's other students, Giri didn't know Sanskrit, he didn't know the vedas, he couldn't understand his master's discourses or at least, nothing about him showed that he did. Throughout Shankracharya's time in Sringeri, Giri served his master most diligently and later accompanied him on his travels, remaining in his personal service.

Giri spent his time washing his master's clothes, cleaning his room, pressing his legs and cooking his meals. The only thing he cared about was how to make his guru's life more comfortable.

"This is my greatest joy, Bhagawan," Giri told Shankracharya, while pressing his legs after a long, tiring day. "I don't understand your discourses and my brain goes numb if I try to learn Sanskrit. My life is worthwhile if my service gave you even one moment of rest."

Shankracharya smiled. "May Ma Sharada bless you," he said raising his hand in benediction.

In the wee hours of the morning, even before Shankracharya got up to give the 4 am discourse to his disciples, Giri was already at the ghat of the Ganges, washing his master's clothes. Soon it was 4 am, but Giri didn't show up. Shankracharya refused to start the class without Giri and said that he would wait for him.

Some ten minutes passed and there was no sign of Giri.

“Why wait for that dunce, Bhagawan?” a learned student reasoned. “Your glorious words of wisdom are not going to get into this thick head anyway.”

Shankracharya maintained his somber look and ignored the question.

“He doesn’t even know the first letter of the Sanskrit alphabet, Guruji,” another said impatiently referring to the fact that not just the scriptural quotes but even the discourses of Shankracharya were in Sanskrit.

“Teaching him is like talking to a wall,” Padamapada, another disciple, said pointing to a wall in the compound.

“We’ll wait,” the guru said firmly.

A few moments later, they heard someone singing. Everyone turned to see who was singing most melodiously. It was Giri. He entered singing a hymn in Sanskrit devoted to his guru. The perfect arrangement of words was created in a new meter that Shankracharya later called ‘*Totaka*’. Everyone was awestruck. While they had been parroting verses from various texts, here was a student with original composition.

The master listened to the entire hymn with great joy as Giri sang eight verses. Right there, Shankracharaya gave him the name ‘Totakacharya’. Acharya means master and the hymn composed by Giri was titled *Totakashtakam*.

When a disciple continues to walk the path with sincerity, diligence and purity, transformation is certain. From an aspirant, he becomes an adept.

DAILY DUTIES OF AN ADEPT

On the path of mantra *sadhana*, there are three types of actions for an adept. They are called *nitya karma* (daily duties), *naimatik karma* (targeted duties) and *kamya prayoga* (application).

Daily Duties (Nitya Karma)

Think of daily duties or *nitya karma* as an employee going to work everyday to mark his presence. For an employee to remain up to date with what's happening in the company, to stay in touch with his colleagues, and to work in line with the vision of the organization, he is expected to show up at the workplace (even if he works from home on some days). In other words, he must stay in touch with the employer throughout his employment.

Nitya karma is something like that. An adept continues to abide by a daily routine to build on the *siddhis* acquired by intense practice or to simply maintain them. Practicing *nitya karma* helps both aspirants and adepts alike to build mindfulness. Daily duties (covered in this chapter) act as subtle constant reminders in the life of a practitioner to stay the course and not lose sight of what he stands for. In the olden days, a guru might ask his disciple to follow his daily duties unfailingly for anywhere between seven and twelve years before he would impart the instructions on how to invoke the mantra (*purushcharana*), which is a type of targeted action (*naimatik karma*).

Targeted (*Naimatik Karma*)

After an aspirant has championed the art and routine of practicing daily duties with reverence, mindfulness and sincerity, the guru, depending on the potential, inclination and readiness of the disciple, imparts the detailed instructions on how to invoke the mantra.

Going back to the example of the employee, targeted karma is like working on a project. You may go to work everyday, but you are likely to be working on a task that is timed and measurable. Similarly, *naimatik karma* is often in the form of a *puruscharana* done for certain duration, only with a specific objective. That specific objective is generally invoking the mantra. It requires intense practice. The nature of daily duties changes when an aspirant undertakes *naimaitik karma* under the guidance of a master.

In this book, under the *sadhana* section, I've given detailed instructions on four different invocations you can do for various outcomes. When performing *sadhanas* in this book, you should try your best to carry out your daily duties. In case you are pressed for time or unable to practice your daily duties, you can simply follow the steps of the *sadhana* because when undertaking any targeted karma (*purushcharana* or *naimaitik karma*), the rites of invocation (as covered in the chapter under the steps of *puruscharana*) take precedence over the daily duties.

Application (*Kamya Prayoga*)

Many mantras come with certain applications (*kamya prayoga*). *Kamya* means desired and *prayoga* means experiment, use or application. *Kamya prayoga* is when the power of a mantra is used to attain a desired outcome. For example, a *mantrin* who has mastered the mantra of *vashikarna* (to control another being) may use it anytime in the future to put it to use. It's like you may buy whatever you can afford if you have already saved that money. Through daily duties you prepare yourself, with targeted action (*naimaitik karma*) you earn and store your energy, and you put that to use by way of an application (*kamya prayoga*).

For a lot of mantras there are no specific applications per se. Many a time, an aspirant simply does *sadhana* to express his gratitude or to have a vision of his deity or to attain mantra *siddhi*. But none of that is done with a view to use the power of mantra for any specific desired outcome, especially material or worldly results. And that is perfectly fine. Such mantras don't come with a *kamya prayoga*. Having said that, when a practitioner has already accumulated plenty of energy of the mantra, he or she is naturally empowered to heal others and grant genuine wishes of others with the sole view of furthering the cause of nature for the welfare of others.

In this chapter, in the section below, I'm covering the daily duties any sincere seeker practicing mantra yoga should follow.

Even when you are not doing any *sadhana*, the path of mantras requires that you follow a certain daily routine. It's okay if you can't follow this on certain days due to family or work commitments, or if you just want to take a break maybe. The assumption, however, is that just like you eat everyday, drink water every day, you also follow your routine day after day. As the saying goes, you are free to break the rules after you have mastered them.

If you are performing the rites of invocation (*puruscharana*), the daily duties may change because the precepts set in the rites of invocation (*purusucharana*) takes precedence over the standard duties. Here are the duties of an aspirant or an adept. Even though I am starting the daily duties with morning, please note that this is not necessarily set in stone. In this day and age when lives are so fast and busy, you could tweak the routine to see what works for you. I'm sharing with you all the nine steps of a daily routine as follows:

1. Waking up

An adept should ideally wake up just before sunrise, after getting about six hours of sleep. In the olden days, most people slept in two parts: about six hours at night and two hours in the afternoon. Their lifestyles allowed that luxury. In most professions, it is not possible to have a siesta, but if yours allows you to, then you must avail it. It's extremely healthy. Even if you napped for more than 15 minutes in the afternoon, you will feel rejuvenated.

If you can't wake up before sunrise because you go to bed late, that's alright too. Just sincerely do the best you can.

Sitting up in your bed, meditate on the form of your guru at the crown of your head. Imagine the smiling face and graceful form of your guru emitting light and filling you with light and bliss. You don't need to devote more than 3-5 minutes on this meditation. Mentally offer your respects to your guru.

Once done, pray to the Lord. You can use your own words or you can use a beautiful prayer from *Lakshmi Tantra* I share below. It is full of devotion. Whether you use your own words or the prayer below, the most important thing is to do it with feeling. The more feeling you have in your prayer the more connected you'll feel and the greater impact your prayer will yield.

Sanskrit (Devanagri)	*Sanskrit (IAST)*
प्रातिकूल्यं परित्यत्तमानुकूल्यं च संश्रितम् ।।	prātikūlyaṃ parityattamānukūlyaṃ ca saṃśritam ।।
मया सर्वेषु भूतेषु यथाशक्ति यथामति ।	mayā sarveṣu bhūteṣu yathāśakti yathāmati ।
अलसस्याल्पशक्तेश्र्च यथावच्चाविजानतः ।।	alasasyālpaśakteśrca yathāvaccāvijānataḥ ।।
उपायाः क्रियमाणास्ते नैव स्युस्तारका मम ।	upāyāḥ kriyamāṇāste naiva syustārakā mama ।
अतोअहम कृपणो दीनो निर्लेपश्र्चाप्यकिंचन ।।	atoahma kṛpaṇo dīno nirlepaśrcāpyakiṃcana ।।

Sanskrit (Devanagri)	*Sanskrit (IAST)*
लक्ष्म्या सह हृषीकेशो देव्या कारुण्यरूपया ।	lakṣmyā saha hṛṣīkeśo devyā kāruṇyarūpayā I
रक्षकः सर्वसिद्धांते वेदान्तेअपि च गीयते ।।	rakṣakaḥ sarvasiddhāṃte vedānteapi ca gīyate I I
यन्मेअस्ति दुस्त्य्जं किंचित् पुत्रदारक्रियादिकम् ।	yanmeasti dustyjaṃ kiṃcit putradārakriyādikam I
समस्तमात्मना न्यस्तं श्रीपते तव पादयोः ।।	samastamātmanā nyastaṃ śrīpate tava pādayoḥ I I
शरणं भव देवेश नाथ लक्ष्मीपते मम ।	śaraṇaṃ bhava deveśa nātha lakṣmīpate mama I
सकृदेवं प्रपन्नस्य कृत्यं नैवान्यदिष्यते ।।	sakṛdevaṃ prapannasya kṛtyaṃ naivānyadiṣyate I I

Translation

I've rejected all feelings of antipathy and have adopted an attitude of friendliness towards all beings to the extent that my ability and mental capacity permit. Since I'm lazy, of limited capacity, and ignorant about the nature of things, the means (that I adopt) can never (be adequate to) save me. Therefore, I am downhearted and poor, without ties, without possessions. I also know that all doctrines (*siddhanta*) and Upanishads (*vedanta*) proclaim that Hrishkesha along with Lakshmi, who is the very embodiment of compassion, is the guardian (source of emancipation). Whatever I possess that is difficult to foresake, such as a wife or sons, all these, O Lord, I offer at thy feet along with myself. O my lord, master of the gods and consort of Lakshmi, be my protector. [Sanjukta Gupta translation of *Lakshmi Tantra*, verses 11.5-16]

2. *Achamana (The first sip of water)*

After praying, the adept takes a sip of water. It is recommended to keep a glass or a bottle of water next to your bed before you go to sleep. In the morning, after meditating for a few minutes as stated earlier, hold the glass of water close to your lips. Chant the mantra of your deity, your guru mantra or the mantra you are initiated into. For a moment, just visualize the heights of the Himalayas or the depths of the ground from where this water has been sourced. It is full of divinity and has the potency of nature.

Gently sip your water with this sentiment. Don't drink cold water out of the fridge. It's best to have the first sips of water of the same temperature as your room.

You may be tempted to think that who has so much time in the morning, but this entire process of waking up mindfully and sipping water shouldn't take you more than a few minutes.

3. *Bathing*

Ideally, an adept should bathe twice a day: once in the morning and once in the evening. If it's not possible to bathe twice a day, then the morning bath is mandatory.

Purify your body and clean your teeth and tongue. Rinse your mouth. Millions of people in India use a tongue cleaner, a very good way to clean your tongue. Some yogic texts also recommend using a strip made from cotton cloth to clean your tongue in the morning.

Chant the following mantra while putting the first mug of water on you (or when you step into the shower if you are using a shower):

Sanskrit (Devanagri)	*Sanskrit (IAST)*
गंगा च यमुने चैव गोदावरी सरस्वती ।	gaṃgā ca yamune caiva godāvarī sarasvatī |
नर्मदे सिंधु कावेरी जलेस्मिन संनिधिम कुरु ॥	narmade siṃdhu kāverī jalesmina saṃnidhima kuru ||

Translation
I invoke the holy presence of Ganga, Yamuna, Godavari, Saraswati, Narmada, Sindhu and Kaveri in this water.

Although remembering the mantras of *nitya karma* won't take anyone more than 50 or so repetitions before memorizing them completely, if you do have trouble in remembering the mantras, you can simply reflect on the meaning and use your own words. As I've said earlier, the sentiment with which you offer is infinitely more important than the language you use to make such an offering.

4. *Entering the Pooja Griha*

If you have a separate pooja room in your home then before entering the pooja room, you should mindfully bow your head for a few seconds and pray to God or the Divine Energy that may you be blessed to sincerely carry out your duties today. Then gently tapping the floor with your right foot, you should say the *astra mantra*. If you have not been imparted an *astra mantra*, you can use the following:

Sanskrit (Devanagri)	Sanskrit (IAST)
ॐ ह्रीं अस्त्राय फट्	oṃ hrīṃ astrāya phaṭ

Once inside, light a lamp and incense and say your daily prayers. Perform the seven core mudras (as shown in the chapter on mudras later in this book). Your daily prayer may include chanting your guru mantra. In addition, it may include meditating for a few minutes depending on what you have been initiated into. If you don't have a guru and you have not been initiated into any mantra, then you could simply chant or meditate on the *gayatri mantra* as follows:

Sanskrit (Devanagri)	*Sanskrit (IAST)*
ॐ भूर्भुवः स्वः	oṃ bhūrbhuvaḥ svaḥ
तत्सवितुर्वरेण्यम	tatsaviturvareṇyama
भर्गो देवस्य धीमहि।	bhargo devasya dhīmahi।
धियो यो नः प्रचोदयात॥	dhiyo yo naḥ pracodayāta॥

Or you could chant any mantra from the other three *sadhanas* provided in this book. What is important is that, above all, we go to our altar to fill ourselves with positivity and compassion. We chant in the morning to express our gratitude for everything God has blessed us with. There's just so much to be grateful for everyday. Early morning chants or mantras are not ways of doing a commercial transaction, where you tell God, "See, I'm chanting your mantra. Now you give me what I'm after." Instead, it's a way of understanding that you go way beyond your individual existence, and that you are bigger than your desires.

What you do on a daily basis is *nitya karma*. I recommend keeping the daily routine short so it doesn't become draggy and boring. If, however, you have the time and the inclination, you could include steps four to fourteen as stated in *Steps in Sadhana* in your daily routine as well.

5. Your first meal

Once you have freshened up and said your prayers, you are ready to have your first meal of the day. I hope you are not in such a mad rush in the morning that you eat your breakfast while driving or commuting to work. If so, try to get up half an hour early. It's doable if you sleep half an hour early. It's possible to sleep earlier than usual if you cut down on your Internet or TV time. Either way, no matter where and how you consume your first meal, say grace before you take the first bite. Gratitude is one of the finest antidotes of negativity and emptiness.

You can say grace in any way you like or you can use any or both of the verses below (with Sanskrit or just their meanings).

Sanskrit (Devanagri)	*Sanskrit (IAST)*
ब्रह्मार्पणं ब्रह्म हविर्ब्रह्माग्नौ ब्रह्मणाहुतम् ।	brahmārpaṇaṃ brahma havirbrahmāgnau brahmaṇāhutam ।
ब्रह्मैव तेन गन्तव्यं ब्रह्म कर्म समाधिना ॥	brahmaiva tena gantavyaṃ brahma karma samādhinā ॥

Translation
It is God alone who is making this offering of food. God is the food. God is the fire accepting this food (and digesting it). Attainment and realization of God is the only worthwhile cause for the one steadfast in selfless deeds.

Sanskrit (Devanagri)	*Sanskrit (IAST)*
हरिं दाता हरिं भोक्ता हरिं अन्नं प्रजापति ।	harir dātā harir bhoktā harir annaṃ prajāpati ।
हरिः सर्व शरीरस्थो भोक्ते भुज्यते हरीः ॥	harir: sarva śarīrastho bhokte bhujyate harī: ॥

Translation
God is the giver, God is the consumer, God is food and the creator of good. God is present in every pore of my body. Verily God alone is granting, consuming and digesting this food.

Ideally, every meal you take should be offered to the Divine with gratitude. With a bit of mindfulness, it's entirely doable. Once you do it for a few weeks, it'll become your second nature. Food becomes *prasadam* when you pray before eating.

6. Living through the day

Your day has begun and it could be a stressful one. There are going to be challenges at work — people you find difficult to get along with, people who don't support you, projects that are way over budget and time, targets that just can't be met. None of this will ever change. We can spend our entire day(s) and life complaining or hoping this will change. You may have some light and easy days, but mostly they'll be tiresome. And that's fine, really.

None of what happens in the external world can take away the one who lives inside you. No doubt, you will be impacted, you may feel hurt, dejected, rejected, down and so on. But all of that is quite temporary.

Your bosses, employers, co-workers, the Prime Minister, the President, economic indicators... these are not the makers of your destiny. All of that has an impact just like what you do will have an impact on those around you, but ultimately, how you feel about what happens to you is your personal matter.

After starting your day beautifully, spend the rest of your day mindfully. Don't speak ill of people. That has never gotten anyone far. As an adept, it's important for you to remember that the mouth that utters the holy names should not spit profanity, obscenity or hurtful words.

It may sound like a lot, but if you practice mindfulness for the first few weeks, it'll become your second nature. Have some personal principles and don't compromise on them. One desirous of walking the path of mantra yoga should chant the mantra of his deity as much as possible. It should be mental chanting.

Scriptures state that there are seven moral ways of acquiring wealth. 1. inheritance (*daaya*), 2. profit (*laabha*), 3. trade (*kraya*),

4. victory (*jaya)* in moral contests, 5. application (*prayoga*) of your skills, 6. working (*karma yoga*) and 7. bonafide gifts (*satpratigraha*).

7. Self-study

From the *Bhagavad Gita* to the *Yoga Sutras* of Patanjali, there's a great deal of emphasis on the importance of self-study (*svadhaya*). Self-study is of two types. First is the study of the self and second is the process of studying scriptures on your own. An adept should do both.

It's important to devote a few minutes to both as part of your routine than do a lot in one go and then not touch the scriptures for a long time.

Self-study (studying of oneself) is the art of contemplative meditation. As a part of studying yourself, you may pick a thought, emotion or an incident and contemplate on why you acted or behaved in a certain manner, or that why you felt what you had felt and so on. Self-study requires that you contemplate your actions, thoughts, feelings, words, gestures and desires. It could be a good exercise to do in the evening before you do your nightly chanting or meditation. Once again, it doesn't have to take tens of minutes. Five to seven minutes are generally sufficient. Don't brood over the past or don't feel guilty, just focus on what you did versus what you should or could have done. Make a mental note and let go of that incident.

The second aspect of self-study is studying a scripture. You could pick the *Bhagavad Gita* or any scripture you connect with. Simply read a verse a day and mull over it. Scriptures are not story books or novels, no matter how interesting they may read. To understand the true meaning and to delve deeper, read a verse (or a chapter) and let it sink in. Reread it and read it yet again. One of the most important things to remember is consistency. Be consistent. Doing a little a day is lot more effective (even practical) than doing a lot on some days.

A *mantrin* should never desecrate a scripture or be blasphemous in word or in thought. Never.

8. Chanting

At least one round of your guru mantra, *ishta mantra* or the mantra of your deity must be done. Depending on the nature of your initiation or the type of tradition, if your guru has asked you to do more, then you must do more. And if you don't have a guru, chant at least one round regardless. One round consists of 108 times chanting using your beads. The chapter on beads explains different types of beads and their effects.

If you are unable to use a rosary or chanting beads, simply chant by counting on your fingers. If you are chanting while you are driving and you can't use your fingers, chant by setting duration. Usually, six to nine minutes are sufficient to mindfully complete a round depending on the length of your mantra.

9. Retiring to bed

Ideally you should have your dinner either before or during sunset. If your lifestyle does not allow that, try to eat at least three hours before you go to sleep. Sleeping on a full stomach leads to a *tamasic* sleep (a sleep where you are completely unaware). Sleep, while it is a suspension of consciousness, is still an opportunity for an adept to chant some more in the form of *ajapa* (chanting without chanting).

After you have washed your face and brushed your teeth, wear light clothes, preferably made from cotton (other light material will also do) and sit on your bed. It's a very good habit to make a small journal entry of any particular incident or learning that you had that day. Don't go on a writing spree, be brief.

Once done, spend five minutes in meditation. You could meditate on your breath (by listening to inhalation and exhalation) or you could meditate on the form of your deity (by visualizing his/

her form) or you could simply meditate on the mantra itself (by chanting mentally and listening to every letter of every word of your mantra).

The best thing to do just before going to bed is to meditate. The next best thing is to read a good book. At any rate, once done with either or both, pray to the Divine expressing your gratitude and seeking forgiveness for any mistakes you might have done in the day. Once again, you can use your own words, or you can use the following prayer:

Sanskrit (Devanagri)	*Sanskrit (IAST)*
करचरण कृतं वाक्कायजं कर्मजं वा ।	karacaraṇa kṛtaṃ vākkāyajaṃ karmajaṃ vā ।।
श्रवणनयनजं वा मानसं वापराधं ।।	śravaṇanayanajaṃ vā mānasaṃ vāparādhaṃ ।
विहितमविहितं वा सर्वमेतत्क्षमस्व ।	vihitamavihitaṃ vā sarvametatkṣamasva ।
जय जय करुणाब्धे श्रीमहादेव शम्भो ॥	jaya jaya karuṇābdhe śrīmahādeva śambho ॥
Translation	
O Lord, please forgive my inappropriate actions done intentionally or inadvertently, prescribed (out of a sense of duty or due to scriptural injunctions) or not prescribed (done out of habit, afflictions and negative emotions), done either through speech, action, sight, words, gestures or mentally. I adore you Bhagawan, the Mahayogi, who is an ocean of mercy. All glories to you.	

It may seem like a lot to do in a day but any additional activities mentioned here should not take you more than 40 minutes. This includes self-study and chanting one round. Rest is simply about building the mindful practice of chanting and compassionate living in your routine.

What if you can't stick to a routine, you ask? I would strongly encourage you to form a routine and follow the daily duties of an adept to the best of your abilities. Having said that, the Goddess states in *Lakshmi Tantra*:

"There is no difference whatsoever in merit between an initiate well-versed in the duties of the five sections of the day and one who is engaged in pronouncing the mantras of Lakshmi."

Eventually, what matters is to live and act with constant memory of God in your mind. This can be attained through mindful chanting. All rituals are designed so you may ultimately live mindfully with a pure heart free of the feelings of jealousy, hatred, envy, covetousness. So, you may have a mind that's stable and positive. This opens you up, it helps you connect with the Divine energy. And a flower that's open is a lot more fragrant than when it's closed.

Mindful *japa* with devotion is the essence of mantra yoga. Therefore, a *mantrin* makes every effort to chant as much as he can. Chanting accumulates energy you can use to elevate yourself or to help others. Lying, false conduct and harmful actions use up your energy. It is one of the primary reasons why many people who chant still don't attain *siddhi* or the rewards of chanting because most of the energy gained through their spiritual practices end up getting absorbed in trivial matters that are not only non-spiritual but detrimental to their spiritual progress.

Here's a brief list of daily dos and don'ts:

Dos

1. Bathe
2. Meditate
3. Say grace before you eat anything
4. Chant at least one round of your mantra
5. Go offline an hour before you go to bed
6. Try to eat and sleep at the same time every day
7. Meditate before going to bed

8. Be charitable wherever and whenever you reasonably can
9. Express your gratitude to the Divine
10. Seek forgiveness for your actions

Don'ts

1. Be a parrot when chanting; chant with reverence and mindfulness
2. Harm, hurt or injure any living being
3. Harbor negativity in your heart. Remind yourself to let go
4. Start your day by checking messages or emails on your phone or tablet
6. End your day watching TV or replying to messages and emails
7. Disclose your *sadhana* or mantra to anyone
8. Abuse your scripture, sadhana, guru or deity
9. Compromise your moral integrity
10. Miss your routine

Āradhāitō yadi haristapasā *tataḥ kim*
Nārādhitō yadi haristapasā tataḥ kim.
Antarvahiryadi haristapasā tataḥ kim
Nāntarvahiryadi haristapasā tataḥ kim.
(*Nārada Pancr*ātra, 1.2.6)

If your worship leads to Śrī Hari, what good is any penance; of what use is any austerity if you are not lead to Śrī Hari. If you worship him within and without, tapas is no longer important; if you do not worship him within and without, how can tapas be of any importance.

INVOKING A MANTRA

- **Six Limbs of a Mantra (*Shadanga*)**
- **Selecting Your Mantra**
- **Exceptions**
- **Checking it for Flaws**
- **Correcting the Flaws in Mantra**
- **Infusing Life in Your Mantra**
- **Chanting Your Mantra**
- **Hurdles in Invocation**
- **Beads and Other Considerations**

SIX LIMBS OF A MANTRA (SHADANGA)

Every mantra has six limbs called *shadanga*. There are some exceptions, however, and they are listed at the end of the next chapter. For every other mantra, though the six limbs are not just six aspects or six elements of a mantra, they are exactly what it says — six limbs. This basically means that with any one of the six missing, a mantra won't be able to work to its full potential. For example, most of us have four limbs and if we lose a leg, we won't be able to run as fast. If we lose an arm too, we'll be severely impaired in many functions. Similarly, a mantra that can be invoked and benefited from only when it comes with all six limbs intact. I've listed the limbs of each mantra sadhana listed in this book. The six limbs are:

Seer (Rishi)

Every mantra that is available to us on our planet was brought to us by some seer. The seer of the mantra is called the rishi of that mantra. It means the one who saw. Mantras are not coined or created; they are only ever seen because all the mantras were given to us by the foremost yogi, Shiva. Everyone else is simply seeing what's already in the universe. In other words, mantras are never invented, they are discovered.

Imagine you come across a book expounding on a technical subject and by the time you are done reading it, you have some questions you would like answered. There are three ways to get those answers. One, you could try figuring it out yourself. Two, you could read more literature on the same subject and see what others have to say. Or three, you could simply contact the author of the book and ask your questions. You could directly benefit from the author's experience and knowledge.

Knowing the seer of a mantra is exercising the third option. If you don't know who first discovered this mantra, you may miss out on many critical aspects of that mantra. For example, all mantras where the great sage Vashistha is the seer, you have much greater chance of mantra *siddhi*, if you lit a lamp made from cow's ghee or if you sat on a *kusha-asana* or a *kambala-asana* because that's what Vasishta used. These little details are generally what a good guru would provide you. Just so you know, for every *sadhana* in this book, I've given all the relevant details sufficient to lead you to *mantra-siddhi*.

Knowing the seer has another point of great and deep significance. Traditionally, mantras are passed on orally, from a guru to a disciple. When you acknowledge the seer of the mantra, you know whom to call upon, you know the lineage you are connected with and you also realize what an immense privilege it is to hear the same mantra from your guru that sages passed on from one to another over a period of several tens, if not hundreds, of thousands of years.

If a mother extends the family by carrying a child in her womb and rearing the baby, a seer extends his spiritual lineage by passing on the mantra. A mantra is the spiritual (eternal and immortal) child of a seer. It is one of the reasons that a sincere guru will not just impart a mantra without examining the intentions and potential of the disciple.

Deity (*Devata*)

Every mantra has a deity (*devata*). The *devata* of a mantra possesses certain traits and qualities that an aspirant wishes to acquire. Every *devata* has a form and attributes that are generally used for the purposes of meditation (*dhyana*). The *devata* represents the potential energy of a mantra. It is to reach this potential that we chant a mantra or become one with it.

The *devata* represents the masculine aspect of a mantra. While I say masculine, I don't mean that the *devata* is a male always. A mantra can have a female deity, and many mantras do have female deities. By masculine aspect, I simply mean the other side of feminine, an aspect which a female deity (*devi*) can possess too.

Seed (*Beeja*)

A mantra without a seed syllable is like the seedless fruit. You can enjoy its taste, you can benefit from its nutrients, but only once. You can't use that fruit to grow a tree and multiply it to have a supply of fruits that will last you a very long time. The seed of a mantra represents its creative energy.

Sometimes, the guru may just give the seed syllables (rather than the actual mantra) to a disciple and only reveal the full mantra over a period. When mantra *sadhana* is done with the knowledge of its seed, it can help in attaining irreversible and remarkable self-transformation.

Energy (Shakti)

Einstein once said, "Nothing happens until something moves." Well, energy (shakti) of a mantra is its kinetic aspect. If *devata* represents the masculine side, shakti signifies the feminine side. Together, they complete the mantra. A mantra without shakti has no application at all.

On the path of mantra yoga, you cannot benefit from a mantra if its energy is not known. It's the movement that makes anything happen. Procreation is movement as is creation. Growth is movement as is evolution. It is by virtue of the shakti of a mantra that we actually put that mantra to use.

Meter (*Chanda*)

All Vedic mantras must adhere to a certain Vedic meter, known as *chanda.* They determine how the various syllables are to be grouped in a mantra. In the ancient days when seers would sometimes scribe on a *burja* or palm leaf, the chances of some letters getting smudged over time or misinterpreting the letters were high, predominantly because the writing instrument would often be a sharpened twig of some tree, or sometimes a small stick (*shalaka*) made from copper, silver or gold. The ink would be made from the color of some fruit or flower. Often such scrawls in small fonts lacked calligraphic excellence. Therefore, to avoid mispronouncing a mantra, it would be assigned a meter that would show the arrangement of syllables.

Even before the days of writing mantras or *sadhanas* on leaves, when everything was transmitted strictly orally, meters were assigned to mantras so the aspirants could recall and chant them correctly. Rhythm in a mantra is as important as rhythm in any musical composition. There are 21 meters in the Vedas, out of which six are most frequently used. The complete list of meters can be found in the detailed notes. The six key ones are as follows:

i. *Gayatri:* This meter comprises 24 syllables in one verse or 3 verses of 8 syllables in each stanza. The famous Gayatri Mantra (covered in a *sadhana* in this book) belongs to a meter with the same name.

ii. *Ushnika:* This meter consists of 28 syllables which may be arranged in 2 verses of 8 syllables each plus one verse of 12 syllables.

iii. *Anushtubh:* A vedic meter that has 32 syllables where 4 verses have 8 syllables each is called Anushtubh.
iv. *Brihati:* A vedic meter comprising 36 syllables with 2 verses of 8 syllables each, plus 1 verse of 12 syllables and 1 verse of 8 syllables is called Brihati.
v. *Pankti:* This meter is made up of 40 syllables arranged in a simple arrangement of 5 verses with each verse having 8 syllables each.
vi. *Trishtubh:* Trishtubh has 44 syllables with 4 verses of 11 syllables each in every stanza.
vii. *Jagati:* Jagati comprises 48 syllables arranged in 4 verses of 12 syllables each in every stanza.

All vedic hymns always belong to a meter.

Kilaka (Lock)

Kilaka refers to the innermost syllables of any mantra. By innermost, I don't mean the letters that are in the middle of a mantra or that the letters are placed in the innermost circle of its accompanying yantra. Here, innermost refers to the most secret, esoteric and potent aspect of the mantra. That is, the ability to put your mantra to use. Think of *kilaka* as a lock. Literally, *kilaka* also means a pin or a bolt. Without *kilaka*, you can accumulate the energy of a mantra but you can't utilize it for any practical purposes. It's like depositing money in your bank account. You can deposit as much as you like but without knowing the pin of your bank card, you can't withdraw that money from the ATM. *Kilaka* is the secret pin code you require to unlock and apply the energy of the mantra towards some attainment.

Sometimes, even if you forget your ATM pin, you can still walk into a bank, furnish your valid proof of identification and generate a new pin. Initiation into a mantra creates that ID proof. When you know the seer (rishi) of the mantra and you are properly initiated into it that is the equivalent of an ID proof. It shows that you are a bonafide individual. It means that you exist in the realm of the mantra science. Initiation into the lineage of the seer is like having a guarantor who can verify your identity.

A pertinent question that arises is, what if you are not initiated into a mantra, how do you go about invoking it? For the four *sadhanas* listed in this book I've given you the work around which begins by invoking the guru within you. For all the other *sadhanas* you may take from other books, I've given in detail various flaws a mantra can have and ways to correct them. I can't promise if an individual can succeed without initiation in all other *sadhanas* you may learn from various texts. But, as far as the four *sadhanas* given in this book, I can tell you with absolute conviction (based on my own experience and research) that lack of initiation is not a hurdle for the sincere *sadhak*.

SELECTING THE RIGHT MANTRA

An adept told me a story once. Somewhere this story underpins the importance of chanting the right mantra.

There was a tantric who had spent his entire life trying to invoke the mantra of Kali but had practically no success. Once he decided to do *shava-sadhana*, a type of sadhana that requires the aspirant to chant the mantra while sitting on a corpse. In *shava-sadhana*, a lamp is lit in the mouth of the corpse. He brought a corpse on a small cart in the woods and set everything up.

It so happened that on a nearby tree a woodcutter was watching this tantric. It was already sunset and the woodcutter had decided to sleep on the tree for the night. With great awe, even fright, he saw how the tantric took off his clothes, lit a lamp, performed some handlocks, sat on the corpse and began chanting the mantra loudly. The powerful chant fell in the ears of the woodcutter, rooting him to the spot.

Night had set in. Birds were back in their nests, jackals howled at a distance and owls occasionally hooted and screeched. Crickets were active as ever. Leaves fluttered in the gentle breeze. Nocturnal animals roamed about. Unfortunately for the tantric, a leopard came in search of prey and attacked the tantric killing him within minutes. It devoured his game and went away as quietly as it had come.

The woodcutter watched the whole ordeal while mentally

praying for his own safety. The corpse looked eerie with a lamp still lit in its mouth. With great courage, he descended from the tree and went near the corpse. Just a few meters from there was the body of the tantric, now no more than a carcass. Even his eyes had been eaten out.

He looked around and for reasons unknown to him decided to recite the mantra he'd heard the tantric chant. He didn't know any of the rituals, he wasn't even initiated, but he'd heard the mantra clearly enough, felt its power, its rhythm and he could recall it correctly. He grabbed hold of the rudraksha rosary the tantric was using and began chanting the mantra. Hardly had he chanted three times that a terrifying form of Kali appeared before him right there.

The woodcutter went cold and sweat broke out. For a moment he felt his heart had stopped pumping. In front of him stood the beautiful ebony Kali, wrathful but glorious. Her hair was loose, her fangs protruding, her tongue red. Eyeballs as dark as the night and eyes sloshed and intoxicated from the wine she drank from the goblet she held in one hand. In another hand, she held a sickle. Her third hand held a freshly severed head while the fourth showered benediction.

"I'm very pleased with you," Devi said. "What do you want?"

The woodcutter could not utter a word. He just stared stupefied, as if struck by lightning. He could have easily died of fright, had the goddess not assumed a calming two-armed form and smiled at him benevolently pacifying him.

"O, Mother Divine," the woodcutter finally found his voice, with his hands folded he said, "The tantric chanted your mantra for over two hours and you did not appear, he gave up his life and yet you did not come to his rescue, and here I'd only just begun reciting and you gave me your vision."

"Two hours?" Devi laughed mellifluously. "He has been calling out to me for more than six lifetimes."

"Oh?" He asked puzzled.

"It was not his time yet," Devi said. "In his next lifetime, he'll have my vision, but you, my son, you died praying to me in your last life. You've been desperate for me for a few thousand years now. That's why your karma brought you here today. For my vision to manifest, only seven more times you had to chant my mantra. You couldn't do it in your previous life, but it happened today. So here I am. Ask for a boon!"

Stories or legends like this are not uncommon to hear on the path of mantra *sadhana* for mantra yoga believes that our affinity with certain deities, sounds or mantras is not just the result of one lifetime but several. Therefore, it is important that you choose your mantra carefully.

Never rush into selecting the mantra you wish to invoke. When you undertake invocation of a mantra, you are making a long-term commitment. You'll be putting in intense energy, time and effort into the entire affair and it greatly helps the cause if selection of a mantra is made after due thought.

Mantras represent your intimate relationship with your deity and as such, the first most important thing to ask yourself is if you feel any affinity towards the deity of the mantra. Because eventually how much strength you are going to draw from your mantra and its deity is primarily dependent on the purity of faith you have in your mantra. Other than checking the flaws in a mantra, there are three ways of ascertaining if a certain mantra is going to be beneficial to you. At least, in one of the three methods, the mantra should be beneficial to you. I've covered here the most important of the three. The remaining two can be found in the detailed notes.

Elemental Compatibility (Kula-Akula Chakra)

Kula means race, tribe, lineage, community or a body. *Akula* is the opposite of *kula*, i.e., something that doesn't belong to a certain *kula*. When Shiva created the original sounds, each letter was assigned an element or category. This is how to ascertain elemental compatibility between you and your mantra.

Please see the table below. It has five elements, namely, wind, fire, earth, water and space. Each letter of the Sanskrit alphabet falls under one of these categories.

Air	*Fire*	*Earth*	*Water*	*Space*
a	i	u	hr	Lr
ā	I	U	hR	Lr
e	ai	o	ou	Am
ka	kha	ga	gha	ṅa
ca	cha	ja	jha	Ña
ṭa	ṭha	ḍa	ḍha	ṇa
ta	tha	da	dha	Na
pa	pha	ba	bha	Ma
ya	ra	la	va	Sh
Sh	Ksha	la	sa	Ha

To check for elemental compatibility, see the first letter of your mantra and the first letter of your name. If they both belong to the same element then the mantra will suit you the most. The chances of you being able to invoke the mantra are extremely high.

If the first letter of an aspirant's name and the first letter of the mantra don't fall in the same category but are still friends (*mitra varga*), the mantra will still be beneficial. If, however, the first letter of the selected mantra and the first letter of an aspirant's name are enemies (*shatru varga*), that mantra is unlikely to be of any benefit to the practitioner. See the table below to know which elements are friends or incompatible with each other.

Friends	Water, earth	If mantra's first letter and your name's first letter fall in water or earth categories (or vice-versa), you can attain mantra *siddhi.*
	Fire, air	If mantra's first letter and your name's first letter fall in fire and air categories (or vice-versa), you can attain mantra *siddhi.*
Enemies	Fire, earth	If mantra's first letter and your name's first letter fall in fire and earth categories (or vice-versa), the mantra won't be beneficial to you.
	Air, earth	If mantra's first letter and your name's first letter fall in the air and the earth categories (or vice-versa), the mantra won't be beneficial to you.

Letters in space category are friends with everyone. Therefore, any mantra where its first letter is governed by space is good for universal chanting.

It is important to note that many mantras have 'Om' as the prefix. For the purposes of assessing elemental compatibility, you can choose to either use or ignore the prefix. Sometimes if you really feel attached to a mantra but it doesn't match with your element, you may consider adopting a spiritual name used only for the purposes of *sadhana.* This was part of the reasons why a guru would give his disciple a new name upon initiation. A spiritual name may be used in healing, application or initiation. With the permission of his guru, an aspirant can replace his common name with his spiritual name.

EXCEPTIONS

When mantras were created by Shiva, there were no exceptions. Any adept practicing a mantra had to be initiated in that mantra as well as check it for flaws and compatibility. The science of mantras evolved over time but legend has it that there was one specific incident that impacted the most. That one incident set many mantras free to be chanted and invoked by anyone.

A devout Brahmin was chanting a verse from the *Rigveda*. This verse became the famous Mrityunjaya Mantra, that is a mantra that can conquer even death (*mrityu*). In his devotional sentiment, with all the reverence and fervor he could muster, he was chanting the following mantra:

oṃ tryambakaṃ yajāmahe sugandhiṃ puṣṭivardhanam
urvārukamiva bandhanān mṛtyormukṣīya māmṛtāt
(The *Rigveda*, 7.59.12)

I worship that fragrant Shiva of three eyes, the one who nourishes all living entities. May he help us severe our bondage with samsara by making us realize that we are never separated from our immortal nature.

The last word *māmṛtāt* comprises two words maa + amritat. *Maa* means my or me and *amritat* means imperishable, immortal and eternal. The opposite of *amritat* is *mritat* which means mortal, perishable and temporary. The Brahmin, though qualified, was wrongly chanting the last word as *ma-mritat* which means my mortal nature. This small mistake was changing the entire meaning of the mantra making it the opposite of what he actually meant.

One such evening when he was chanting, Shiva was roaming the universe with his divine consort Parvati, the Goddess. They came closer to earth and passed over the Brahmin.

Shiva chuckled hearing him chant the mantra.

"O Devi," he said, "this Brahmin is ignorantly asking for bondage and not liberation by incorrectly chanting the mantra. If he goes on like this, he'll never attain moksha."

"The world will certainly blame you for that, my Lord," Devi said. "You are the creator of all the mantras. He's chanting out of extreme devotion and reverence. He doesn't even know that you will grant him the opposite of what he seeks. No average person can understand the intricacies of the language that evolved from your *damaru*. You alone are the perfect grammarian."

Shiva stopped mid-air and pondered over the matter for a few seconds. "I hear you, Devi," he said somberly, "but I can't interfere in the natural energy radiated by the mantras. A sun in any solar system will always exude heat, it can't emit coldness. It must follow the natural dharma. So too will mantras only emanate their energy based on how they are chanted."

"There must be some solution, Nath," Devi pleaded. "At least, there should be no ill-effects. Maybe the energy of the mantra could be neutralized. After all, no matter how much heat sun radiates, stones don't catch fire nor does water. At least, a sincere devotee should be protected."

"That is why initiation is important, hence the need for all the precepts and checks," Shiva reasoned.

"Agreed, but no one should be deprived from participating in your sonic creation just because of initiation. Grant them pardon, Lord. Show them the way."

Shiva looked at Devi for a brief moment and then gazed in the far distant space as if scanning all the universes in the whole of creation, as if taking stock of all the mantras that floated in that creation, the mantras his damaru had created.

"From this day on, all Vedic mantras are exempt from phonetic and compatibility checks. Even if an uninitiate were to chant, no harm would befall on him."

Shiva went on to narrate a list of conditions that mantras fulfilling those conditions would be considered exceptions and those chanting or invoking such mantras will only benefit from the positives and not be affected by the negatives.

"My own mantra of five letters, *Om Namah Shivaya*, will also be exempt as will be all mantras imparted by any female practitioner because you live in all females, Devi, and today with your intervention, mankind will benefit in a big way."

Realizing that Sanskrit required great phonetic precision, Shiva also created another class of mantras called the Sabar Mantras. They are self-invoked (*svyama-siddha*) mantras that are used for a variety of worldly purposes. But most importantly, with that boon, Shiva set free millions of mantras. The conditions under which a mantra may be exempt are given at the end of this chapter.

There are many mantras that are used for chanting, spiritual progress and other purposes and they don't have the six limbs as stated earlier. Most of these mantras have become famous over the last few thousand years, some only in the last few hundred years. It is quite possible for a chant to be a mantra and still not conform to the framework of mantra science. As always there are exceptions to the rule. In mantra yoga as well, there are many mantras that can be taken up by anyone with or without initiation (though initiation is always recommended). Anyone can chant these mantras without worrying about whether or not the mantra is beneficial to them. It doesn't mean they are any less effective, it simply means that over the last few thousand years, these mantras have been invoked and passed on by enough adepts for the welfare of others that they are beyond personal invocation. And, therefore, they no longer require the usual rigors of mantra yoga.

There are some medicines for which you must have prescription and then there are some you can just procure over the counter. It's not that off-the-shelf medicines are not effective; it's just that they are unlikely to kill someone or cause damage. Those meds are freely available. Anyone can buy them without consulting a doctor or having a prescription in their hands. Think of mantras that are exempt from the standard requirements in mantra yoga to be like off-the-shelf medication — effective, harmless, but temporary.

Most bhakti mantras such as Hare Krishna Hare Krishna Krishna Krishna Hare Hare, Hare Rama Hare Rama Rama Rama Hare Hare, many self-invoked (*svayam siddha*) mantras, etc., don't have the six limbs. It also depends a great deal on the guru. If the guru invoked a certain mantra and decides to pass it on to his or her disciples in a way that's not traditional or scriptural, those mantras can still work provided you are initiated into such a mantra. For all other mantras, it's of immense benefit to actually follow the process.

Rudrayamalam and other scriptures are quite clear on the mantras that don't need special assessments. Here are the mantras that don't require any compatibility or other considerations in the Kali Yuga.

1. A mantra your guru has initiated you in
2. Any mantra of Krishna
3. A mantra that's given to you in a dream
4. When a mantra is imparted by a female adept even not as initiation
5. A mantra comprising only one seed syllable
6. A mantra comprising only three seed syllables
7. A mantra that contains more than twenty letters
8. All vedic mantras (There are a lot of non-vedic mantras)
9. A mantra of five letters
10. A mantra of eight letters

For any mantra to be effective, particularly if it doesn't fall in the above ten categories, it requires initiation, proper invocation and complete adherence to the tenets of mantra yoga.

FLAWS IN MANTRAS

In *Rudrayamalam*, Shiva says to Devi:

maṃtradoṣāṃstu vijñāya guruḥ pariharet kṣaṇāt,
anyathā sa guruḥ śiṣyaṃ nihantyevācirāt dhruvam.
tena tatparihāraṃca śṛṇu devi! Samāhitā,
parihāraprakārantu vakṣye yogeṣu tatvataḥ.

A guru must correct the flaws of a mantra otherwise both the guru and the disciple are headed for downfall (by compromising the tradition). O Devi! The scriptures are clear about how to correct those flaws. I shall expound on those, pay attention.

Imagine trying to produce beautiful music with a flute that has a crack in it. You may still be able to create some melody, your music may not be cacophonous, but the music you will produce from a broken instrument won't be the desired one. Similarly, when it comes to mantras, the music of energy that you create with the melody of a mantra is greatly impacted by the quality of your mantra.

If your mantra has flaws, they must be corrected beforehand. When you are given a mantra by your guru, chances are your guru might have considered or even corrected these flaws beforehand (provided your guru possesses adequate working knowledge of the science of mantras). But, if you are uninitiated into your chosen mantra or unaware of its flaws, the chances of success are quite grim.

Once again though, for the four *sadhanas* listed in this book, I've given you the procedure to correct any flaws in these mantras.

Sometimes, even after doing everything right, an aspirant does not attain mantra *siddhi*. All too often it can also happen due to flaws in your selection of mantra.

Mantric scriptures state many potential flaws in a mantra, out of which fifty are the important ones and applicable even in this day and age. Out of those fifty, six flaws are most common. I'm listing the six common flaws here, the remaining forty-four, with explanation, can be found under 'Detailed Notes' at the end of this book.

1. *Dagdha:* When chanting is done with unnecessary additional sounds of "yo, ee, ya, yo". This is one of the most common flaws. Frequently, *sadhaks* when restless, will start chanting a mantra fast, or slow when feeling lazy. In doing so, they often distort the phonetic harmony that exists in the mantra. And, when that harmony is breached, the mantra yields either no results or undesirable results.
   For example, chanting '*Om Namah Shivay*' as '*Om Namah Shivaya*' will attach *dagdha* flaw to this mantra changing the phonetics, and therefore, application and outcome of this mantra. Like playing any musical instrument requires great precision, correct chanting of mantra too requires a certain phonetic accuracy at the minutest level. The best way to overcome this flaw is to maintain consistency of speed, rhythm and alertness while chanting your mantra. Rather than chanting fast when restless, you could slow down instead, for example. This will help you in being mindful and alert.
2. *Trasta:* To chant other mantras along with the mantra you are initiated into. When carrying out a *sadhana*, one must stick to the procedure given by the guru. Any other mantras must be chanted only if they are a part of your *sadhana*. If you do two

sadhanas at a time or chant other mantras thinking your main mantra is not potent enough, you won't attain success in any of the *sadhanas* by default.

If you want to source water from earth, you must bore many hundreds of feet at the same point. If you dig ten feet and then think that there's no water here and so I must go and dig a well elsewhere, it won't help. You can go wherever you like but digging ten feet here and ten feet there will never get you to the source of water in the ground. Similarly, to invoke the latent energy within you through the power of mantra, we must keep digging at the same point. Make one mantra your everything and go after it with full zeal, discipline and mindfulness. Results most certainly come through for the one who is patient and persistent.

3. *Garvita:* If you haven't acquired a mantra through proper tradition, it is inherently flawed. For example, a guru maybe giving mantra instructions to another disciple and you happen to drop into that conversation, adopting the mantra as your own. It creates a flaw in the mantra called *garvita*. A most common occurrence of this is when someone you know shares with you that they benefited from a certain mantra. They are not entitled to initiate you into the mantra and yet you take the mantra from them and start chanting. Such a mantra is not going to yield the desired results.
4. *Mattah:* When a mantra is acquired from a book without getting instruction from your guru, the mantra is said to have *mattah dosha*. *Garvita* and *mattah* are the two most common forms of flaws in a mantra. While we are at it, I would like to spell out clearly that the four *sadhanas* mentioned in this book have been practiced, invoked and awakened by me. I forego any holding and grant you the privilege to benefit from them without attracting *mattah* or *garvita dosha*. It's for the welfare of our fellow sisters and brothers that I've chosen to deviate from the norm. Anyone sincerely following the procedure stated in those

four *sadhanas* will derive benefit. Provided, of course, that the *sadhak* believes in the science of mantras and tries it sincerely.

5. *Chinna:* This applies if your guru has recommended a specific place for your mantra *sadhana*, or if the *sadhana* explicitly states selection of a certain place. When an aspirant ignores this instruction and tries to awaken the mantra at a place of his or her own choice, the mantra is called *chinna*.

   There's no doubt that a conducive environment is an important requirement in mantra *siddhi*. If you wish to be an Olympian swimmer, sooner or later, you'll have to practice in an Olympic-size pool. You'll have to replicate those conditions you are going to be swimming in while going for the gold medal. In mantra science, too, certain mantras can only be invoked at certain places.

   Woods, caves, mountain peaks and the banks of a river are generally good places. It all depends on the nature of your mantra. Some mantras, for example, can only be invoked in a cremation ground.

6. *Stambhita:* When ignoring guru's instructions completely, a practitioner chooses to go according to what he sees fit, the mantra is said to be *stambhita*. *Stambhita* means that which has stopped and *stambhita dosha* implies that the potency of the mantra is blocked due to breaking from the tradition. If for any reason the practitioner still goes his way, it's not that they can't awaken the mantra, it's just that by starting a new tradition, they are signing up for greater effort than is required. The lineage of siddhas and the original seer of the mantra who imparted the instructions won't be there to assist the practitioner.

   Once you've reached an advanced level, after you have invoked a mantra, you can modify some of the practices based on your individual temperament. You can add to your guru's instructions and not replace them completely. It's 'in addition to' and not 'instead of'. Many *sadhaks* make the mistake of simply taking the mantra from their guru and ignoring his/her instructions. When you are initiated into a mantra but you don't make a sincere attempt to follow the instructions of the guru who initiated into such mantra, the flaw of *stambhita* applies to the mantra.

CORRECTING FLAWS IN A MANTRA

We don't live in a perfect world. It's so hard to find a good guru, and even when you do find the perfect guru, he or she is often not available to answer your personal queries and so on. The good news is that not having the guru, or not having a guru at all, doesn't mean that you can't succeed on the path of mantra yoga. At the end of the day, it's quite simple: pick your mantra, correct its flaws and begin invoking it with all the discipline, reverence and faith you can find within.

By now, you already know some measures you can take to select the right mantra. Further, in this book, I share four mantra *sadhanas* any aspirant can undertake. Plus, I've shared the process of invoking a mantra in detail. Even if you select a mantra that's exempted from checks, initiation, etc., I still strongly recommend that you correct its flaws anyway. I've followed this process in all major *sadhanas* of mine and benefitted immensely.

In this chapter, I share with you the process to correct the flaws in a mantra. It is an eight-step process. This has to be done only once, on the first day of whenever you start invoking a new mantra. Here are the eight steps:

1. Acquiring the mantra sentiment (Mantra *Bhavana*)

When an aspirant continues to walk the path of mantra yoga, eventually there comes a time when he becomes one with his mantra (*mantramayi*). To reach that state, it's important to imbibe the energy of a mantra in you so it becomes a part of your being. There are two ways to do that.

1. Add 'Om Aim Hreem Shreem' as prefix and suffix to your mantra and chant it 1000 times in one sitting. So, if your mantra is '*Om Namah Shivaya*', it becomes '*Om Aim Hreem Shreem Om Namah Shivaya Shreem Hreem Aim Om*'.
2. If you have access to a clean river, lake, stream or pond then simply stand in it during sunrise, add the prefix '*Om*' to your mantra and chant it 1000 times. For example, if your mantra is '*Om Namah Shivaya*', stand in water so that it is at least knee-deep (this is equally effective though it should ideally be waist-deep) and chant '*Om Om Namah Shivaya*' 1000 times.

2. Praying to your guru (Guru *Dhyana*)

Even if you don't have a guru in human form, do pray to your guru as a part of correcting the flaws in a mantra. The original seer of the mantra could be your guru, your inner voice could be your guru, the universe or God could be your guru. You could simply chant the following mantra three times.

gururbrahmā gururviṣṇurgururdevo maheśvaraḥ,
gurureva paraṃ brahma tasmai śrīgurave namaḥ.

If you have the time and devotion, you can also chant the full *stotra* (only once) which is given in detailed notes with meaning.

3. Crowning your deity (*Kulluka*)

This is done by touching the crown of your head and chanting your mantra three times and then chanting the crown of your deity seven times. Every mantra has a deity and the crowning (*kulluka*) is always done of the deity and not of the mantra per se. Usually, most mantra *sadhanas* will specify the crowning mantra, but in case they don't, you can use:

a. *Aim Hreem Shreem* for all feminine (devi) mantras
b. *Kha sa phrem* for all masculine mantras (*devata*) mantras
c. *Om bhram jam sam* for all neutral (*napunsaka*) mantras

If you know the class of your deity, you can then also use the table below to be more specific:

Type of Sadhana		*Crowning Mantra*
1	*Shaiva* (all mantras where Shiva is the deity)	*Om Haraum*
2	*Shakta* (all mantras where Devi is the deity)	*Aim Hreem Shreem*
3	*Vaishnava* (all mantras where Vishnu is the deity)	*Om Namo Narayanaya*
4	*Saur* (all mantras where Sun is the deity)	*Om Ashvatejasya Swaha*
5	*Ganpatya* (all mantras where Ganesha is the deity)	*Om Gam Jram Namah*

Just to reiterate, when crowning your deity, simply touch the crown of your head and chant your main mantra three times. Thereafter, chant the crowning mantra seven times. Keep touching the crown of your head throughout.

4 Bridging your mantra (*Mahasetu*)

Since any verbal chanting of the mantra particularly involves the throat plexus (*vishuddhi* chakra), bridging of the mantra is performed to, as the name says, bridge the gap between the energy of the mantra and our speech.

Mantra bridging is performed exactly in the same manner as crowning of the mantra with only one difference: when bridging, just touch your throat plexus rather than the crown of your head.

So, when bridging your mantra, touch your throat and chant your main mantra three times. Thereafter, chant the bridging mantra seven times. Keep touching your throat throughout. For your bridging mantra, simply refer to the table under point number three above. Your bridging mantra is the same as the crowning mantra.

5 Protective shield (*Bandhan*)

Though the word *bandhan* means to tie, in mantra *sadhana*, the process of bandhan means to create a protective shield around you so that other energies don't interfere with the energy of the mantra you are trying to invoke.

A mantra *sadhana* may have a specific *bandhan* mantra and in case nothing is specified, simply use the one based on the table below:

Type of Sadhana		*Shield Mantra*
1	*Shaiva* (all mantras where Shiva is the deity)	*Om Raudraye Swaha*
2	*Shakta* (all mantras where Devi is the deity)	*Hreem Kleem Shreem*
3	*Vaishnava* (all mantras where Vishnu is the deity)	*Om Narasimhaya Swaha*
4	*Saur* (all mantras where Sun is the deity)	*Om Suryaye Phat*
5	*Ganpatya* (all mantras where Ganesha is the deity)	*Om Gam Gam Vaushat*

The protective shield is created by chanting the shield mantra a total of 400 times. You can use beads or anything else for counting. You can also use your fingers. Or you may just set aside three minutes for chanting in each direction and not worry about counting. Follow the process below:

1. Face east and chant 100 times or for 3 minutes
2. Face south and chant 100 times or for 3 minutes
3. Face west and chant 100 times or for 3 minutes
4. Face north and chant 100 times or for 3 minutes

The five steps above correct most of the flaws in mantra by aligning its energy with your own and in the immediate surroundings around you. Once done, you are ready to infuse life into your mantra. Please note that correction of flaws and infusing life into your mantra is only done once at the beginning of your mantra *sadhana*. So, it may seem like a lot but if you go through it patiently, one step at a time, you'll cover it in no time.

INFUSING LIFE IN A MANTRA

Infusing life in a mantra is done by way of performing ten *samskaras*, or a rite of passage.

Think of mantra *siddhi* as your child made from pure energy. The ten *samskaras* ensure proper upbringing of this child so he is obedient, wise, compassionate and competent.

In Sanatana Dharma, every important milestone of life is linked to a Vedic celebration, for life is a celebration. We celebrate when we are grateful, happy, full, when we want to share and give. Each milestone is called a rite of passage or *samskara*. *Gautam Sutras* list forty-eight *samskaras*, out of which, sixteen are the most common ones (you can find them in 'Detailed Notes'). Similarly, since on the path of mantra yoga, a mantra is considered to have living energy, it also undergoes ten important rites of passage where the adept brings it to life.

An important point to note, however, is that you don't need to do all the ten *samskaras*, especially if your guru has initiated you into the mantra and given you instructions on how to invoke it. Also, these ten samskaras are only done as part of your targeted karma (*naimaitik karma*, i.e., when you are performing the rites of invocation, *puruscharana*) and not as a part of your daily duties (*nitya karma*, i.e., when you are just chanting on a daily basis).

If, you have attained the mantra on your own, or in a dream, I strongly recommend you perform the ten samskaras diligently. I can tell you from my personal experience that this greatly heightens the chances of attaining mantra siddhi. Here are the ten samskaras.

Janana

Janana is the first *samskara*. *Janana* means to give birth. It is the equivalent of conception (*garbadhana*) *samskara* in Vedic Dharma. To do *janana samskara*, you require *bhojpatra* (bark of a tree and is 100 per cent bio degradable).

Make an ink by mixing *chandan* and *kumkum*. Now facing eastwards, sit on your asana. Take separate small pieces of *bhojpatra* and write the letters of your mantra; one letter on one piece of *bhojpatra*. Let it dry. Once done, take the letters written on *bhojpatra* and immerse it in a river, stream or an ocean.

On another piece of *bhojpatra*, write your entire mantra. This becomes the asana of your mantra. This can be put at the base of your lamp throughout your *puruscharana* or you can put it below your *yantra* or you can just keep it at your altar. Yantras or mandalas are drawings that visually capture the energy field of the mantra. For the sake of simplicity, I've stayed away from the use of yantras in sadhanas elucidated in this book. Once your *puruscharana* is complete, the *bhojapatra* must be immersed in water.

Deepan

Deepan is to ignite the light in a mantra — the light of life. It is similar to *pumsvana samskara* which is performed in Vedic dharma when a soul has already taken the form of an embryo.

To do *deepan samskara*, you need to enclose the mantra with the '*hamsa*' mantra and chant one thousand times. For example, if your mantra is '*Om Namaha Shivaya*', you need to chant '*Hamsa Om Namaha Shivaya SoHam*' one thousand times. *Deepan samskara* signifies your desire and intention to bring the mantra into your own world (like one day the child leaves the womb and enters your world).

Bodhan

Bodhan is the process of infusing consciousness in the energy of a mantra. The energy of a mantra that has been infused with consciousness can guide on many facets of life. It polishes your inner voice and paves way for you to communicate with and be guided by the universal energy around you.

To do *bodhan samskara*, you need to enclose the mantra with the seed syllable '*hroom*' and chant your mantra five thousand times. For example, if your mantra is '*Om Namaha Shivaya*', chant '*Hroom Om Namaha Shivaya Hroom*' five thousand times.

Tadan

Tadan means two things. First, to chastize and second, a solemn act. When it comes to mantra yoga, the *samskara* of *tadana* is the solemn act of chastizing your mantra. It needs to be gently chastized because when it goes out there and interacts with the universal energy, it is going to meet resistance and other obstacles. By gently chastising it now, you prepare it for the future.

By doing various mantra *samskara*, we are preparing the mantra to have a life of its own. That's what *siddhi* is. A conglomerate of energy, potent enough to make things happen for you, that you have available for your use at your beck and call. It is only possible if you make the energy of your mantra strong enough to take care of itself.

Tadan is done by enclosing the mantra with the seed syllable 'phat' and by chanting it one thousand times. For example: Phat Om Namah Shivaya Phat.

Abhishek

The mantra is fully grown now. Think of *abhishekam* as coronation. It is done to acknowledge that the mantra is assuming a life of its own from this moment. You recognize that the energy of the mantra is mature enough to handle its own energy. Remember that you have brought the energy of the mantra into your world and given it a new life, like two parents procreate from what was already there and give birth to a new child.

To do *abhishekam*, you need to scribble the mantra on *bhojpatra*. Take a small vessel of water and chant '*Rom Hansa Om*' on the water. Now take a leaf of peepul, *bilva* or *bahera* tree and pour it on the *bhojpatra* 108 times, chanting the mantra alongside. Chant your mantra, take water in the leaf and pour it on the *bhojapatra*. Do it 108 times. If you can't procure peepul, *bilva* or *bahera* tree leaves, then simply join your ring finger and thumb, dip it in the water and sprinkle it on the *bhojpatra*.

Vimalikaran

Vimalikaran means purification and *vimalikarana samskara* means the act of purification. The living energy of the mantra is young enough to be aggressive, even hurtful. After its coronation, the mantra is infused with new power. *Vimalikarna samskara* purifies and pacifies the energy of the mantra.

Vimalikaran is done by enclosing your mantra with '*Om Trom Vashat*' and chanting it 1000 times. For example, the mantra '*Om Namah Shivaya*' will become '*Om Trom Vashat Om Namah Shivaya Vashat Trom Om*'.

Jeevan

The mantra is ready to be independent now. It's ready to lead a life of its own. It has acquired enough energy to serve your cause. The rationale is that even if you bring up a child with all the right qualities, at some point in time, he has to be independent so that he may go out and earn a living and support you as well in the process. A dependent child can't really support his parents.

To do *jeevan samskara*, enclose the mantra with '*svadha vashat*' by prefixing and suffixing it to your mantra. Therefore, the mantra will become '*Svadha Vashat Om Namah Shivaya Vashat Svadha*'.

Tarpan

The mantra is not only independent but mature enough so that you can now release it out in the world to interact with the universal energy and remove obstacles from your path. Now you don't have to watch out for your mantra. It goes out and does its job for you.

Take half a cup of cow's milk, half a cup of water and a few drops of ghee. Chant your mantra 100 times while doing libations in the same vessel. This is how *tarpan samskara* is performed.

Gopan

Only a mantra that is mature can protect you. After the *tarpan samskara*, *gopan samskara* is done. *Gopan* means protection. In this *samskara*, you remind your mantra, you infuse in it the subconscious energy that its primary responsibility is to protect you.

Gopan samskara is performed by enclosing your mantra with the seed syllable of '*hreem*' and chanting it 1000 times. For example, the mantra '*Om Namah Shivaya*' will become '*Hreem Om Namah Shivaya Hreem*'.

Apyaayan

There are two words in Sanskrit closely related to each other. One is *apyayana*, which means union. And the other is *aapyaayana*, which means advancement, gladness and satiated.

This is the final stage of the *samskara* where living energy of the mantra has attained union with you, leaving you satiated with a wave of bliss. From this moment on, you are ready to infuse potency in this mantra by performing *puruscharana* of the mantra. *Puruscharana* is creating spiritual and energetic wealth of the mantra you may use at a later date.

Apyaayan samskara is done by enclosing the mantra with the seed syllable '*hrom*'. Therefore, the mantra '*Om Namah Shivaya*' will become '*Hrom Om Namah Shivaya Hrom*'.

Once you have performed the ten *samskaras*, you are ready to do a *puruscharana* of your mantra. A pertinent question that arises is what are these seed syllables and why do you have to do *samskara* before you can truly awaken the energy in a mantra?

Generally, the intention behind invoking a mantra is to not only attain a certain benefit from it but to be able to do so repeatedly. A mantra invoked by *purushcharana* is like seedless fruit. It's tasty, nutritious and ripe, but you can only eat it once. When you awaken the mantra by doing various *samskaras* that require seed syllables, essentially what you are getting is a seeded fruit. Which means that not only do you enjoy the fruit but with the seed you have, you can plant a tree reaping the same fruit repeatedly and in abundance.

HOW TO CHANT YOUR MANTRA

You have selected your mantra, you know how to go about invoking it, you know the various steps to infusing life in your mantra. Now, you've arrived at one of the most important aspects of mantra *sadhana*, i.e., how to chant the mantra. The most common mistake people make is to chant without feeling or chant just for the sake of it. Such chanting does not bring the promised rewards. I learned it the hard way after years and years of practice.

I would sincerely follow all the steps required by various *sadhanas*, do *japa* as per the instructions and yet, I didn't feel any difference in my life or my mindset. Eventually, I discovered that quality and quantity are both important in mantra *sadhana*. Chanting a mantra a few thousand times or even a few hundred thousand times does not necessarily amount to spiritual progress. The quality in chanting must be there. As I wrote earlier, devotion and faith are two most important ingredients on the path of mantra *sadhana*.

Devotion and faith are synonymous to spiritual love. When you love someone, time just flies in their company, there's little to no boredom. Without love, your *sadhana* is reduced to dry performance of mechanical rituals making you only more rigid and angry. When you undertake a prolonged or an intense mantra *sadhana*, it is natural that at times you'll feel lazy, sleepy, bored, tired and so on. That's okay. It's human. These are common hurdles and there are ways to overcome them. A lack of interest at times doesn't mean that you lack devotion or faith.

To get past emotional and mental hurdles (in the form of negative feelings and restive tendencies of the mind), you have to understand the four types of chanting. *Vigyan Bhairav Tantra* states that there are only two types of mantras. They are, one, mantras that are internalized (*citta-yukta-mantra*) and two, mantras that are uttered (*dhvani-yukta-mantra*). When it comes to chanting (*japa*), the mantras that are internalized are far more effective than those that are chanted out loud. Having said that, switching between the four forms of chanting helps you in maintaining the freshness and lucidity of the mind. Here are the four types of *japa* and ways to use them in your *sadhana*:

1. Spoken chanting (*Vachika japa*)

This is the first and lowest form of chanting. It's called *vachika*. *Vachika* means a word that's been verbalized and uttered. We communicate with the external world through spoken words alone. Whether those words are written or uttered, they are classified as spoken words. The use of spoken words is purely to strengthen our connection with the external world.

Mantra *sadhana*, however, is an inward process. Chanting aloud like the relentless chirping of a cricket does not take you closer to your inner world.

In mantra yoga, all hymns, odes and eulogies to God or your deity can be sung out loud as they evoke positive feelings of devotion and celebration but mantra chanting is almost always done internally. It takes a great deal of practice to chant your mantra internally without losing your concentration. *Vachika japa* is audible to everyone around you. It represents physical consciousness (*vaikhari*).

2. Whispered chanting (*Upanshu japa*)

The second type of japa is called *upanshu*. *Upanshu* is whispering. In this form of chanting, only your lips move, only just. When you are whispering your mantra, your mind naturally concentrates a bit more. One of the fundamental precepts of mantra *sadhana* is to not disclose your mantra to others. In whispered word (*upnashu japa*), you whisper so discreetly that you are almost inaudible. Only you are able to listen to what you are chanting. Whispered chanting is better than spoken chanting. It represents mental consciousness (*madhyama*).

3. Mental chanting (*Mansika japa*)

Mental chanting or *mansika japa* is when there's no external sound in your chanting and even your lips don't move. A common misconception is that mental chanting is chanting your mantra loud in your mind. That's not really *mansika japa*. The correct way to do mental chanting is to recall your mantra with concentration, one word at a time.

If you are simply chanting in your mind, you'll discover that very soon even though you are chanting the mantra mentally, your mind is already thinking about a million other things. This is not effective. If, however, you recall the mantra mentally one word at a time, you are able to maintain much superior concentration. Recollection allows you to draw upon the sonic energy generated by your mantra.

Mental *japa* is ten times more effective than the first type of *japa*. It represents intellectual consciousness (*pashyanti*). It is important to note that the sound it is associated with is called *pashyanti*, means that which is seen (as opposed to spoken). In mental chanting, you repeatedly visualize the mantra in your mind's eye.

4. Unspoken chanting (*Ajapa*)

Unspoken chanting is not something you do per se. This fourth form of *japa* is called *ajapa* which means that which is not chanted. It is no longer a conscious act. It is something that happens to you. When you continue to sincerely chant your mantra in the first three stages with mindfulness and over a long period of time, you naturally reach the fourth stage of *japa*.

In unspoken chanting (*ajapa*), you find yourself mentally chanting all the time, the sonic energy of the mantra continues to accumulate in you. You are able to continue your chanting even when you are operating normally throughout the day doing other chores. As soon as you get up in the morning, you realize that you are already chanting your mantra.

Some scriptures say that in the *ajapa* state you are even chanting while you are asleep. I'm not sure if that's indeed the case as I don't have any scientific data, at least nothing that I could validate personally. It is possible to chant your mantra as part of lucid dreaming or yogic sleep and it's something I've experimented with as well. But, I'll not get into those details at this stage as it remains outside the scope of this book and is not directly relevant to mantra yoga.

Unspoken chanting (*ajapa*) represents transcendental consciousness (*para*).

Both spoken and whispered chanting come under the category of mantras that are uttered (*dhvani-yukta-mantra*). Mental and unspoken chanting, on the other hand, is internalized mantra (*citta-yukta-mantra*). The mantra remains the same but how you chant makes all the difference. The softer you chant your mantra, the closer you get to the source.

A sage, with his disciples, was taking a morning stroll by the Ganges and chanting the holy names. There was a couple in the distance – they were distressed and were shouting at each other. It turned out that the man's wife had lost her gold necklace while taking a dip in the Ganges. Her husband unleashed a flurry of filthy slurs and she was shouting back in equal fury.

The saint stopped, turned towards his disciples and said, "Why do people shout in anger?"

One of the disciples replied, "Because when we lose our calm, we shout."

"Granted," said the sage, "but, why should you raise your voice when the other person is just next to you? It's not that he's hearing you better that way. You can still make your point without shouting at the top of your voice."

They offered various answers, none with any revelation.

Finally, the sage spoke:

"When two people are angry at each other, their hearts are no longer close; their emotions are divided and they are miles apart. To cover that distance, they yell. The angrier they are, the louder they shout. Anger immediately creates a distance. They are unable to hear each other; shouting is how they believe they can be heard.

"And, what happens when two people fall in love? They don't shout at each other but talk softly, because their hearts are very close. There's little or no distance between them.

"When they love each other even more, they exchange even less words, they murmur, they whisper, yet they hear each other better, their bond strengthens, love prospers. Finally, they may not even whisper, they only look at each other; silence becomes more potent than speech."

So it is with chanting. As you develop a stronger bond with God or your deity, chanting becomes a part of your life. You whisper, you laugh, you cry for your deity. You call upon Him continuously like two people deeply in love but separated miss each other.

At a practical level, when undertaking any mantra *sadhana*, try doing only the third type of *japa* (mental chanting) as much as possible. When you feel lazy or sleepy during your *sadhana*, simply switch to the first or the second type (spoken or whispered) for a few minutes. When your mind is invigorated by spoken chanting, come back to mental chanting. This is one of the best ways to do mantra chanting with mindfulness and alertness.

HURDLES IN INVOCATION

The path of mantra yoga is like any other path with hurdles and challenges. There are inner, outer and spiritual obstacles any sincere seeker is bound to experience. The keyword here is '*sincere seeker*'. Any aspirant who's not really serious or committed will neither encounter the challenges nor reap the rewards, for you only get to the choppy waves when you venture deeper in the ocean. Mantra *sadhana* is no different.

In the beginning, you begin with enthusiasm, hope, expectations and determination but most people quit even as the journey starts to take shape, as they move towards the point of no return. Transformation, while immensely rewarding, can be painful and it certainly doesn't come easy. The path of mantra *sadhana* is not the one for quick results. Like anything worthwhile, it requires sustained effort over a period of time. Let me walk you through various obstacles you'll hit during your journey and how to overcome them.

Fear

Fear is not a challenge in the beginning, not during your *nitya karma* (daily invocations) anyway. But, when you begin to embark on other aspects of mantra yoga, notably *puruscharna*, which is a *naimaitik karma* (for a specific purpose), you can't just sit in the comfort and confines of your home. Your *sadhana* may take you to secluded places, remote areas... maybe to caves, woods or even cremation grounds, depending on the nature of your *sadhana*.

When you are all by yourself, in solitude, doing *puruscharna*, all kinds of fear may grip you. It could be the worries of the future, it could be the guilt from the past or it could simply be your experiences with energy and your deity that may invoke fear in you. Even some of the most courageous aspirants quit at this juncture. Don't. Hold. Stay the course. Keep on pursuing your *sadhana*. If you've hit a state of fear on account of your experiences with the sonic energy of the mantra, you must be doing it right. You are closer to the final *siddhi*.

I remember during the days of my intense *sadhana* or the numerous *purushcharanas* I did, whenever I hit that point of fear due to hallucinations, visions or other challenges, I would simply tell myself, "Don't worry, you are not going to die. Don't quit." I reminded myself that I didn't want to live without finding my truth anyway. In other words, you have to give yourself some affirmation to keep going.

If you are initiated into a tradition by your guru, you've absolutely nothing to worry about. The entire lineage of *siddhas*, the gurus in the tradition who existed before you will protect you. They have a vested interest in protecting their tradition as well as protecting those who have invested faith in them. When you hit the highest point of fear, you will break free and will experience an incredible sense of fearlessness.

Swami Karunananda was initiated by a great tantric guru and I'd known Swami for a good few years. Before I renounced, whenever he stopped by in my city, he would always stay at my place. We would have lovely conversations stretching well into the late hours. He was 74 years old at the time and I was 27. He would gently fall asleep and I would watch the soft glow on his face. He spoke most softly and was a carefree soul. In his saffron robes, you could never guess that Swami Karunananda was also an adept, the kind of tantric well versed into *vamachara* — the left-handed path of tantra.

For more than forty years, at the instruction of his guru, he never missed his practice on the new moon night, no matter where he was. Every *amavasya*, he would go to the nearest cremation ground, disrobe completely, spread his seat next to a funeral pyre and take out the human skull and two bones he always carried discreetly in his bag and begin his tantric ritual. I asked him once if he felt any fear being all alone, stark naked, next to a funeral pyre in a cremation ground in the dead of the night.

"Not anymore," he said. "But it wasn't always like this."

"When I was barely 19," he continued, "my guru sent me away to do my first tantric *sadhana* in the woods. It was a ritual I had to do at night. 'Once in the woods, don't look back until you reach your spot,' my guru had said, 'and, the great Bhairava will test you but don't come back to me without completing this ritual.'

"I thought I was very brave and could overcome any fear," Swami Karunanda said smilingly, "but that was hardly the case. In the deep and dark woods of Girnar, I began walking just when the sun was setting. The spot my guru had told me was at least a four hour walk into the jungle. I had to reach there by 11 pm, get ready and start the ritual by midnight and finish by 4 am.

"Everything was almost fine when there was still a bit of sunlight. I could see what lay ahead of me, I could see to my left and to my right. I could hear birds tweeting and their mating calls but that was about it. Soon dusk turned to night and I took out my torch. Torches were not common in those days but my master had lent me his. After about an hour of walking, I had this eerie feeling that someone was following me. It was most scary. I began walking faster but it wouldn't stop."

Swami Karunananda paused to take a breath and then continued, "At first, I tried to dismiss it as the sound of ruffling leaves or just my imagination but it was way too clear. I so wanted to turn back and see if there was anyone or was it just my mind whipping up hallucinations but my guru had specifically forbidden me from turning back. My heart began thumping and I stopped walking.

Within a few seconds, that being stopped following me and came closer to me. I thought I would die; I was so scared. I nearly wet myself when it started breathing so close to me. I felt its warm breath fanning my neck and the sound of labored breathing. I held my own breath to make sure it wasn't my own breathing sound. It wasn't."

Swami Karunananda's face turned serious but he kept on narrating the story, "In hindsight it might have been nothing but I was so scared at the time. All alone in the woods. Well, not all alone actually, I'm certain my master was there with me. His energy protected me. Anything could have gone wrong. Girnar, at the time, was infested with serpents, lions, foxes, wolves, hyenas and jackals. I resumed walking and it started following me. A little later, a voice shouted close to my ear, "Karunananda!". Believe me, I thought I had died already or all this was a dream. I stood there trembling and I began crying. 'Guruji, guruji, save me,' I called out to my guru.

"I heard the howling of jackals at a distance, a bird took off from a nearby tree and every sound drove me insane, every little sound felt like my death warrant. 'I don't want any *siddhis*, guruji,' I cried. 'I just want to serve you. I'm coming back.' I nearly turned but in that tiny fraction of a moment something changed in me. A voice inside me said, 'What are you afraid of?' I felt it was my master instructing me.

"Till date, I don't know if anyone actually followed me. My master wouldn't tell me anything about it whenever I asked him. And I don't know why I was so scared, but all I know is that very moment my fear subsided and I felt a sort of elation. In that elation, I ran through the woods and towards my spot. You should never run through the woods, it draws unnecessary attention from wild animals, but I was past caring. After running for about half an hour, I started walking again and I made it to the spot by 10.30 pm.

"I don't know what exactly happened but I was no longer scared. I felt so fearless that I began dancing. 'I dare you to come in front of me whoever you are, if you are,' I shouted. Of course, no one came.

I disrobed, spread my seat and sat on the ground and waited for the watch to tick 11. I completed my ritual fearlessly and walked out of the woods a new person in the morning. Since then, I have never been afraid of doing any *sadhana*, anywhere, in any condition, at any time of the day or night."

I know exactly what Swami Karunananda means, perhaps you do too. I remember when I had to walk to a river in the middle of a night and complete a ritual, away in the Himalayas, far from any civilization, for a moment you do feel fear. But that's the thing; the mind has a strange clinging to fear. It shows its hesitation even if you decide to take something as harmless as a cold bath. It forces you to stop for a moment before you pour cold water on yourself.

There is only one way to overcome your fear and that is by understanding it. Once you understand the nature of your fear(s), whether they are fears on the path of *sadhana* or in real life, it begins to disintegrate. For, understanding allows you to be prepared to not just handle the fear but the consequences it brings. As you walk through, and not run away, from your fears, you gain this incredible strength, which invariably is the potent seed of transformation.

Like clouds, fears appear laden and heavy, but when you are in the sky passing through them, you discover no matter how real these clouds are, they are not strong or full enough to resist you. Even a tiny pebble can easily pierce through them.

Fear is not just a feeling or an emotion; it's a phase, a stage. Any worthwhile pursuit will have it. You can walk away from it and abandon your pursuit or you can walk into it and experience the exhilaration that only attainment of a goal brings.

Impatience

I have devoted more than two decades to my own meditative practices, and my specialization and area of interest was always mantra yoga and tantra *sadhana*. These involved long hours of meditating on a sound, on a form, and bringing mantras to life. There is one flaw that hurt me the most whenever I failed. This is the same problem I see in hundreds of seekers I meet every year. It's a common issue arising from our get-rich-quick mentality.

There is absolutely no way to hasten the process of invocation. None whatsoever. Impatience will not only compromise your practice, but it is at the root of most challenges we face when invoking a mantra. When you are impatient, you are restless naturally. It's harder to focus; your mind wanders in different directions. With an unfocused mind the chances of making mistakes are much higher. I can't stress enough that you must have faith and patience if you are serious about seeing the results from mantra yoga.

There is a joke I tell often. There were four men crossing the river on a boat. One of them was a Muslim, one Hindu, a Christian and a Sikh. Midway, they realized that the boat was sinking. There was a crack on the surface that turned into a gash. It was too long to cover with hands. Worse still, no one knew how to swim. They looked at each other helplessly as the boat plummeted fast. Soon they would be floating like corpses on the river, they felt. But, they had faith, staunch faith.

The Muslim went first. Seeing no avenue, he shouted loudly, "Yah Allah!" and jumped in the river. Allah came and saved him.

The Christian went next. "Save me, my lord Jesus Christ!" he screamed of the top of his lungs and jumped. Sure enough, Christ, his savior, manifested and rescued him.

The Sikh gentleman also called upon God, he shouted, "Waheguru!" and jumped. A divine light of *Nirankar*, the formless God, appeared and safely led him to the riverbank.

The Hindu was left alone. He called out to his favorite God, Shiva first. But no one came. He went on to pray to Krishna. Still no one came. He called out to the benevolent Rama and yet there was no sign of anyone. He prayed fervently to Devi. No one came. And so, he drowned.

As soon as he died, he found himself in heaven.

"Due to your good karma and for remembering God in the last moments of your life, you are granted a permanent place in heaven. You are free from the sufferings on earth."

"I don't care about a permanent place," he retaliated stamping his foot and clenching his fists. "I just want to know why no one showed up to rescue me. Is there no God?"

God appeared before him and said, "Of course, I was about to come but you kept changing your position. First you called out to Shiva, I took a trident and damaru, donned a lion hide and summoned Nandi. Just when I was about to leave and reach you within a second, you began calling out to Krishna. I immediately put on a crown with a peacock feather. I wore *pitambara*, my yellow attire. I took on the discus, tucked in my flute and called for my divine chariot to be with you within a moment, but showing no faith, you started calling out to Rama. Immediately, I changed my attire, put a different *tilak* on, carried my bow and quiver and boarded my chariot, but you began praying to Devi. Once again, I assumed a differnt form, carried different implements, summoned my lion to come to you but by then, you had drowned."

It's quite important to see the message behind the humor in this anecdote. More often than not, aspirants lose their patience and faith. They think, "I've been chanting this mantra, nothing has happened, so let me try something different. I heard from so-and-so that such-and-such mantra is a lot more powerful and solved their problems. Or, I heard that there's this *siddha*, some adept, who gives out ancient mantras, I'd better get one quickly," and so on.

Kabir says beautifully:

Bhaur bhooli khasam ke bahut kiya vibichar,
Satguru aani bataya poorbala bartar.

Like a promiscuous one, I went around my beloved's back and sought pleasures from other partners (This means, I lost faith in my deity and went around praying to other gods thinking they were more powerful). But, when my guru entered into my life, he helped me stay focused and pray to the one I'd been praying to in all my lifetimes.

Once again, I have to emphasize an important point: By following mantra yoga, or even simple intense meditation or devotion, you can even manifest divinity in a stone. The absoluteness of the mantra is not as important as the sincerity of your practice. No matter how plain your deity may sound, if you are persistent, results will come through. Never make the mistake of abandoning your practice thinking some other one is simpler. That way you start all over again. Build on what you know, grow from where you already are rather than going back to square one. When it comes to mantra yoga, all you have to do is follow the tradition and instructions of your guru, and practice with patience and sincerity.

One step at a time, one mantra at a time, one word, one letter at a time. With patience, discipline and truthfulness, you keep walking. Results most definitely come through for such an aspirant. For, if not for a sincere seeker then for who else would the deity manifest, who else would be more qualified to reap the rewards?

Physical pain or disability, an unfavorable environment, procrastination, laziness, doubt and self-doubt are other common hurdles on the path of mantra yoga. The best way to overcome them is to continue with faith and mindfulness, one step at a time. Patiently, sincerely.

Beads

What type of rosary or chanting beads you use plays an important role in attaining mantra *siddhi*. It is important to consecrate the rosary when you first get it (covered later in this chapter). It is best to keep your rosary in a bag that no one touches other than you throughout your *sadhana*. Ideally, you should even wash the bag yourself.

There are rosaries with 27, 54 or 108 beads. The most common is

108 beads and is most suitable for mantra *sadhana*. So, the number of beads in your rosary should be 108. The 109th bead usually sits at the top and is called *meru*. When one round of 108 is complete, a *sadhak* should not go over the beads but turn over the rosary. In other words, you don't cross the 109th bead but turn over the rosary and start from the beginning. There is very good reason behind it.

Generally, when you do intense *sadhanas* where you may be chanting several tens of rounds at a stretch, it's normal for the mind to lose its sharpness and focus. Chanting then becomes a mere mechanical activity (which must be avoided at all costs). Chanting must be done with reverence, alertness, faith and mindfulness. By remembering to turn over the chanting beads at the completion of one round brings you back to the present moment and refreshes your concentration.

Different beads have different results. In all mantra *sadhanas* of Ganapati, Devi, Shiva and other energies, rosary made of aksha nuts – commonly known as rudraksha – or eleocarpus seeds is most auspicious.

In all mantra *sadhanas* of Vishnu and Krishna, *tulasi mala* – rosary made from *tulasi* beads is most suitable. For spiritual progress, use Rama *tulasi* (white beads) and Krishna *tulasi* (dark beads) for material endeavors.

Rosary made of sandalwood beads is universally good for any sadhana. Once again, *shweta chandan* (white sandalwood) for spiritual progress and *rakta chandan* (red sandalwood) for material progress. Further, in all Devi *sadhanas*, if you choose sandalwood beads, you are better off using red sandalwood.

Rosary made from the beads of treated mercury is used in some tantric mantras of Shiva.

For *siddhi* in the mantra of Lakshmi, the goddess of wealth, best results come from using the rosary made from *kamal gatta* (lotus beads).

For specific *sadhanas* leading to an expansion of consciousness through mantra yoga, *sphatika* (crystal) is most efficacious.

In many sadhanas of lower forms of masculine energy (demigods) *moonga* (coral) beads have a definitive effect.

For peace of mind, longevity and fame, a rosary made from white pearls is useful.

Rosary made from the beads spun from cotton or silk yarn is used to simply aid general purpose chanting.

Rosary of gold beads is used in rituals intended to worship the ancestors or with a view to attain a desired material outcome.

Beads of silver or copper are used in *sadhanas* done with a view to attain victory in the battlefield.

Many *sadhanas* of lower forms of energies (like *yakshinis*) use beads made of tin.

Lead beads, especially in some tantric *sadhanas*, are used in mastery over even lower forms of energies like *rakshas* and *pischas*.

Rosary made from the beads of turmeric can be used by a householder to ward off evil spirits.

Bell-metal beads are used in mastery over vampire spirits (*vetala*).

Brass beads are used in chanting of mantras, especially a special class of mantras called Sabra Mantras, to gain control of serpents and reptile.

For great wisdom, beads of topaz (red topaz) either strung or studded in silver are used.

There are other types of beads and rosaries made from sapphire, bones, *siyar singi*, claws of owl or lion, clay, charcoal, wood obtained from *gular* (cluster fig tree) or *shami* tree (Prosopis *cineraria*) that are used in many tantric *sadhanas*, generally with a view to harm someone. I do not wish to expound on them publicly nor have I any practical insight into these beads for I've never used them.

I have, however, personally experimented with at least nine different types of rosaries in many *sadhanas* over two decades and I can tell you that the selection of beads does have a noticeable impact on the quality of your *sadhana*, and therefore, the outcome.

Once you have sourced the beads, you can string them yourself. While the color and type of thread makes a difference as well, for the sake of simplicity and practicality, you can use red thread braided properly to make it strong. If you procure the beads already strung into a rosary, your job is simpler. Either way, you must consecrate the beads. Every new *sadhana* is always performed with a rosary consecrated exclusively for that *sadhana*. Once you complete your sadhana, you can either wear those beads or immerse them in water. You must not pass on those beads to an unknown person nor should any other mantra *sadhana* be done on the rosary that's been already used for a *sadhana*. You can, however, do the same *sadhana* again on your beads.

Consecrating your rosary

Here's how to consecrate your rosary:

1. Soak them in water overnight. Ideally, you should put drops of *Gangajal* in that water. After it gushed forth from Vishnu's toe, Shiva captured Ganga in his matted locks before allowing her to descend on earth. Since Shiva first revealed the mantras that are used in all *samskaras* (from conception to death), *Gangajal* is used in all purificatory rights. In case, you don't have access to *Gangajal*, cover the pot of water with your hands (left hand

Sanskrit (Devanagri)	*Sanskrit (IAST)*
गंगा च यमुने चैव गोदावरी सरस्वती ।	gaṃgā ca yamune caiva godāvarī sarasvatī |
नर्मदे सिंधु कावेरी जलेस्मिन संनिधिम कुरु ॥	narmade siṃdhu kāverī jalesmina saṃnidhima kuru ||
Translation	
I invoke the holy presence of Ganga, Yamuna, Godavari, Saraswati, Narmada, Sindhu and Kaveri in this water.	

resting on the right hand) and whisper the following mantra. If your guru has imparted you a special mudra for consecrating the beads, use it at this time.

2. The next morning, take the rosary out of water. Offer the water in the pot at the root of any plant or tree. If you can't do that, you can drink that water. If you can't do that, pour it on your head while bathing. Under no circumstances should the water just be thrown or flushed down the toilet. Everything, all ingredients, elements in the course of mantra *sadhana* must be treated with reverence. No reverence means no success.
3. Do *pancho*, *dasho* or *shodosha upchara* depending on your resources.
4. Chant one round of Ganapati Mantra on it. If you have not been initiated into any mantra of Ganesha, simply use the one that's used to pay obeisance to Ganesha, the slayer of obstacles.

Om Ganeshaya Namah.

5. Chant one round of Guru Mantra on it. If you have not been initiated by any guru into a mantra, then simply chant the name of your guru on the chanting beads. If you don't yet have a guru in your life, you can chant the following mantra:

Om Gurubhayo Namah.

6. Chant one round of Astra Mantra on it. Generally, an Astra Mantra is imparted by the guru again. If you don't have a guru or your guru hasn't given you any, use the Astra Mantra specific to that *sadhana*. In this book, I list four *sadhanas* with their respective Astra Mantras. You can use them.
7. Chant one round of Gayatri Mantra. Once again, there are many forms of Gayatri Mantra, but here we are concerned with the mantra of Vedmata Gayatri, also known as Savitur Gayatri. Here's the mantra:

Sanskrit (Devanagri)	*Sanskrit (IAST)*
ॐ भूर्भुवः स्वः	oṃ bhūrbhuvaḥ svaḥ
तत्सवितुर्वरेण्यम	tatsaviturvareṇyama
भर्गो देवस्य धीमहि।	bhargo devasya dhīmahi I
धियो यो नः प्रचोदयात॥	dhiyo yo naḥ pracodayāta II

8. Chant three rounds of your *sadhana* mantra on these beads. The *sadhana* mantra is the mantra you are specifically consecrating the beads for.
9. Touch the beads on your forehead and chant the mantra of Ganesha, Guru, Astra, Gayatri and Sadhana mantra one more time. Only once each.
10. Put the rosary in your bead bag. Hold out both your palms in the open with the bag resting in it and chant the following mantra seven times with reverence:

Sanskrit (Devanagri)	*Sanskrit (IAST)*
माले माले महामाले सर्व तत्त्व स्वरूपिणी,	māle māle mahāmāle sarva tattva svarūpiṇī,
चतुर्वस्त्वयी-न्यस्तस्तस्मान्मे सिद्धि दाभवः	caturvastvayī-nyastastasmānme siddhi dābhavaḥ

Your beads are now consecrated for you and ready to be used for your *sadhana*.

In the advanced stages of *sadhana*, generally in your guru's direction, physical beads are not used for *sadhana*. Instead, what's used is *akshamala*. Briefly put, *akshmala* is the use of *Brahmi* script (the original script of Sanskrit) in lieu of physical beads. When using *akshmala*, each letter of the Sanskrit alphabet is used as a bead. Using *akshmala* is an excellent way of improving your concentration, but it's only effective in the advanced stages of the *sadhana* when an aspirant has already attained a certain mastery over mindfulness. When using *akshmala*, simply append the letter of the Sanskrit alphabet in front of your mantra and go through the entire alphabet. Once you reach the end, you can begin a new round. For example, let's say your mantra is *Om Namah Shivaya*. This is how you'll use *akshmala*:

a *Om namah shivaya*
aa *Om namah shivaya*
i *Om namah shivaya*
I *Om namah shivaya*

and so on till you reach the last letter of the alphabet.

Lamp

There are three aspects of a lamp that matter in a mantra *sadhana*. They are the actual material and quality of lamp, the type and material of wick used and the oil used to burn the wick.

Lamps made from gold, silver, brass are good for any *sadhana*. If an aspirant can't procure a lamp made from any of these three metals, an earthen lamp is universally acceptable and good for all *sadhanas*. Certain sadhanas, especially tantric *sadhanas,* require lamps made from bones, human skull or skulls of various animals. Lamp made from just copper is never advised. Brass lamp is the most common lamp used in mantra *sadhana*, followed by silver lamp.

Different types of oils are used for different *sadhanas*. If the *sadhana* you are undertaking is quiet about what kind of oil you should use, you can then use either clarified butter (ghee) or sesame seed oil (*tila*). If you are in a cold place, it's best to use sesame seed oil because ghee settles and thickens, almost freezes, quickly in cold temperatures. Other oils commonly used are mustard oil and castor oil (*eranda*). In some tantric *sadhanas*, oils extracted from the fat of other animals and reptiles are also used.

The wick is best made from cotton. It can be braided or a single thick strand.

The lamp, oil and wick must be checked for cleanliness and purity before using them. A *sadhak* should ensure that there are no tiny creatures or insects at all.

Direction

Ideally, you should be facing east, north or north-east while doing your *nitya karma* (daily pooja). Different *sadhanas* require the *sadhak* to face different direction. If your guru doesn't mention anything or there's no mention of the direction in the *sadhana*, follow the principles below:

1. North, east or north-east are good for all *sadhanas* where you do *japa* in the morning. Any *sadhana* that is done for peace and prosperity can be done facing east, north or north-east.
2. Specifically, for material progress relating to wealth, face west
3. Invoking your ancestors is done by facing south
4. Meditation, yoga, *sadhana* for wisdom and knowledge should be done facing north
5. Any *sadhana* done after sunset or at night should be done facing west

Clothing

Once again, the rules of clothing differ from one *sadhana* to another. This includes the type and color of clothing you can wear. If your guru hasn't given any instructions or if the notes on *sadhana* don't say anything about it, you can follow the principles below:

1. Wear loose and comfortable clothing.

2. They should be made from natural material like cotton, wool or silk. Cotton is most preferable.
3. Ideally you should not have more than two pieces of clothing on your body
4. If you are in cold weather, however, feel free to don a blanket or wear warm clothing. Your body should be comfortable so you may focus on your *sadhana*
5. For all devi *sadhana*, you can wear red colored clothing
6. For all *devata sadhana*, you can wear either white or yellow
7. For all other *sadhanas* (of neutral mantras, for example), you can wear white clothing

Seat (Asana)

The type of asana (seat/mat) you select has an impact on the quality of your *sadhana*. Asana is the only thing separating you from the energy of the earth. A good asana should support you throughout your sadhana. In the Hindu tradition, all gods are seated on some asana. Vishnu on *ananta-shesha*, Shiva on lion's hide, Brahma on a lotus and so on.

Every day when you sit down to do your *sadhana*, take a bit of water in your hands and chant:

Sanskrit (Devanagri)	*Sanskrit (IAST)*
ॐ अस्य श्री आसन महामंत्रस्य-पृथिव्या	oṃ asya śrī āsana mahāmaṃtrasya-pṛthivyā
मेरुपृष्ठ ऋषिः सुतलं छन्दः **कूर्मो** देवता आसने विनियोगः।	merupṛṣṭha ṛṣiḥ sutalaṃ chandaḥ kūrmo devatā āsane viniyogaḥ |

The following mantra is chanted to pray to the earth and to express our gratitude to Mother Earth for patiently bearing our weight and for providing us a place to sit by using her as an asana.

Sanskrit (Devanagri)	*Sanskrit (IAST)*
पृथ्वीत्वया घृता लोका देवित्वं विष्णुना घृता ।	pṛthvītvayā ghṛtā lokā devitvaṃ viṣṇunā ghṛtā I
त्वं च धारय मा देवि पवित्रं कुरु चासनम् ।।	tvaṃ ca dhāraya mā devi pavitraṃ kuru cāsanam II

Put this water in the small vessel kept aside to collect water.

Now take bit more water in your right palm and chant the following mantra.

Sanskrit (Devanagri)	*Sanskrit (IAST)*
योगासनाय नमः	yogāsanāya namaḥ
वीरासनाय नमः	vīrāsanāya namaḥ
शरासनाय नमः	śarāsanāya namaḥ
ॐ ह्रीं क्लीं आधार शक्ति कमलासनाय नमः	oṃ hrīṃ klīṃ ādhāra śakti kamalāsanāya namaḥ

Put this water just in front of you.

There are many types of asanas. I'm listing the ones most commonly used.

1. *Kambla-asana (blanket):* An asana made from blanket is the best asana which is easily available and is universally good for almost all kinds of *sadhanas*. More than 80 per cent of the *sadhanas* I did in my life were on *kambla-asana*. It is called a *sarva-siddhi* asana — an asana good for all kinds of attainment.
2. *Vyaghra or Mriga Charma (Lion hide or deer hide):* I don't recommend using lion hide or deer hide for any of your *sadhanas* because a) It is not compassionate to kill another living entity just so you may sit on their skin and chant a mantra. b) Wildlife poaching is illegal pretty much everywhere. Nevertheless, for your

information, there are many *sadhanas*, in particular, *sadhanas* of *yakshinis* and other celestial beings, where lion hide is used. Deer hide is used in *sadhanas* of intense penance and repentance leading to self-purification.

3. *Kusha-asana (Kusha grass): Kusha-asana* is made by weaving together strands of *kusha* and making a mat out of them. It is used for spiritual and material progress.
4. *Reshami-asana (Silk):* A seat made from silk is used in many *sadhanas* where you are trying to attract something specific in your life.
5. A seat made from wood or to sit directly on a stone and do mantra *japa* is prohibited and is considered ominous.

In many tantric *sadhanas*, various hides such as that of a cow, dog, horse, buffalo, sheep, etc., are used. The two most popular ones in mantra yoga are lion and deer hides, though.

Diet

Many *puruscharanas* require a special diet. It differs from *sadhana* to *sadhana*. If your mantra *sadhana* is quiet about any particular kind of diet, you can then follow the dietary principles below. A general rule of thumb is that your diet should be strictly vegetarian. Dairy products are allowed. Meat, seafood, eggs, or any by-products of meat of any nature (gelatin, etc.) should be avoided at all costs.

It's best to eat food that is easy to digest, wholesome and freshly cooked. The diet that's particularly suited for most *sadhanas* is called *havishya-anna*. Simply put, *havishya-anna* involves not eating any beans, lentils, grains, pulses and legumes. Therefore, items like peas, all lentils, corn, wheat, rice are prohibited. You can eat potatoes, any fruit, any vegetable (except peas), dairy products ideally made from cow's milk, rock salt and jaggery. Processed salt and sugar are prohibited.

If you choose to keep your standard diet with foodgrains and all, follow the principles below:

Mung dal (split beans), sesame seeds, rice, wheat, peas, cow's milk, yogurt, ghee, jaggery, rock salt are permitted.

Processed salt, meat, alcohol, carrots, *masoor* and *arhara* daal, stale food, oats are to be avoided.

Other kinds of excitatory foods we consume for our body and mind are to be avoided as well. Notably, sexual intercourse or any sexual activity, telling lies, sensual talks, harsh words and cunningness are prohibited. Scriptures also prohibit unusual hairdos. Practice as much silence as you reasonably can.

BOOK TWO

THE PRACTICES

RITES OF INVOCATION

- **Invoking the deity**
- **Awakening your mantra (nyasa)**
- **Self-identification with your deity (mudras)**
- **Essential steps in invocation**

The Sanskrit term of rites of invocation is *purushcharana*. After an aspirant has been initiated and has practiced the mantra for a while, generally with the guru's permission, he goes ahead to invoke the energy of the mantra. *Purusha* means the one that's entered into the city (*pura*). Our body is known as the city of nine gates. *Charana* means steps, stages or even feet. From head to toe when you invoke the mantra, it's *puruscharana*. Or when you work on step by step invocation, whereby a certain living energy enters into the city (*pura*) of your mantra, the process is called *puruscharana*.

In this section, I cover the rites of invocation.

INVOKING THE DEITY

Once you invite your deity into your world, you effectively bring the energy of the mantra into your own energy field. Even though I'm using the word energy, the path of mantra yoga requires immense faith and devotion in your deity. By energy, I don't mean merely the scientific meaning or use of the word. Instead, when I say energy in the context of mantra yoga, I'm particularly referring to the deity of the mantra, say Lord Shiva, an energy operating at a certain frequency and you are connecting with that energy using your mantra which is an oral representation of Shiva, the deity.

There are nine steps to attain that union before you become one with the deity. The more mindfully, reverently you perform the steps below, the more effective will be your *japa* and consequently, you'll have much better chances of attaining mantra *siddhi*.

Here are the nine steps:

Avahana

Avahana means to invite. You begin by inviting your deity in your world. This is shown by using the *avahani* mudra and then placing a flower either on the yantra (mandala or geometrical field), on the statue or the picture of your deity or at the base of the lamp if you are not using a yantra, statue or a picture. With *avahana*, you recognize that this energy exists and is dear to you and you want it to connect with your individual energy.

Place your thumbs at the root of your little fingers and join your hands together. This is called the *avahani* mudra.

Chant the mantra of your deity and add the words '*avahyami*' in the end and display the *avahani* mudra.

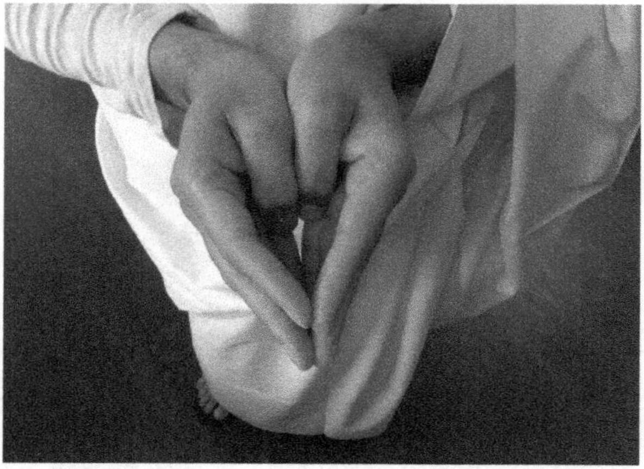

Sthapana

Once you've invited your deity, an appropriate place is offered for the divine energy to sit. This process is called establishment

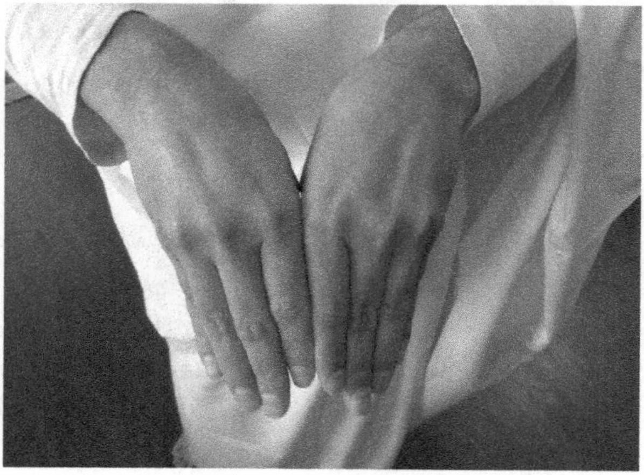

(*sthapana*). Like invitation, this is done with reverence. With *sthapna*, you welcome the deity to take a seat and establish itself in your energy field.

Direct the *avahani* mudra towards the ground and open your palms. This is called the *sthapani* mudra.

Chant the mantra of your deity and add the words, '*sthapyami*', in the end and show the *sthapani* mudra.

Sannidhana

Sannidhana is done to bring the energy closer to you. It's created from the word *sannidhaya* to be in proximity which in turn has come from the word *sanna,* which means to be together. Proximity simply refers to being physically close to someone. You could be standing close to your enemy. Being together implies the mental quality of a sense of belonging towards each other. The act of *sannidhana* is to befriend the energy you have invited.

Make a fist with each hand, join those two fists together and raise the thumbs. This is the *sannidhapini* mudra.

Chant your mantra and add '*sannidhim kuru*' in the end and display the *sannidhapini* mudra.

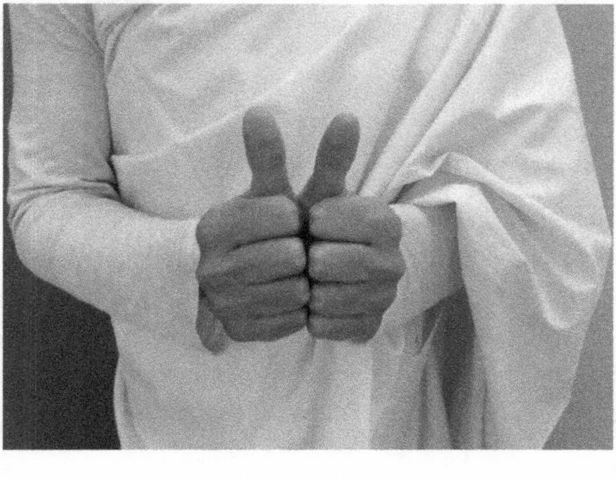

Sannirodhan Sambodhana

This is to gratefully and gleefully address your deity. Your deity has arrived in your world, express your happiness at this. This is done by either chanting a short hymn dedicated to your deity or the *dhyana shloka*. If you have neither, simply just chant your mantra and display the mudra below.

When you tuck in your thumbs in their respective fists and turn these fists over, this is called *sambodhini* or *sannirodhini* mudra.

After chanting your mantra and while showing the mudra, just chant, 'Jaya Devi! *Suswagatam*!' if you are invoking feminine energy, or 'Jaya Deva! *Suswagatam*!' if you are invoking the masculine energy.

Sammukhikaran

Sammukhikarana means to present. In *sammukhikarana*, you mentally present various offerings like a glass of water, or a cool drink, or fanning your deity. All of this is done mentally while you visualize with utmost reverence and devotion.

When fists formed in the *sambodhini* mudra are turned upwards, this is called *sammukhikarana* mudra.

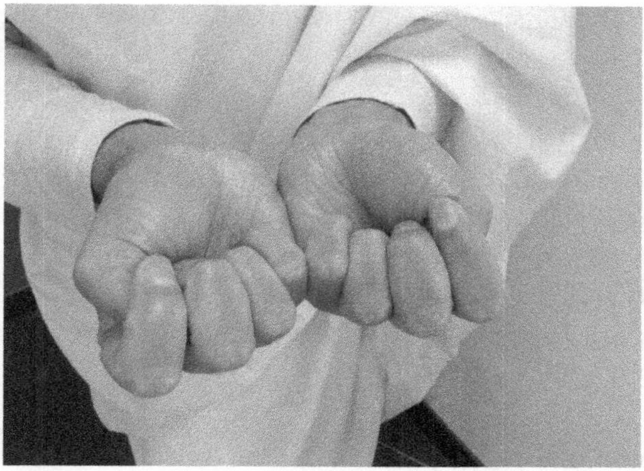

Chant your mantra and add '*sarvam samarpyami*' in the end. Finish by showing the *sammukhikarana* mudra.

Sakalikaran

Created from the word *sakala*, *sakalikaran* is to make it complete, to fulfill one's promise and to include everything. It also means low

sound. *Sakalikaran* is the act of merging your energy in the energy of the deity so you become one.

This is done by performing the *shadanga nyasa* with your *ishta* mantra. In all the previous five steps, you would chant your mantra loud but in skalikaran after performing the nyasa, simply whisper your mantra.

The joining your palms next to your heart in the posture of namaste is called *sakalikaran* mudra.

Finish *sakalikarana* by performing the *sakalikaran* mudra and whispering your mantra.

Avagunthana

After *sakalikarana*, now you possess the qualities of your deity. The literal meaning of *avagunthana* is to veil or conceal. You are covering your new energy so they may not disperse out there. Imagine a lamp lit out in the sun versus the one that's lit in a dark room. The same lamp's presence will be felt lot more in a closed room.

Mantra yoga places great emphasis on keeping your *sadhana* and attainments to yourself and only using them for your and others welfare. Talking about your *sadhana* wastes your energy

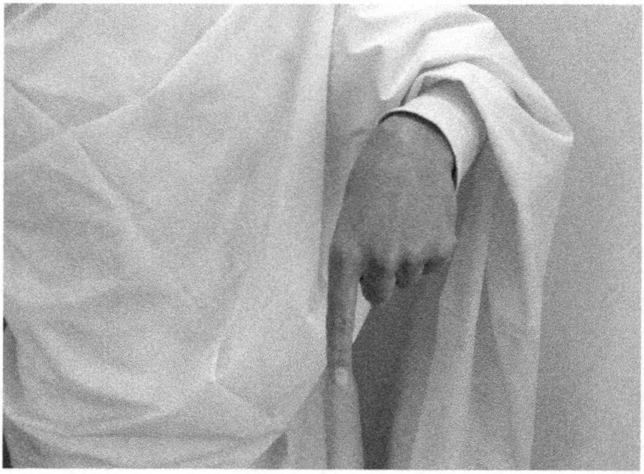

and in mantra science, it's all about preservation and channelizing your energy.

Now that you are infused with the energy of your deity, you want to cover it so you may do your *sadhana* and build up this energy in you.

To make a fist with your left hand while keeping the left index finger out and pointing it at the ground and turning the index finger anti clockwise is called *avagunthana* mudra.

Avagunthana is done by mentally chanting your mantra and performing the *avagunthana* mudra.

Amartikaran

You want to give life to your energy you have just received. You are the receptacle of the energy of your deity and with *amaritkarna*, you ensure that this energy stays alive in you.

It's much like a patient receiving a kidney transplant. Initially, there's great danger that the patient's body may reject the transplant as a foreign object. To avoid this, the patient undergoes a number of treatments and remains on heavy medication so that gradually his body may accept the new organ.

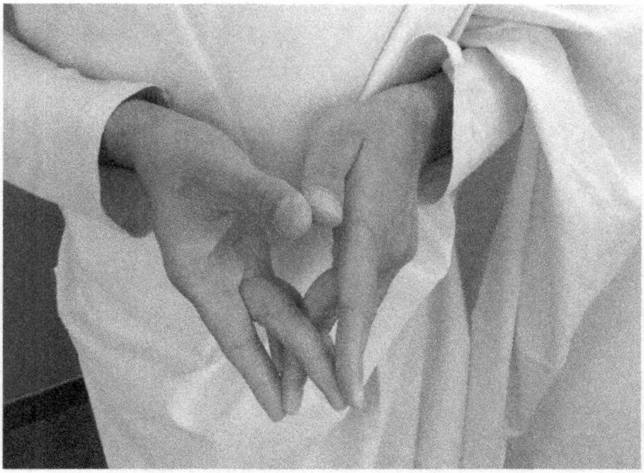

Amaratikaran is something like that for energy. When you invoke the deity, bring him into your world, establish his energy in yours, initially this can cause ripples in your consciousness. Those ripples could be in the form of suppressed and negative emotions, or feelings of fear, despair or ego. To smoothen the process, *amaratikaran* is one of the important steps.

Dhenu mudra is shown for *amaratikarna*. Dhenu mudra is performed by bringing your palms together. The tip of the right index finger should touch the tip of the left middle finger while the tip of the left index finger should touch the tip of the right middle finger. The tip of the right ring finger should touch the tip of the left little finger while the tip of the left ring finger should touch the tip of the right ring finger. Join both thumbs at their tips. Point it downwards. This is the auspicious *dhenu* mudra.

Chant the mantra of your deity but give a *samputa* of the *amrita beeja* (vam) by appending it in the front and at the end. Finish by showing the *dhenu* mudra.

Paramikaran

Paramikarana means to supremify, it means to elevate something to the most supreme level. A deity that was originally invited now

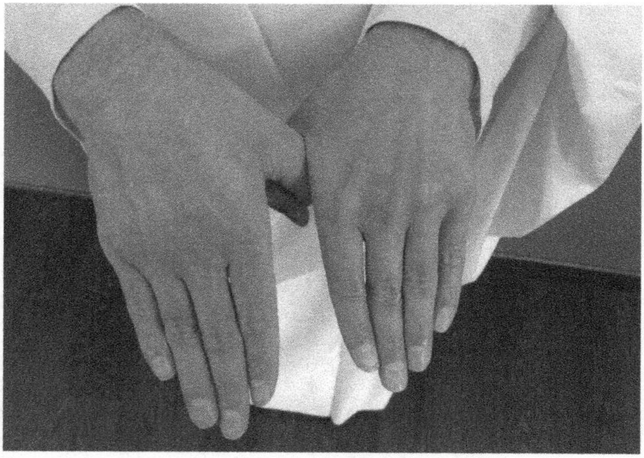

lives in you. By *amartikaran*, you've accepted the deity in your body and immortalized its energy in you. With *paramikaran*, you realize your own supreme divinity. You have brought another dimension of consciousness to operate in your normal world. It's incredibly powerful. It is the dawning of wisdom, the beginning of awakening.

Entwine both thumbs and spread out your hands (keeping fingers of the respective hands joined together). This is called the *paramikaran* mudra.

Chant your mantra and then say '*aham brahmasmi*' three times. Finish by showing the *paramikaran* mudra.

NYASA

You have arrived at one of the most important aspects of mantra sadhana – *nyasa*. In fact, *nyasa* and mudra (covered in the next section) are two most critical factors in mantra *siddhi*. Knowledge of these is what differentiates an aspirant from an adept.

Nyasa means two things. First and foremost, it refers to the consecration rites. Consecration rites of the body, that is. The idea is to really prepare your body and mind so that it becomes a worthy receptacle to hold the divine energy of your deity; you pretty much have to become the deity yourself. *Nyasa* is consecrating yourself with various letters of the mantra, of the Sanskrit alphabet, and other elements (such as the seer of your mantra, asterism, etc.) for self-purification.

Nyasa is also a synonym of *nikshepa* which means to abandon or put away. If I wish to possess the powers of the deity of a mantra, it is obvious that I must have the same strength, attribute, purity of mindset as my deity. *Nyasa* is done with that view.

Different *sadhanas* have different *nyasas* and for all the *sadhanas* listed in this book, I've covered the *nyasas* against each *sadhana* under that section. There's one *nayasa*, however, you can perform regardless. It is called *matrika nyasa*. *Matrika* are the fifty letters of the Sanskrit alphabet. There are three variations of this consecration. They are sequence-of-creation (*srishti-krama*), sequence-of-sustenance (*stithi-krama*) and sequence-of-destruction (*samhara-krama*).

For all householders or people aspiring material progress, sequence-of-creation is recommended. Here is how to do it properly starting with application (*viniyoga*):

Application (*Viniyoga*)

Take a bit of water in your right palm from the water pot for offering (*arghya patra*) and chant the following mantra. (The type, use and arrangement of water pots are covered in detail in Arrangement of Pots (*Patrasadan*) in Detailed Notes.

Sanskrit (Devanagri)	*Sanskrit (IAST)*
ॐ अस्य श्री मातृका न्यास मन्त्रस्य ब्रह्मा ऋषिः गायत्री छन्दः मातृका सरस्वती देवी देवता हलो	oṃ asya śrī mātṛkā nyāsa mantrasya brahmā ṛṣiḥ gāyatrī chandaḥ mātṛkā sarasvatī devī devatā halo
बीजानि स्वराः शक्त्यः (क्षं कीलकं) अखिलातप्ये न्यासे विनियोगः ।	bījāni svarāḥ śaktyaḥ (kṣaṃ kīlakaṃ) akhilātapye nyāse viniyogaḥ ।

After chanting the mantra above, leave the water in your palm in the plate next to you.

Nyasa of the sages (rsyādi-nyāsa:)

Sanskrit (Devanagri)	*Sanskrit (IAST)*	*Touch with right hand your...*
ॐ अं ब्रह्मणे ऋष्ये नमः आं शिरसि ।	oṃ aṃ brahmaṇe ṝṣye namaḥ āṃ śirasi ।	Top of your head
ॐ इं गायत्री छन्दसे नम ईं मुखे ।	oṃ iṃ gāyatrī chandase nama īṃ mukhe ।	Lips

Sanskrit (Devanagri)	*Sanskrit (IAST)*	*Touch with right hand your...*
ॐ उं सरस्वती देवतायै नमः ऊं हृदि ।	oṃ uṃ sarasvatī devatāyai namaḥ ūṃ hradi ।	Heart
ॐ एं हल्भ्यो बीजेभ्यो नमः ऐं गुह्ये ।	oṃ eṃ halbhyo bījebhyo namaḥ aiṃ guhye ।	Groin
ॐ ओं स्वरेभ्यो शक्तिभ्यो नमः औं पादयोः ।	oṃ oṃ svarebhyo śaktibhyo namaḥ auṃ pādayoḥ ।	Feet (your feet may be tucked in if you are sitting cross legged. Simply touch that region of the feet.)
ॐ अं क्षं कीलकाय नमः अः सर्वांगे ।	oṃ aṃ kṣaṃ kīlakāya namaḥ aḥ sarvāge ।	Whole body. This is done by rolling your right hand over your head and then doing Namaste by bringing both hands closer to your heart and joining your palm.

After performing *nyasa* of the sages (ṝṣyādi nyāsa:), now perform the *nyasa* of the hands (*kara-nyāsa*) as per the table below followed by the six-limbed mantra *nyasa* in the subsequent table.

Nyasa of the hands (kara *nyāsa*)

Sanskrit (Devanagri)	*Sanskrit (IAST)*	*Handlock (Mudra)*	*Gesture with both hands*
ॐ अं कं खं गं घं ङं आं अंगुष्ठाभ्यां नमः ।	oṃ aṃ kaṃ khaṃ gaṃ ghaṃ ṅaṃ āṃ aṃguṣṭhābhyāṃ namaḥ ।	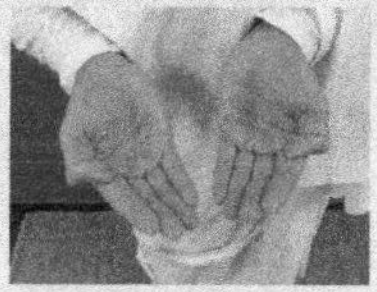	Touch the tip of your thumb at the base of your index finger.
ॐ इं चं छ जं झं ञं ईं तर्जनीभ्यां नमः ।	oṃ iṃ caṃ cha jaṃ jhaṃ ñaṃ īṃ tarjanībhyāṃ namaḥ ।		Touch the tip of your thumb to the tip of your index finger.
ॐ उं टं ठं डं ढं णं ऊं मध्यमाभ्यां नमः ।	oṃ uṃ ṭaṃ ṭhaṃ ṅaṃ ḍhaṃ ṇaṃ ūṃ madhyamābhyāṃ namaḥ ।	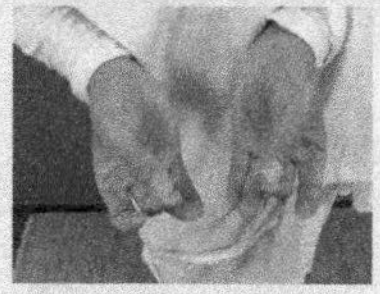	Touch the tip of your thumb to the tip of your middle finger.
ॐ एं तं थं दं धं नं ऐं अनामिकाभ्यां नमः ।	oṃ eṃ taṃ thaṃ daṃ dhaṃ naṃ aiṃ anāmikābhyāṃ namaḥ ।	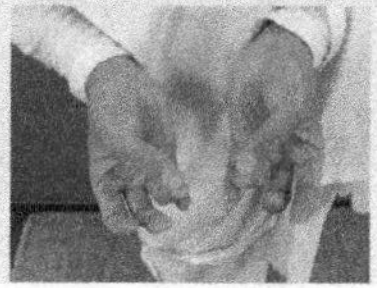	Touch the tip of your thumb to the tip of your ring finger.

Sanskrit (Devanagri)	*Sanskrit (IAST)*	*Handlock (Mudra)*	*Gesture with both hands*
ॐ ओं पं फं बं भं मं औं कनिष्ठिभ्यां नमः ।	oṃ oṃ paṃ phaṃ baṃ bhaṃ maṃ auṃ kaniṣṭhibhyāṃ namaḥ ।	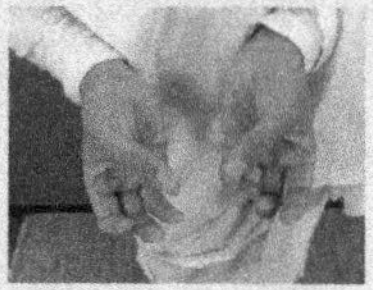	Touch the tip of your thumb to the tip of your little finger.
ॐ अं यं रं लं वं शं षं सं हं लं क्षं अः करतलकरपृष्ठाभ्यां नमः ।	oṃ aṃ yaṃ raṃ laṃ vaṃ śaṃ ṣaṃ saṃ haṃ laṃ kṣaṃ aḥ karatalakarapṛṣṭhābhyāṃ namaḥ ।		Touch the back of your left hand with the back of your right hand and then clap softly.

Six-Limbed Mantra Nyasa (Shadanga mantra nyāsa)

Sanskrit (Devanagri)	*Sanskrit (IAST)*	*Posture*	*Description*
ॐ अं कं खं गं घं ङं आं हृदयाय नमः ।	oṃ aṃ kaṃ khaṃ gaṃ ghaṃ ṅaṃ āṃ hṛdayāya namaḥ ।		Touch your heart region with your right hand.
ॐ इं चं छ जं झं ञं ईं शिरसे स्वाहा ।	oṃ iṃ caṃ cha jaṃ jhaṃ ñaṃ īṃ śirase svāhā ।		Touch your forehead with your right hand keeping the index finger away.
ॐ उं टं ठं डं ढं णं ऊं शिखायै वषट् ।	oṃ uṃ ṭaṃ ṭhaṃ ṅaṃ ḍhaṃ ṇaṃ ūṃ śikhāyai vaṣaṭ ।		Make a fist with right hand and extend your thumb. Now touch the crown of your head with your thumb.

Sanskrit (Devanagri)	*Sanskrit (IAST)*	*Posture*	*Description*
ॐ एं तं थं दं धं नं ऐं कवचाय हुम् ।	oṃ eṃ taṃ thaṃ daṃ dhaṃ naṃ aiṃ kavacāya hum I		Touch your shoulders by crossing your hands. Generally, in Devi Pooja, left hand is on top of the right and in *Devata* Pooja, right on top of the left. This is, however, just a guideline and not a rule.
ॐ ओं पं फं बं भं मं औं नेत्रत्रयाय वौषट् ।	oṃ oṃ paṃ phaṃ baṃ bhaṃ maṃ auṃ netratrayāya vauṣaṭ I		Spread your right hand and touch your right eye with your index finger, forehead with the middle finger and left eye with the ring finger simultaneously. *Netra-traya* means the three eyes.
ॐ अं यं रं लं वं शं षं सं हं लं क्षं अः अस्त्राय फट् ।	oṃ aṃ yaṃ raṃ laṃ vaṃ śaṃ ṣaṃ saṃ haṃ laṃ kṣaṃ aḥ astrāya phaṭ I		Take the right hand over your head and then bring it back in front of you to clap softly.

Once you are done with the *nyasa* of sages and hands, you've arrived at the last step of the *matrika nyasa*. This is done by touching various parts of your body while you chant the *matrika* (the fifty letters of the Sanskrit alphabet). This is called *nyasa* of the limbs or body (*amga nyasa*). When *nyasa* is done with devotion and feeling, your mind and body starts to feel one with the mantra, as if you are made of sound yourself. Energy begins to flow and your consciousness becomes a fertile ground to receive divine grace. When performing the nyasa, the body part is always touched with the right hand unless noted otherwise.

Nyasa of the Limbs (amga nyāsa)

	Mantra Sanskrit (Devanagri)	*Sanskrit (IAST)*	*Touch your...*
1	ॐ अं नमः ललाटे ।	oṃ aṃ namaḥ lalāṭe I	Forehead
2	ॐ आं नमः भ्रूमध्ये ।	oṃ āṃ namaḥ bhrūmadhye I	The point between your brows (glabella)
3	ॐ इ नमः दक्षनेत्रे ।	oṃ i namaḥ dakṣanetre I	Right eye
4	ॐ ईं नमः वामनेत्रे ।	oṃ īṃ namaḥ vāmanetre I	Left eye
5	ॐ उं नमः दक्षकर्णे ।	oṃ uṃ namaḥ dakṣakarṇe I	Right ear
6	ॐ ऊं नमः वामकर्णे ।	oṃ ūṃ namaḥ vāmakarṇe I	Left ear
7	ॐ ॠं नमः दक्षनासायाम् ।	oṃ ṝṃ namaḥ dakṣanāsāyām I	Right nostril

Mantra Sanskrit (Devanagri)		Sanskrit (IAST)	Touch your...
8	ॐ ॠं नमः वामनासायाम् ।	oṃ ṝṃ namaḥ vāmanāsāyām I	Left nostril
9	ॐ ऌं नमः दक्षगण्डे ।	oṃ lṛṃ namaḥ dakṣagaṇḍe I	Right cheek
10	ॐ ॡं नमः वाम गण्डे ।	oṃ lṝṃ namaḥ vāma gaṇḍe I	Left cheek
11	ॐ एं नमः ऊधर्वोष्ठे ।	oṃ eṃ namaḥ ūdharvoṣṭhe I	Upper lip
12	ॐ ऐं नमः अधरोष्ठे ।	oṃ aiṃ namaḥ adharoṣṭhe I	Lower lip
13	ॐ ओं नमः ऊधर्वदन्तपंक्तौ ।	oṃ oṃ namaḥ ūdharvadantapaṃktau I	Upper teeth
14	ॐ औं नमः अधोदन्तपंक्तौ ।	oṃ auṃ namaḥ adhodantapaṃktau I	Lower teeth
15	ॐ अं नमः मूर्ध्नि ।	oṃ aṃ namaḥ mūrdhni I	Head
16	ॐ अः नमः मुखे ।	oṃ aḥ namaḥ mukhe I	Entire face (Just gently put your nose with your right palm to cover your face)
17	ॐ कं नमः दक्षबाहुमूले ।	oṃ kaṃ namaḥ dakṣabāhumūle I	Right bicep (with left hand)
18	ॐ खं नमः दक्षबाहुमूले (कूर्परे) ।	oṃ khaṃ namaḥ dakṣabāhumūle (kūrpare) I	Right elbow (with left hand)

Mantra Sanskrit (Devanagri)		Sanskrit (IAST)	Touch your...
19	ॐ गं नमः दक्षबाहुमूले मणिबन्धे ।	oṃ gaṃ namaḥ dakṣabāhumūle maṇibandhe ।	Right wrist (with left hand)
20	ॐ घं नमः दक्षबाहुमूले हस्तांगुलिमुले ।	oṃ ghaṃ namaḥ dakṣabāhumūle hastāṃgulimule ।	Base of right-hand fingers (with left hand)
21	ॐ ङं नमः दक्षबाहुमूले हस्तांगुल्यग्रे ।	oṃ ṅaṃ namaḥ dakṣabāhumūle hastāṃgulyagre ।	Tip of right-hand fingers (with left hand)
22	ॐ चं नमः वाम बाहुमूले ।	oṃ caṃ namaḥ vāma bāhumūle ।	Left bicep
23	ॐ छं नमः वाम (कूर्परे) ।	oṃ chaṃ namaḥ vāma (kūrpare) ।	Left elbow
24	ॐ जं नमः वाम मणिबन्धे ।	oṃ jaṃ namaḥ vāma maṇibandhe ।	Left wrist
25	ॐ झं नमः वाम हस्तांगुलिमूले ।	oṃ jhaṃ namaḥ vāma hastāṃgulimūle ।	Base of left-hand fingers
26	ॐ ञं नमः वाम हस्तांगुल्यग्रे ।	oṃ ñaṃ namaḥ vāma hastāṃgulyagre ।	Tip of left-hand fingers
27	ॐ टं नमः दक्षिण पाद मूले ।	oṃ ṭaṃ namaḥ dakṣiṇa pāda mūle ।	Right thigh
28	ॐ ठं नमः दक्षिण जानुनि ।	oṃ ṭhaṃ namaḥ dakṣiṇa jānuni ।	Right knee
29	ॐ ड़ं नमः दक्षिण गुल्फे ।	oṃ ḍaṃ namaḥ dakṣiṇa gulphe ।	Right ankle

	Mantra Sanskrit (Devanagri)	*Sanskrit (IAST)*	*Touch your...*
30	ॐ ढं नमः दक्षिण पादांगुलिमूले ।	oṃ ḍha ṃ namaḥ dakṣiṇa pādāṃgulimūle ।	Base of the right-foot toes
31	ॐ णं नमः दक्षिण पादांगुल्यग्रे ।	oṃ ṇaṃ namaḥ dakṣiṇa pādāṃgulyagre ।	Tip of the right-foot toes
32	ॐ तं नमः वाम पादमूले ।	oṃ taṃ namaḥ vāma pādamūle ।	Left thigh
33	ॐ थं नमः वाम जानुनि ।	oṃ thaṃ namaḥ vāma jānuni ।	Left knee
34	ॐ दं नमः वाम गुल्फे ।	oṃ daṃ namaḥ vāma gulphe ।	Left ankle
35	ॐ धं नमः वाम पादांगुलिमूले ।	oṃ dhaṃ namaḥ vāma pādāṃgulimūle ।	Base of the left-foot toes
36	ॐ नं नमः वाम पादांगुल्यग्रे ।	oṃ naṃ namaḥ vāma pādāṃgulyagre ।	Tip of the left-foot toes
37	ॐ पं नमः दक्षिणपार्श्वे ।	oṃ paṃ namaḥ dakṣiṇapārśve ।	Right ribs
38	ॐ फं नमः वाम पार्श्वे ।	oṃ phaṃ namaḥ vāma pārśve ।	Left ribs
39	ॐ बं नमः पृष्ठे ।	oṃ baṃ namaḥ pṛṣṭhe ।	Back
40	ॐ भं नमः नाभौ ।	oṃ bhaṃ namaḥ nābhau ।	Navel
41	ॐ मं नमः उदरे ।	oṃ maṃ namaḥ udare ।	Stomach
42	ॐ यं त्वगात्मने नमः हृदि ।	oṃ yaṃ tvagātmane namaḥ hradi ।	Heart
43	ॐ रं असृगात्मने नमः दक्षांसे ।	oṃ raṃ asṛgātmane namaḥ dakṣāṃse ।	Right shoulder

	Mantra Sanskrit (Devanagri)	*Sanskrit (IAST)*	*Touch your...*
44	ॐ लं मांसात्मने नमः ककुदि ।	oṃ laṃ māṃsātmane namaḥ kakudi I	Back of your neck (cervix)
45	ॐ वं मेदात्मने नमः वामांसे ।	oṃ vaṃ medātmane namaḥ vāmāṃse I	Left shoulder
46	ॐ शं अस्थ्यात्मने नमः हृदयादि दक्ष हस्तान्तम् ।	oṃ śaṃ asthyātmane namaḥ hṛdayādi dakṣa hastāntam I	Heart to the end of your right hand (by rolling your left hand over it).
47	ॐ षं मज्जात्मने नमः हृदयादिवाम हस्तान्तम् ।	oṃ ṣaṃ majjātmane namaḥ hṛdayādivāma hastāntam I	Heart to the end of your left hand (by rolling your right hand over it).
48	ॐ सं शुक्रात्मने नमः हृदयादिदक्षपादान्तम् ।	oṃ saṃ śukrātmane namaḥ hṛdayādidakṣapādāntam I	Heart to the end of your right foot (by rolling your right hand over it).
49	ॐ हं आत्मने नमः हृदयादिवामपादान्तम् ।	oṃ haṃ ātmane namaḥ hṛdayādivāmapādāntam I	Heart to the end of your right foot (by rolling your right hand over it).
50	ॐ क्षं प्राणात्मने नमः मुखे ।	oṃ kṣaṃ prāṇātmane namaḥ mukhe I	Face

This *nyasa* can be done daily if you have time or only during the rites of invocation. The most important thing is to not turn nyasa (or any other aspect of mantra invocation) into a mechanical act. It's imperative to do it with a devotional sentiment and feeling. The more mindful and aware you are while you do *nyasa*, mudra or chanting, the more you stand to gain and the closer you get to mantra *siddhi*.

HAND LOCKS (MUDRAS)

I once heard that the only way to get into a certain sought-after monastery, run by a young abbot, was to win a debate with him. He rarely lost. One day, they found out that a great scholar was visiting them with the intention to challenge the abbot for a debate. The abbot didn't want to lose to the scholar and tarnish his own image. He asked his younger brother, who had only one eye and was barely literate, to hold a colloquy with the scholar.

"Me?" The young one exclaimed. "I know nothing."

"You can just keep quiet throughout the debate," the abbot suggested. "I'm sure the scholar will get frustrated and leave."

After much prodding and with much reluctance, the younger brother agreed. Surely enough, the scholar arrived and challenged them for a debate. The illiterate brother received the guest and the stage was set. The abbot chose to stay back in the office and not even watch the debate for he knew that there was going to be no debate but a mere mockery of his brother.

Some fifteen minutes later, the abbot saw that the scholar was approaching him in a hurried manner. Expecting a big brawl, he wanted to hide from his guest but the scholar was already there before he could do anything.

Taking a deep bow, the scholar said, "I've never met anyone as intelligent as your brother. He's incredible. I must go and refer to our scriptures again and spend a few more years in gaining deeper knowledge."

"My... my brother?" the abbot stuttered.

"Yes. He's incredible. Without uttering a word, he showed how superior his intelligence is."

"Please tell me what happened," requested the abbot.

"Well," the scholar replied somberly, "I raised one finger in the air to indicate that God is one. He raised two in response saying but there exists duality. I raised three to tell him that all is governed by the three modes of material nature (*sattva*, *rajas* and *tamas*). He immediately joined all fingers and formed a fist to say that regardless, the whole creation is one. At that, I had no come back. I knew he was a much greater scholar. I felt ashamed to challenge someone of his stature. I raised my one hand to tell him that he has understood the clapping of one hand. He's Buddha. I immediately came out of the hall."

The scholar left and refused to even have a meal.

A few minutes later, the unlettered brother came running to the abbot and screamed, "Where is he?"

"My brother!" the abbot said bursting with joy. "I didn't know you were such a great scholar. He was all praises for you."

"Forget that. First tell me where he is hiding. I want to teach him a lesson."

"Lesson? Why? What happened?"

"What happened, you ask me? He was an arrogant scoundrel. As soon as he sat down he raised one finger to poke fun at me saying that I only have one eye. Still, I maintained my calm and raised two fingers implying that it's okay, at least he had two eyes. But, this wasn't enough for him and he raised three fingers saying, between the two of us we only have three eyes. This was too much. I raised my fist to say that if he didn't stop, I would punch him. And that visitor, that rascal, showed me a slap in return. Immediately after that he got up and left the hall."

Our gestures can mean different things to different people. They differ from culture to culture. Mudras are gestures too. In Sanskrit, mudra means a gesture performed with our limbs or any part of our body. Even a simple raise of an eyebrow is a mudra. They play a critical role in correct mantra *sadhana* provided you show the right gestures. Different mantras require different mudras for gestures mean different things to different entities.

Our actions reach where our words can't. Literally. Imagine you have been stranded on an island for a few days. You are the only one there and every day you desperately wish that someone come looking for you, or just pass by or that you spot a ship. A few days pass by, you even yell and scream but there's no one there to hear you. With each passing moment, you only think of finding a way to rescue yourself. You even write 'Help' in big letters on the sandy beach but every so often, the waves come and wash it away. Besides, you could easily be in an area where anyone flying overhead may overlook or not even understand what you've scribbled on the beach. Your desperation builds as does your hopelessness.

And then one day, you spot a helicopter passing overhead. It's flying at an altitude of a few thousand feet. No matter how loudly you yell, they are unlikely to hear you. The distance is great. And yet, you may only have to jump and wave your hands a couple of times before you have their attention. Your gesture immediately accomplished what your deepest desire, thoughts, words, scribbles couldn't for so many days. They see the animated you and know immediately that you require help.

There are primarily four types of mudras.

1. **Hand gestures (Hasta mudra)**
   As the name suggests, these are performed with hands only. They are also known as hand locks. Out of the four types of mudras, mantra yoga only makes use of hand gestures. Hand gestures are the only ones we are concerned with at the moment.
2. **Head gestures (Manna mudra)**
   Mudras performed with eyes, ears, nose, tongue and lips are called *manna* mudras. These are frequently used in kundalini, agohra and *hatha* yoga.

3. **Postural gestures (Kaya mudra)**
   Gestures performed with your body are called postural gestures. *Kaya* means body. All asanas in yoga are postural gestures basically.
4. **Locks (Bandhas)**
   Bandhas are commonly used in hatha yoga. They can be a combination of asanas and hand locks and head gestures.

To a beginner on the path of mantra *sadhana*, mudras often appear to be an insignificant exhibition of some gestures. An adept knows better though. To an experienced practitioner, correct understanding and performance of mudras can make all the difference between success and failure. Mudras differ from *sadhana* to *sadhana* and I've detailed the appropriate mudras for each *sadhana* in the relevant chapters. Having said that, there are seven core mudras that should be performed daily anyway. These can be performed at any time throughout the day, even multiple times if you like.

In the world of mudras, each finger refers to a different element. Our body that is made up of five elements of earth, water, fire, air, space is a colony of these elements. When Shiva created the mantras, he created the elements and all sensory phenomena from such elements. Therefore, mantras can be used to gain mastery over elements or to channelize them. Mudras prepare our body to harness the energy gained from mantra chanting. It's performing the right gesture like that person stranded on an island so you can draw attention of the cosmic energy.

Our little finger represents water, ring finger the earth, middle finger space, index finger air and thumb signifies fire. Touching the tip of the finger with your thumb balances the element represented by the finger. Touching the tip of your finger to the base of your thumb pacifies the element represented by the finger. Touching the tip of the thumb to the base of your finger boosts the element represented by the finger. Touching the tip of your thumb with all the fingers pacifies the element represented by the thumb (which is always fire). Mudras can be performed with one hand or both hands. Whenever you can, use both hands for more effectiveness.

Here are the seven core mudras that should be performed as part of your daily duties.

1. Shunya Mudra

Shunya means void, empty, ab initio, original. *Shunya* represents creation, the universe, the vast expanse. We begin by showing the *shunya* mudra first so we merge our individual ego in the supreme consciousness.

This is done by keeping your palms up and tucking the middle fingers with your thumbs as illustrated below.

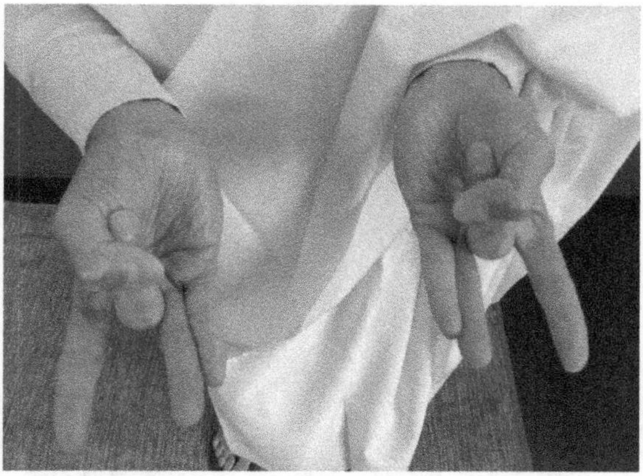

2. Prana Mudra

Prana regulates the vital life force in your body. Bring your ring and little fingers together and join them at the tip of your thumbs. Extend your index and middle fingers. See the illustration below.

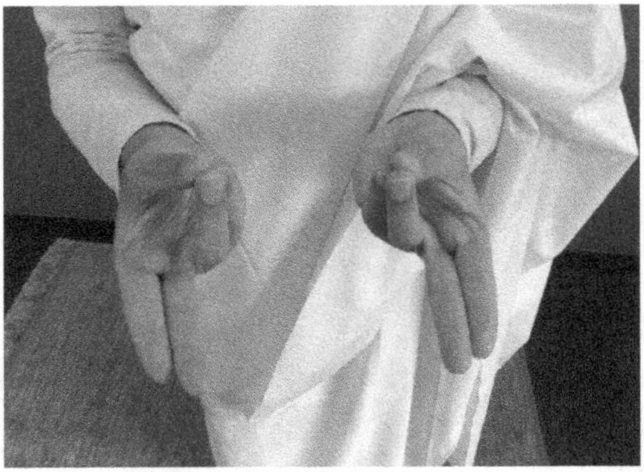

3. Apana Mudra

Apana mudra regulates the descending energy. Bring your ring and middle fingers together and join them at the tip of your thumbs. Extend your index and little fingers as per the illustration below.

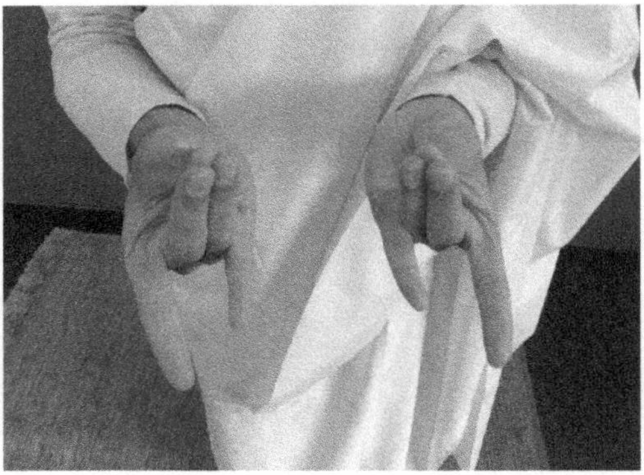

4. Samana Mudra

This mudra regulates the thermal energy. *Samana* mudra is performed by bringing all your fingers together and joining them at the tip of your thumbs as shown in the following illustration.

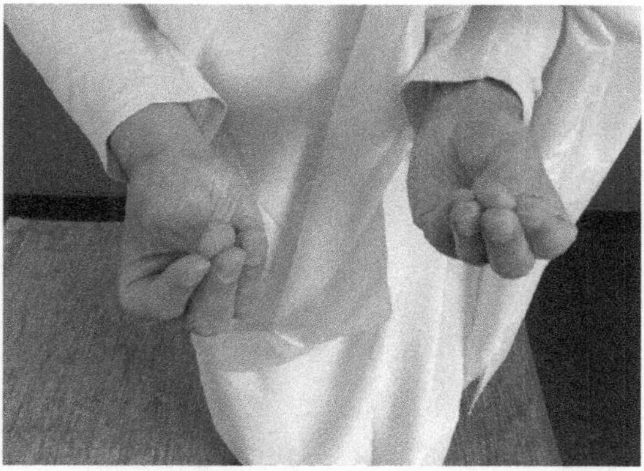

5. Udana Mudra

Udana mudra regulates the ascending energy. Bring all your fingers together and join them at the tip of your thumbs. Now extend the index finger out. In some traditions, the little finger is extended in lieu of the index finger. Personally, I find extending index finger more effective. Feel free to choose what works best for you. If unsure, simply follow the illustration below.

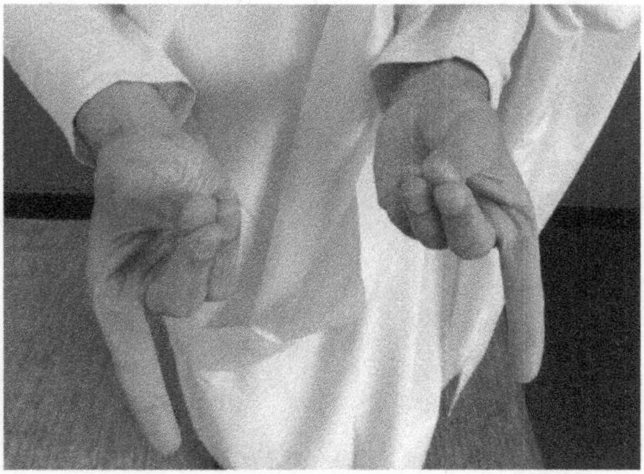

6. Vyana Mudra

Vyana mudra regulates the diffusive energy. Bring your index and middle finger together and join them at the tip of your thumbs. Extend the little and ring fingers as shown in the illustration below.

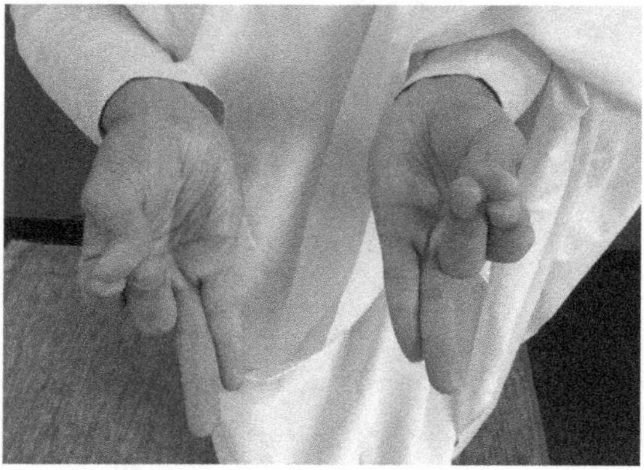

7. Dhyana Mudra

Dhyana means meditation. *Dhayana* mudra is meditative gesture. There are three different ways of performing *dhyana* mudra. I have shown all three below. First common way is to join your index

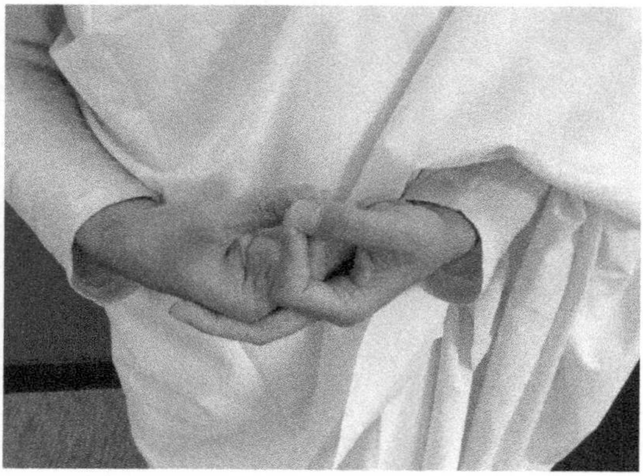

finger at the tip of your thumb to form a circle. Do this with both hands and now rest your left hand on your right as shown in the illustration.

The second method is by resting your right hand on your left and joining the thumbs at the tip to form a circle.

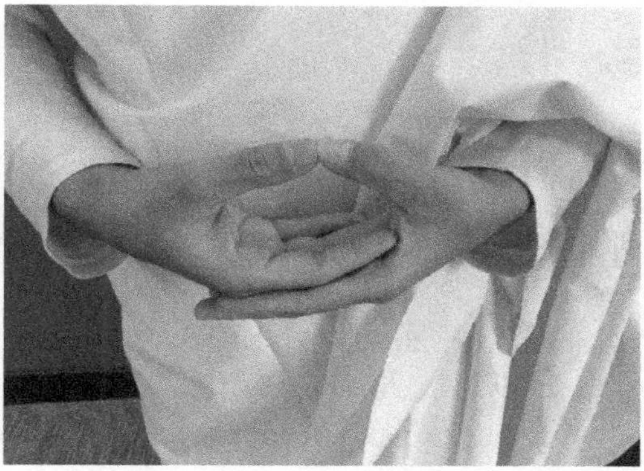

The third way is to crisscross your fingers of both hands and leave them relaxed.

How to do mudras correctly

1. Ideally your hands should be clean. Particularly, when it comes to mantra yoga, mudras are divine gestures designed to bridge the gap between you and your deity, therefore cleanliness is a must.
2. Just sit in a relaxed manner in any posture comfortable to you.
3. Gently rub your hands together for a few seconds. Seven to ten seconds should be sufficient.
4. Place your right hand on your navel and left hand on top of your right hand. The middle of your palm should be on top of your belly button or *manipura* chakra. Within about 15 seconds, you'll start to feel a flow of warm energy. (Try it to experience it. You'll not feel the same flow by placing your hands anywhere else on your body.) Stay in this position for about a minute.
5. Perform each mudra one by one. Yogic mudras require that you exert certain pressure and so on. In mantra *sadhana*, however, you just have to gently perform the mudra without exerting any pressure at all and hold a mudra for roughly 10 seconds each.

ESSENTIAL STEPS IN THE RITES OF INVOCATION (*PURUSHCHARANA*)

There are forty standard steps in any *sadhana* (*naimatika karma*). By *sadhana* I mean *anushthana* or *puruscharana*. Most *anushthanas* have additional or different steps too. Generally, they are given by the guru. I have, however, provided those steps for each of the four *sadhanas* enumerated in this book.

The following things are required to do your *anushthana*:

1. Four small vessels made from copper, silver or gold carrying water and a small spoon. One will be used for purificatory rights, second for offerings, third for *tarpana* and fourth for *marjana*.
2. A small saucer where you may drop water after symbolically washing hands
3. Your bowl containing your *tilakam*
4. A butter lamp where you can put a cotton wick and light it
5. Ghee for lighting your lamp. Mustard oil, *airand* or oil from sesame seeds can also be used. Some *sadhanas* require different kinds of oils.
6. Incense or *dhoopam*
7. Flowers if easily available
8. Sweets if easily available. Even a few grains of sugar will do.

9. Your mat where you will sit. What type of asana you use is dependent on what kind of *sadhana* it is. It has been detailed in the chapter on Seats.
10. Chanting beads. These differ from *sadhana* to *sadhana* and have been expounded on in the chapter on Beads.

Steps in *Sadhana*

1. Bathe

In all *sattvik* mantra *sadhanas*, regardless of what time of the day or night they are done, an aspirant begins by purifying and cleaning his body. A bath is non-negotiable requirement of all mantra *sadhanas*. Ever since I can recall, I've never missed taking my bath in the morning. A sincere aspirant should not eat anything prior to taking bath. This rule does not apply to patients (who must eat something in the morning so they may take their medication, etc.), pregnant women (they are free to eat as per their needs), elderly people (if you are above 75 in particular or even if you are above 70) and children below the age of seven.

Chant the following mantra while putting the first mug of water on you (or when you step into the shower if you are taking a shower):

Sanskrit (Devanagri)	*Sanskrit (IAST)*
गंगा च यमुने चैव गोदावरी सरस्वती ।	gaṃgā ca yamune caiva godāvarī sarasvatī |
नर्मदे सिंधु कावेरी जलेस्मिन संनिधिम कुरु ॥	narmade siṃdhu kāverī jalesmina saṃnidhima kuru ||
Translation	
I invoke the holy presence of Ganga, Yamuna, Godavari, Saraswati, Narmada, Sindhu and Kaveri in this water.	

2. Put on fresh clothes

Once you've taken your bath and brushed your teeth, you should put on fresh clothes. Often householders keep their pooja clothes separate and wear them everyday while only washing them once a week or more or less. While that is okay when it comes to *nitya karma*, or daily duties of an adept, it is not okay to do so during your *anushthana*. If weather conditions or due to other challenges (like lack of water, resources and so on), you can't put on a fresh cloth everyday, that's alright. But throughout your *anushthana*, you should make every attempt to wear washed/fresh clothes for pooja everyday.

3. Entering the sanctum sanctorum or opening your altar

If you have a separate pooja room in your home then before entering the pooja room, you should mindfully bow your head for a few seconds and pray to God or the Divine Energy that may you be blessed to sincerely carry out your duties. Then gently tapping the floor with your right foot, one should say the Astra Mantra. The Astra Mantra is different for each *sadhana* usually. If your *sadhana* has not provided you with Astra Mantra, then use the following:

'Om Hrim Astraya Phat!'

4. Purification

Once inside the pooja *griha*, you begin by purifying yourself and the energies around you. Use your left hand to take a bit of water using the spoon in your vessel and put it in the right one. Chant the following mantra:

om apavitrah pavitro vā
sarvāvasthāṁ gato api vā
yaḥ smaret puṇḍarīkākṣaṁ
sa bahya abhyantaraṁ śuciḥ

No matter how one is, whether he is clean or unclean, in what ever state he may be, the one who remembers Lord Pundarikasha is at once purified both internally and externally.

Sprinkle the water in your hand above you and around you.

5(a). Self-Purification (Achamana)

Water is consecrated and drunk three times while performing *achamana*. It's done three times to purify you at emotional, mental and physical level. To purify you in your waking, sleeping and dreaming state. To purify the three modes of material nature, that is, goodness, passion and ignorance. To infuse you with knowledge, existence, bliss (*sat-chit-anand*). To ignite your potential, kinetic and creative energies.

With your left hand, using the spoon again, put some water in your right hand and say the following mantra:

Om Keshvaya Namah
Drink the water.

Put one more spoon and say the following mantra.

Om Madhavaya Namah
Drink the water.

One more spoon and say the following mantra:

Om Narayanaya Namaha
Drink the holy water.

5(b). Prakshalana

Once you have done the *achamana* three times, take some more water in your right hand (a spoonful is usually enough) and symbolically wash both your hands while saying the following mantra:

'Om Pundarikakshaya Namah'

6. Lighting the lamp

Now light the lamp. Lamp is lit as a symbol of divine energy in living form, for fire has living energy. This is the view of the Vedas, that's why Agni has been deemed God. It does not discriminate. Lamp is lit to indicate that we want to dispel the darkness from our lives. It is lit to symbolize that let the light of knowledge and bliss be lit in our hearts too. You can simply use your guru mantra while lighting the lamp or chant the following mantra:

Om agni jyotir jyotir agnih swaha
Suryo jyoti jyotir suryah swaha
Agnir varcho jyotir varchah swaha
Suryo varcho jyotir varchah swaha
Jyoti suryah suryo jyotih swaha

(May the Divine Energy bring the power of Agni in this lamp. The light of this lamp is Agni, and Agni is this lamp... *svaha*, let all afflictions burn.)

7. Invoking Ganesha (Ganesh Dhyana)

All vedic, mantric, tantric and puranic poojas must begin with Ganapti. This is a scriptural injunction and I find no reason to violate it. Even in the *sadhanas* of Sabara Mantras (non-vedic mantras that belong to neither the Vedas or Vedanagas), all *sadhanas* begin by meditating on Lord Ganesha. You can just pray to Ganesha either by any mantra you may already know or by folding your hands and reciting any or both mantras:

Sanskrit (Devanagri)	*Sanskrit (IAST)*
वक्रतुण्ड महाकाय सूर्यकोटि समप्रभ ।	vakratuṇḍa mahākāya sūryakoṭi samaprabha ।

निर्विघ्नं कुरु मे देव सर्वकार्येषु सर्वदा ॥	nirvighnaṃ kuru me deva sarvakāryeṣu sarvadā ll

Translation

O Lord Ganesha of curved trunk, magnificent body exuding the radiance of countless suns, please be by my side and help me complete my task.

Sanskrit (Devanagri)	*Sanskrit (IAST)*
सुमुखश्च-एकदंतश्च कपिलो गज कर्णक:	sumukhaśca-ekadaṃtaśca kapilo gaja karṇaka:
लम्बोदरश्व विकटो विघ्ननाशो विनायक:	lambodaraśva vikaṭo vighnanāśo vināyaka:
धूम्रकेतुर्गणाध्यक्षो भालचन्द्रो गजानन:	dhūmraketurgaṇādhyakṣo bhālacandro gajānana:
द्वादशैतानि नामानि य: पठेच्छर्णुयादपि	dvādaśaitāni nāmāni ya: paṭheccharṇuyādapi
विद्यारम्भे विवाहे च प्रवेशे निर्गमे तथा	vidyārambhe vivāhe ca praveśe nirgame tathā
संग्रामें संकटे चैव विघ्नस्तस्य न जयते।	saṃgrāmeṃ saṃkaṭe caiva vighnastasya na jayate l

Translation

O Ganesha of beautiful face, one tusk, crimson red and elephant ears. O beautiful pot-bellied Ganesha who is hard on enemies, slayer of obstacles and a great spiritual perceptor. O Ganesha who is sometimes the color of smoke, the chief of ganas, who sports a moon on his forehead and walks like an elephant, whoever chants these twelve names of yours before studying, marrying, entering a new home, in battlefield, in distress (or embarking on any important journey of their lives) is sure to receive your help.

8. Handlocks for Ganesha (Ganesh Mudra)

Show the following three mudras of Ganesha.

First mudra of Ganesha:

a. Bring your left hand closer to your chest with the back of your hand facing your chest.
b. Curl your left hand a little and grab it with your right hand to form the mudra below.

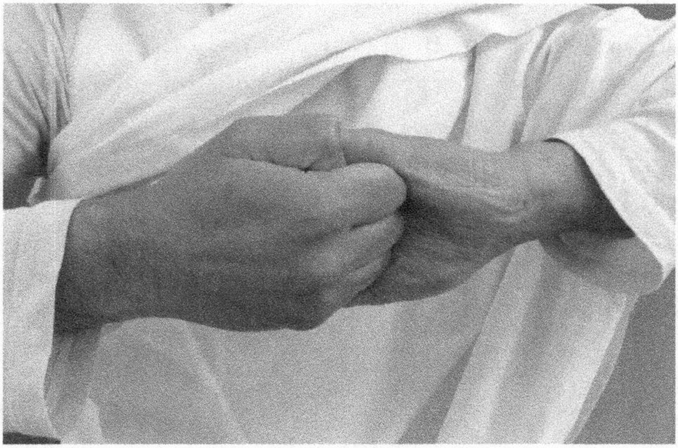

Second mudra of Ganesha:

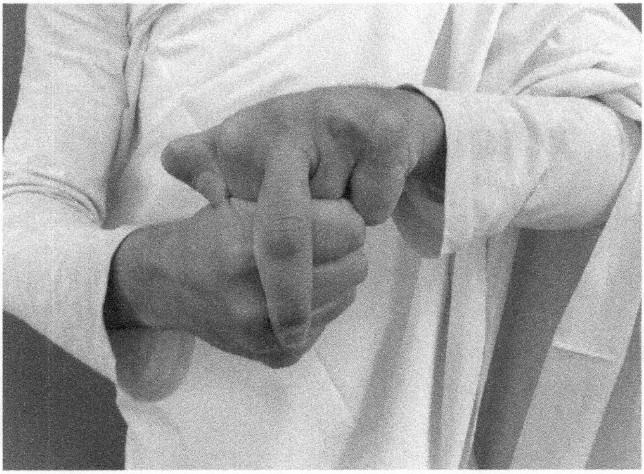

a. Tuck index and ring fingers of your left hand in your right fist.
b. Let the middle finger of your left hand remain outside to form the trunk of Ganesha.
c. Slightly protrude the thumb and little finger of your left hand to form the ears of Ganesha.

Third mudra of Ganesha:

a. It's exactly the same as the second mudra, just that Ganesha is made with the right hand.
b. Tuck index and ring fingers of your right hand in your left fist.
c. Let the middle finger of your right hand remain outside to form the trunk of Ganesha.
d. Slightly protrude the thumb and little finger of your right hand to form the ears of Ganesh as per the image below.

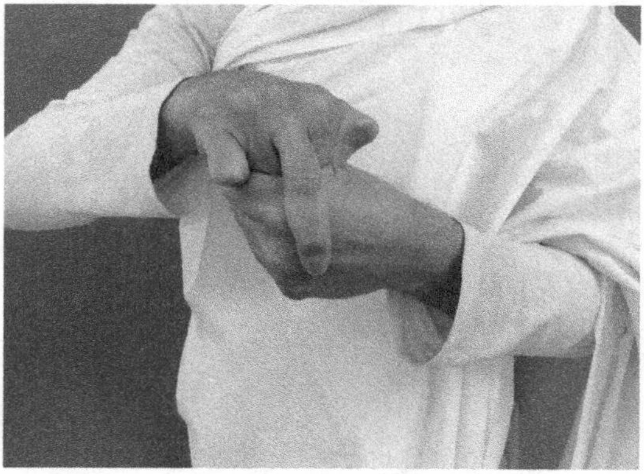

9. Chanting the hymn of auspiciousness (*Svastivachana*)

A chant to invite and invoke the vedic energies around you is done at this stage. It is usually done by chanting a specific hymn called *svastivachana*. You can either chant the *svastivachana* or just the following verses taken from the *Rigveda* (1.89.8):

Sanskrit (Devanagri)	Sanskrit (IAST)
ॐ भद्रं कर्णेभिः शृणुयाम देवाः ।	oṃ bhadraṃ karṇebhiḥ śṛṇuyāma devāḥ I
भद्रं पश्येमाक्षभिर्यजत्राः	bhadraṃ paśyemākṣabhiryajatrāḥ
स्थिरैरङ्गैस्तुष्टुवागँसस्तनूभिः	sthirairaṅgaistuṣṭuvāgaṁsa-stanūbhiḥ
व्यशेम देवहितं यदायूः	vyaśema devahitaṃ yadāyūḥ
स्वस्ति न इन्द्रो वृद्धश्रवाः	svasti na indro vṛddhaśravāḥ
स्वस्ति नः पूषा विश्ववेदाः	svasti naḥ pūṣā viśvavedāḥ
स्वस्ति नस्ताक्षर्यो अरिष्टनेमिः	svasti nastākṣaryo ariṣṭanemiḥ
स्वस्ति नो ब्रुहस्पतिर्दधातु ।	svasti no bruhaspatirdadhātu I
ॐ शान्तिः शान्तिः शान्तिः	oṃ śāntiḥ śāntiḥ śāntiḥ

Translation

May we only hear auspicious sounds with our ears and may only see divine things with our eyes. May we lead a stable life of health and prosperity with gratitude throughout the lifespan granted to us. May Indra of great renown protect us. May the omniscient Poosha protect us. May Lord Garuda destroy all harm and negativity. May Brihaspati protect us.

10. Meditating on your guru (*Guru dhyana*)

Now that you have purified yourself and the environment around you by invoking various energies, it is time to meditate on your guru. Call upon your guru by offering a flower if you have your guru's picture or you can simply visualize your guru's form and chant the following mantra with reverence:

Sanskrit (Devanagri)	*Sanskrit (IAST)*
गुरुर्ब्रह्मा गुरुर्विष्णुर्गुरुर्देवो महेश्वरः	gururbrahmā gururviṣṇurgururdevo maheśvaraḥ ।
गुरुरेव परं ब्रह्म तस्मै श्रीगुरवे नमः ॥	gurureva paraṃ brahma tasmai śrīgurave namaḥ ॥

Translation
Guru is Brahma, Guru is Vishnu, Guru is Shiva himself. Guru is verily Para-Brahma (Supreme Soul). Humble obeisance and salutations to my guru.

11. Chanting the guru mantra (*Guru* mantra *japa*)

Now, you should chant your guru mantra 11, 21 or 108 times depending on either the routine given to you by your guru or your own usual routine. It's important to be consistent throughout your *sadhana*. So, it's better to commit to 11 and do it properly than do 108 on the first day out of your enthusiasm and then struggling to do even 20 the next day. Guru mantra is usually not the mantra you are initiated into. That could be your *ishta* mantra or could even be (and generally is) a specific mantra for your *sadhana*. Guru mantra is given by the guru that contains the guru's secret name imparted only to the initiates. If your guru has not made any such distinction (most mantra adepts will do though), you can then either chant your *ishta* mantra as your guru mantra or simply take the name of your guru eleven times as your guru mantra.

12. Obeisance to all siddhas

Offer your respects and gratitude to all the siddhas, sages, seers and gurus of the past. Generally, this mantra can differ from tradition to tradition but if your guru is not a mantra adept (therefore not knowing this mantra) or hasn't initiated you into this mantra. Simply chant the following:

Sanskrit (Devanagri)	*Sanskrit (IAST)*
ॐ दिव्यौघ नमः	oṃ divyaugha namaḥ
ॐ सिद्धौघ नमः	oṃ siddhaugha namaḥ
ॐ मानवौघ नमः	oṃ mānavaugha namaḥ
Translation	
My obeisance to all the siddhas of divine bodies. My obeisance to all the siddhas of the past who are no more in their physical bodies. My obeisance to all the siddhas who are either still in a human body or can assume one.	

13. Meditating on your deity (*Ishta dhyana*)

Ishta generally means desired. *Ishta-devata* is the deity or the form of God you generally pray to. Your current *sadhana* may well be to invoke your *ishta* or it may be to attain mantra siddhi or some other divine entity. For example, on your usual days you may be praying to Krishna, etc. but now you are trying to invoke Goddess Durga. In this case, your *ishta* is Krishna, whereas the deity of your mantra is Durga. Before you can awaken the mantra of your deity, an aspirant is required to meditate on his *ishta-devata* as well. If, however, the deity you are trying to invoke is *your ishta-devata*, simply meditate on the form of your *ishta*.

Your *ishta-devata* could be any god, goddess from any religion for that matter. Religion is not important in *sadhana*, for *sadhana* is a religion in its own right. If you don't have an *ishta-devata*, simply meditate on the deity of your mantra.

14. Chanting the preliminary mantra (*Ishta* mantra *japa*)

Preliminary mantra is the mantra of your *ishta-devata.* Chant the mantra of your *ishta-devata* 11, 21 or 31 times. Once again, be consistent throughout your *sadhana.* If you don't have an *ishta-mantra*, then the mantra of your deity is your *ishta-mantra.* If you don't have a mantra or a deity, then none of what I'm talking about here applies because please remember that these steps are not for the daily pooja but specifically for doing *anushthanas.*

15. Praying to Mother Earth (*Prithvi pooja*)

Draw a triangle on the floor, right in front of you with water. It's a symbolic triangle. If you are trying to invoke a masculine mantra the triangle should point upwards (towards the deity) and if you are invoking a feminine mantra, the triangle should point downwards. Put a dot with water right in the middle of the triangle and put a flower in the middle (on top of the dot) and say the following mantra:

Sanskrit (Devanagri)	*Sanskrit (IAST)*
ह्रीं आधारशक्तये नमः	hrīṃ ādhāraśaktaye namaḥ
Translation	
My obeisance to the primordial energy that is sustaining the entire creation.	

Take a moment to mentally express your gratitude to Mother Nature, Mother Earth, for blessing you with the privilege and that ground where you are able to sit now and invoke divine energies.

16. Taking the vow (*Sankalpa*)

Sankalpa is only taken on the very first day of your *sadhana.* As a part of *sankalpa*, you announce your intention to the universe. You take a vow that for the next so many days, you'll do this much of *japa* dedicated to so and so deity to attain such and such outcome. Remember, it's only done on the very first day of the *sadhana.*

When you violate your *sankalpa*, your *sadhana* is compromised and you must either start from the beginning or seek a remedial measure from your guru. For example, if in your *sankalpa*, you state that you will chant four thousand mantras everyday for the next forty days but you miss one day or chant less one day, this compromises your *sadhana.* You must reset the counter and start all over again. I'm giving you a trimmed down vedic mantra below for the simplest form of *sankalpa.* Or, you can simply take water in your right palm, put a few grains of rice and a flower and do the *sankalpa* in any language you know. Fill in the blanks:

I ...*(your full name)* ... born in ... *(state your* gotra. *If you don't know your* gotra, *simply say* Narayana gotra *for everyone is a child of the Divine)* ... on ... *(state your date of birth)* hereby vow to do a *puruscharana* of ... *(the name of your mantra, like Gayatri, Sri Suktam, Guru Mantra, etc.)* ... over the next ... *(state the number of days you'll be chanting the mantra over, for example, 40, 90, 100, 300 and so on)* days... so I may become a worthy recipient of your grace and attain the desired outcome.

Keep the water, rice and flower aside. You can immerse it in the water on any day convenient to you or simply leave it at the root of a tree or a plant. Any plant except cactus is permitted.

17. Mantra breathing (Mantra *shvasa*)

Start by completely and gently exhaling from both nostrils before you can begin the mantra breathing process below:

With your right thumb, close your right nostril and breathe in deeply from the left. While breathing in, chant the mantra of your deity.

Now, lift the thumb from your right nostril and close your left nostril by placing the index finger of your right-hand. Exhale gently. Chant your mantra while exhaling.

Keep the same hand position and deeply inhale from your right nostril now. Chant the mantra while inhaling from your right nostril.

Now, lift your index finger from the left nostril and put your thumb on the right nostril to close it. Gently exhale from your left nostril and chant your mantra while exhaling.

This is one round of inhalation-exhalation which involves inhaling from your left, exhaling from your right, inhaling from your right and exhaling from your left.

Do three rounds of mantra breathing.

18. Application (*Viniyoga*)

The word *viniyoga* means application. Unlike *sankalpa*, *viniyoga* is chanted every day throughout your *sadhana*. A *sadhana* under one *sankalpa* can have multiple *viniyogas* (as you'll see in the *sadhana* of *Sri Sukta*). There's no standard *viniyoga* that I can give you as it changes from mantra to mantra. In the four *sadhanas* given in this book, I've provided separate *viniyoga* at all applicable places.

Viniyoga is done by taking water in your right palm and then leaving that water in the tiny saucer after you've chanted the *viniyoga*. Just a rule of thumb: only in the case of *achamana*, you drink the water and only when washing your hands, you leave it on the floor. Only while *sankalpa*, you keep it aside with the flower (there are going to be barely a few drops anyway). During all the other aspects when you keep water in your right palm, almost always it's left in the saucer unless otherwise stated.

19. Purification of hands (*Kara shuddhi*)

Kara shuddhi refers to purification of the hands before you begin *nyasa* (the next step). It is done by chanting the seed syllable of your mantra and washing your hands while you chant it. Three times the hands are washed and three times the seed syllable is chanted. Once again, you wash your hands by taking a bit of water in the right hand and then symbolically washing both hands with it to your left side.

You can keep a small towel with you to wipe your hands everytime you use water. This is completely at your discretion.

There's no specific seed syllable I can give you for *kara shuddhi* because, once again, like *viniyoga*, they are different for each *sadhana*. Some *sadhanas* don't require *kara shuddhi*. As far as the *sadhanas* in this book are concerned, I've given the mantra of *kara shuddhi* wherever applicable. At times the process of *kara shuddhi* can also vary. Wherever applicable, I've noted in this book.

20. Unification with the mantra (*Nyasa*)

I've detailed the meaning, types and process of nyasa under the chapter with the same name. Once you have done *kara shuddhi*, *nyasa* is performed at this stage. It is one of the most important steps in *sadhana*. With *nyasa*, you establish various letters of the mantra in you. You become the deity yourself.

21. Preliminary mantra chanting (*Purva* mantra *japa*)

Once you have mentally established yourself as the deity and have completed the process, an aspirant chants the *moola* mantra (the mantra of the deity) sixteen times. Generally, the number of times this chanting is done is dependent on the *tithi* (date) in the lunar calendar but to keep things simple, just chant sixteen times every day throughout your *sadhana*. Once again, please remember that this is not your guru mantra but the main mantra you are doing *puruscharana* of.

22. Preliminary handlocks (*Purva* mudras)

Mudras are handlocks and I've explained their significance in the chapter with the same name. Each *sadhana* generally has some mudras that are shown before and after the *japa* throughout your *sadhana*. Mudras differ from *sadhana* to *sadhana*. There are seven standard handlocks you can show before you begin your *sadhana* though. I've detailed those in the chapter on mudras.

23. Sixteen offerings (*Shodashopchara*)

Shodasha means sixteen and *upchara* means offerings. *Upchara* also means treatment, solution or cure. In the current context, however, it means offering. *Shodashopchara* refers to the sixteen offerings you can make to the deity. If you don't have the time or resources to make sixteen offerings, you can make ten (*dashopchara*) or five (*panchopchara*) offerings as well.

The most important thing to remember is to be consistent. If you make five offerings on the first day, stick to five for the rest of your *puruscharana*. If you do sixteen offerings on day one, you must do sixteen everyday throughout your *puruscharana* and so on.

I've narrated the various offerings in *Types of Offerings (Upacharas)* under Detailed Notes.

24. Invoking the mantra (Mantra *samskara*)

Any mantra *samskaras* are done at this stage. In the chapter on correcting the flaws in a mantra I've already stated the various types of *samskaras*. You should do the *samskara* if either your guru has instructed or it's mentioned in the *sadhana* (for every *sadhana* in this book, I've mentioned what *samskara* you need to do) or if your earlier attempt did not yield mantra *siddhi*. Mantra *samskara* are extremely important for the attainment of *siddhi* on the path of mantra yoga. All too often, I've seen seekers fail because they ignored mantra *samskara*. If you truly believe that mantras are living energies and we are trying to invoke that, it's only natural that we treat this sonic vibration as we would treat any living entity — with care.

25. Meditation on your mantra (Mantra *dhyana*)

You are only one step away from starting your mantra chanting now. *Dhyana* is meditating on the deity of the mantra before you begin *japa*. It's usually done by *dhyana shloka* that differs from *sadhana* to *sadhana*. If you can read basic Sanskrit (even if you don't understand it), I've given all Sanskrit shlokas in transliteration making it easier for anyone to read), I encourage you to read the *dhyana shloka* in Sanskrit. I've provided meanings next to every *dhyana* mantra so you may rejoice in the beauty each such *shloka* has and so that you may meditate correctly on the form.

26. Mantra chanting (*Moola* mantra *japa*)

The chanting begins at this step. Now you dip your hand into the bead bag (*gaumukhi*) and start chanting the mantra. The degree and quality of results directly depend on the purity of your faith, discipline and concentration. The more mindful you are while chanting, the quicker and greater the results. Rather than just parroting a mantra without any feeling (which won't result in much), it's important to do it with a sense of devotion and gratitude. To be able to do a *sadhana* is considered a great privilege in mantra yoga. Be grateful for this privilege.

27. Post *japa* handlocks (*Uttara* mudra)

Once your *japa* is complete, the mudras post the *sadhana* are shown now. They differ from *sadhana* to *sadhana* and not every *sadhana* has handlocks to be shown upon completion. Please refer to the relevant *sadhana* to know which mudras are performed. For every *sadhana* given in this book, I've documented the relevant mudras. If no handlocks are given simply show the two mudras below in the order shown.

Gratitude handlock (Anjali mudra)

Simply join your palms and bring them to your chest. This is the normal gesture to do namaste as well.

Liberation handlock (Samhara or nirvana mudra)

Stretch out your left arm with palm facing downwards. Stretch your right arm and turn it over. Put the back of your right hand on the back of your left hand. Crisscross the fingers and turn the hand inward and bring them to your chest. This looks like the inverted gratitude handlock. See the image below.

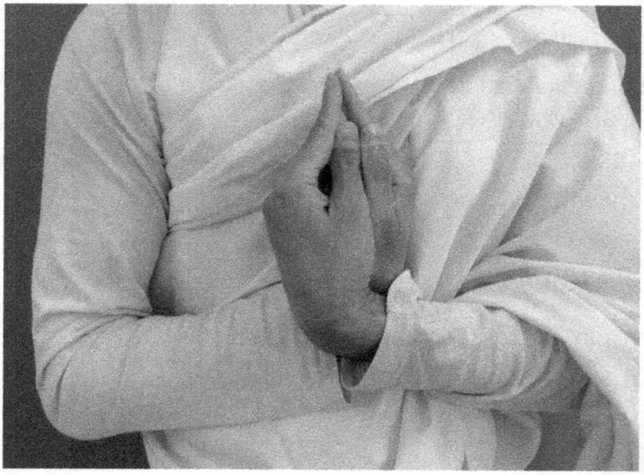

28. Offering your chanting (*Japa samarpana*)

When your *japa* is complete, it should be offered to the deity of the mantra so its vibrations are released in the universe and it may be used for the welfare of all sentient beings. When doing *japa samarpana*, visualize that your deity has manifested before you. If you chanted a feminine mantra, offer it in the left hand of the goddess and if you chanted a masculine mantra, offer it in the right hand of your deity. If your mantra was of neutral nature, offer it in the left hand still because Devi represents kinetic energy, energy in motion. Offer your prayer with the mantra below:

Sanskrit (Devanagri)	*Sanskrit (IAST)*
अभिष्ट सिद्धिं मे देहि शरणागत वत्सले, भक्त्या समर्पये तुभ्यं जपमेवर्चनम् ॥	abhiṣṭa siddhiṃ me dehi śaraṇāgata vatsale, bhaktyā samarpaye tubhyaṃ japamevarcanam ॥
Translation	
Please grant me your benediction (the desired outcome) O Devi, refuge of the one who seeks you, your devotee here surrenders and offers all my *japa* and prayers to you.	

You can chant the following mantra after offering your chanting to reinforce that you pray for the welfare of everyone around you.

Sanskrit (Devanagri)	*Sanskrit (IAST)*
ॐ सर्वे भवन्तु सुखिनः	oṃ sarve bhavantu sukhinaḥ
सर्वे सन्तु निरामयाः ।	sarve santu nirāmayāḥ ।
सर्वे भद्राणि पश्यन्तु	sarve bhadrāṇi paśyantu

मा कश्चिदद्दुःखभाग्भवेत् ।	mā kaścidduḥkhabhāgbhavet I
ॐ शान्तिः शान्तिः शान्तिः ॥	oṃ śāntiḥ śāntiḥ śāntiḥ II

Translation

May all sentient beings be at peace,
May no one suffer from illness,
May all see what is auspicious,
May no one suffer.
Om peace, peace, peace.

29. Freeing all energies (*Visarjana*)

In this step thanking the energies of the deity who presented themselves while you propitiated the Divine Energy and chanted your mantra, we allow those energies to return to their abode. We request prosperity and wisdom to stay with us, so we may continue to do good karma and work for the welfare of our entire world. It can be done with any words you wish to choose or you can chant the simple mantra below:

If praying to the feminine energy (Devi)	
Sanskrit (Devanagri)	*Sanskrit (IAST)*
गच्छ गच्छ परं स्थानं स्वस्थानं परमेश्वरि । पूजाराधनकाले च पुनरागमनाय च ॥ तिष्ठ तिष्ठ परस्थाने स्वस्थाने परमेश्वरि । यत्र ब्रह्मादयो देवाः सर्वे तिष्ठन्ति मे हृदि ॥	gaccha gaccha paraṃ sthānaṃ svasthānaṃ parameśvari I pūjārādhanakāle ca punarāgamanāya ca II tiṣṭha tiṣṭha parasthāne svasthāne parameśvari I yatra brahmādayo devāḥ sarve tiṣṭhanti me hṛdi II

Translation
May all energies return to their abode and I humbly request your presence again when I pray to you next. May all energies may take their seats in their respective abodes. May the supreme energy reside in my heart.

If praying to the masculine energy (Devata)	
Sanskrit (Devanagri)	*Sanskrit (IAST)*
गच्छ गच्छ परं स्थानं स्वस्थानं परमेश्वरः। पूजाराधनकाले च पुनरागमनाय च ॥ तिष्ठ तिष्ठ परस्थाने स्वस्थाने परमेश्वरः । यत्र ब्रह्मादयो देवाः सर्वे तिष्ठन्ति मे हृदि ॥	gaccha gaccha paraṃ sthānaṃ svasthānaṃ parameśvaraḥ । pūjārādhanakāle ca punarāgamanāya ca ॥ tiṣṭha tiṣṭha parasthāne svasthāne parameśvaraḥ । yatra brahmādayo devāḥ sarve tiṣṭhanti me hṛdi ॥
Translation	
May all energies return to their abode and I humbly request your presence again when I pray to you next. May all energies may take their seats in their respective abodes. May the supreme energy reside in my heart.	

30. Seeking forgiveness (*Kshama prarthana)*

No matter how perfect an aspirant may be, it's normal and natural that during the course of the *japa, sadhana*, one might have made some mistakes. Those could be errors in pronouncing the mantras, lack of faith, devotion or not properly purifying the ingredients. Or, chanting with an impure mind, heart or mouth. Once again you can do so with any words you wish to use, for, sentiment is more important than language or you can use the verses below to seek forgiveness.

Sanskrit (Devanagri)	*Sanskrit (IAST)*
अपराधसहस्त्राणि	aparādhasahastrāṇi
क्रियन्तेऽहर्निशं मया ।	kriyantesharniśaṃ mayā I
दासोऽयमिति मां मत्वा क्षमस्व	dāsosyamiti māṃ matvā kṣamasva
परमेश्र्वरि ॥	parameśrvari II
आवाहनं न जानामि न जानामि	āvāhanaṃ na jānāmi na jānāmi
विसर्जनम् ।	visarjanam I
पूजां चैव न जानामि क्षम्यतां	pūjāṃ caiva na jānāmi kṣamyatāṃ
परमेश्र्वरि ॥	parameśrvari II
मन्त्रहीनं क्रियाहीनं भक्तिहीनं	mantrahīnaṃ kriyāhīnaṃ
सुरेश्र्वरि ।	bhaktihīnaṃ sureśrvari I
यत्पूजितं मया देवि परिपूर्ण	yatpūjitaṃ mayā devi paripūrṇa
तदस्तु मे ॥	tadastu me II

Translation
O Devi, I must have committed thousands of mistakes and errors in chanting your names. Please forgive me for my errors like a good master forgives his servant.
I don't know how to invite you nor do I know how to see you off. I don't know how to pray to you, please forgive me for my ignorance.
I am without the knowledge of mantras, actions or devotion, O Goddess. And yet, I dare to pray to you. Please grant me your grace.

If you are invoking a masculine mantra (like the mantra of Ganapati or any other god) use the following mantra:

Sanskrit (Devanagri)	Sanskrit (IAST)
अपराधसहस्त्राणि क्रियन्तेऽहर्निशं मया । दासोऽयमिति मां मत्वा क्षमस्व परमेश्र्वर ॥ आवाहनं न जानामि न जानामि विसर्जनम् । पूजां चैव न जानामि क्षम्यतां परमेश्र्वर ॥ मन्त्रहीनं क्रियाहीनं भक्तिहीनं सुरेश्र्वर । यत्पूजितं मया देव परिपूर्ण तदस्तु मे ॥	aparādhasahastrāṇi kriyantesharniśaṃ mayā I dāsosyamiti māṃ matvā kṣamasva parameśrvara II āvāhanaṃ na jānāmi na jānāmi visarjanam I pūjāṃ caiva na jānāmi kṣamyatāṃ parameśrvara II mantrahīnaṃ kriyāhīnaṃ bhaktihīnaṃ sureśrvara I yatpūjitaṃ mayā deva paripūrṇa tadastu me II

Translation
O Supreme Soul, I must have committed thousands of mistakes and errors in chanting your names. Please forgive me for my errors like a good master forgives his servant. I don't know how to invite you nor do I know how to see you off. I don't know how to pray to you, please forgive me for my ignorance, O Bhagawan. I am without the knowledge of mantras, actions or devotion, O God. And yet, I dare to pray to you. Please grant me your grace.

31. Fire offerings (*Yajna*)

There are many types of *yajnas* but the particular one I'm referring to here is known as *havan* or *homam*, a *yajna* that involves fire offerings. When you do pooja involving external ingredients (as opposed to inner worship), to do fire offerings is imperative. The rites of *puruscharana* require that one tenth of your *japa* must be done as *havan*. I have shown how to do a basic *yajna* in the chapter titled Yajna. Most *yajnas* have the same beginning and a similar ending but a different middle which is often based on making fire offerings using the mantra of your deity. Further, while there are standard ingredients that are used in most *yajnas*, the ingredients can actually vary vastly when you do a *yajna* as part of a *puruscharana*. I've listed the *yajna* ingredients and requirements for each *sadhana* separately under the *sadhana* notes.

32. Libations (*Tarpana*)

Tarpana are water offerings or libations, as they are usually called, made to the deity of your mantra. For each *sadhana,* the mantras used for libations differ a great deal, for they depend on the deity of the mantra. Once again, the ritual of *tarpana* has been elaborated in the chapter under the same heading. Here's how to do *tarpana*:

The number of libations is one tenth of the number of offerings made in *yajna*. There are four different types of *tarpana* and each one is done with a different mudra. I'm sharing with you the simplest version that does not require you to learn any specific mudra.

Take your spoon and the small vessel of water you have next to you. Lift your spoon, take some water in it, chant the mantra of your deity, add 'tarpyami' at the end of the mantra, and pour the water back into the vessel. Do it as many times as the *sadhana* requires you to. In the end, offer this water to the sun as stated in the last step.

33. Coronation (*Marjana* or *abhishekam*)

Marjana or *abhishekam* is an important part of closing. Remember, the *nyasa* you'd done in the beginning? *Nyasa* made you a shrine where you house the mantric energy of the deity. If you recall, nyasa was placing various letters of the mantra throughout your body. *Marjana* is done to honor yourself, to consecrate yourself and to offer yourself the same treatment as is met out to gods because you now carry the energy of the mantra.

The number of offerings done in *marjana* is one-tenth the number of libations. To do *marjana*, take vessel number two containing water.

Joining your thumb and ring finger, dip it in water and sprinkle on your head with the same mudra.

In the end, you can either offer this water to the sun (you can mix it with the water used for *tarpana*) or you can pour this water in the root of any tree. Both are equally effective.

34. Charity (*Sadhak bhojan* or Brahmin *bhojan*)

Sadhak bhojan is usually done not everyday of your *sadhana* but on the last day when you complete your *sadhana*. The idea is to feed the God in living entities. It is also a moment of celebration that you successfully completed your intense routine spread over so many days. In the olden times, an aspirant would either be part of a *gurukul* where there would be other aspirants and feeding them would be enough. Or, an aspirant would gather a certain number of Brahmins. They would come together and with beautiful vedic chants energize the whole environment. The aspirant would feed them.

Depending on where you live, it may be difficult to do either. So, you can do something else which is equally effective. Simply set aside whatever you can every day, an amount of money that would buy at least one meal for a person or whatever you can reasonably afford. If you are really pressed financially and can't set aside even Rs. 50 or a dollar a day, then simply set aside a handful of dry fruits every day. At the end of your *sadhana*, offer them to a fellow aspirant who's also walking the path. If you can't find that, offer it to a Brahmin who serves in a temple or chants vedic mantras daily. If you can't find that Brahmin, then offer it to any orphanage. If there's no orphange, you can give it at any oldage home. If you can't find even that, feed it to the birds. If by some rare chance, you can't do that either then immerse it in a stream, river or the ocean. The idea is that someone other than you or your own family should partake of your offerings so whatever you did tangibly also helps someone else.

35. Seeking again forgiveness (*Kshama prarthana*)

Repeat the hymn of forgiveness as in step number 30 for there might have been mistakes in your actions from step 31 – 34.

36. Offering water to the sun (*Surya arghya*)

Step outside and offer the water to the sun. You do that by facing the sun. If due to weather conditions or the time of the day, you can't see the sun, simply face the direction the sun rises in. Chanting the mantra of your deity, simply raise the vessel of water above your head and pour it on the ground.

These thirty-six steps are performed everyday when you do the *puruscharana* of any mantra. It's common for an aspirant to pick and choose the steps based on their convenience. Please don't do that. If you don't feel like doing all the steps, it's better to not do the *sadhana* altogether. If you are serious about mantra *siddhi* and benefits, diligently work through every single step with faith and devotion. You may feel overwhelmed at first but trust me once you get the hang of it, it'll just all come to you naturally like flying comes to a bird.

If for some reason, you can't get your head around this, you have the option to do inner *sadhana* where you worship the deity within you and none of the physical ingredients are used. The process of inner worship appeals to many and is often more practical, too. Having said that, it requires an aspirant to build supreme one-pointed concentration and that is not an easy task. In other words, there's no shortcut. But, those who walk through fire come out as pure gold.

A guiding principle

Successful performance of invocation requires that you do *japa* (chanting) of your mantra as required by the *sadhana* of that mantra or as instructed by the guru. This is followed by fire offerings (*yajna*). The number of offerings (*ahuti*) made in a *yajna* are usually equivalent to the ten percent of your *japa*. Libations (*tarpana*) are ten percent of *yajna*. Coronation (*marjana* or *abhishekam*) is done equivalent to ten percent of your *yajna*. This is followed by charity (*sadhak bhojan*) which is ten percent of coronation.

For example, if you do *japa* of 100,000, you'll do fire offering (*yajna*) of 10,000 offerings, libations (*tarpana*) of 1,000 offerings, coronation (*marjana*) of 100 offerings and charity by serving food (*sadhak bhojan*) to 10 people. Further assume that you did *japa* of 100,000 over 40 days which means everyday you chanted 2,500 times. This means that you could do *yajna* every day, offering 250 oblations (*ahutis*), libations 25 times and coronation three times.

Serving of food is usually done at the end of your *puruscharana* because it may not be feasible to find someone everyday. In rites of invocation that last several months, usually the aspirant sets aside a bit of money every day, enough to buy one meal. At the end of *puruscharana*, that money is either donated to a worthy recipient (scriptures usually recommend a Brahmin or a saint), or food grains, etc., are bought and a meal is hosted for several people.

In case you are not able to do *yajna*, *tarpana*, *marjana* or *sadhak bhojana*, scriptures allow doing double the *japa* for the missed aspect to compensate. For example, let's say you have to do *yajna* with 250 fire offerings, but you are not able to do so. To make up for it, you can do *japa* 500 times.

BOOK THREE

SADHANAS

śvapāko jalpāko bhavati madhupākopamagirā
nirātaṅko raṅko viharati ciraṃ koṭikanakaiḥ |
tavāparṇe karṇe viśati manuvarṇe phalamidaṃ
janaḥ ko jānīte janani japanīyaṃ japavidhau ||

Even a simpleton becomes an eloquent orator. A poor and miserable man becomes an emperor, forever moving around fearlessly. Such is the result if even one letter of your mantra falls in one's ears, who among the mortals, O Mother, can ever comprehend the immense rewards that a properly done sadhana of you can bring.
(Devi Aparadha Kshamapana Stotram, 6).

ACTUAL SADHANA

- **Ganesha (for blessings & grace)**
- **Guru (for permission & guidance)**
- **Gayatri (for spiritual growth & wisdom)**
- **Sri Suktam (for material progress)**
- **Rites of Atonement (Prayashchitta)**
- **How To Make Fire Offerings (Yajna)**

Based on tradition and lineage, the path of mantra *sadhana* requires the aspirant to do certain preliminary *sadhanas* before they can embark on the main ones. Assuming you don't belong to any particular tradition or that your guru is not an expert in mantra yoga or that you don't have a guru at all, I've listed here in detail two preliminary *sadhanas* (Ganesha *Sadhana* and Guru *Sadhana*) and four primary *sadhanas*. Don't get carried away by all four. Pick one *sadhana* and perfect it.

If you have read the book till here, you now know all there is to know about mantra yoga. (In Detailed Notes after this section, I've covered many aspects I merely touched upon in the previous chapters).

Now that you fully understand various aspects, steps and dimensions of mantra *sadhana*, you are ready to take a plunge into its fascinating world. In this section, I share with you the four different *sadhanas*.

For each *sadhana*, I've explained every step. Based on your temperament or needs, you may choose to do one or the other, but it's imperative that you do Ganesha *Sadhana* first anyway. I also highly recommend that you do Guru *Sadhana* as well to invoke the guru within you for future guidance. No mantra *sadhana* is performed without praying to Ganesha and Guru first.

Remember that mantra yoga is a tradition and to benefit from it fully, you must honor the tradition. If you don't care about lineage, tradition and the rest, mantra yoga is not for you. Rather, you'll gain more from simple meditation. If, however, you are keen to follow this path, I'm elucidating four *sadhanas* for you, assuming you are not initiated into any of these mantras. And even if you are already initiated but would like to experience mantra *sadhana* in its entirety, you are welcome to experiment with the *sadhanas* I share in this section.

Before you begin, please make sure that you have read the previous sections at least twice (if not three times), because if you understand thoroughly, you'll perform the *sadhanas* more effectively.

GANESHA SADHANA

वक्रतुण्ड महाकाय सूर्यकोटि समप्रभ ।
निर्विघ्नं कुरु मे देव सर्वकार्येषु सर्वदा ॥

vakratuṇḍa mahākāya sūryakoṭi samaprabha |
nirvighnaṃ kuru me deva sarvakāryeṣu sarvadā ||

My obeisance to Lord Ganesha of curved trunk, gigantic body radiating like the brilliance of countless suns. I pray for success in all my endeavors.

The tradition of mantra yoga requires that Lord Ganesha be invoked before every major prayer. I strongly recommend that you do Ganesha *Sadhana* before taking on any mantra *sadhana*. By following any tradition, you benefit from it. Besides, it's a simple *sadhana* that can be done in 30 days at the most.

How long does it take

The *puruscharana* of this *sadhana* requires that you chant the mantra of Ganesha (shared ahead) 1,25,000 times in 15 or 30 days.

When can you start this sadhana

Start on the fourth night of the waxing or waning moon. Chant the mantra in the wee hours (starting ninety minutes before the sunrise) or at night. The most important thing is to stick to the same routine throughout your *puruscharana*. For example, if you begin chanting at 5 am on day one, it's important to start it exactly at the same time for the next 30 days.

Who can do this sadhana

Anybody, of any age, religion, ability or background can do this with or without initiation. Since this *puruscharana* lasts a minimum of 40 days, women who are menstruating can continue their *sadhana* without any reservations whatsoever. You must observe complete abstinence throughout the *puruscharana*. However, there's no *dosha* (issue) in case of wet dreams or any other involuntary release of sexual fluids.

Diet

Throughout your *puruscharna*, you should be on a strict vegetarian diet. Dairy is allowed but no meat, seafood or eggs. No onion or garlic either. Be careful about eating biscuits, cakes, cheeses and supplements that may contain animal-derived ingredients.

Lamp

Only a brass lamp should be used in this *puruscharana*, with the wick made from cotton. It is permissible to use braided cotton thread (like the common sacred red thread, *mauli*, for example, or any other) to use as a wick. Use pure ghee only to light the lamp.

Direction

The aspirant should face east or north while doing the chanting and the *yajna*.

Clothing

Wear yellow-colored clothing. Ideally, you should wear no more than two pieces of loose yellow-cloth on your body — one to cover your lower body and the other to cover the upper portion. If you are in a very cold place, you can either use a heater in your room to keep it warm or sew your upper cloth with a woolen shawl. Women can wear a yellow saree, a blouse, etc.

Seat

The best seat will be a blanket on which you should spread a yellow cloth. The nature of this *sadhana* requires you to sit on the floor. If you are unable to do that, you may try sitting in a chair and setting up a table in front with lamp, pots, etc. Personally, I have never experimented with that. If you do, please feel free to share the results of your *sadhana*.

Other than a blanket, you can also take a standard meditation cushion or use any seat made out of cotton.

Seat made of *kusha* grass is also permissible for this *sadhana*.

Posture

Try to keep your posture still while you chant with utmost mindfulness, faith and devotion. Please allow me to remind you that mantra *sadhana* is not about reckless chanting of a mantra just for the sake of ticking off an item. It is the soulful process of becoming one with your deity so that you may elevate yourself spiritually, materially and emotionally.

Requirements for this *sadhana*:

1. A brass lamp.
2. Ghee and wick for your lamp.
3. Five small water pots, a small spoon and a saucer. They can be of silver, copper or brass. This is the standard for every sadhana and details on how to lay out the patra (pots) can be found in the chapter Arrangement of Pots (i) in Detailed Notes.

4. Sweetmeat, jaggery or honey (to make the madhuparka offering).
5. Standard ingredients for fire-offerings (yajna) as mentioned in the chapter How to Make Fire Offerings (Yajna).
6. In addition to those ingredients, you would also need firewood. You can use either wood from a sacred fig (Ficus religiosa. Common name: peepul), mango (Magnifera indica, Common name: aam or aamra) or palasha (Butea monosperma. Common name: plasha or dhak). You can also use the wood from deodar (Cedrus deodara. Common name: devadaru) or teak (Tectona grandis. Common name: sagaun or sheesham).
7. Chanting beads of rudraksha or sandalwood.
8. A lot of faith, devotion and discipline.

I strongly recommend you to make a daily checklist in line with the 36 steps I enumerate below. Also, do make a daily list of what all you require and procure it beforehand.

The Mantra

Sanskrit (Devanagri)	*Sanskrit (IAST)*
ॐ वक्रतुंडाय हुं ।	oṃ vakratuṃḍāya huṃ ।

Before You Begin

We must seek permission from the Divine Mother before undertaking Ganesha *Sadhana*. The simplest way to do this is, after sunset, take a bath and sit at your altar. Take a bit of water in your right hand and mentally call upon the Divine Mother in the form of Gayatri and seek her permission that She and other forces of nature allow you to complete your *sadhana*. Leave the water in the plate next to you.

Next, do 30 rounds of Gayatri Mantra with rudraksha beads. Use the same beads to commence your *puruscharana* the next day.

One round is 108 times. Thirty rounds will be chanting your mantra 108 x 30 = 3,240 times. I always used to chant 10,000 times before doing any major *puruscharana*. But, 30 rounds will suffice too. Once the 30 rounds are done, sleep at the same place where you finished chanting the mantra. Here's the mantra again for your reference.

Sanskrit (Devanagri)	*Sanskrit (IAST)*
ॐ भूर्भुवः स्वः तत्सवितुर्वरेण्यम भर्गो देवस्य धीमहि। धियो यो नः प्रचोदयात॥	oṃ bhūrbhuvaḥ svaḥ tatsaviturvareṇyama bhargo devasya dhīmahi । dhiyo yo naḥ pracodayāta ॥

Translation
May we abide in the Supreme Energy that is eternal, transcendental, radiant, perfect, divine. May such divine grace always guide us on the path of righteousness.

How to perform the rites of invocation (*puruscharana*)

Every day, throughout your *puruscharna*, the first few steps will be the same. Step number 17 (taking the vow – *sankalpa*) is done only on the first night. For all the remaining days you don't need to do this step. All the steps are as follows. Please note that the details of each one of these steps and how to perform it, etc., can be found in the chapter *Essential Steps in the Rites of Invocation (Puruscharana).* Wherever this *sadhana* deviates from the standard instructions, I've given the details next to that step.

Remember though that one night before commencing this *sadhana*, you've to seek permission from Vedmata Gayatri.

Here are the 36 steps of Ganesha *Sadhana*:

1. Bathe
2. Put on fresh clothes
3. Clean your altar (enter the sanctum sanctorum)
   Set up your altar by laying the pots as per *Arranging the Pots (Patrasadana)* in Detailed Notes. Make sure you wash all the pots and the lamp every day before using it.
4. Purify the surroundings
   Self purification (*Achamana*)
5. Wash your hands (*Hasta prakshalana*)
6. Light the lamp. (You can also light incense at this stage if you like, but it's optional).
7. Invoke Ganesha
   Yes, that's right. Even for the *sadhana* of Ganesha, we have to invoke him first anyway.
8. Show three handlocks for Ganesha (Ganesh mudra)
9. Chant the Vedic hymn of auspiciousness (*Svastivachana*)
10. Meditate on your guru (Guru *dhyana*)
11. Chant your guru mantra (Guru mantra *japa*)
12. Offer obeisance to all siddhas
13. Meditate on your deity (*Ishta dhyana*)
    If you pray to a specific god, pray to that diety now or simply meditate on Ganesha using the mantra below.

Sanskrit (Devanagri)	*Sanskrit (IAST)*
वक्रतुण्ड महाकाय सूर्यकोटि समप्रभ । निर्विघ्नं कुरु मे देव सर्वकार्येषु सर्वदा ॥	vakratuṇḍa mahākāya sūryakoṭi samaprabha । nirvighnaṃ kuru me deva sarvakāryeṣu sarvadā ॥

Translation
My obeisance to Lord Ganesha of curved trunk, gigantic body radiating like the brilliance of countless suns. I pray for success in all my endeavors.

14. Chant the preliminary mantra (*Ishta* mantra *japa*)
    If you have been initiated into any mantra, chant that mantra now 11, 21 or 31 times. If you have never been initiated into a mantra by a guru, simply chant the Gayatri Mantra.
15. Pray to Mother Earth (*Prithvi* Pooja)
16. Take the vow (*Sankalpa*)
    This is done only on the first night. You don't have to chant the standard vow in Sanskrit because to do that properly, you will either need to consult a pandit who can tell you the exact lunar dates, arrangement of planets and various other astrological aspects that are taken into consideration while chanting a vow, or you are required to have that knowledge yourself. The chances of committing mistakes that way remain high. It's much simpler and better to make your pact with the universe by saying out loud your vow in whatever language you know. The text of the vow is given in step 16 in the chapter *Essential Steps in the Rites of Invocation (Puruscharana).*
17. Mantra breathing (Mantra *shvasa*)
18. Application (*Viniyoga*)

Sanskrit (Devanagri)	*Sanskrit (IAST)*
ॐ अस्य श्रीगणेशमंत्रस्य भार्गवऋषि:, अनुष्टुप्छन्द:, विघ्नेशो देवता, वं बीजम्, यं शक्ति:, ममाभीष्टसिद्धये जपे विनियोग:।	oṃ asya śrīgaṇeśamaṃtrasya bhārgavarṣi:, anuṣṭupchandaḥ, vighneśo devatā, vaṃ bījam, yaṃ śakti:, mamābhīṣṭasiddhaye jape viniyoga:।

19. Purification of hands (*Kara shuddhi*)
    Chant the following mantras and show the appropriate mudras to perform the purification of the hands.

Sanskrit (Devanagri)	Sanskrit (IAST)	Handlock (Mudra)	Gesture with both hands
ॐ वं नमः अंगुष्ठाभ्यां नमः ।	oṃ vaṃ namaḥ aṃguṣṭhābhyāṃ namaḥ ।	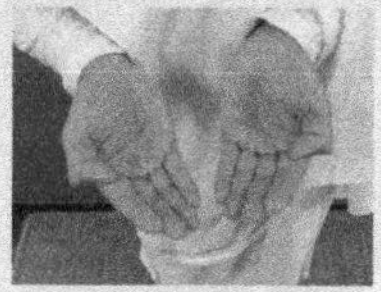	Touch the tip of your thumb at the base of your index finger.
ॐ क्रं नमः तर्जनीभ्यां नमः ।	oṃ kraṃ namaḥ tarjanībhyāṃ namaḥ ।	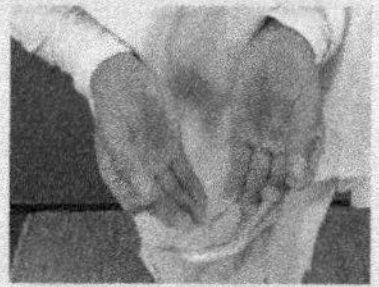	Touch the tip of your thumb to the tip of your index finger.
ॐ तुं नमः मध्यमाभ्यां नमः ।	oṃ tuṃ namaḥ madhyamābhyāṃ namaḥ ।	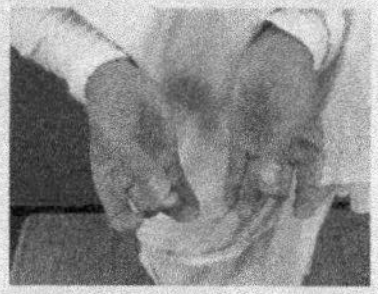	Touch the tip of your thumb to the tip of your middle finger.
ॐ डां नमः अनामिकाभ्यां नमः ।	oṃ ḍāṃ namaḥ anāmikābhyāṃ namaḥ ।	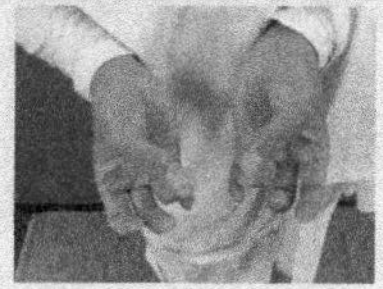	Touch the tip of your thumb to the tip of your ring finger.

Sanskrit (Devanagri)	*Sanskrit (IAST)*	*Handlock (Mudra)*	*Gesture with both hands*
ॐ यं नमः कनिष्ठिकाभ्यां नमः ।	oṃ yaṃ namaḥ kaniṣṭhikābhyāṃ namaḥ ।	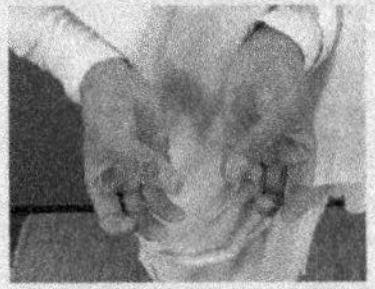	Touch the tip of your thumb to the tip of your little finger.
ॐ हुं नमः करतलकरपृष्ठाभ्यां नमः ।	oṃ huṃ namaḥ karatalakarapṛṣṭhābhyāṃ namaḥ ।		Touch the back of your left hand with the back of your right hand and then clap softly.

20. Unification with the mantra (Mantra *nyasa*)

Please do all the *nyasas* shown below:

Nyasa of the sages (Rishyadi-nyasa)		
Sanskrit (Devanagri)	*Sanskrit (IAST)*	*Touch with your right hand your...*
ॐ भार्गवर्षये नमः शिरसि ।	oṃ bhārgavarṣaye nama: śirasi I	Head
ॐ अनुष्टुप्छन्दसे नमः मुखे ।	oṃ anuṣṭupchandase nama: mukhe I	Face
ॐ विघ्नेशदेवतायै नमः हृदि ।	oṃ vighneśadevatāyai nama: hradi I	Heart
ओं वं बीजाय नमः गुह्ये ।	oṃ vaṃ bījāya namaḥ guhye I	Groin
ॐ यं शक्तये नमः पादयोः ।	oṃ yaṃ śaktaye namaḥ pādayoḥ I	Feet
ॐ विनियोगाय नमः सर्वांगे ।	oṃ viniyogāya namaḥ sarvāge I	Take the right hand over your head and then bring it back in front of you to clap softly.

Six-Limbed Mantra Nyasa (Shadanga mantra nyāsa)

Sanskrit (Devanagri)	*Sanskrit (IAST)*	*Posture*	*Description*
ॐ वं नमः हृदयाय नमः ।	oṃ vaṃ namaḥ hṛdayāya namaḥ ।		Touch your heart region with your right hand.
ॐ क्रं नमः शिरसे स्वाहा ।	oṃ kraṃ namaḥ śirase svāhā ।		Touch your forehead with your right hand keeping the index finger away.
ॐ तुं नमः शिखायै वषट् ।	oṃ tuṃ namaḥ śikhāyai vaṣaṭ ।		Make a fist with right hand and extend your thumb. Now touch the crown of your head with your thumb.

Sanskrit (Devanagri)	Sanskrit (IAST)	Posture	Description
ॐ डां नमः कवचाय हुं ।	oṃ ḍāṃ namaḥ kavacāya huṃ I		Touch your shoulders by crossing your hands. Generally, in Devi Pooja, left hand is on top of the right and in Devata Pooja, right on top of the left. This is, however, just a guideline and not a rule.
ॐ यं नमः नेत्रत्रयाय वौषट् ।	oṃ yaṃ namaḥ netratrayāya vauṣaṭ I		Spread your right hand and touch your right eye with your index finger, forehead with the middle finger and left eye with the ring finger simultaneously. Netra-traya means the three eyes.
ॐ हुं नमः अस्त्राय फट् ।	oṃ huṃ namaḥ astrāya phaṭ I		Take the right hand over your head and then bring it back in front of you to clap softly.

Nyasa of the letters (Mantra varna nyasa)

Sanskrit (Devanagri)	*Sanskrit (IAST)*	*Touch with your right hand your...*
ॐ वं नमः भ्रूमध्ये ।	oṃ vaṃ namaḥ bhrūmadhye I	Between your brows
ॐ क्रं नमः कण्ठे ।	oṃ kraṃ namaḥ kaṇṭhe I	Throat
ॐ तुं नमः हृदये ।	oṃ tuṃ namaḥ hradaye I	Heart
ॐ डां नमः नाभौ ।	oṃ ḍāṃ namaḥ nābhau I	Navel
ॐ यं नमः लिंगे ।	oṃ yaṃ namaḥ liṃge I	Groin
ॐ हुं नमः पादयो ।	oṃ huṃ namaḥ pādayo I	Feet

21. Preliminary mantra chanting (*Purva* mantra *japa*)
    Upon completion of the *nyasas*, chant Ganesha Mantra 21 times.
22. Preliminary handlocks (*Purva* mudra)
    Show the preliminary handlocks as per step 22 in *Essential Steps in the Rites of Invocation (Puruscharana).*
23. Sixteen, ten or five offerings.
    Now make sixteen, ten or five offerings as per step 23 in *Essential Steps in the Rites of Invocation (Puruscharana).*
24. Invoke the mantra (Mantra *samskara*)
    This mantra does not require any *samskara*. This has been invoked by the lineage I belong to.
25. Meditate on your mantra (Mantra *dhyana*)
    Simply use the mantra shared in step 13 and meditate on your mantra (by repeating it mindfully) for roughly five minutes.
26. Mantra chanting (*Moola* mantra *japa*)
    Chant 40 rounds of your mantra (*vakrtundaya hum*) every day for 30 days.

27. Post-*japa* handlocks (*Uttara* mudra)
    Show the standard handlocks as stated in step 27 in *Essential Steps in the Rites of Invocation (Puruscharana).*
28. Offering of chanting (*Japa samarpana*)
    Make an offering of the *japa* to Ganesha. You can find the mantra and process as stated in step 28 in *Essential Steps in the Rites of Invocation (Puruscharana).*
29. Freeing all energies (*Visarjana*)
    All the energies who participated in your *sadhana* for the night are now given a send-off with this step. Please follow the instructions given in step 29 in *Essential Steps in the Rites of Invocation (Puruscharana).*
30. Seeking forgiveness (*Kshama prarthana*)
    It's now time to seek forgiveness for any mistakes of omission or commission committed out of ignorance or otherwise. The mantra and process of seeking forgiveness is detailed in step 30 in *Essential Steps in the Rites of Invocation (Puruscharana).*
31. Fire offerings (*Yajna*)
    The process of *yajna* has been detailed in the chapter *How to Make Fire Offerings (Yajna).* For this *sadhana*, you'll require different ingredients every night. I've listed those ingredients for each night under the appropriate section.
32. Libations (*Tarpana*)
    Please follow the instructions as given in step 32 in *Essential Steps in the Rites of Invocation (Puruscharana).* Your mantra for libations will also change every night and I've noted that under each night.
33. Coronation (*Marjana* or *abhishekam*)
    Once again, you can read about *marjana* in step 33 in *Essential Steps in the Rites of Invocation (Puruscharana).* For each night, I've provided the appropriate mantra for *marjana* in the notes below.
34. Charity (*Sadhak bhojan* or Brahmin *bhoj*)
    By the time you finish your *japa*, *yajna*, etc., for the night, it would be early morning. You can then set aside some money

you can give to a believer of Devi (Devi upasaka) so he may buy his own meal. Or, you can cook a meal and serve it to him for breakfast. Or, you can have a meal cooked by anyone else but serve it yourself. Whatever is convenient for you, can work. It's important to do it with the sentiment of charity.

35. Seek forgiveness again (*Kshama prarthana*)
    Repeat the hymn of forgiveness as in step 30 for there might have been mistakes in your actions from step –31-34.
36. Offer water to the sun (*Surya arghya*)
    Follow the instructions given in step 36 in *Essential Steps in the Rites of Invocation (Puruscharana).*

GURU SADHANA

गुरुर्ब्रह्मा गुरुर्विष्णुर्गुरुर्देवो महेश्वरः ।
साक्षात परं ब्रह्म तस्मै श्रीगुरवे नमः ॥
अखण्डमण्डलाकारं व्याप्तं येन चराचरम् ।
तत्पदं दर्शितं येन तस्मै श्रीगुरवे नमः ॥

gururbrahmā gururviṣṇurgururdevo maheśvaraḥ ।
sākṣāta paraṃ brahma tasmai śrīgurave namaḥ ॥
akhaṇḍamaṇḍalākāraṃ vyāptaṃ yena carācaram ।
tatpadaṃ darśitaṃ yena tasmai śrīgurave namaḥ ॥

Humble obeisance to my guru, the supreme being, who is no different to Brahma, Vishnu or Rudra.
Humble obeisance to my guru whose form pervades the entire universe, the one who is the indweller of all animate and inanimate entities.

Not all of us are fortunate to have a guru and sometimes even if we do, our guru may not necessarily be an expert in various esoteric sciences. How do you progress then? It is easier than you might think. The best way is to awaken your inner guru. You can align various energies in the universe in a manner that the light within you guides you on the path or may send someone your way to provide that guidance to you.

Long before taking *sannyasa* initiation, I did Guru *Sadhana* to receive guidance from various energies in the universe. Just like a river is quietly guided to the sea, like a calf to its mother, like a sperm to its egg, you too can be guided by the quiet but powerful forces of the universe.

My personal experience says that doing Guru *Sadhana* with faith and hope can open doors to an incredible spiritual portal.

How long does it take

The *puruscharana* of this sadhana requires that you chant the mantra of Guru (shared ahead) 1,25,000 times in 30 days.

When can you start this *sadhana*

Start on any new moon night. Chant the mantra in the wee hours of the morning (starting 90 minutes before sunrise) or at night. The most important thing is to stick to the same routine throughout your *puruscharana*. So, if you begin chanting at 5 am on day one, it's important to start it exactly at the same time for the next 30 days.

Who can do this *sadhana*

If you don't have a guru in human form, I strongly recommend that you do this *sadhana* before undertaking the major ones. If you do have a guru, doing this *sadhana* is optional. In any case, doing this will benefit you. Any man or woman, of any age, religion, ability or background can do this *sadhana* with or without initiation. Since this *puruscharana* lasts a minimum of 40 days, women who are menstruating can continue their *sadhana* without any reservations whatsoever. Complete abstinence must be practiced throughout the *puruscharana*. There's no *dosha* (issue) in case of wet dreams or any other involuntary release of sexual secretions. Voluntarily though, any form of sexual gratification is strictly forbidden.

Diet

Throughout your *puruscharna*, you should be on a strict vegetarian diet. Dairy is allowed but no meat, seafood or eggs. No onion or garlic either. Be careful about eating biscuits, cakes, cheeses and supplements that may contain animal-derived ingredients.

Lamp

A silver or a brass lamp is used in this *puruscharana*, with a cotton wick. You can also use braided cotton thread (like the common sacred red thread, for example, or any other) to use as a wick. Use only pure ghee to light the lamp.

Direction

Face northeast or north while doing the chanting and the *yajna*.

Clothing

Wear white clothing. Ideally you should wear no more than two pieces of white loose cloth on your body — one to cover your lower body and the other to cover the upper. If you are in a very cold place, you can either use a heater in your room or sew your upper cloth with a woolen shawl. Women can wear a white saree, blouse, etc., or any other comfortable white clothing.

Seat

The best seat is a blanket on which you should spread a white cloth. The nature of this *sadhana* requires you to sit on the floor. If you are unable to do that, you may try sitting in a chair and setting up a table in front with lamp, pots, etc. Personally, I have never experimented with that. If you do, please feel free to share the results of your *sadhana*.

Other than a blanket, you can also take a standard meditation cushion or use any seat made of cotton.

Seat made out of *kusha* grass is also permissible for this *sadhana*.

Posture

Try to maintain the stillness of your posture while you chant with utmost mindfulness, faith and devotion. Please allow me to remind you that mantra *sadhana* is not about reckless chanting of a mantra just for the sake of ticking off an item. It is the soulful process of becoming one with your deity, so you may elevate yourself spiritually, materially and emotionally.

Requirements for this *sadhana*

1. A brass or a silver lamp.
2. Ghee and wick for your lamp.
3. Five small water pots, a small spoon and a saucer. They can be of silver, copper or brass. This is the standard for every sadhana and details on how to layout the pots (*patra*) can be found in the chapter *Arrangement of Pots (Patrasadan)* in Detailed Notes.
4. Sweetmeat, jaggery or honey (to make the *madhuparka* offering).
5. Standard ingredients for fire-offerings (*yajna*) as mentioned in the chapter *How to Make Fire Offerings (Yajna).*

   In addition to those ingredients, you will need firewood.

   You can use either wood from a sacred fig (Ficus *religiosa*. Common name: peepul), mango (Magnifera *indica*, Common name: *aam* or *aamra*) or palasha (Butea *monosperma*. Common name: *plasha* or *dhak*). You can also use the wood from deodar (Cedrus *deodara*. Common name: *devadaru*) or teak (Tectona *grandis*. Common name: *sagaun* or *sheesham*).

6. Chanting beads of rudraksha or sandalwood.
7. A lot of faith, devotion and discipline.

I strongly recommend you to make a daily checklist in line with the 36 steps I enumerate below. Also, do make a daily list of what all you require and procure it beforehand.

The Mantra

Sanskrit (Devanagri)	*Sanskrit (IAST)*
ॐ गं गुरवे नमः ।	oṃ gaṃ gurave namaḥ ।

Before You Begin

We must seek permission from the Divine Mother before undertaking this *sadhana*. The simplest way to do that is after sunset, take a bath and sit at your altar. Take a bit of water in your right hand and mentally call upon the Divine Mother in the form of Gayatri and seek her permission that may She and other forces of nature allow you to complete Her sadhana. Leave the water in the plate next to you.

Next, do 30 rounds of chanting of the Gayatri Mantra with rudraksha beads. Use the same beads to commence your *puruscharana* the next day.

One round is 108 times. Thirty rounds will be chanting your mantra 108 x 30 = 3,240 times. I always used to chant 10,000 times before doing any major *puruscharana*. But, 30 rounds will suffice too. Once done with your *sadhana*, sleep at the same place where you chanted the Gayatri Mantra. Here's the mantra again for your reference.

Sanskrit (Devanagri)	Sanskrit (IAST)
ॐ भूर्भुवः स्वः तत्सवितुर्वरेण्यम भर्गो देवस्य धीमहि। धियो यो नः प्रचोदयात॥	oṃ bhūrbhuvaḥ svaḥ tatsaviturvareṇyama bhargo devasya dhīmahi । dhiyo yo naḥ pracodayāta ॥

Translation
May we abide in the Supreme Energy that is eternal, transcendental, radiant, perfect, divine. May such divine grace always guide us on the path of righteousness.

How to perform the rites of invocation (*puruscharana*)

Every day, throughout your puruscharna, the first few steps will be the same. Only step 17 (taking the vow – *sankalpa*) is done on the first night alone. For all the remaining days, you don't need to do this step. All the steps are as follows. Please note that the details of each one of this step, how to perform it, etc., can be found in the chapter *Essential Steps in the Rites of Invocation (Puruscharana).* Wherever this *sadhana* deviates from the standard instructions, I've given the details next to that step.

Remember though that one night before commencing this *sadhana*, you've to seek permission from Vedmata Gayatri.

Here are the 36 steps of Guru *Sadhana.*

1. Bathe
2. Put on fresh clothes
3. Clean your altar (enter the sanctum sanctorum)
   Set up your altar by laying the pots as per *Arranging the Pots (Patrasadana)* in Detailed Notes. Make sure you wash all the pots and the lamp every day before using it.
4. Purify the surroundings
5. Self-purification (*Achamana*)

Wash your hands (*Hasta prakshalana*)

6. Light the lamp. (You can also light incense at this stage if you like, but it's optional).
7. Invoke Ganesha
8. Show three handlocks for Ganesha (Ganesh mudra)
9. Chant the Vedic hymn of auspiciousness (*Svastivachana*)
10. Meditate on your guru (Guru *dhyana*)

Sanskrit (Devanagri)	*Sanskrit (IAST)*
गुरुर्ब्रह्मा गुरुर्विष्णुर्गुरुर्देवो महेश्वरः ।	gururbrahmā gururviṣṇurgururdevo maheśvaraḥ I
साक्षात परं ब्रह्म तस्मै श्रीगुरवे नमः ॥	sākṣāta paraṃ brahma tasmai śrīgurave namaḥ II
अखण्डमण्डलाकारं व्याप्तं येन चराचरम् ।	akhaṇḍamaṇḍalākāraṃ vyāptaṃ yena carācaram I
तत्पदं दर्शितं येन तस्मै श्रीगुरवे नमः ॥	tatpadaṃ darśitaṃ yena tasmai śrīgurave namaḥ II

Translation

Humble obeisance to my guru, the supreme being, who is no different to Brahma, Vishnu or Rudra.

Humble obeisance to my guru whose form pervades the entire universe, the one who is the indweller of all animate and inanimate entites.

11. Chant your guru mantra (Guru mantra *japa*)
    Simply chant the mantra of this *sadhana* 21 times.
12. Offer obeisance to all siddhas
13. Meditate on your deity (*Ishta dhyana*)
    If you pray to a specific god, pray to that diety now. Otherwise, chant the mantra of this *sadhana* 21 times more.
14. Chant the preliminary mantra (*Ishta* mantra *japa*)

If you have been initiated into any mantra, chant that mantra now 11, 21 or 31 times. If you have never been initiated into a mantra by a guru, simply chant the Gayatri Mantra.

15, Pray to Mother Earth (*Prithvi* pooja)

16. Take the vow (*Sankalpa*)

    This is done only on the first night. You don't have to chant the standard vow in Sanskrit because to do that properly you will either need to consult a pandit who can tell you the exact lunar dates, arrangement of planets and various other astrological aspects that are taken into consideration while chanting a vow, or you have to have that knowledge. The chances of committing mistakes that way remain high. It's much simpler and better to make your pact with the universe by saying your vow out loud in whatever language you know. The text of vow is given in step 16 in the chapter *Essential Steps in the Rites of Invocation (Puruscharana).*

17. Mantra breathing (Mantra *shvasa*)

18. Application (*Viniyoga*)

    This will change every night for 16 nights and is detailed under the respective section.

19. Purification of hands (*Kara shuddhi*)

    Chant the following mantras and show the appropriate mudras to perform purification of the hands.

Sanskrit (Devanagri)	*Sanskrit (IAST)*	*Handlock (Mudra)*	*Gesture with both hands*
ॐ गं नमः अंगुष्ठाभ्यां नमः ।	oṃ gaṃ namaḥ aṃguṣṭhābhyāṃ namaḥ ।	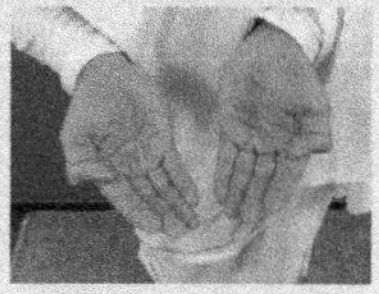	Touch the tip of your thumb at the base of your index finger.
ॐ गुं नमः तर्जनीभ्यां नमः ।	oṃ guṃ namaḥ tarjanībhyāṃ namaḥ ।	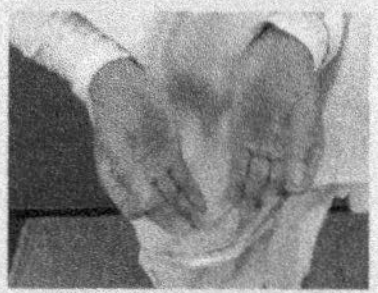	Touch the tip of your thumb to the tip of your index finger.
ॐ रं नमः मध्यमाभ्यां नमः ।	oṃ raṃ namaḥ madhyamābhyāṃ namaḥ ।	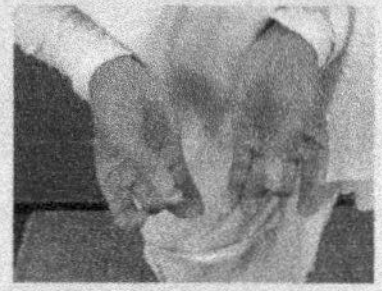	Touch the tip of your thumb to the tip of your middle finger.
ॐ वें नमः अनामिकाभ्यां नमः ।	oṃ veṃ namaḥ anāmikābhyāṃ namaḥ ।	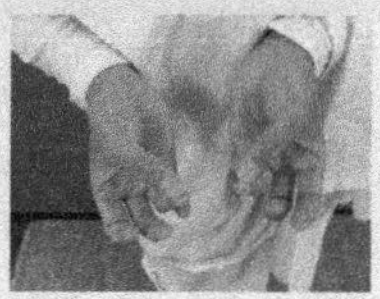	Touch the tip of your thumb to the tip of your ring finger.

Sanskrit (Devanagri)	*Sanskrit (IAST)*	*Handlock (Mudra)*	*Gesture with both hands*
ॐ नं नमः कनिष्ठिकाभ्यां नमः ।	oṃ naṃ namaḥ kaniṣṭhikābhyāṃ namaḥ ।	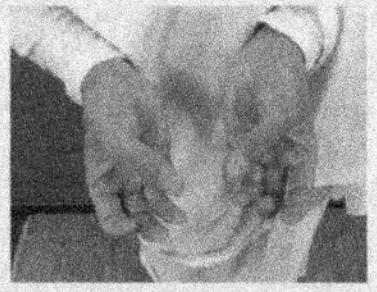	Touch the tip of your thumb to the tip of your little finger.
ॐ मं नमः करतलकरपृष्ठाभ्यां नमः ।	oṃ maṃ namaḥ karatalakarapṛṣṭhābhyāṃ namaḥ ।	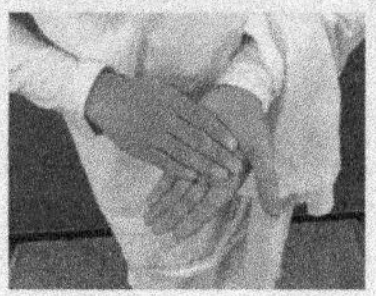	Touch the back of your left hand with the back of your right hand and then clap softly.

20. Unification with the mantra (Mantra *nyasa*)
    Please do all the *nyasas* shown below:

Nyasa of the sages *(Rishyadi nyasa)*

Sanskrit (Devanagri)	*Sanskrit (IAST)*	*Touch with your right hand your...*
ॐ नारायणर्षये नमः शिरसि ।	oṃ nārāyaṇarṣaye nama: śirasi ।	Head
ॐ गायत्रिछन्दसे नमः मुखे ।	oṃ gāyatrichandase nama: mukhe ।	Face
ॐ रुद्रादेवतायै नमः हृदि ।	oṃ rudrādevatāyai nama: hradi ।	Heart
ॐ गं बीजाय नमः गुह्ये ।	oṃ gaṃ bījāya namaḥ guhye ।	Groin
ॐ रं शक्तये नमः पादयोः ।	oṃ raṃ śaktaye namaḥ pādayoḥ ।	Feet
ॐ विनियोगाय नमः सर्वांगे ।	oṃ viniyogāya namaḥ sarvāṃge ।	Take the right hand over your head and then bring it back in front of you to clap softly.

Six-Limbed Mantra Nyasa (Shadanga mantra nyāsa)

Sanskrit (Devanagri)	*Sanskrit (IAST)*	*Posture*	*Description*
ॐ गं नमः हृदयाय नमः ।	oṃ gaṃ namaḥ hṛdayāya namaḥ I	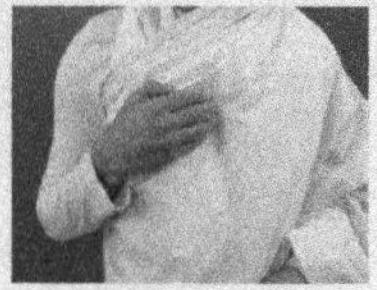	Touch your heart region with your right hand.
ॐ गुं नमः शिरसे स्वाहा ।	oṃ guṃ namaḥ śirase svāhā I		Touch your forehead with your right hand keeping the index finger away.
ॐ रं नमः शिखायै वषट् ।	oṃ raṃ namaḥ śikhāyai vaṣaṭ I		Make a fist with right hand and extend your thumb. Now touch the crown of your head with your thumb.

Sanskrit (Devanagri)	*Sanskrit (IAST)*	*Posture*	*Description*
ॐ वें नमः कवचाय हुं ।	oṃ veṃ namaḥ kavacāya huṃ ।		Touch your shoulders by crossing your hands. Generally, in Devi Pooja, left hand is on top of the right and in Devata Pooja, right on top of the left. This is, however, just a guideline and not a rule.
ॐ नं नमः नेत्रत्रयाय वौषट् ।	oṃ naṃ namaḥ netratrayāya vauṣaṭ ।		Spread your right hand and touch your right eye with your index finger, forehead with the middle finger and left eye with the ring finger simultaneously. Netra-traya means the three eyes.
ॐ मं नमः अस्त्राय फट् ।	oṃ maṃ namaḥ astrāya phaṭ ।		Take the right hand over your head and then bring it back in front of you to clap softly.

Nyasa of the letters (Mantra varna nyasa)

Sanskrit (Devanagri)	*Sanskrit (IAST)*	*Touch with your right hand your...*
ॐ गं नमः भ्रूमध्ये ।	oṃ gaṃ namaḥ bhrūmadhye I	Between your brows
ॐ गुं नमः कण्ठे ।	oṃ guṃ namaḥ kaṇṭhe I	Throat
ॐ रं नमः ह्रदये ।	oṃ raṃ namaḥ hradaye I	Heart
ॐ वें नमः नाभौ ।	oṃ veṃ namaḥ nābhau I	Navel
ॐ नं नमः लिंगे ।	oṃ naṃ namaḥ liṃge I	Groin
ॐ मं नमः पादयो ।	oṃ maṃ namaḥ pādayo I	Feet

21. Preliminary mantra chanting (*Purva* mantra *japa*)
    Upon completion of the *nyasa*, chant Gayatri Mantra 21 times.
22. Preliminary handlocks (*Purva* mudra)
    Show the preliminary handlocks as per step 22 in *Essential Steps in the Rites of Invocation (Puruscharana).*
23. Sixteen, ten or five offerings.
    Now make sixteen, ten or five offerings as per step 23 in *Essential Steps in the Rites of Invocation (Puruscharana).*
24. Invoke the mantra (Mantra *samskara*)
    This mantra does not require any *samskara*. This has been invoked by the lineage I belong to.
25. Meditate on your mantra (Mantra *dhyana*)
    Simply use the mantra shared in step 13 and meditate on your mantra (by repeating it mindfully) for roughly five minutes.
26. Mantra chanting (*Moola* mantra *japa*)

Chant 40 rounds of your mantra (*Om gum guruve namah*) every day for 30 days.

27. Post-*japa* handlocks (*Uttara* mudra)
Show the standard handlocks as stated in step 27 in *Essential Steps in the Rites of Invocation (Puruscharana).*
28. Offering of chanting (*Japa samarpana*)
Make an offering of the *japa* to the guru. You can find the mantra and process as stated in step 28 in *Essential Steps in the Rites of Invocation (Puruscharana).*
29. Freeing all energies (*Visarjana*)
All the energies who participated in your *sadhana* for the night are now given a send off with this step. Please follow the instructions given in step 29 in *Essential Steps in the Rites of Invocation (Puruscharana).*

30 Seeking forgiveness (*Kshama prarthana*)
It's now time to seek forgiveness for any mistakes of omission or commission commited out of ignorance or otherwise. The mantra and process of seeking forgiveness is detailed in step 30 in *Essential Steps in the Rites of Invocation (Puruscharana).*

31. Fire offerings (*Yajna*)
The process of *yajna* has been detailed in the chapter *How to Make Fire Offerings (Yajna).* For this *sadhana*, you require different ingredients every night. I've listed those ingredients for each night under the appropriate section.
32. Libations (*Tarpana*)
Please follow the instructions as given in step 32 in *Essential Steps in the Rites of Invocation (Puruscharana).* Your mantra for libations will also change every night and I've noted that under each night.
33. Coronation (*Marjana* or *abhishekam*)
Once again, you can read about *marjana* in step 33 in *Essential Steps in the Rites of Invocation (Puruscharana).* For each night, I've provided the appropriate mantra for *marjana* in the notes below.
34. Charity (*Sadhak bhojan* or Brahmin *bhoj*)

By the time you'll finish your *japa, yajna,* etc., for the night, it would be early morning. You can then either set aside some money you can give to a believer of Devi (Devi *upasaka*) so he may buy his own meal. Or, you can cook a meal and serve it to the person for breakfast. Or, you can have a meal cooked by anyone else but serve it yourself. Whatever is convenient for you works. It's important to do it with the sentiment of charity.

35. Seek forgiveness again (*Kshama prarthana*)
    Repeat the hymn of forgiveness as given in step 30 for there might have been mistakes in your actions from step –31-34.
36. Offer water to sun (Surya *arghya*)
    Follow the instructions given in step in *Essential Steps in the Rites of Invocation (Puruscharana).*

GAYATRI SADHANA

ॐ बालां विद्यां तु गायत्रीं लोहितां चतुराननाम् ।
रक्ताम्बरद्वयोपेतामक्षसूत्रकरां तथा ॥
कमण्डलुधरां देवी हंसवाहनसंस्थिताम् ।
ब्रह्माणी ब्रह्मदैवत्यां ब्रह्मलोकनिवासिनीम् ॥
मन्त्रेनावाहयेद्देवीमायान्ती सूर्यमण्डलात् ।

oṃ bālāṃ vidyāṃ tu gāyatrīṃ lohitāṃ caturānanām ।
raktāmbaradvayopetāmakṣasūtrakarāṃ tathā ॥
kamaṇḍaludharāṃ devī haṃsavāhanasaṃsthitām ।
brahmāṇī brahmadaivatyāṃ brahmalokanivāsinīm ॥
mantrenāvāhayeddevīmāyāntī sūryamaṇḍalāt ।

The youthful Devi, emerging like the radiance of sun, is an embodiment of the highest wisdom. She is of red color and has four faces. She holds rudraksha beads in one hand and a water pot in the other. Mounted on a swan, she's like Saraswati. She resides and abides in the absolute Brahman and is a consort of Brahma.

The *sadhana* of the Gayatri Mantra is one of the most powerful *sadhanas*. It bestows wisdom on the practitioner. Those looking for material success often either underestimate or completely discard Gayatri *Sadhana* as irrelevant. The truth, however, is that it is with wisdom alone that you can progress materially and maintain your status.

If there's only one *sadhana* you wish to do in your life, I would recommend this one. If there's one mantra you wish to impart, let it be this one.

Mother Divine in the form of Gayatri is called Vedmata, the mother of Vedas. No mantra *sadhana* is ever done without first seeking permission from the Divine Mother. There are 24 different mantras of Gayatri (different energies and deities have their own Gayatri Mantra) but the one that we are concerned with, the one that's also the most popular as well as the only mantra of the mother of Vedas, is called Savitur Gayatri, for Her name is Savitri. Savitur is the name used for both sun and the Divine Mother. Just like the sun is a source of light for us, the basis of all sustenance and creation on our planet, Gayatri is a source of light for our consciousness, the basis of all our intellectual and intuitive faculties.

As part of your routine, chanting at least one round of Gayatri (108 times) with rudraksha beads is recommended. In my personal experience and view though, whenever we try to make something a must-do-daily thing, we often lose the devotional sentiment attached to it. And mantra yoga without devotion is like a melon without any sweetness. To keep the devotion alive, it's better to chant this mantra whenever you can — while bathing, walking, running, sitting, thinking, driving — whenever you have a spare moment, mindfully chant this mantra with whatever reverence you can muster.

Once you start to feel a bit of devotion (it may take days, weeks or months for you, depending on your temperament), I recommend undertaking one of the most pious and potent *sadhanas* ever known to mankind: the *sadhana* of Vedmata Gayatri.

Any wisdom that you find in my books, I owe it all to Mother Divine. As a child, while growing up, there had come a time when all I was doing when not talking (or sleeping) was chanting this mantra. Like the other *sadhanas* I've shared in this book, I can personally vouch for the incredible efficacy of this mantra.

You make this mantra your own by chanting it mentally as much as you can and Mother Divine will become yours. Your face will glow and drip with unmistakable bliss. Even if others got a glimpse of you, they'll experience peace, let alone your glance falling on them. Your darshan will evoke intense emotions of love and positivity. This happens naturally to the one who attains the siddhi of the Gayatri Mantra. Faith, discipline, purity and devotion are required to become one with Vedmata Gayatri.

In this section below, I share with you how to do *puruscharana* of the Gayatri Mantra.

How long does it take

There are three ways to do a Gayatri *puruscharana.* First is the standard *puruscharana,* designed for beginners. Most people complete this in 40 days. It entails chanting the Gayatri Mantra 125,000 times in 40 days. Or, simply 30 rounds (1 round = 108 times) everyday using your chanting beads.

The second *puruscharana* is done by intermediate practitioners. It involves chanting the mantra 2,400,000 times. Like any other *puruscharana,* only the chanting you do while seated properly, in your posture, after purificiation, etc., counts. (Chanting done while walking, eating, etc., does not count for the purposes of *puruscharana.*) It usually takes twenty-four months or two years to complete this *puruscharana.* If all you are doing is this *puruscharana* or if you do it with greater instensity, you may complete it in 18 months.

The third and the highest form of *puruscharana* is undertaken by advanced practitioners. I would recommend that you embark on this only if you've already done at least three *puruscharanas* of the first type (requiring 125,000 *japas*). One of the worst things you can do is to take a vow (*sankalpa*) of a *puruscharana* and not complete it. This is an act of great misdemeanor in mantra yoga. When you decide to do something and don't give your best to carry it out, it weakens your willpower. Your mind stops taking you seriously. This *puruscharana,* the third type, involves chanting the Gayatri Mantra 32 lac times.

It usually takes two years and eight months to complete this *puruscharana*. Those special few who embark on it also take three years. Such serious and sincere aspirants are extremely rare in this day and age.

There is no relaxation of rules for the longer *puruscharana*. The same principles of diet, abstinence and conduct apply to all three types. I must remind you here that just reckless or mindless chanting has no place or respect in mantra yoga. Your chanting must be done with devotion and mindfulness. I cannot stress this point enough. When you sit down to chant, do so patiently and mindfully, listening to your own voice, every word, every letter of your mantra. It will get tiring at times, but keep going if you care to go till the end.

When can you start this *sadhana*

You can start this *sadhana* on any full moon day. You can carry out the routine in the morning or at night. Praying to the Divine Mother in the form of Gayatri in the morning is Vedic worship while the exactly same routine when undertaken at night becomes Her tantric method of worship. The main thing is to be consistent. If you start a *puruscharana* by doing just one session of chanting in the morning, follow that till you complete the *puruscharana*. If you start your *sadhana* by chanting only in the evening, stick to that till the end. It is also perfectly fine to split your session into mornings and evenings. Once again, if you do that, make sure you follow the same routine till you finish your *puruscharana*. Please note that at the beginning of every session, you've to do purification, *nyasa* and all the other steps as specified later in this chapter.

Who can do this *sadhana*

Any person, of any age, religion, ability or background can do this *sadhana* with or without initiation. Since this *puruscharana* lasts a minimum of 40 days, women who are menstruating can continue their *sadhana* without any reservations whatsoever. Complete abstinence must be practiced throughout the *puruscharana*. There's no *dosha* (issue) in case of wet dreams or any other involuntary release of sexual secretions. Voluntarily though, any form of sexual gratification is strictly forbidden.

Diet

Throughout your *puruscharna*, you should be on a strict vegetarian diet. Dairy is allowed but no meat, seafood or eggs. No onion or garlic either. Be careful of eating biscuits, cakes, cheeses and supplements that may contain animal-derived ingredients.

Lamp

The lamp used in this *puruscharana* can be made of brass. An earthen lamp can also be used. The wick must be of cotton. It is permissible to use braided cotton thread (like the common sacred red thread, *mauli*, for example, or any other) to use as a wick. The oil used in the lamp should be either ghee or sesame oil. If you are doing this *sadhana* in a cold region (as Diwali often falls in winter and it can be very cold in some parts of the world), I would recommend using sesame oil as ghee solidifies very quickly and it may put out your lamp. Once again, it's important to be consistent. If you start your *sadhana* by lighting a ghee lamp, stick to that throughout your *puruscharana*.

Direction

The aspirant should face east, north or northeast while doing the chanting and the *yajna*.

Clothing

Any color is okay but the best are red, yellow and white. Ideally you should wear no more than two pieces of red, yellow or white, loose-cloth on your body — one to cover your lower body and the other to cover the upper part. If you are in a very cold place, you can either use a heater in your room or sew your upper cloth with a woolen shawl. Women can wear a saree, blouse, etc.

Seat

The best seat will be a blanket on which you should spread the same colored cloth you cover your body with. Or, if you are wearing regular clothes (and not one of the three colors mentioned in the previous section) while doing *puruscharana*, you can just put a yellow cloth on your seat. The nature of this *sadhana* requires you to sit on the floor. If you are unable to do that, you may try sitting in a chair and setting up a table in front of you with lamp, pots, etc. Personally, I have never experimented with that. If you do, please feel free to share the results of your *sadhana*.

Other than a blanket, you can also take a standard meditation cushion or use any seat made from cotton.

Seat made out of *kusha* grass is also permissible for this *sadhana*.

Posture

Try to maintain stillness of your posture while you chant with utmost mindfulness, faith and devotion. Please allow me to remind you that mantra *sadhana* is not about reckless chanting of a mantra just for the sake of ticking off an item in your list. It is the soulful process of becoming one with your deity so you may elevate yourself spiritually, materially and emotionally.

What all will you need to do this *sadhana*

1. A lamp (brass or earthen)
2. Ghee or sesame oil and wick for your lamp
3. Five small water pots, a small spoon and a saucer. They can be of silver, copper or brass. This is the standard for every *sadhana* and details on how to layout the pots (*patra*) can be found in the chapter *Arrangement of Pots (Patrasadan)* in Detailed Notes.

4. Standard ingredients for fire offerings (*yajna*) as mentioned in the chapter *How to Make Fire Offerings (Yajna).*
5. In addition to those ingredients, you will need firewood. You can use either wood from a sacred fig (Ficus *religiosa.* Common name: peepul), mango (Magnifera *indica,* Common name: *aam* or *aamra*) or palasha (Butea *monosperma.* Common name: *plasha* or *dhak*). You can also use the wood from *deodar* (Cedrus *deodara.* Common name: *devadaru*) or teak (Tectona *grandis.* Common name: *sagaun* or *sheesham*).
6. Chanting beads made from rudraksha
7. A lot of faith, devotion and discipline

   I strongly recommend that after going through this chapter, you make a daily checklist in line with the 36 steps I enumerate below. Also, make a daily list of what all you require; it's better to procure everything in advance.

The Mantra

Sanskrit (Devanagri)	*Sanskrit (IAST)*
ॐ भूर्भुवः स्वः	oṃ bhūrbhuvaḥ svaḥ
तत्सवितुर्वरेण्यम	tatsaviturvareṇyama
भर्गो देवस्य धीमहि।	bhargo devasya dhīmahi।
धियो यो नः प्रचोदयात॥	dhiyo yo naḥ pracodayāta॥

Before You Begin

We must seek permission from the Divine Mother before undertaking Her *sadhana.* The simplest way to do this is to take a bath and sit at your altar after sunset. Take a bit of water in your right hand and mentally call upon the Divine Mother in the form of Gayatri and seek permission that may She and other forces of nature allow you to complete Her sadhana. Leave the water in the plate next to you.

Next, do 30 rounds of the Gayatri Mantra with rudraksha beads. Use the same beads to commence your *puruscharana* the next day.

One round is 108 times. Thirty rounds will be chanting your mantra 108 x 30 = 3240 times. I always chant 10,000 times before doing any major *puruscharana*. But 30 rounds will suffice too. Once done, go to sleep in the same place where you chanted the Gayatri Mantra. Here's the mantra again for your reference.

Sanskrit (Devanagri)	*Sanskrit (IAST)*
ॐ भूर्भुवः स्वः तत्सवितुर्वरेण्यम भर्गो देवस्य धीमहि। धियो यो नः प्रचोदयात॥	oṃ bhūrbhuvaḥ svaḥ tatsaviturvareṇyama bhargo devasya dhīmahi । dhiyo yo naḥ pracodayāta ॥
Translation	
May we abide in the Supreme Energy that is eternal, transcendental, radiant, perfect, divine. May such divine grace always guide us on the path of righteousness.	

How to perform the rites of invocation (*Puruscharana*)

Every day, throughout your *puruscharna*, the first few steps will be the same. However, step 17 (taking the vow – *sankalpa*) is done only on the first night. For all the remaining days, you don't need to do this step.

All the steps are as follows. Please note that the details of each of these steps and how to perform it, etc., can be found in the chapter *Essential Steps in the Rites of Invocation (Puruscharana)*. Wherever this *sadhana* deviates from the standard instructions, I've given the details next to that step.

Remember though that one night before commencing this *sadhana*, you've to seek permission from Vedmata Gayatri.

Here are the 36 steps of Gayatri *Sadhana*.

1. Bathe
2. Put on fresh clothes

3. Clean your altar (enter the sanctum sanctorum)
   Set up your altar by laying the pots as per *Arranging the Pots (Patrasadana)* in Detailed Notes. Make sure you wash all the pots and the lamp every day before using it.
4. Purify the surroundings
5. Self purification (*Achamana*)
   Wash your hands (*Hasta prakshalana*)
6. Light the lamp (You can also light incense at this stage if you like, but it's optional).
7. Invoke Ganesha
8. Show three handlocks for Ganesha (Ganesh mudra)
9. Chant the Vedic hymn of auspiciousness (*Svastivachana*)
10. Meditate on your guru (Guru *dhyana*)
11. Chant your guru mantra (Guru mantra *japa*)
12. Offer obeisance to all siddhas
13. Meditate on your deity (*Ishta dhyana)*
   If you pray to a specific god, pray to that deity now or simply meditate on Mother Divine using the mantra below.

Sanskrit (Devanagri)	*Sanskrit (IAST)*
ॐ बालां विद्यां तु गायत्रीं लोहितां चतुराननाम् । रक्ताम्बरद्वयोपेतामक्षसूत्रकरां तथा ॥ कमण्डलुधरां देवी हंसवाहनसंस्थिताम् । ब्रह्माणी ब्रह्मदैवत्यां ब्रह्मलोकनिवासिनीम् ॥	oṃ bālāṃ vidyāṃ tu gāyatrīṃ lohitāṃ caturānanām । raktāmbaradvayopetāmakṣa sūtrakarāṃ tathā ॥ kamaṇḍaludharāṃ devī haṃsavāhanasaṃsthitām । brahmāṇī brahmadaivatyāṃ brahmalokanivāsinīm ॥

Translation
The youthful, glorious and beautiful Devi is an embodiment of the highest wisdom. She is of red color and has four faces. She holds rudraksha beads in one hand and a water pot in the other. Mounted on a swan, She's like Saraswati. She resides and abides in the absolute Brahman and is a consort of Brahma.

14. Chant the preliminary mantra (*Ishta* mantra *japa*)
    If you have been initiated into any mantra, chant that mantra now 11, 21 or 31 times. If you have never been initiated into a mantra by a guru, simply chant the Gayatri Mantra.
15. Pray to Mother Earth (*Prithvi* pooja)
16. Take the vow (*Sankalpa*)
    This is done only on the first night. You don't have to chant the standard vow in Sanskrit because to do that properly, you will either need to consult a pandit who can tell you the exact lunar dates, arrangement of planets and various other astrological aspects that are taken into consideration while chanting a vow, or you have to have that knowledge. The chances of committing mistakes that way remain high. It's much simpler and better to make your pact with the universe by saying out loud your vow in whatever language you know. The text of vow is given in step 16 in the chapter *Essential Steps in the Rites of Invocation (Puruscharana).*
17. Mantra breathing (Mantra *shvasa*)
18. Application (*Viniyoga*)

Sanskrit (Devanagri)	*Sanskrit (IAST)*
सप्तव्याहृतीनां जमदग्नि-भरद्वाज अत्रि-गौतम-कश्यप-विश्वामित्र-वसिष्ठा ऋषयः ।	saptavyāhratīnāṃ jamadagni-bharadvāja atri-gautama-kaśyapa-viśvāmitra-vasiṣṭhā ṛṣayaḥ ।
गायत्र्युष्णिगनुष्टुब्बृहती-पंक्तिस्त्रिष्टुब्जगत्यश्छन्ददांसि ।	gāyatryuṣṇiganuṣṭubbṛhatī-paṃktistriṣṭubjagatyaśchandadāṃsi ।
अग्नि-वायु-सूर्य-बृहस्पति-वरुणेन्द्र-विश्वेदेवा देवताः ।	agni-vāyu-sūrya-bṛhspati-varuṇendra-viśvedevā devatāḥ ।
सर्वपापक्षयार्थे जपे विनियोगः ।	sarvapāpakṣayārthe jape viniyogaḥ ।

19. Purification of hands (*Kara shuddhi*)
    Chant the following mantras and show the appropriate mudras to perform purification of the hands.

Sanskrit (Devanagri)	*Sanskrit (IAST)*	*Handlock (Mudra)*	*Gesture with both hands*
ऐं अंगुष्ठाभ्यां नमः।	aiṃ aṃguṣṭhābhyāṃ namaḥ।	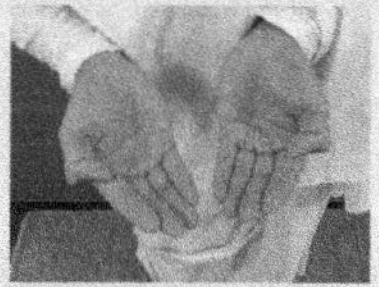	Touch the tip of your thumb at the base of your index finger.
ह्रीं तर्जनीभ्यां नमः।	hrīṃ tarjanībhyāṃ namaḥ।		Touch the tip of your thumb to the tip of your index finger.
श्रीं मध्यमाभ्यां नमः।	śrīṃ madhyamābhyāṃ namaḥ।		Touch the tip of your thumb to the tip of your middle finger.
ऐं अनामिकाभ्यां नमः।	aiṃ anāmikābhyāṃ namaḥ।	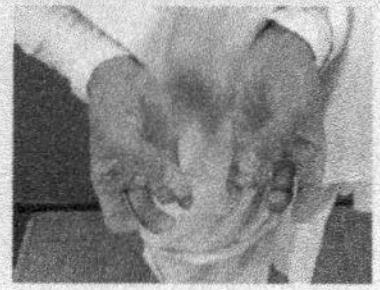	Touch the tip of your thumb to the tip of your ring finger.

Sanskrit (Devanagri)	*Sanskrit (IAST)*	*Handlock (Mudra)*	*Gesture with both hands*
ह्रीं कनिष्ठिकाभ्यां नमः।	hrīṃ kaniṣṭhikābhyāṃ namaḥ।	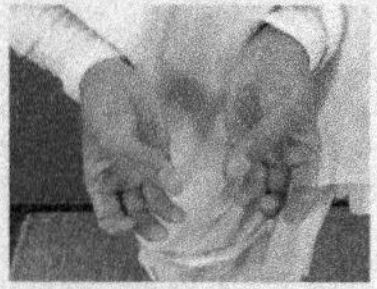	Touch the tip of your thumb to the tip of your little finger.
श्रीं करतलकरपृष्ठाभ्यां नमः।	śrīṃ karatalakara pṛṣṭhābhyāṃ namaḥ।	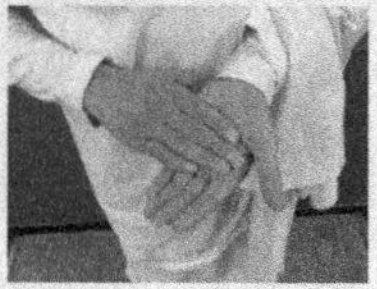	Touch the back of your left hand with the back of your right hand and then clap softly.

Unification with the mantra (Mantra *nyasa*)
Please do all the *nyasas* shown below:

Nyasa of the sages (Rishyadi nyasa)

Sanskrit (Devanagri)	*Sanskrit (IAST)*	*Touch with your right hand your*
ॐ गायत्र्या विश्वामित्र ऋषिः नमः शिरसि ।	oṃ gāyatryā viśvāmitra ṛṣiḥ namaḥ śirasi ।	head
गायत्रीछन्दसे नमः मुखे ।	gāyatrīchandase namaḥ mukhe ।	mouth
सविता देवता नमः हृदये ।	savitā devatā namaḥ hradaye ।	heart
जपोपनयने विनियोगः नमः सर्वांगे ।	japopanayane viniyogaḥ namaḥ sarvāṃge ।	Take the right hand over your head and then bring it back in front of you joining your hands near your heart in the posture of Namaste.
ॐ विश्वामित्र ऋषये नमः शिरसि ।	oṃ viśvāmitra ṛṣaye namaḥ śirasi ।	head
गायत्रीछन्दसे नमः मुखे ।	gāyatrīchandase namaḥ mukhe ।	mouth
सवितृदेवतायै नमः हृदये ।	savitṛdevatāyai namaḥ hradaye ।	heart
विनियोगाय नमः सर्वांगे ।	viniyogāya namaḥ sarvāṃge ।	Take the right hand over your head and then bring it back in front of you joining your hands near your heart in the posture of Namaste.

Nyasa of the Primal Energy (Pranava nyasa)

Sanskrit (Devanagri)	*Sanskrit (IAST)*	*Touch with your right hand your*
ॐ ब्रह्म ऋषये नमः शिरसि।	oṃ brahma ṛṣaye namaḥ śirasi।	head
गायत्रीछन्द से नमः मुखे ।	gāyatrīchanda se namaḥ mukhe ।	mouth
ॐ परमात्मादेवतायै नमः हृदि ।	oṃ paramātmādevatāyai namaḥ hradi ।	heart
विनियोगाय नमः सर्वांगे ।	viniyogāya namaḥ sarvāṃge ।	Take the right hand over your head and then bring it back in front of you joining your hands near your heart in the posture of Namaste.

Sanskrit (Devanagri)	*Sanskrit (IAST)*	*Gesture with both hands*
ॐ तत्सवितुब्रह्मणे अंगुष्ठाभ्यां नमः ।	oṃ tatsavitubrahmaṇe aṃguṣṭhābhyāṃ namaḥ ।	Touch the tip of your thumb at the base of your index finger.
ॐ वरेण्यं विष्णवे तर्जनीभ्यां नमः ।	oṃ vareṇyaṃ viṣṇave tarjanībhyāṃ namaḥ ।	Touch the tip of your thumb to the tip of your index finger.
ॐ भर्गो देवस्य रुद्राय मध्यमाभ्यां नमः।	oṃ bhargo devasya rudrāya madhyamābhyāṃ namaḥ।	Touch the tip of your thumb to the tip of your middle finger.

Sanskrit (Devanagri)	*Sanskrit (IAST)*	*Gesture with both hands*
ॐ धीमहि ईश्वराय अनामिकाभ्यां नमः ।	oṃ dhīmahi īśvarāya anāmikābhyāṃ namaḥ ।	Touch the tip of your thumb to the tip of your ring finger.
ॐ धियो यो नः सदाशिवाय कनिष्ठिकाभ्यां नमः ।	oṃ dhiyo yo naḥ sadāśivāya kaniṣṭhikābhyāṃ namaḥ ।	Touch the tip of your thumb to the tip of your little finger.
ॐ प्रचोदयात् सर्वात्मने करतलकरपृष्ठाभ्यां नमः ।	oṃ pracodayāt sarvātmane karatalakarapṛṣṭhābhyāṃ namaḥ ।	Touch the back of your left hand with the back of your right hand and then clap softly.

Six-Limbed Mantra Nyasa (Shadanga mantra nyāsa)

Sanskrit (Devanagri)	*Sanskrit (IAST)*	*Posture*	*Description*
ॐ तत्सवितुर्ब्रह्मणे हृदयाय नमः ।	oṃ tatsavitubrahmaṇe hradayāya namaḥ I		Touch your heart region with your right hand.
ॐ वरेण्यं विष्णवे शिरसे स्वाहा ।	oṃ vareṇyaṃ viṣṇave śirase svāhā I		Touch your forehead with your right hand keeping the index finger away.
ॐ भर्गो देवस्य रुद्राय शिखायै वषट् ।	oṃ bhargo devasya rudrāya śikhāyai vaṣaṭ I		Make a fist with right hand and extend your thumb. Now touch the crown of your head with your thumb.

Sanskrit (Devanagri)	Sanskrit (IAST)	Posture	Description
ॐ धीमहि ईश्वराय कवचाय हुम् ।	oṃ dhīmahi īśvarāya kavacāya hum ।		Touch your shoulders by crossing your hands. Generally, in Devi Pooja, left hand is on top of the right and in Devata Pooja, right on top of the left. This is, however, just a guideline and not a rule.
ॐ धियो यो नः सदाशिवाय नेत्रत्रयाय वौषट् ।	oṃ dhiyo yo naḥ sadāśivāya netratrayāya vauṣaṭ ।		Spread your right hand and touch your right eye with your index finger, forehead with the middle finger and left eye with the ring finger simultaneously. Netra-traya means the three eyes.
ॐ प्रचोदयात् सर्वात्मने अस्त्राय फट् ।	oṃ pracodayāt sarvātmane astrāya phaṭ ।		Take the right hand over your head and then bring it back in front of you to clap softly.

Nyasa of the Verses (*Pada nyasa*)

Sanskrit (Devanagri)	*Sanskrit (IAST)*	*Touch with your right hand your*
ॐ तत् नमः शिरसि ।	oṃ tat namaḥ śirasi I	Head
ॐ सवितुर्नमः भ्रुवोर्मध्ये ।	oṃ saviturnamaḥ bhruvormadhye I	Between your brows (glabella)
ॐ वरेण्यं नमः नेत्रयोः ।	oṃ vareṇyaṃ namaḥ netrayoḥ I	Both eyes
ॐ भर्गो नमः मुखे ।	oṃ bhargo namaḥ mukhe I	Face (Palm touching your nose)
ॐ देवस्य नमः कण्ठे ।	oṃ devasya namaḥ kaṇṭhe I	Throat
ॐ धीमहि नमः हृदये ।	oṃ dhīmahi namaḥ hradaye I	Heart
ॐ धियो नमः नाभौ ।	oṃ dhiyo namaḥ nābhau I	Navel
ॐ यो नमः गुह्ये ।	oṃ yo namaḥ guhye I	Groin
ॐ नः नमः जानुनोः ।	oṃ naḥ namaḥ jānunoḥ I	Knees
ॐ प्रचोदयात् नमः पादयोः ।	oṃ pracodayāt namaḥ pādayoḥ I	Feet
ॐ आपोज्योति रसो मृतं ब्रह्मभूर्भवः स्वरोमिति शिरसि ।	oṃ āpojyoti raso mṛtaṃ brahmabhūrbhavaḥ svaromiti śirasi I	Head
ॐ तत्सवितुरवरेण्यम् नमः नाभ्यादिपादांगुलिपर्यन्तम् ।	oṃ tatsavituravareṇyam namaḥ nābhyādipādāṃguliparyantam I	Roll your hand from your navel to your toes.
ॐ भर्गो देवस्यधीमहि नमः हृदयादिनाभ्यान्तं ।	oṃ bhargo devasyadhīmahi namaḥ hradayādinābhyāntaṃ I	Roll your hand from your heart to navel.
ॐ धियो यो नः प्रचोदयात् नमः मूर्धादिहृदयान्तम् ।	oṃ dhiyo yo naḥ pracodayāt namaḥ mūrdhādihradayāntam I	Roll your hand from your head to your heart.

Nyasa of the Letters (Mantra varna nyasa)

Sanskrit (Devanagri)	*Sanskrit (IAST)*	*Touch with your right hand your*
ॐ भूः नमः ह्रदयेः ।	oṃ bhūḥ namaḥ hradayeḥ ।	Heart
ॐ भुवः नमः मुखे ।	oṃ bhuvaḥ namaḥ mukhe ।	Face
ॐ स्वः नमः दक्षांसे ।	oṃ svaḥ namaḥ dakṣāṃse ।	Right shoulder
ॐ महः नमः वामांसे ।	oṃ mahaḥ namaḥ vāmāṃse ।	Left shoulder
ॐ जनः नमः दक्षिणपार्श्वे ।	oṃ janaḥ namaḥ dakṣiṇapārśve ।	Right rib
ॐ तपः नमः वामपार्श्वे ।	oṃ tapaḥ namaḥ vāmapārśve ।	Left rib
ॐ सत्यं नमः जठरे ।	oṃ satyaṃ namaḥ jaṭhare ।	Stomach
ॐ तत् नमः पादांगुलिमुलेषु ।	oṃ tat namaḥ pādāṃgulimuleṣu ।	Feet
ॐ सं नमः गुल्फ्योः ।	oṃ saṃ namaḥ gulphyoḥ ।	Ankles
ॐ विं नमः जानुनोः	oṃ viṃ namaḥ jānunoḥ	Knees
ॐ तुं नमः पादमुलयोः ।	oṃ tuṃ namaḥ pādamulayoḥ ।	Thighs
ॐ वं नमः लिंगे ।	oṃ vaṃ namaḥ liṃge ।	Groin
ॐ रें नमः नाभौ ।	oṃ reṃ namaḥ nābhau ।	Navel
ॐ णिं नमः ह्रदये ।	oṃ ṇiṃ namaḥ hradaye ।	Heart
ॐ यं नमः कण्ठे ।	oṃ yaṃ namaḥ kaṇṭhe ।	Throat
ॐ भं नमः हस्तागुलिमुलेषु ।	oṃ bhaṃ namaḥ hastāgulimuleṣu ।	Hands
ॐ ग्रों नमः मणिबंध्योः ।	oṃ groṃ namaḥ maṇibaṃdhyoḥ ।	Wrists
ॐ दें नमः कूपरयोः ।	oṃ deṃ namaḥ kūparrayoḥ ।	Elbows

Sanskrit (Devanagri)	Sanskrit (IAST)	Touch with your right hand your
ॐ वं नमः बाहूमूलयोः ।	oṃ vaṃ namaḥ bāhūmūlayoḥ ।	Biceps
ॐ स्यं नमः अस्ये ।	oṃ syaṃ namaḥ asye ।	Mouth
ॐ धीं नमः नासापुटयोः ।	oṃ dhīṃ namaḥ nāsāpuṭayoḥ ।	Nostrils
ॐ मं नमः कपोलयोः ।	oṃ maṃ namaḥ kapolayoḥ ।	Cheeks
ॐ हिं नमः नेत्रयोः ।	oṃ hiṃ namaḥ netrayoḥ ।	Eyes
ॐ धिं नमः कर्णयोः ।	oṃ dhiṃ namaḥ karṇayoḥ ।	Ears
ॐ यों नमः भ्रूमध्ये ।	oṃ yoṃ namaḥ bhrūmadhye ।	Glabella
ॐ यों नमः मस्तके ।	oṃ yoṃ namaḥ mastake ।	Forehead
ॐ नं नमः पश्चिमवक्त्रे ।	oṃ naṃ namaḥ paścimavaktre ।	Left cheek
ॐ प्रं नमः उत्तरवक्त्रे ।	oṃ praṃ namaḥ uttaravaktre ।	Upper part of your face (forehead again)
ॐ चों नमः दक्षिणवक्त्रे ।	oṃ coṃ namaḥ dakṣiṇavaktre ।	Chin
ॐ दं नमः पुर्ववक्त्रे ।	oṃ daṃ namaḥ purvavaktre ।	Right cheek
ॐ यां नमः मूर्ध्नि ।	oṃ yāṃ namaḥ mūrdhni ।	Head
ॐ तं् नमः सर्वांगे ।	oṃ tṃ namaḥ sarvāṃge ।	Roll your right hand over your entire body and clap softly.

21. Preliminary mantra chanting (*Purva* mantra *japa*)
    Upon completion of the *nyasa*, chant the Gayatri Mantra 21 times.
22. Preliminary handlocks (*Purva* mudra)
    Gayatri *sadhana* has 24 handlocks that are performed before you begin the chanting and eight that are performed after you are done chanting.
    The 24 preliminary handlocks are as follows:

Handlock (Mudra)		*Gesture with both hands*
सुमुखम् (sumukham)		Turn your palm downwards and join all the fingers of both hands.
सम्पुटम् (sampuṭam)		Form a bracket with your palms facing each other.
विततम् (vitatam)		Open your hands and let both palms face each other.
विस्तृतम् (vistṛtam)		Increase the distance between your palms from the previous mudra and turn them slightly up.
द्विमुखम् (dvimukham)	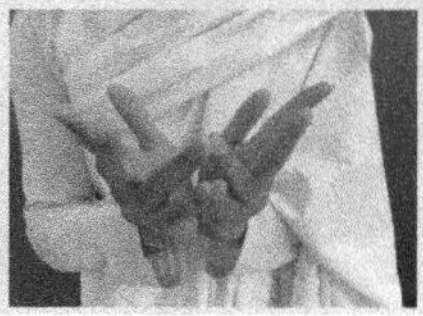	Join little and ring fingers of both hands.

Handlock (Mudra)		*Gesture with both hands*
त्रिमुखम् (trimukham)		Keeping the earlier mudra intact, join middle fingers as well now.
चतुर्मुखम् (caturmukham)		Keeping the previous mudra as it is, join the index fingers as well.
पञ्चमुखम् (pañcamukham)		Now join the thumbs too.
षण्मुखम् (ṣaṇmukham)		Keeping your hands joined, now unjoin and spread the thumbs and little fingers.
अधोमुखम् (adhomukham)	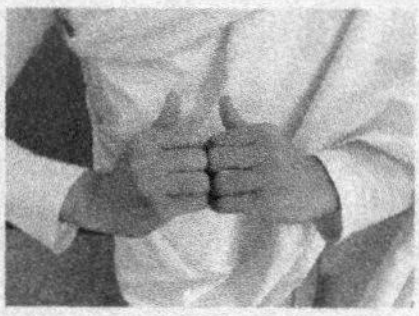	Bend your fingers and turn your hands over so the back of right-hand fingers touch the back of left-hand fingers.
व्यापकाञ्जलिकम् (vyāpakāñjalikam)		Turn these hands over and spread so both palms now face upwards with hands together.
शकटम् (śakaṭam)		Turn your hands over (palms facing down) and join index fingers and thumbs.

Handlock (Mudra)		*Gesture with both hands*
यमपाशम् (yamapāśam)		Entwine your index fingers and let the right-hand hang.
ग्रथितम् (grathitam)		Entwine all fingers and form one fist.
उन्मुखोन्मुखम् (unmukhonmukham)	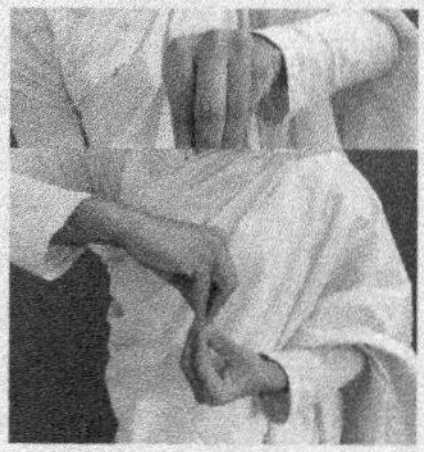	Bring all fingers together of both hands. First rest your right-hand on top of the left and then left on top of right.
प्रलम्बम् (pralambam)	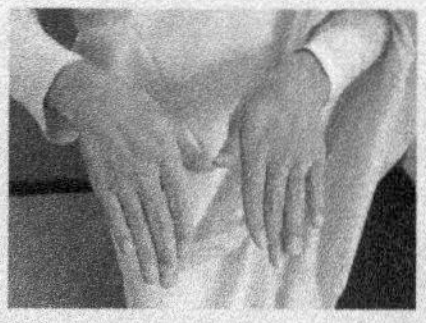	Turn both your hands and let palms face down. Join gently at the tip of the thumbs.
मुष्टिकम् (muṣṭikam)	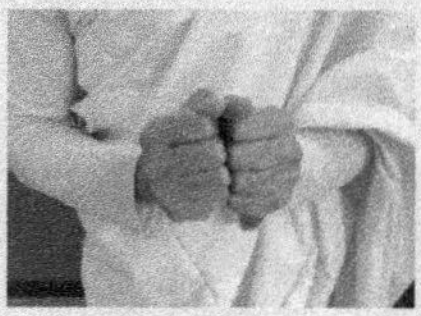	Keep your thumbs out and make fists with both hands.
मत्स्यः (matsyaḥ)	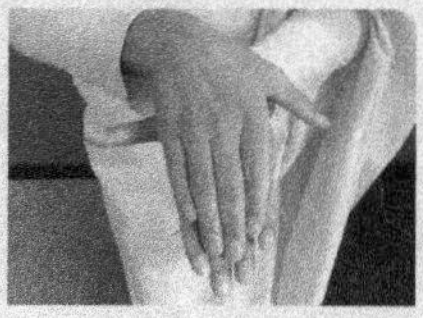	Rest your right-hand on your left (palms facing down). Spread your thumbs and twiddle your thumbs a bit.

Handlock (Mudra)		*Gesture with both hands*
कूर्मः (kūrmaḥ)		Spread your left-hand. Turn index and middle fingers keeping the other fingers extended. Do the same with your right-hand. Now turn your right on and let it rest on your left with index fingers, thumbs and little fingers touching at the tips. There are other ways of showing this mudra but this is the one I practice and got from my guru.
वराहकम् (varāhakam)	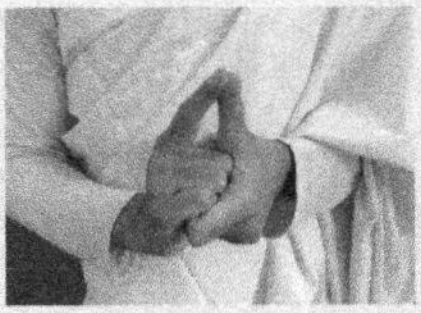	Grab four fingers of your left hand (except your thumb) with right middle, ring and little fingers. Join the tip of right index finger with the left thumb.
सिंहाक्रान्तम् (siṃhākrāntam)		Raise both your hands as in benediction, the back of your palms facing you. (Like in a hands-up posture)
महाक्रान्तम् (mahākrāntam)		Keep the same posture but turn your hands so your palms are facing your ears.

Handlock (Mudra)		*Gesture with both hands*
मुद्गरम् (mudgaram)	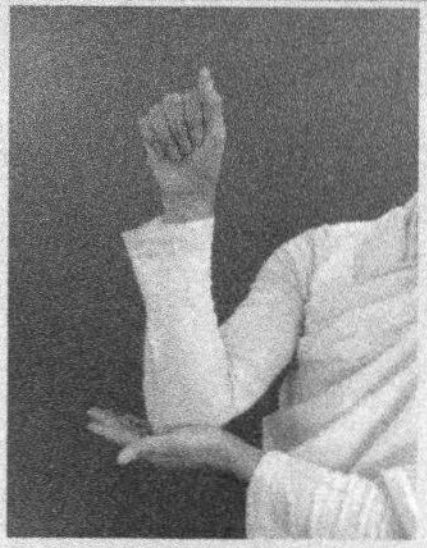	Make a fist with your right-hand and then rest the right elbow on your left.
पल्लवम् (pallavam)	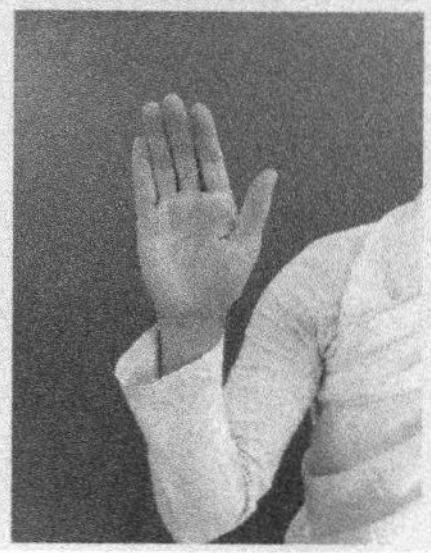	Raise your right-hand to your shoulder in benediction.

23. Sixteen, ten or five offerings.
    Now make sixteen, ten or five offerings as per step 23 in *Essential Steps in the Rites of Invocation (Puruscharana).*
24. Invoke the mantra (Mantra *samskara*)
    The mantra of Gayatri was cursed by Brahma, Vashishta and Vishvamitra. Therefore, chant the following mantras seven times every day before you do the mantra *japa* to absolve the mantra of the curse of the sages (*shaap vimochana*). Usually, application (*viniyoga*) is required here, but if you chant the following mantras, seven times each, every day, throughout the course of your *puruscharana*, you don't need to do *viniyoga* separately for this step.

Brahma Shaap Vimochana

Sanskrit (Devanagri)	*Sanskrit (IAST)*
ॐ गायत्रीब्रह्मेत्युपासीत यद्रूपं ब्रह्मविदो विदुः ।	oṃ gāyatrībrahmetyupāsīta yadrūpaṃ brahmavido viduḥ ।
तां पश्यन्ति धीराःसुमनसा वाचामग्रतः ।	tāṃ paśyanti dhīrāḥsumanasā vācāmagrataḥ ।
ॐ वेदान्तनाथाय विद्दहे हिरण्यगर्भाय धीमहि ।	oṃ vedāntanāthāya viddahe hiraṇyagarbhāya dhīmahi ।
तन्नो ब्रह्म प्रचोदयात् ।	tanno brahma pracodayāt ।
ॐ देवी गायत्री त्वं ब्रह्मशापविमुक्ता भव ।	oṃ devī gāyatrī tvaṃ brahmaśāpavimuktā bhava ।
Vasishta Shaap Vimochana	
ॐ सोहमर्कमयं ज्योतिरात्मज्योतिरहं शिवः ।	oṃ sohamarkamayaṃ jyotirātmajyotirahaṃ śivaḥ ।
आत्मज्योतिरहं शुक्रः सर्वज्योतिरसोस्म्यहम् ।	ātmajyotirahaṃ śukraḥ sarvajyotirasosmyaham ।
ॐ देवी गायत्री त्वं वसिष्ठशापविमुक्ता भव ।	oṃ devī gāyatrī tvaṃ vasiṣṭhaśāpavimuktā bhava ।
Vishvamitra Shaap Vimochana	
ॐ गायत्रीं भजाम्यग्निमुखीं विश्वगर्भाः यदुद्भवा देवाश्चिक्ररे विश्वसृष्टिं तां कल्याणीमिष्टकरीं प्रपघे ।	oṃ gāyatrīṃ bhajāmyagnimukhīṃ viśvagarbhāḥ yadudbhavā devāśckrire viśvasṛṣṭiṃ tāṃ kalyāṇīmiṣṭakarīṃ prapaghe ।
यन्मुखान्निः सृतो खिलवेदगर्भः ।	yanmukhānniḥ sṛto khilavedagarbhaḥ ।
औं देवी गायत्री त्वं विश्वामित्रशापद्विमुक्ता भव ।	oṃ devī gāyatrī tvaṃ viśvāmitraśāpadvimuktā bhava ।

Sanskrit (Devanagri)	*Sanskrit (IAST)*
तथा चः सोहमर्कमयं ज्योतिरर्को ज्योतिरहं शिवः ।	tathā caḥ sohamarkamayaṃ jyotirarko jyotirahaṃ śivaḥ ।
आत्मज्योतिरहं शुक्रः शुक्रज्योतिरसोहमोम् ।	ātmajyotirahaṃ śukraḥ śukrajyotirasohamom ।
महोविष्णुमहेशेशे दिव्य सिद्धि सरस्वती ।	mahoviṣṇumaheśeśe divya siddhi sarasvatī ।
अजरे अमरे चैव दिव्ययोनि नमोस्तुते ।।	ajare amare caiva divyayoni namostute ।।

25. Meditate on your mantra (Mantra *dhyana*)
    There are many meditations on Mother Divine in the form of Gayatri. Personally, I keep it very simple and meditate upon Her using the core mantra. You can do the same.

Sanskrit (Devanagri)	*Sanskrit (IAST)*
ॐ भूर्भुवः स्वः तत्सवितुर्वरेण्यम भर्गो देवस्य धीमहि। धियो यो नः प्रचोदयात॥	oṃ bhūrbhuvaḥ svaḥ tatsaviturvareṇyama bhargo devasya dhīmahi। dhiyo yo naḥ pracodayāta॥

Translation
May we abide in the Supreme Energy that is eternal, transcendental, radiant, perfect, divine. May such divine grace always guide us on the path of righteousness.

26. Mantra chanting (*Moola* mantra *japa*)
    Depending on the nature and length of your *puruscharana*, chant your mantra now. Remember to keep the same count everyday of your *puruscharana*. For example, if you chant 30 rounds on

the first day, chant 30 rounds every day till your *puruscharna* is complete.

27. Post-*japa* handlocks (*Uttara* mudra)

    There are eight handlocks (mudras) that are shown at the completion of your *japa*. Rather than showing the standard handlocks as stated in *Essential Steps in the Rites of Invocation (Puruscharana)*, simply show the handlocks below.

Handlock (Mudra)		*Gesture with both hands*
धेनू (dhenū)	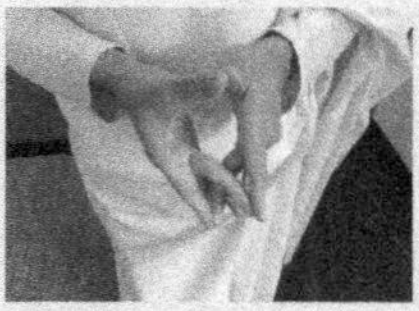	Join right index finger at the tip of the left middle finger while the left index finger should touch the tip of the right middle finger. The right ring finger should touch the tip of the left little finger while the left ring finger should touch the tip of the right ring finger. Join both thumbs at their tips. Point it downwards.
ज्ञानम् (jñānam)	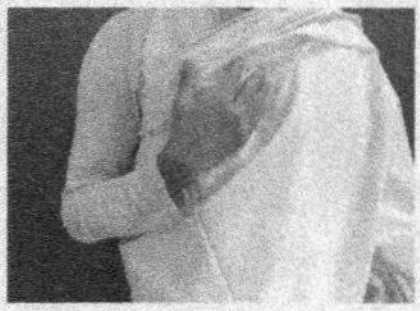	Touch your heart with your right-hand. The left is usually in vairagya mudra (the one below) while the right touches your heart.
वैराग्य (vairāgya)		Join index fingers with the thumbs and spread out the rest.

Handlock (Mudra)		*Gesture with both hands*
योनि (yoni)	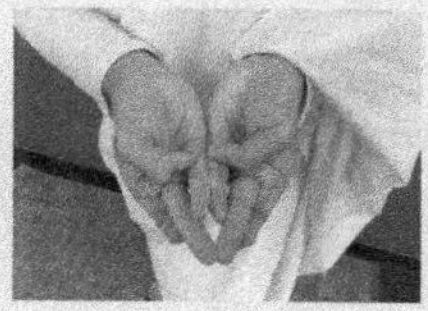	Grab right ring finger with left index finger and right index finger with left ring finger. Join the two middle fingers at the tip. Let the two little fingers rest on it. Put tips of your thumbs at the base of the little fingers and you have the auspicious yoni mudra.
शंख (śaṃkha)		Grab your left thumb with your four fingers of the right-hand. Let four fingers of the left-hand cover your right fist with left index finger joining at the tip with the right thumb.
पन्कजम् (pankajam)		A budding lotus is shown by joining all your fingers but opening the index fingers. You can also spread out all the fingers to show this mudra.
लिङ्गम् (liṅgam)		Crisscross fingers of both hands and stick out the right thumb.
निर्वाणम् (nirvāṇam)		This is also called samahara mudra and has been explained in the chapter on mudras.

28. Offering of chanting (*Japa samarpana*)
    Make an offering of the japa to your deity. You can find the mantra and process as stated in step 28 in *Essential Steps in the Rites of Invocation (Puruscharana).*
29. Freeing all energies (*Visarjana*)
    All the energies who participated in your sadhana for the night are now given a send off with this step. Please follow the instructions given in step 29 in *Essential Steps in the Rites of Invocation (Puruscharana).*
30. Seeking forgiveness (*Kshama prarthana*)
    It's now time to seek forgiveness for any mistakes of omission or commission committed out of ignorance or otherwise. The mantra and process of seeking forgiveness is detailed in step 30 in *Essential Steps in the Rites of Invocation (Puruscharana).*
31. Fire offerings (*Yajna*)
    The process of *yajna* has been detailed in the chapter *How to Make Fire Offerings (Yajna).* For this *sadhana*, you require different ingredients every night. I've listed those ingredients for each night under the appropriate section.
32. Libations (*Tarpana*)
    Please follow the instructions as given in step 32 in *Essential Steps in the Rites of Invocation (Puruscharana).* Your mantra for libations will also change every night and I've noted that under each night.
33. Coronation (*Marjana* or *abhishekam*)
    Once again, you can read about *marjana* in step 33 in *Essential Steps in the Rites of Invocation (Puruscharana).* For each night, I've provided the appropriate mantra for *marjana* in the notes below.
34. Charity (*Sadhak bhojan* or Brahmin *bhoj*)
    By the time you'll finish your *japa, yajna,* etc., for the night, it would be early morning. You can then either set aside some money you can give to a believer of Devi (Devi *upasaka*) so he may buy his own meal. Or, you can cook a meal and serve it to him for breakfast. Or, you can have a meal cooked by anyone

else but serve it yourself. Whatever is convenient for you works. It's important to do it with the sentiment of charity.

35. Seek forgiveness again (*Kshama prarthana*)
    Repeat the hymn of forgiveness as in step 30 for there might have been mistakes in your actions from step –31-34.
36. Offer water to the sun (Surya *arghya*)
    Follow the instructions given in step 36 in *Essential Steps in the Rites of Invocation (Puruscharana).*

SRI SUKTAM SADHANA

विश्वारणे नमस्तुभ्यं नमो विश्वविभूतये
सर्वसामपि सिद्धिनां नमस्ते मूलहेतवे ।।

आदिदेवात्मभूताये नारायणकुटुम्बिनि
समस्तजगदाराध्ये नमस्ते पद्मयोनये ।।

viśvāraṇe namastubhyaṃ namo viśvavibhūtaye
sarvasāmapi siddhināṃ namaste mūlahetave ||

ādidevātmabhūtāye nārāyaṇakuṭumbini
samastajagadārādhye namaste padmayonaye ||

I salute thee, the source of the universe, adoration to thee who abides in the universe as its glory, O primary cause of all (spiritual) ability (acquired through mantra-worship), I salute thee, who art identical with the primeval God and art Narayana's spouse. O universally propitiated, lotus-born (goddess), I prostrate myself before thee. (Lakshmi Tantra, Trans. Sanjukta Gupta, Motilal Banarsidass. 2002.)

In 2008, I had started a business in India along with a partner. That same year, we bought a factory. We'd ordered new machinery that would take almost a month to arrive. The timing was such that for one month, our new factory wouldn't have any staff other than the caretaker. The management team would be operating from the corporate headquarters that was in a different city, some 70 km away.

I saw this as a golden opportunity to do the *sadhana* of *Sri Suktam* lasting 16 nights.

In 2010, I renounced the world.

Here's the thing though: the business we had started back then is still going strong and it turned over more than Rs 100 crore last year. (Though as a renunciant I'm no longer associated with that company in any way.) Of course, this was not just because of the *sadhana* of *Sri Suktam*, but also due to the immense hard work, smart thinking and relentless execution by my partner and staff. Having said that, I believe, when the seed is divine and healthy, the probability of a sapling turning into a tree remains incredibly high.

Originating from the *Rigveda*, *Sri Suktam* is the most powerful *sadhana* anyone can undertake. It is a *puruscharna* of 16 nights. When done correctly, it tunes your energy with the cosmic energy around you to aid your material progress. Here I share the rites of *puruscharana*, but any aspirant has to earn his right to do the *Sri Sukta Sadhana*, which is gained by diligently following a certain routine for a period of 960 days.

Your first reaction may be a sense of disbelief, thinking, 960 days! "I don't have 960 days or the discipline to follow a routine for 960 days," you may say. Well, if that's the case, I strongly recommend not to waste your time reading more about this *sadhana*. You can do just the Ganesha or Guru *Sadhana*. You can try doing the *puruscharana* of this *sadhana* too without following a regimen but the results are going to be miniscule. Nature is a giant ship that turns slowly. There's nothing called an overnight *sadhana*. If you wish to align the forces of nature using mantra yoga so you are in harmony, it'll take some time.

To do *Sri Sukta purushcharana* successfully, following the schedule for 960 days is pretty much non-negotiable. To carry out the routine requires approximately 45 minutes (excluding the time you may take to bathe every morning).

The daily injunctions are as follows:

1. Your routine (*nitya karma*) for 960 days
2. Bathe every morning
3. Light a lamp at the altar and apply a light saffron *tilak* on your forehead. This *tilak* can be very light if you like, so light that no one will be able to see it. Simply keep a few strands of saffron in a small bowl and add a few drops of water to it. Touch it with your ring finger on your forehead. This will be your *tilak*. Just add a bit of water everyday and add more saffron whenever needed.
4. Chant *Sri Suktam* 11 times in the morning after your bath
5. Meditate on Sri and Vishnu for five minutes and seat them in your heart most gloriously
6. Chant *Sri Suktam* every evening/night for five times (bathing at this time is advisable though not mandatory. You can simply wash your face, hands and feet, rinse your mouth and apply *tilak* on your forehead.) Light an evening lamp at your altar.
7. Meditate for five minutes before going to bed (you can meditate while sitting on your bed). Once again, seat Sri (Devi) and Vishnu in your heart chakra.

During these 960 days, the practitioner must remain completely vegetarian. No meat, no seafood and no eggs. Dairy is okay; garlic and onions are also okay. The original scriptural injunction requires that the aspirant subsist on the milk (and milk products) of Kapila cow, but I'm imparting to you the way I practiced and benefited from it. *Sampradaya* (tradition) is one of the basic tenets of mantra science. If you follow my tradition, you only need to worry about the rules I state here. Abstinence is not required during these 960 days but it'll be a requirement during the rites of *puruscharana* lasting 16 nights.

If you unintentionally eat something inappropriate (a cake or biscuits containing eggs, for example, or, products containing gelatin, etc.) or break any of the six rules above, the aspirant must do rites of expiation (*prayaschita*). I've detailed the rites of expiation for this *sadhana* later in this book.

If, however, you intentionally violate the principles above, your *sadhana* stands compromised. You must reset the counter and start from the beginning.

If you are unable to follow any of the rules above due to genuine sickness, you must catch up later. For example, if due to an injury or illness, you couldn't bathe one day, the next day, you must do double the amount of chanting and meditation. Similarly, if you were on a long international flight, let's say, and couldn't bathe in the morning, you must make up for this loss by chanting and meditating twice as much the next day.

Diligently follow this rule for three years and you'll be ready to do the transformational *puruscharana* of Mother Divine.

How long does it take

The *puruscharana* is of 16 nights but as I stated earlier, ideally an aspirant should follow a daily routine for 960 days.

When can you start this *sadhana*

The *puruscharana* of *Sri Suktam* can only be done once a year starting on the night of Diwali. When you start on the night of Diwali, it'll conclude on the 16th night. Please consult the *panchangam* or the Indian calendar to know the date of Diwali. Diwali, according to the Gregorian calendar, changes every year because like most other festivals of Sanatana Dharma, Diwali too is based on the lunar calendar.

Who can do this *sadhana*

Any man or woman (irrespective of whether a woman is menstruating during, before or after the *puruscharana*) of any age, religion, ability or background can perform this *sadhana* with or without initiation. Complete abstinence must be practiced throughout the *puruscharana*. There's no *dosha* (issue) in case of wet dreams or any other involuntary release of sexual fluids. Voluntarily though, any form of sexual gratification is strictly forbidden.

Diet

During the 16-night *sadhana*, you should be on a strict vegetarian diet. Dairy is allowed but no meat, seafood or eggs. No onion or garlic either. Be careful of eating biscuits, cakes, cheeses, supplements, etc., that may contain animal-derived ingredients.

Lamp

The lamp lit in this *puruscharana* can be made of any metal. Even an earthen lamp can be used. The wick must be made of cotton. It is permissible to use braided cotton thread (like the common sacred red thread, *mauli*, for example, or any other) to use as a wick. The oil used in the lamp should be either ghee or sesame oil. If you are doing this sadhana in a cold region (as Diwali often falls in winter and it can be very cold in some parts of the world), I would recommend using sesame oil as ghee solidifies very quickly and it may put out your lamp.

Direction

The aspirant should face east, north or northeast while doing the chanting and the *yajna*.

Clothing

Use red-colored clothing only. Ideally you should wear no more than two pieces of red-colored loose cloth on your body — one to cover your lower body and the other to cover the upper part. If you are in a very cold place, you can either use a heater in your room or sew your upper cloth with a woolen shawl. Women can wear a saree, blouse, etc. Women are allowed to do this *sadhana* even if they are menstruating during these 16 nights. This is a tantric *sadhana* and poses no restrictions based on an aspirant's sex, sexuality or physiology.

Seat

The best seat will be a blanket on which you should spread a red-colored cloth. Your clothes and the color of your seat should be red. The nature of this *sadhana* requires you to sit on the floor. If you are unable to do that, you may try sitting on a chair and setting up a table in front of you with lamp, pots, etc. Personally, I have never experimented with that. If you do, please feel free to share the results of your *sadhana.*

Other than a blanket, you can also take a standard meditation cushion or use any seat made out of cotton.

Seats made of *kusha* grass are also permissible for this *sadhana.*

Posture

Try to maintain the stillness of your posture while you chant with utmost mindfulness, faith and devotion. Please note that mantra *sadhana* is not about reckless chanting of a mantra just for the sake of ticking off an item from your list. It is the soulful process of becoming one with your deity so you may elevate yourself spiritually, materially and emotionally.

Requirements for this *sadhana*

1. A lamp (silver, brass or any other metal. Earthen lamp is fine, too)
2. Ghee to light your lamp
3. Sixteen wicks for 16 nights.
4. Five small water pots, a small spoon and a saucer. They can be

of silver, copper or brass. This is the standard for every *sadhana* and details on how to layout the pots (*patra*) can be found in the chapter *Arrangement of Pots (Patrasadan)* in Detailed Notes.

5. Sweetmeat, jaggery or honey (to make the *madhuparka* offering)
6. Different ingredients are needed for the fire offerings (*yajna*) each day for 16 days. They have been listed against the respective days.
7. In addition to those ingredients, you will need firewood. You can use either wood from a sacred fig (Ficus *religiosa*. Common name: peepul), mango (Magnifera *indica*, Common name: *aam* or *aamra*) or *palasha* (Butea *monosperma*. Common name: *plasha* or *dhak*). You can also use the wood from *deodar* (Cedrus *deodara*. Common name: *devadaru*) or *teak* (Tectona *grandis*. Common name: *sagaun* or *sheesham*).
8. Chanting beads made from rudraksha or lotus seeds (*kamal gatta*)
9. A lot of faith, devotion and discipline

I strongly recommend that after going through this chapter you make a daily checklist in line with the 36 steps I enumerate below. Do make a daily list of what all you require and procure everything in advance so that you don't miss out on the golden opportunity of completing your *sadhana* for the lack of ingredients or so on.

The Mantra

The mantra of this *sadhana* changes every night for the 16 nights. I've specified it in the appropriate subsequent sections under Night 1, Night 2 and so on.

Before You Begin

This *sadhana* starts on the night of Diwali. But, a night prior to starting this *sadhana* (that is the night before Diwali), you have to seek permission from Vedmata Gayatri, the mother of the Vedas.

The simplest way to do that is to sit at your temple after bathing, after sunset. Take a bit of water in your right hand and mentally call upon the Divine Mother in the form of Gayatri and seek Her permission that may She and other forces of nature allow you to complete *Sri Suktam Sadhana*. Leave the water in the plate next to you.

Next, do 30 rounds of chanting of *Savitur* Gayatri Mantra. You can use rudraksha or chandan beads. If you have used any other chanting beads in the past to chant the Gayatri Mantra, you can use the same rosary. Please make sure that you don't use these beads for chanting any other mantra (including *Sri Suktam*).

One round is 108 times, so 30 rounds will be 108 x 30 = 3240. I always used to chant 10,000 times before doing any major *puruscharana*. But, 30 rounds will suffice too. After finishing, sleep at the same place where you chanted the Gayatri Mantra. Here's the Gayatri Mantra again for your reference.

Sanskrit (Devanagri)	*Sanskrit (IAST)*
ॐ भूर्भुवः स्वः तत्सवितुर्वरेण्यम भर्गो देवस्य धीमहि। धियो यो नः प्रचोदयात॥	oṃ bhūrbhuvaḥ svaḥ tatsaviturvareṇyama bhargo devasya dhīmahi। dhiyo yo naḥ pracodayāta॥

The Source Hymn (Sri Suktam)

The entire *sadhana* is based on *Sri Suktam* that contains 17 verses. A verse is invoked every night, hence the *sadhana* of 16 nights. You can find *Sri Suktam* below in both Sanskrit and IAST transliteration and the meaning of this beautiful hymn.

	Sanskrit (Devanagri)	*Sanskrit (IAST)*
1	हिरण्यवर्णां हरिणीं सुवर्णरजतस्रजाम् । चन्द्रां हिरण्मयीं लक्ष्मीं जातवेदो म आवह ॥	hiraṇyavarṇāṃ hariṇīṃ suvarṇarajatasrajām । candrāṃ hiraṇmayīṃ lakṣmīṃ jātavedo ma āvaha ॥
2	तां म आवह जातवेदो लक्ष्मीमनपगामिनीम् । यस्यां हिरण्यं विन्देयं गामश्वं पुरुषानहम् ॥	tāṃ ma āvaha jātavedo lakṣmīmanapagāminīm । yasyāṃ hiraṇyaṃ vindeyaṃ gāmaśvaṃ puruṣānaham ॥
3	अश्वपूर्वां रथमध्यां हस्तिनादप्रबोधिनीम् । श्रियं देवीमुपह्वये श्रीर्मा देवी जुषताम्	aśvapūrvāṃ rathamadhyāṃ hastinādaprabodhinīm । śriyaṃ devīmupahvaye śrīrmā devī juṣatām ॥
4	कां सोस्मितां हिरण्यप्राकारामार्द्रां ज्वलन्तीं तृप्तां तर्पयन्तीम् । पद्मे स्थितां पद्मवर्णां तामिहोपह्वये श्रियम् ॥	kāṃ sosmitāṃ hiraṇyaprākārāmārdrāṃ jvalantīṃ tṛptāṃ tarpayantīm । padme sthitāṃ padmavarṇāṃ tāmihopahvaye śriyam ॥
5	चन्द्रां प्रभासां यशसा ज्वलन्तीं श्रियं लोके देवजुष्टामुदाराम् । तां पद्मिनीमीं शरणमहं प्रपद्ये'लक्ष्मीर्मे नश्यतां त्वां वृणे ॥	candrāṃ prabhāsāṃ yaśasā jvalantīṃ śriyaṃ loke devajuṣṭāmudārām । tāṃ padminīmīṃ śaraṇamahaṃ prapadye'lakṣmīrme naśyatāṃ tvāṃ vṛṇe ॥
6	आदित्यवर्णे तपसो'धिजातो वनस्पतिस्तव वृक्षो'थ बिल्वः । तस्य फलानि तपसानुदन्तु मायान्तरायाश्च बाह्या अलक्ष्मीः ॥	ādityavarṇe tapaso'dhijāto vanaspatistava vṛkṣo'tha bilvaḥ । tasya phalāni tapasānudantu māyāntarāyāśca bāhyā alakṣmīḥ ॥

	Sanskrit (Devanagri)	Sanskrit (IAST)
7	उपैतु मां देवसखः कीर्तिश्च मणिना सह । प्रादुर्भूतो'स्मि राष्ट्रे'स्मिन् कीर्तिमृद्धिं ददातु मे ॥	upaitu māṃ devasakhaḥ kīrtiśca maṇinā saha I prādurbhūto'smi rāṣṭre'smin kīrtimṛddhiṃ dadātu me II
8	क्षुत्पिपासामलां ज्येष्ठामलक्ष्मीं नाशयाम्यहम् । अभूतिमसमृद्धिं च सर्वां निर्णुद मे गृहात् ॥	kṣutpipāsāmalāṃ jyeṣṭhāmalakṣmīṃ nāśayāmyaham I abhūtimasamṛddhiṃ ca sarvāṃ nirṇuda me gṛhāt II
9	गन्धद्वारां दुराधर्षां नित्यपुष्टां करीषिणीम् । ईश्वरीं सर्वभूतानां तामिहोपह्वये श्रियम् ॥	gandhadvārāṃ durādharṣāṃ nityapuṣṭāṃ karīṣiṇīm I īśvarīṃ sarvabhūtānāṃ tāmihopahvaye śriyam II
10	मनसः काममाकूतिं वाचः सत्यमशीमहि । पशूनां रूपमन्नस्य मयि श्रीः श्रयतां यशः ॥	manasaḥ kāmamākūtiṃ vācaḥ satyamaśīmahi I paśūnāṃ rūpamannasya mayi śrīḥ śrayatāṃ yaśaḥ II
11	कर्दमेन प्रजाभूता मयि सम्भव कर्दम । श्रियं वासय मे कुले मातरं पद्ममालिनीम् ॥	kardamena prajābhūtā mayi sambhava kardama I śriyaṃ vāsaya me kule mātaraṃ padmamālinīm II
12	आपः सृजन्तु स्निग्धानि चिक्लीत वस मे गृहे । नि च देवीं मातरं श्रियं वासय मे कुले ॥	āpaḥ sṛjantu snigdhāni ciklīta vasa me gṛhe I ni ca devīṃ mātaraṃ śriyaṃ vāsaya me kule II
13	आर्द्रां पुष्करिणीं पुष्टिं पिङ्गलां पद्ममालिनीम् । चन्द्रां हिरण्मयीं लक्ष्मीं जातवेदो म आवह ॥	ārdrāṃ puṣkariṇīṃ puṣṭiṃ piṅgalāṃ padmamālinīm I candrāṃ hiraṇmayīṃ lakṣmīṃ jātavedo ma āvaha II

	Sanskrit (Devanagri)	Sanskrit (IAST)
14	आर्द्रां यः करिणीं यष्टिं सुवर्णां हेममालिनीम् । सूर्यां हिरण्मयीं लक्ष्मीं जातवेदो म आवह ॥	ārdrāṃ yaḥ kariṇīṃ yaṣṭiṃ suvarṇāṃ hemamālinīm | sūryāṃ hiraṇmayīṃ lakṣmīṃ jātavedo ma āvaha ||
15	तां म आवह जातवेदो लक्ष्मीमनपगामिनीम् । यस्यां हिरण्यं प्रभूतं गावो दास्यो'श्वान् विन्देयं पूरुषानहम् ॥	tāṃ ma āvaha jātavedo lakṣmīmanapagāminīm | yasyāṃ hiraṇyaṃ prabhūtaṃ gāvo dāsyo'śvān vindeyaṃ pūruṣānaham ||
16	यः शुचिः प्रयतो भूत्वा जुहुयादाज्यमन्वहम् । सूक्तं पञ्चदशर्चं च श्रीकामः सततं जपेत् ॥	yaḥ śuciḥ prayato bhūtvā juhuyādājyamanvaham | sūktaṃ pañcadaśarcaṃ ca śrīkāmaḥ satataṃ japet ||

	Translation
1	Invoke for me, O Agni, the Goddess Lakshmi who is radiant like gold, beautiful yellow in hue, adorned with garlands of silver and gold, magnanimous like the moon and an embodiment of wealth and prosperity.
2	O Agni! Invoke for me the Goddess who will stay by my side and bless me so I may acquire material wealth of gold, cows, horses and attendants.
3	I invoke Sri, the resplendent Mother Divine who is the Goddess of prosperity, most gloriously accompanied by her retinue of horses in the front, chariots in the middle and whose arrival is announced by the trumpeting of elephants. May she come and bless me.

Translation

4 I invoke Sri of the lustre of burnished gold, beautiful like the lotus she's seated on, the ever smiling, benevolent, Mother Divine who is the Goddess of prosperity, an embodiment of Absolute Bliss, who is blazing with splendour. She grants the wishes of her devotees.

5 I seek refuge at the lotus feet of the Goddess who is as beautiful and bright as the moon, who blazes with illustriousness, who is adored by the gods and exceedingly munificent. May my misfortunes end. I invoke thee.

6 O Mother Divine, resplendent as the sun! As a result of thy glories and penance have the sacred plants like bilva come into existence. May the fruits of (such penance) destroy all inauspiciousness arising out of my impure thoughts and ignorant actions.

7 With thy grace, O Mother! I'm living in a blessed country. May Kubera (the guardian lord of wealth) and Kirti (fame) come to me. May the Gods bestow upon me fame and prosperity.

8 With thy grace and my efforts, I shall ward off inauspiciousness and distressing poverty as hunger, thirst and the like. O Lakshmi! Dispel from my home every misfortune and insufficiency.

9 I invoke Sri, Mother Divine who's the supreme controller of all beings, who can be perceived through heady fragrance, who is beyond defeat and threat, who is ever virtuous and abundant.

10 O Mother Divine, Goddess of prosperity, May we enjoy the fulfilment of our noble desires, may we be blessed with the veracity of speech, wealth and abundant foodgrains. May prosperity and fame reside in thy devotee.

Translation	
11	O Kardama! Make her who was born to Kardama (i.e., to you) abide with me. Make the Goddess of Prosperity who is the mother of the universe and wears garlands of lotuses, dwell in our family.
12	Let the waters produce oily products (like butter) in my house. O Chiklita, dwell in my house and make the Goddess of Prosperity, the Divine Mother, also dwell in my family.
13	O Jataveda! Bring to me the extremely benign Lakshmi who is reddish in complexion, who dwells in lakes and who possesses the Moon's brilliance and gold in abundance.
14	O Jataveda! Bring to me the extremely benign Lakshmi of a golden complexion who dwells in lakes, who is the bestower of plenty, who wears a garland of gold, who is resplendent like the sun and abounds in wealth.
15	O Jataveda! Bring to me that Lakshmi who will not forsake me and by whose grace I may obtain in plenty gold, cows, maids, horses and men servants.
16	He who is desirous of becoming prosperous should, after making himself pure and controlling his senses, make daily offerings of melted butter in the fire. He should also repeat always the above stanzas of mantras.

How to perform the rites of invocation (Puruscharana)

As I wrote earlier, if you've followed the daily routine (*nitya karma*) everyday for nearly three years, you are most certainly ready to perform the rites of invocation (*purushcharana*). If, however, you haven't done three years yet or not at all, you can still try this *sadhana* to catch a glimpse, but I remain skeptical about seeing any significant results without following the daily routine first for 960 days.

Every night, for 16 nights, you'll be invoking a different mantra. But every night, the first few steps will be the same. Step 17 (taking the vow – *sankalpa*) will be done only on the first night. For all the remaining days, you don't need to do this step. All the steps are as follows. Please note that the details of each one of these steps and how to perform it, etc., can be found in the chapter *Essential Steps in the Rites of Invocation (Puruscharana).* Wherever this *sadhana* deviates from the standard instructions, I've given the details next to that step.

Remember though that one night before commencing *Sri Suktam Sadhana*, you've to seek permission from Vedmata Gayatri. I've stated the procedure in an earlier section in this chapter '*Before you begin*'.

Here are the 36 steps of *Sri Suktam Sadhana.*

1. Bathe
   This *sadhana* starts after sunset. Even if you bathed in the morning – something an aspirant must always do – take a bath again every night before commencing the rites.
2. Put on fresh clothes
3. Clean your altar (enter the sanctum sanctorum)
   Set up your altar by laying the pots as per *Arranging the Pots (Patrasadana)* in Detailed Notes. Make sure you wash all the pots and lamp every day before using it.
4. Purify the surroundings
5. Self purification (*Achamana*)
   Wash your hands (*hasta prakshalana*)
6. Light the lamp (You can also light incense at this stage if you like, but it's optional).
7. Invoke Ganesha
8. Show three handlocks for Ganesha (Ganesh mudra)
9. Chant the Vedic hymn of auspiciousness (*Svastivachana*)
10. Meditate on your guru (Guru *dhyana*)

11. Chant your guru mantra (Guru mantra *japa*)
12. Offer obeisance to all siddhas
13. Meditate on your deity (*Ishta dhyana*)
    If you pray to a specific god, pray to that diety now or simply meditate on Mother Divine using the mantra below.

Sanskrit (Devanagri)	*Sanskrit (IAST)*
सिन्दूरारुण विग्रहां त्रिनयनां माणिक्यमौलि स्फुरत्	sindūrāruṇa vigrahāṃ trinayanāṃ māṇikyamauli sphurat
तारा नायक स्हेखरां स्मितमुखी मापीन वक्ष्होरुहाम् ।	tārā nāyaka shekharāṃ smitamukhī māpīna vakṣhoruhām I
पाणिभ्यामलिपूर्ण रत्न चष्हकं रक्तोत्पलं बिभ्रतीं	pāṇibhyāmalipūrṇa ratna caṣhakaṃ raktotpalaṃ bibhratīṃ
सौम्यां रत्न घटस्थ रक्तचरणां ध्यायेत् परांम्बिकाम् ।।	saumyāṃ ratna ghaṭastha raktacaraṇāṃ dhyāyet parāṃmbikām II

Translation
Meditate on the Divine Mother as shining in a buxom vermilion-red body. She has three eyes. Sporting a resplendent crown studded with rubies and crescent moon, with a beautiful smiling face and a splendid bust, she is holding a cup studded with jewels and brimming with a heady drink made from honey and water. In her other hand, she holds most delicately a twirling red lotus.

14. Chant the preliminary mantra (*Ishta* mantra *japa*)
    If you have been initiated into any mantra, chant that mantra now 11, 21 or 31 times. If you have never been initiated into a mantra by a guru, simply chant the mantra of this *sadhana*. (For each night, there's a different mantra. So refer to that particular night to see which mantra you should be chanting).
15. Pray to Mother Earth (*Prithvi* pooja)

16. Take the vow (*Sankalpa*)
    This is done only on the first night. You don't have to chant the standard vow in Sanskrit because to do that properly you will either need to consult a pandit who can tell you the exact lunar dates, arrangement of planets and various other astrological aspects that are taken into consideration while chanting a vow, or you have to have that knowledge yourself. The chances of committing mistakes that way remain high. It's much simpler and better to make your pact with the universe by saying your vow out loud in whatever language you know. The vow is given in step 16 in the chapter *Essential Steps in the Rites of Invocation (Puruscharana).*
17. Mantra breathing (Mantra *shvasa*)
18. Application (*Viniyoga*)
    This will change every night for 16 nights and is detailed under the respective section.
19. Purification of hands (*Kara shuddhi*)
    Chant the following mantras and show the appropriate mudras to perform purification of the hands.

Sanskrit (Devanagri)	Sanskrit (IAST)	Handlock (Mudra)	Gesture with both hands
ऐं अंगुष्ठाभ्यां नमः।	aiṃ aṃguṣṭhābhyāṃ namaḥ।	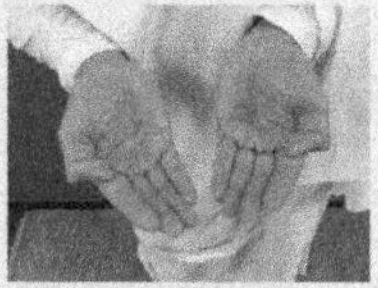	Touch the tip of your thumb at the base of your index finger.
ह्रीं तर्जनीभ्यां नमः।	hrīṃ tarjanībhyāṃ namaḥ।	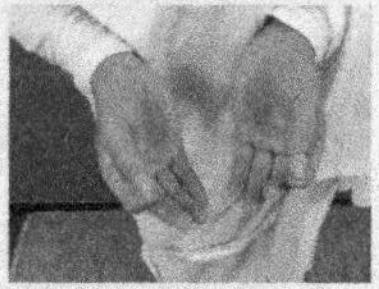	Touch the tip of your thumb to the tip of your index finger.
श्रीं मध्यमाभ्यां नमः।	śrīṃ madhyamābhyāṃ namaḥ।	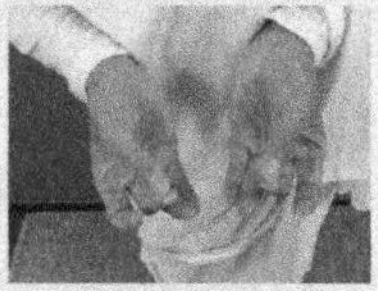	Touch the tip of your thumb to the tip of your middle finger.
ऐं अनामिकाभ्यां नमः।	aiṃ anāmikābhyāṃ namaḥ।	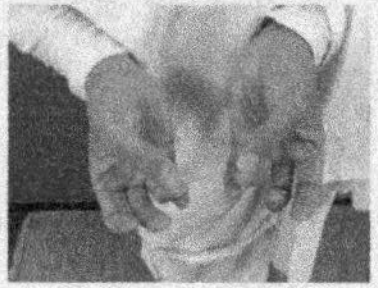	Touch the tip of your thumb to the tip of your ring finger.

Sanskrit (Devanagri)	*Sanskrit (IAST)*	*Handlock (Mudra)*	*Gesture with both hands*
ह्रीं कनिष्ठिकाभ्यां नमः।	hrīṃ kaniṣṭhikābhyāṃ namaḥ।	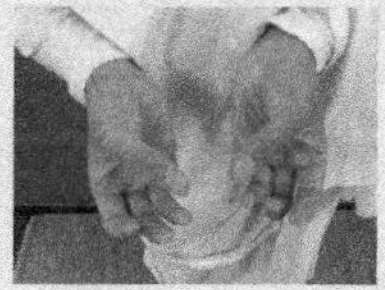	Touch the tip of your thumb to the tip of your little finger.
श्रीं करतलकरपृष्ठाभ्यां नमः।	śrīṃ karatalakara pṛṣṭhābhyāṃ namaḥ।	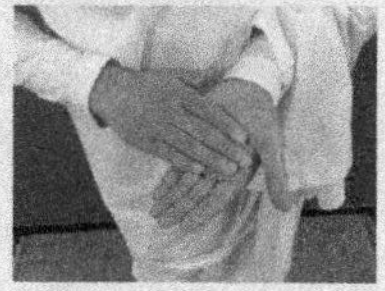	Touch the back of your left hand with the back of your right hand and then clap softly.

20. Unification with the mantra (Mantra *nyasa*)
    In this *sadhana*, mantra *nyasa* will change every night. I've given details of such *nyasa* against relevant nights.
21. Preliminary mantra chanting (*Purva* mantra *japa*)
    Once you are done with the *nyasa*, chant your mantra of that particular night 16 times.
22. Preliminary handlocks (*Purva* mudra)
    Show the following four mudras:

Handlock (Mudra)	*Handlock (Mudra)*	*Gesture with both hands*
Dhenu	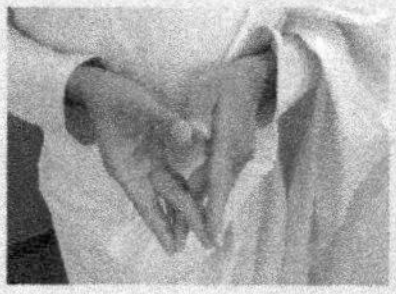	Join right index finger at the tip of the left middle finger while the left index finger should touch the tip of the right middle finger. The right ring finger should touch the tip of the left little finger while the left ring finger should touch the tip of the right ring finger. Join both thumbs at their tips. Point it downwards.
Kalash		Form a fist with your right and hold the fist with your left hand. There's an alternate way as well of Kalash mudra: make fists with both hands and bring them together.
Matasya	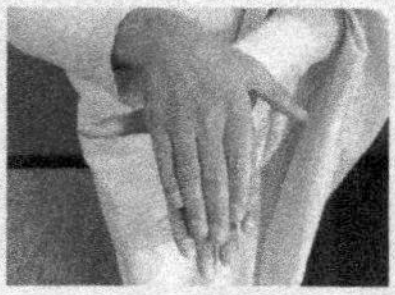	Join all fingers and spread the thumbs. Let the right-hand rest on your left.

Handlock (Mudra)	Handlock (Mudra)	Gesture with both hands
Paash		Entwine the two index fingers and let the right hand hang down.

23. Sixteen offerings (*Shodoshopchara*)
    Please make the following 16 offerings every night:

I. Invoke with the first verse

Fold your hands in the pose of 'Namaste' and bring them close to your heart. Chant the following verse to invoke the grace of Devi.

hiraṇya-varṇāṁ hariṇīṁ suvarṇa-rajata-srajām,
candrāṁ hiraṇmayīṁ lakṣmīṁ jātavedo ma āvaha.

II. Welcome with the second verse

Believing that Devi has come, chant the second verse to welcome Her.

tāṁ ma āvaha jātavedo lakṣmī-mana-pagāminīm,
yasyāṁ hiraṇyaṁ vindeyaṁ gāmaśvaṁ puruṣānaham.

III. Offer a seat with the third

Chant the third verse of *Sri Suktam* to offer Her a seat.

aśva-pūrvāṁ ratha-madhyāṁ hasti-nāda-pramodinīm,
śriyaṁ devīm-upahvaye śrīrmā devīr-juṣatām.

IV. Offer arghya and padya with the fourth

Offer Her water and wash Her feet by chanting the fourth verse. Simply take water from the water-offering pot (*arghya patra*) and put it in the plate next to you. And then take water from the washing pot and put it in the plate again. The verse has to be chanted only once.

kāṁ sosmitāṁ hiraṇya-prākārām-ārdrāṁ jvalantīṁ tṛptāṁ tarpayantīm,
padme sthitāṁ Padma-varṇāṁ tāmih-opahvaye śriyam.

V. Offer achmana with the fifth

This is not an aspirant doing *achmana* but offering *achmana* to the deity. So, take a spoonful of water from the water pot (*achmana patra*) and put it in the plate next to you.

candrāṁ prabhāsāṁ yaśasā jvalaṁtīṁ śriyaṁ loke deva-juṣṭāmudārām,
tāṁ padminīmīṁ śaraṇamahaṁ prapadye alakṣmīrme naśyatāṁ tvāṁ vṛṇe.

VI. Offer water oblation with the sixth

Take a spoonful of water from the water-offering pot (*arghya patra*) and put it in the plate while you chant the verse below.

ādityavarṇe tapaso'dhijāto vanaspatistava vṛkṣo'tha bilvaḥ,
tasya phalāni tapasā nudantu māyāntarāyāśca bāhyā alakṣmīḥ.

VII. Mentally bathe Devi with the seventh

Take a spoonful of water from the pot containing water for washing (*padyam*) and put it in the plate. Chant the verse below.

upaitu māṁ devasakhaḥ kīrtiśca maṇinā saha
prādurbhūto'smi rāṣṭre'smin kīrtimṛddhiṁ dadātu me.

VIII. Offer Her clothing with the eighth verse

Take two flowers or any small pieces of fresh clothes and put them by the feet of your deity. If you are not using any idol or yantra, you can then leave this next to the lamp. (Make sure you maintain safe distance between lamp and the clothes to prevent any fire hazard.)

kṣutpipāsāmalāṁ jyeṣṭhāmalakṣmīṁ nāśayāmyaham,
abhūtimasamṛddhiṁ ca sarvāṁ nirṇuda me gṛahāt.

IX. Offer ornaments with the ninth verse of Sri Suktam

Take a flower as an ornament and offer it to your deity, yantra or the lamp. Chant the verse below.

gandhadvārāṁ durādharṣāṁ nityapuṣṭāṁ karīṣiṇīm,
īśvarīṁ sarvabhūtānāṁ tāmihopahvaye śriyam.

If your financial resources permit, you can offer full length clothes and ornaments of gold, silver, etc., and at the end of 16 nights, you can give that in charity to someone who is either a Devi *upasaka* or leads a sattvik life. The recipient can be male or female.

X. Offer Her perfume with the tenth verse

Take a spoonful of water from the pot containing fragrant water and put it in the plate next to you. Chant the verse below while you do that.

manasaḥ kāmamākūtiṁ vācaḥ satyamaśīmahi,
paśūnāṁ rūpamannasya mayi śrīḥ śrayatāṁ yaśaḥ.

XI. Offer flowers with the eleventh verse

Take one or more flowers, recite the verse below and offer the flower(s) at the lamp. The following verse is to be recited while you make the offering.

kardamena prajā bhūtā mayi sambhava kardama,
śriyaṁ vāsaya me kule mātaraṁ padmamālinīm.

XII. Offer incense with the twelfth verse

If you are burning incense, turn it clockwise in front of the lamp, idol or the *yantra*. In case you are not burning incense, simply close your eyes and offer it mentally. Make the offering with the verse below.

āpaḥ sṛjantu snigdhāni ciklīta vasa me gṛhe,
nica devīṁ mātaragï śriyaṁ vāsaya me kule.

XIII. Offer lit lamp with the thirteenth verse

If you have lit a lamp in front of an idol, picture or *yantra*, simply lift the lamp and turn it clockwise once while chanting the following verse. If you are praying to the lamp itself, just touch the base of the lamp while reciting the verse.

ārdrāṁ puṣkariṇīṁ puṣṭiṁ suvarṇāṁ hemamālinīm,
sūryāṁ hiraṇmayīṁ lakṣmīṁ jātavedo ma āvaha.

XIV. Offer madhuparka with the fourteenth

Generally, *madhuparka* is made by mixing honey with ghee. For convenience and practical purposes, you can use just honey or any sweetmeat (even jaggery) to make an offering to Devi. Please chant the verse below. At the end of your pooja, you can offer this sweetmeat to anyone. If there's no one, feel free to eat it yourself.

ārdrāṁ yaḥ kariṇīṁ yaṣṭiṁ piṅgalāṁ padmamālinīm,
candrāṁ hiraṇmayīṁ lakṣmīṁ jātavedo ma āvaha.

XV. Eulogize (prapanna aarti) with the fifteenth

Simply fold your hands in 'Namaste', close to your heart, and chant the verse below.

tāṁ ma āvaha jātavedo lakṣmīmanapagāminīm,
yasyāṁ hiraṇyaṁ prabhūtaṁ gāvo dāsyo'śvānvindeyaṁ puruṣānaham.

XVI. Salutation with Sri Gayatri

The 16th verse of *Sri Suktam* is not chanted to make the 16th offering. Instead, the Laxmi Gayatri Mantra is chanted, primarily because the 16th verse forms spelling out the benefits of chanting (*phala shruti*) this hymn.

ōm mahādevyai ca vidmahe viṣṇupatnī ca dhīmahi,
tanno lakṣmīḥ pracodayāt.

Once you are done with making the 16 offerings, you are ready to proceed to step 24 in the rites of *puruscharana.*

24. Invoke the mantra (Mantra *samskara*)
    Mantra *samskara* is not required for this *sadhana.*
25. Meditate on your mantra (Mantra *dhyana)*
    Every night, offer the following prayer to Mother Divine. This marks the completion of the 25 steps. You are now ready to do the mantra chanting as per the next step.

Sanskrit (Devanagri)	*Sanskrit (IAST)*
विश्वारणे नमस्तुभ्यं नमो विश्वविभूतये सर्वसामपि सिद्धिनां नमस्ते मूलहेतवे ॥	viśvāraṇe namastubhyaṃ namo viśvavibhūtaye sarvasāmapi siddhināṃ namaste mūlahetave ॥
आदिदेवात्मभूताये नारायणकुटुम्बिनि समस्तजगदाराध्ये नमस्ते पद्मयोनये ॥	ādidevātmabhūtāye nārāyaṇakuṭumbini samastajagadārādhye namaste padmayonaye ॥

Translation

(I salute thee, the source of the universe, adoration to thee who abides in the universe as its glory, O primary cause of all (spiritual) ability (acquired through mantra worship), I salute thee, who art identical with the primeval God and art Narayana's spouse. O universally propitiated, lotus-born (goddess), I prostrate myself before thee.

26. Mantra chanting (*Moola* mantra *japa*)
    If you recall, *Sri Suktam* has 16 verses and each night you will chant a different verse. Every night, there are some seed syllables that are appended at the beginning and end of the verse. Your mantra every night is going to be different. The number of times you have to chant every night can also vary. At the end of the steps in this *puruscharana*, I've detailed all the requirements and instructions for each day separately. For now, let me enumerate the next steps for you.
27. Post-*japa* handlocks (*Uttara* mudra)
    Once you are done with your *japa*, show the mudras as per step 27 in *Essential Steps in the Rites of Invocation (Puruscharana).*
28. Offering of chanting (*Japa samarpana*)
    Make an offering of the *japa* to your deity. You can find the mantra and process as stated in step 28 in *Essential Steps in the Rites of Invocation (Puruscharana).*
29. Freeing all energies (*Visarjana*)
    All the energies who participated in your *sadhana* for the night are now given a send off with this step. Please follow the instructions given in step 29 in *Essential Steps in the Rites of Invocation (Puruscharana).*
30. Seeking forgiveness (*Kshama prarthana*)
    It's now time to seek forgiveness for any mistakes of omission

or commission committed out of ignorance or otherwise. The mantra and process of seeking forgiveness is detailed in step 30 in *Essential Steps in the Rites of Invocation (Puruscharana).*

31. Fire offerings (*Yajna*)
    The process of *yajna* has been detailed in the chapter *How to Make Fire Offerings (Yajna).* For this *sadhana*, you'll require different ingredients every night. I've listed those ingredients for each night under the appropriate section.
32. Libations (*Tarpana*)
    Please follow the instructions as given in step 32 in *Essential Steps in the Rites of Invocation (Puruscharana).* Your mantra for libations will also change every night and I've noted that under each night.
33. Coronation (*Marjana* or *abhishekam*)
    Once again, you can read about *marjana* in step 33 in *Essential Steps in the Rites of Invocation (Puruscharana).* For each night, I've provided the appropriate mantra for *marjana* in the notes below.
34. Charity (*Sadhak bhojan* or Brahmin *bhoj*)
    By the time you'll finish your *japa*, *yajna*, etc., for the night, it would be early morning. You can then either set aside some money that you can give to a believer of Devi (Devi *upasaka*), so he can buy his own meal. Or, you can cook a meal and serve it to him for breakfast. Or, you can have a meal cooked by anyone else but serve it yourself. Whatever is convenient for you works. It's important to do it with the sentiment of charity.
35. Seek forgiveness again (*Kshama prarthana*)
    Repeat the hymn of forgiveness as in step 30 for there might have been mistakes in your actions from step –31-34.
36. Offer water to the sun (Surya *arghya*)

Follow the instructions given in step 36 in *Essential Steps in the Rites of Invocation (Puruscharana).*

The section below details your night-by-night routine and instructions for 16 nights of Sri Suktam Sadhana. For each night, your mantras for chanting, *yajna*, libation, coronation, etc., will change. I've noted them duly. At the beginning of each night, you'll find a table that lists the relevant mantras, the number of times you need to chant it and different ingredients required for the *yajna.*

Night 1

It always takes a bit longer on the first day compared to all the other days because all steps are new and it takes more time to perform each step.

Night 1

Chanting (Japa)	
Mantra Sanskrit (Devanagri)	ॐ आं ह्रीं श्रीं क्लीं ब्लूं सौं रं वं श्रीं । ॐ श्री ह्रीं श्रीं नमः । हिरण्यवर्णां हरिणीं सुवर्णरजतस्रजाम् । चन्द्रां हिरण्मयीं लक्ष्मीं जातवेदो म आवह ॥ नमो श्रीं ह्रीं श्रीं ॐ । आं ह्रीं श्रीं क्लीं ब्लूं सौं रं वं श्रीं ॐ ।।
Mantra Sanskrit (IAST)	oṃ āṃ hrīṃ śrīṃ klīṃ blūṃ sauṃ raṃ vaṃ śrīṃ । oṃ śrī hrīṃ śrīṃ namaḥ । hiraṇyavarṇāṃ hariṇīṃ suvarṇarajatasrajām । candrāṃ hiraṇmayīṃ lakṣmīṃ jātavedo ma āvaha ॥ namo śrīṃ hrīṃ śrīṃ oṃ । āṃ hrīṃ śrīṃ klīṃ blūṃ sauṃ raṃ vaṃ śrīṃ oṃ ।।

Count	Chant this mantra 1000 times.
Fire offerings (Yajna)	
Mantra	Same as above. Just add 'Om Svaha' (Skt: ॐ स्वाहा, oṃ svāhā) at the end of your mantra. Therefore, say the mantra, say Om Svaha and then make an offering in the fire pit.
Count	108 times.
Ingredients for fire-offerings	Ghee — 200 grams Raisins (50 grams) — 50 grams Havan Samagri — 1 packet White sesame seeds — 50 grams Red sandalwood — One small piece
Instructions	Follow the standard procedure of fire offerings as stated in *How to Make Fire Offerings (Yajna)*. 1. Mix raisins, havan samagri and white sesame seeds. 2. Put five tablespoons of melted ghee in it. Mix it thoroughly. 3. After you have made 108 offerings (ahuti), offer the last one with the small piece of red sandalwood. Dip it in ghee or put a bit of ghee in it and offer it in the fire pit. 4. Conclude by pouring any remaining ghee from the 200 grams you set aside for this yajna. 5. If you feel the fire going off while you do yajna, feel free to pour more ghee on the fire. Keep the fire alive.

Libations (Tarpana)	
Mantra	Same as the mantra above for chanting. Just add 'tarpyami' (Skt: तर्प्यामि, tarpyāmi) at the end of your mantra.
Instructions	Say the mantra, take a bit of water as per the instructions in step 32 in Essential Steps in the Rites of Invocation (Puruscharana), and add 'tarpyami' in the end when you put water back in the vessel.
Coronation (Marjana or Abhishekam)	
Mantra	Same as the mantra above for chanting. Just add 'marjyami' (Skt: मार्जयामि, mārjayāmi) at the end of your mantra.
Instructions	Say the mantra, take a bit of water as per the instructions in step 33 in Essential Steps in the Rites of Invocation (Puruscharana), and add 'marjyami' in the end when you put water back in the vessel.

Follow the 36 steps of the rites of invocation but please note that vow — step 16 is to be performed only on the first night. The rest of the steps remain the same. *Nyasa*, application (*viniyoga*) and mantra will change every night. Mantra has been already specified in the previous table, *viniyoga* and *nyasa* are as follows.

Application (Viniyoga)

Sanskrit (Devanagri)	*Sanskrit (IAST)*
ॐ अस्य श्री हिरण्यवर्णां इति श्री सूक्त प्रथम मंत्रस्य चिक्लीत ऋषि, श्री महाविद्या	oṃ asya śrī hiraṇyavarṇāṃ iti śrī sūkta prathama maṃtrasya ciklīta ṛṣi, śrī mahāvidyā

सर्वसिद्धि प्रदायै देवता, सर्वार्थ साधक शक्ति, श्री बीजं, भुवनेशी महाविद्या, ह्रीं उत्कीलन, सर्व मंगल कारिण्यै भगवती लक्ष्मी प्रसाद सिद्धयर्थ प्रथम मंत्र जपे विनियोगः ।	sarvasiddhi pradāyai devatā, śrī bījaṃ, sarvārtha sādhaka śakti, bhuvaneśī mahāvidyā, hrīṃ utkīlana, sarva maṃgala kāriṇyai bhagavatī lakṣmī prasāda siddhayartha prathama maṃtra jape viniyogaḥ I

Follow the standard procedure of viniyoga by taking a bit of water in your palm (as explained in step 18 in Essential Steps in the Rites of Invocation).

Perform the *nyasa* as per the tables below, in that order, starting with the *Nyasa* of the Sages (*Rishyadi nyasa*)

Nyasa of the Sages **(***Rishyadi nyasa***)**

Sanskrit (Devanagri)	*Sanskrit (IAST)*	*Touch with your right-hand your...*
श्री कर्दम चिक्लीत ऋषयै नमः सहस्रारे शिरसि ।	śrī kardama ciklīta ṛṣayai namaḥ sahasrāre śirasi I	Crown of the head
भागवती श्री सर्वसिद्धिप्रदायै नमः द्वादशारै हृदि ।	bhāgavatī śrī sarvasiddhipradāyai namaḥ dvādaśārai hradi I	Heart
सर्वार्थ साधक शक्त्यै नमः दशारे नाभौ ।	sarvārtha sādhaka śaktyai namaḥ daśāre nābhau I	Navel
श्रीं बीजाय नमः षडारे योनौ ।	śrīṃ bījāya namaḥ ṣaḍāre yonau I	Groin

Sanskrit (Devanagri)	*Sanskrit (IAST)*	*Touch with your right-hand your...*
भुवनेशी श्री विद्यायै नमः षोडशारे कण्ठे ।	bhuvaneśī śrī vidyāyai namaḥ ṣoḍaśāre kaṇṭhe ।	Throat
रजोगुणाय नमः अंतरारै मनसि ।	rajoguṇāya namaḥ aṃtarārai manasi।	Heart (again)
रसना ज्ञानेन्द्रियाय नमः चेतसी ।	rasanā jñānendriyāya namaḥ cetasī।	Mouth (just open your mouth a bit while touching).
वाक् कर्मेन्द्रियाय नमः कर्मेन्द्रिये ।	vāk karmendriyai namaḥ karmendriye।	Lips
मध्यम स्वराय नमः कंठमूले ।	madhyama svarāya namaḥ kaṃṭhamūle।	Base of your throat (the soft area just below the Adam's apple).
भुतत्वाय नमः चतुरारे गुदे ।	bhutatvāya namaḥ caturāre gude।	Lower back (near your anus but keep your clothes on and just touch your lower back symbolically).
विद्या कलायै नमः करतले ।	vidyā kalāyai namaḥ karatale।	The palm of your left hand
ह्रीं उत्कीलनाय नमः पादयोः ।	hrīṃ utkīlanāya namaḥ pādayoḥ।	Feet

Sanskrit (Devanagri)	*Sanskrit (IAST)*	*Touch with your right-hand your...*
प्रवाहिनी मुद्रायै नमः सर्वांगे ।	pravāhinī mudrāyai namaḥ sarvāṃge	Whole body (Do this by rolling your right hand over your upper body by bringing it around and then clapping gently).

Now perform the *nyasa* of the hands (*kara nyasa*). The mudras are the same as in step 17 (purification of the hands) of this chapter. You can see the illustrations in the table below; I am providing the description again.

Nyasa of the Hands (*Kara Nyasa*)

Sanskrit (Devanagri)	*Sanskrit (IAST)*	*Gesture with both hands*
ॐ हिरण्यवर्णां अंगुष्ठाभ्यां नमः ।	oṃ hiraṇyavarṇāṃ aṃguṣṭhābhyāṃ namaḥ।	Touch the tip of your thumb at the base of your index finger.
श्रीं हरिणीं तर्जनीभ्यां स्वाहा ।	śrīṃ hariṇīṃ tarjanībhyāṃ svāhā।	Touch the tip of your thumb to the tip of your index finger.
ह्रीं सुवर्णरजतस्त्रजाम् मध्यमाभ्यां वषट् ।	hrīṃ suvarṇarajatastrajām madhyamābhyāṃ vaṣaṭ ।	Touch the tip of your thumb to the tip of your middle finger.

Sanskrit (Devanagri)	*Sanskrit (IAST)*	*Gesture with both hands*
श्रीं चन्द्रां हिरण्मयीं लक्ष्मीं अनामिकाभ्यां हुं ।	śrīṃ candrāṃ hiraṇmayīṃ lakṣmīṃ anāmikābhyāṃ huṃ ।	Touch the tip of your thumb to the tip of your ring finger.
ऐं जातवेदो कनिष्ठिकाभ्यां वौषट् ।	aiṃ jātavedo kaniṣṭhikābhyāṃ vauṣaṭ ।	Touch the tip of your thumb to the tip of your little finger.
सौः ममावह करतलकरपृष्ठाभ्यां फट् ।	sauṃḥ mamāvaha karatalakarapṛṣṭhābhyāṃ phaṭ ।	Touch the back of your left hand with the back of your right hand and then clap softly.

Now do the final *nyasa* by performing six-limbed mantra *nyasa*. The mudras for this are the same as shown in the chapter on *nyasa*. I am providing them in this chapter once again for your reference.

Six-Limbed Mantra Nyasa (Shadanga Mantra Nyāsa)

Sanskrit (Devanagri)	*Sanskrit (IAST)*	*Posture*	*Description*
ॐ हिरण्यवर्णां हृदयाय नमः ।	oṃ hiraṇyavarṇāṃ hradayāya namaḥ I	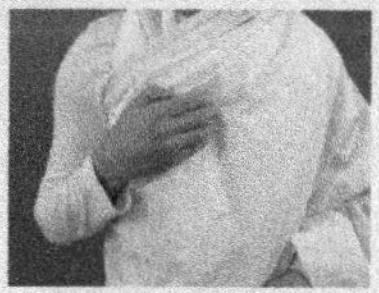	Touch your heart region with your right-hand.
श्रीं हरिणीं शिरसे स्वाहा ।	śrīṃ hariṇīṃ śirase svāhā I		Touch your forehead with your right-hand keeping the index finger away.
ह्रीं सुवर्णरजतस्त्रजाम् शिखायै वषट् ।	hrīṃ suvarṇarajatastrajām śikhāyai vaṣaṭ I		Make a fist with right-hand and extend your thumb. Now touch the crown of your head with your thumb.

Sanskrit (Devanagri)	Sanskrit (IAST)	Posture	Description
श्रीं चन्द्रां हिरण्मयीं लक्ष्मीं कवचाय हुं ।	śrīṃ candrāṃ hiraṇmayīṃ lakṣmīṃ kavacāya huṃ I		Touch your shoulders by crossing your hands. Generally, in Devi Pooja, left-hand is on top of the right and in Devata Pooja, right on top of the left. This is, however, just a guideline and not a rule.
ऐं जातवेदो नेत्रत्रयाय वौषट् ।	aiṃ jātavedo netratrayāya vauṣaṭ I		Spread your right-hand and touch your right eye with your index finger, forehead with the middle finger and left eye with the ring finger simultaneously. Netra traya means the three eyes.
सौः म आवह अस्त्राय फट् ।	sauḥ mamāvaha astrāya phaṭ I		Take the right-hand over your head and then bring it back in front of you to clap softly.

Night 2

Chanting (Japa)		
Mantra Sanskrit (Devanagri)	ॐ आं ह्रीं श्रीं क्लीं ब्लूं सौं रं वं श्रीं । ॐ श्रीं हीं श्रीं नमः । तां म आवह जातवेदो लक्ष्मीमनपगामिनीम् । यस्यां हिरण्यं विन्देयं गामश्वं पुरुषानहम् ॥ नमो श्रीं हीं श्रीं ॐ । आं ह्रीं श्रीं क्लीं ब्लूं सौं रं वं श्रीं ॐ ।।	
Mantra Sanskrit (IAST)	oṃ āṃ hrīṃ śrīṃ klīṃ blūṃ sauṃ raṃ vaṃ śrīṃ I oṃ śrīṃ hīṃ śrīṃ namaḥ I tāṃ ma āvaha jātavedo lakṣmīmanapagāminīm I yasyā hiraṇyaṃ vindeyaṃ gāmaśvam puruṣānaham II namo śrīṃ hrīṃ śrīṃ oṃ I āṃ hrīṃ śrīṃ klīṃ blūṃ sauṃ raṃ vaṃ śrīṃ oṃ II	
Count	Chant this mantra 1000 times.	
Fire offerings (Yajna)		
Mantra	Same as above. Just add 'Om Svaha' (Skt: ॐ स्वाहा, oṃ svāhā) at the end of your mantra. Therefore, say the mantra, say 'Om Svaha' and then make an offering in the fire pit.	
Count	108 times.	
Ingredients for fire-offerings	Ghee	200 grams
	White rice (50 grams)	50 grams
	Havan Samagri	1 packet
	Black sesame seeds	50 grams
	Jaggery	50 grams
	White sandalwood	One small piece

Instructions	Follow the standard procedure of fire offerings as stated in How to Make Fire Offerings (Yajna). Mix white rice, havan samagri, jaggery and black sesame seeds. Put five tablespoons of melted ghee in it. Mix it thoroughly. After you have made 108 offerings (ahuti), offer the last one with the small piece of white sandalwood. Dip it in ghee or put a bit of ghee in it and offer it in the firepit. Conclude by pouring any remaining ghee from the 200 grams you set aside for this yajna. If you feel the fire going off or dousing while you do yajna, feel free to pour more ghee on the fire. Keep the fire alive.
Libations (Tarpana)	
Mantra	Same as the mantra above for chanting. Just add 'tarpyami' (Skt: तर्प्यामि, tarpyāmi) at the end of your mantra.
Instructions	Say the mantra, take a bit of water as per the instructions in step 32 in Essential Steps in the Rites of Invocation (Puruscharana), and add 'tarpyami' in the end when you put water back in the vessel.
Coronation (Marjana or Abhishekam)	
Mantra	Same as the mantra above for chanting. Just add 'marjyami' (Skt: मार्जयामि, mārjayāmi) at the end of your mantra.
Instructions	Say the mantra, take a bit of water as per the instructions in step 33 in Essential Steps in the Rites of Invocation (Puruscharana), and add 'marjyami' in the end when you put water back in the vessel.

Follow the 36 steps of the rites of invocation but please note that vow — step 16 — is to be performed only on the first night. The rest of the steps remain the same. The *Nyasa*, application (*viniyoga*) and mantra will change every night. Mantra has been already specified in the previous table, *viniyoga* and nyasa are as follows.

Application (Viniyoga)

Sanskrit (Devanagri)	*Sanskrit (IAST)*
ॐ अस्य श्री तां म आवह इति श्री सूक्त द्वित्य मंत्रस्य श्री कर्दम चिक्लीत ऋषि, भगवती सर्वकाम प्रदायै देवी, ज्योति शक्ति, श्रीं बीज, कमला महाविद्या, क्लीं उत्कीलन, सर्व मंगल कारिण्यै भगवती लक्ष्मी प्रसाद सिद्धयर्थ द्वितीय मंत्र जपे विनियोगः ।	oṃ asya śrī tāṃ ma āvaha iti śrī sūkta dvitya maṃtrasya śrī kardama ciklīta ṛṣi, bhagavatī sarvakāma pradāyai devī, śrīṃ bīja, jyoti śakti, kamalā mahāvidyā, klīṃ utkīlana, sarva maṃgala kāriṇyai bhagavatī lakṣmī prasāda siddhayartha dvitīya maṃtra jape viniyogaḥ I
Follow the standard procedure of viniyoga by taking a bit of water in your palm (as explained in step 18 in Essential Steps in the Rites of Invocation).	

Perform the *nyasa* as per the tables below, in that order, starting with Nyasa of the Sages (*Rishyadi nyasa*)

Nyasa of the Sages (*Rishyadi Nyasa*)

Sanskrit (Devanagri)	*Sanskrit (IAST)*	*Touch with your right hand your...*
श्री कर्दम चिक्लीत ऋषये नमः सहस्रारे शिरसि ।	śrī kardama ciklīta ṛṣaye namaḥ sahasrāre śirasi I	Crown of the head

Sanskrit (Devanagri)	*Sanskrit (IAST)*	*Touch with your right hand your...*
भगवती सर्वकामप्रदायै देव्यै नमः द्वादशारे हृदि ।	bhagavatī sarvakāmapradāyai devyai namaḥ dvādaśāre hradi I	Heart
ज्योतिशक्तयै नमः दशारे नाभौ ।	jyotiśaktayai namaḥ daśāre nābhau I	Navel
श्रीं बीजाय नमः षडारे योनौ ।	śrīṃ bījāya namaḥ ṣaḍāre yonau I	Groin
भुवनेश्वरी महाविद्यायै नमः षोडशारे कंठे ।	bhuvaneśvarī mahāvidyāyai namaḥ ṣoḍaśāre kaṃṭhe I	Throat
रजोगुणाय नमः अंतरारे मनसि ।	rajoguṇāya namaḥ aṃtarāre manasi I	Heart (again)
श्रोत्र ज्ञानेन्द्रियाय नमः ज्ञानेन्द्रिये ।	śrotra jñānendriyāya namaḥ jñāneindraye I	Ears
वाक् कर्मेन्द्रियाय नमः कर्मेन्द्रिये ।	vāk karmendriyāya namaḥ karmendriye I	Lips
उच्स्वराय नमः कंठमूले ।	ucsvarāya namaḥ kaṃṭhamūle I	Base of your throat (the soft area just below the Adam's apple)
भुतत्वाय नमः चतुरारे गुदे ।	bhutatvāya namaḥ caturāre gude I	Lower back (near your anus but keep your clothes on and just touch your lower back symbolically)
विद्या कलायै नमः करतले ।	vidyā kalāyai namaḥ karatale I	The palm of your left hand

Sanskrit (Devanagri)	*Sanskrit (IAST)*	*Touch with your right hand your...*
क्लीं उत्कीलनाय नमः पादयोः ।	klīṃ utkīlanāya namaḥ pādayoḥ I	Feet
संकोचिनी मुद्रायै नमः सर्वांगे ।	saṃkocinī mudrāyai namaḥ sarvāṃge I	Whole body (Do this by rolling your right-hand over your upper body by bringing it around and then clapping gently)

Now perform the *nyasa* of the hands (*kara nyasa*). The mudras are the same as in step 17 (purification of the hands) of this chapter. You can see the illustrations in the table below; I am providing the description again.

Nyasa of the Hands (*Kara Nyasa*)

Sanskrit (Devanagri)	*Sanskrit (IAST)*	*Gesture with both hands*
ॐ तां म आवह अंगुष्ठाभ्यां नमः ।	oṃ tāṃ ma āvaha aṃguṣṭhābhyāṃ namaḥ I	Touch the tip of your thumb at the base of your index finger.
श्रीं जातवेदो तर्जनीभ्यां स्वाहा ।	śrīṃ jātavedo tarjanībhyāṃ svāhā I	Touch the tip of your thumb to the tip of your index finger.
ह्रीं लक्ष्मीमनपगामिनीम् मध्यमाभ्यां वषट् ।	hrīṃ lakṣmīmanapagāminīm madhyamābhyāṃ vaṣaṭ I	Touch the tip of your thumb to the tip of your middle finger.

Sanskrit (Devanagri)	Sanskrit (IAST)	Gesture with both hands
श्रीं यस्यां हिरण्यं अनामिकाभ्यां हुं ।	śrīṃ yasyāṃ hiraṇyaṃ anāmikābhyāṃ huṃ I	Touch the tip of your thumb to the tip of your ring finger.
ऐं विन्देयं कनिष्ठिकाभ्यां वौषट् ।	aiṃ vindeyaṃ kaniṣṭhikābhyāṃ vauṣaṭ I	Touch the tip of your thumb to the tip of your little finger.
सौः गामश्वं पुरुषानहम् करतलकरपृष्ठाभ्यां फट् ।	sauṃḥ gāmaśvaṃ puruṣānahaṃ karatalakarapṛṣṭhābhyāṃ phaṭ I	Touch the back of your left-hand with the back of your right-hand and then clap softly.

Now do the final *nyasa* by performing six-limbed mantra nyasa. The mudras for this are the same as shown in Night 1. I'm giving the description again.

Six-Limbed Mantra *Nyasa* (*Shadanga* Mantra *Nyāsa*)

Sanskrit (Devanagri)	Sanskrit (IAST)	Description
ॐ तां म आवह हृदयाय नमः ।	oṃ tāṃ ma āvaha hradayāya namaḥ I	Touch your heart region with your right-hand.
श्रीं जातवेदो शिरसे स्वाहा ।	śrīṃ jātavedo śirase svāhā I	Touch your forehead with your right-hand keeping the index finger away.

Sanskrit (Devanagri)	*Sanskrit (IAST)*	*Description*
ह्रीं लक्ष्मीमनपगामिनीम् शिखायै वषट् ।	hrīṃ lakṣmīmanapagāminīm śikhāyai vaṣaṭ ।	Make a fist with right-hand and extend your thumb. Now touch the crown of your head with your thumb.
श्रीं यस्यां हिरण्यं कवचाय हुं ।	śrīṃ yasyāṃ hiraṇyaṃ kavacāya huṃ ।	Touch your shoulders by crossing your hands.
ऐं विन्देयं नेत्रत्रयाय वौषट् ।	aiṃ vindeyaṃ netratrayāya vauṣaṭ ।	Spread your right-hand and touch your right eye with your index finger, forehead with the middle finger and left eye with the ring finger simultaneously.
सौंः गामश्वं पुरुषानहम् अस्त्राय फट् ।	sauṃḥ gāmaśvaṃ puruṣānaham astrāya phaṭ ।	Take the right-hand over your head and then bring it back in front of you to clap softly.

Night 3

Chanting (Japa)	
Mantra Sanskrit (Devanagri)	ॐ आं ह्रीं श्रीं क्लीं ब्लूं सौं रं वं श्रीं ॐ श्रीं ह्रीं श्रीं नमः । अश्वपूर्वां रथमध्यां हस्तिनादप्रबोधिनीम् । श्रियं देवीमुपह्वये श्रीर्मा देवी जुषताम् ॥ नमो श्रीं ह्रीं श्रीं ॐ । ॐ आं ह्रीं श्रीं क्लीं ब्लूं सौं रं वं श्रीं ॐ ।।
Mantra Sanskrit (IAST)	oṃ āṃ hrīṃ śrīṃ klīṃ blūṃ sauṃ raṃ vaṃ śrīṃ oṃ śrīṃ hrīṃ śrīṃ namaḥ I aśvapūrvāṃ rathamadhyāṃ hastinādaprabodhinīm I śriyaṃ devīmupahvaye śrīrmā devī juṣatām II namo śrīṃ hrīṃ śrīṃ oṃ I oṃ āṃ hrīṃ śrīṃ klīṃ blūṃ sauṃ raṃ vaṃ śrīṃ oṃ II
Count	Chant this mantra 1000 times.

Fire offerings (Yajna)		
Mantra	Same as above. Just add '*Om Svaha*' (Skt: ॐ स्वाहा, oṃ svāhā) at the end of your mantra. Therefore, say the mantra, say '*Om Svaha*' and then make an offering in the fire pit.	
Count	Make fire offerings 108 times.	
Ingredients for fire-offerings	Ghee	200 grams
	Almonds (50 grams)	50 grams
	Havan Samagri	1 packet
	White sesame seeds	50 grams
	Red sandalwood	One small piece

Instructions	Follow the standard procedure of fire offerings as stated in *How to Make Fire Offerings (Yajna).* 1. Mix almonds, *havan samagri* and white sesame seeds. 2. Put five tablespoons of melted ghee in it. Mix it thoroughly. 3. After you have made 108 offerings (*ahuti*), offer the last one with the small piece of red sandalwood. Dip it in ghee or put a bit of ghee in it and offer it in the fire pit. 4. Conclude by pouring any remaining ghee from the 200 grams you set aside for this *yajna.* If you feel the fire going off or dousing while you do *yajna*, feel free to pour more ghee on the fire. Keep the fire alive.
Libations (Tarpana)	
Mantra	Same as the mantra above for chanting. Just add '*tarpyami*' (Skt: तर्प्यामि, tarpyāmi) at the end of your mantra.
Instructions	Say the mantra, take a bit of water as per the instructions in step 32 in *Essential Steps in the Rites of Invocation (Puruscharana)*, and add '*tarpyami*' in the end when you put water back in the vessel.
Count	Do libations 11 times.
Coronation (Marjana or Abhishekam)	
Mantra	Same as the mantra above for chanting. Just add '*marjyami*' (Skt: मार्जयामि, mārjayāmi) at the end of your mantra.

Instructions	Say the mantra, take a bit of water as per the instructions in step 33 in Essential Steps in the Rites of Invocation (*Puruscharana*), and add '*marjyami*' in the end when you put water back in the vessel.
Count	Do coronation 11 times.

Follow the 36 steps of the rites of invocation but please note that vow – step 16 is to be performed only on the first night. The rest of the steps remain the same. The *nyasa*, application (*viniyoga*) and mantra will change every night. The mantra has been already specified in the previous table; *viniyoga* and nyasa are as follows.

Application (Viniyoga)

Sanskrit (Devanagri)	*Sanskrit (IAST)*
ॐ अस्य श्री अश्वपूर्वां रथमध्यां इति श्रीसूक्त तृतीय मन्त्रस्य श्री चिक्लीत कर्दम ऋषि, महालक्ष्मी देवता, पद्मावती शक्ति, श्रीं बीज, मातंगी महाविद्या, क्रों उत्कीलन, सर्व मंगल कारिण्यै भगवती लक्ष्मी प्रसाद सिद्धयर्थ तृतीय मंत्र जपे विनियोगः ।	oṃ asya śrī aśvapūrvāṃ rathamadhyāṃ iti śrīsūkta tṛtīya mantrasya śrī ciklīta kardama ṛṣi, mahālakṣmī devatā, padmāvatī śakti, śrīṃ bīja, mātaṃgī mahāvidyā, kroṃ utkīlana, sarva maṃgala kāriṇyai bhagavatī lakṣmī prasāda siddhayartha tṛtīya maṃtra jape viniyogaḥ ।

Follow the standard procedure of *viniyoga* by taking a bit of water in your palm (as explained in step 18 in *Essential Steps in the Rites of Invocation*).

Perform the *nyasa* as per the tables below, in that order, starting with *Nyasa* of the Sages (*Rishyadi Nyasa*)

Nyasa of the Sages (Rishyadi Nyasa)

Sanskrit (Devanagri)	*Sanskrit (IAST)*	*Touch with your right-hand your...*
श्री चिक्लीत कर्दम ऋषयै नमः सहस्त्रारे शिरसि ।	śrī ciklīta kardama ṛṣayai namaḥ sahastrāre śirasi ।	Crown of the head
महालक्ष्मी देवतायै नमः दद्वादशारे हृदि ।	mahālakṣmī devatāyai namaḥ dadvādaśāre hradi ।	Heart
पद्मावती शक्त्यै नमः दशारे नाभौ ।	padmāvatī śaktyai namaḥ daśāre nābhau ।	Navel
श्रीं बीजाय नमः षडारे योनौ ।	śrīṃ bījāya namaḥ ṣaḍāre yonau ।	Groin
मातंगी महाविद्यायै नमः षोडशारे कण्ठे ।	mātaṃgī mahāvidyāyai namaḥ ṣoḍaśāre kaṇṭhe ।	Throat
रजोगुणाय नमः अंतरारे मनसि ।	rajoguṇāya namaḥ aṃtarāre manasi ।	Heart (again)
स्वः ज्ञानेन्द्रायाय नमः ज्ञानेन्द्रिये ।	svaḥ jñāneindrāyāya namaḥ jñānei ndraye ।	Ears
वाक् कर्मेन्द्रियाय नमः कर्मेन्द्रिये ।	vāk karmendriyāya namaḥ karmendriye ।	Lips
मध्यम स्वराय नमः कंठमूले ।	madhyama svarāya namaḥ kaṃṭhamūle ।	Base of your throat (the soft area just below the Adam's apple)

Sanskrit (Devanagri)	*Sanskrit (IAST)*	*Touch with your right-hand your...*
आकाश तत्वाय नमः चतुरारे गुदे ।	ākāśa tatvāya namaḥ caturāre gude I	Lower back (near your anus but keep your clothes on and just touch your lower back symbolically)
शांति कलायै नमः करतले ।	śāṃti kalāyai namaḥ karatale I	The palm of your left hand
क्रों उत्किलनाय नमः पादयोः ।	kroṃ utkilanāya namaḥ pādayoḥ I	Feet
योनि मुद्रायै नमः सर्वांगे ।	yoni mudrāyai namaḥ sarvāṃge I	Whole body (do this by rolling your right-hand over your upper body by bringing it around and then clapping gently)

Now perform *nyasa* of the hands (*kara nyasa*). The mudras are the same as in step 17 (purification of the hands) of this chapter. You can see the illustrations in that table; I am providing the description again.

Nyasa of the Hands (_Kara Nyasa_)

Sanskrit (Devanagri)	*Sanskrit (IAST)*	*Gesture with both hands*
ॐ अश्वपूर्वां अंगुष्ठाभ्यां नमः ।	oṃ aśvapūrvāṃ aṃguṣṭhābhyāṃ namaḥ I	Touch the tip of your thumb at the base of your index finger.
रथमध्यां तर्जनीभ्याम् स्वाहा ।	rathamadhyāṃ tarjanībhyām svāhā I	Touch the tip of your thumb to the tip of your index finger.

Sanskrit (Devanagri)	Sanskrit (IAST)	Gesture with both hands
हस्तिनादप्रबोधिनीम् मध्यमाभ्यां वषट् ।	hastinādaprabodhinīm madhyamābhyāṃ vaṣaṭ ।	Touch the tip of your thumb to the tip of your middle finger.
श्रियं अनामिकाभ्यां हुं ।	śriyaṃ anāmikābhyāṃ huṃ ।	Touch the tip of your thumb to the tip of your ring finger.
देविमुपह्वये नेत्रत्रयाय वौषट् ।	devimupahvaye netratrayāya vauṣaṭ ।	Touch the tip of your thumb to the tip of your little finger.
श्रीर्मा देवि जुषताम् करतलकरपृष्ठ फट् ।	śrīrmā devi juṣatām karatalakarapṛṣṭha phaṭ ।	Touch the back of your left-hand with the back of your right-hand and then clap softly.

Now do the final *nyasa* by performing six-limbed mantra *nyasa*. The mudras for this are the same as shown in Night 1. I'm giving the description again.

Six-Limbed Mantra *Nyasa* (*Shadanga* Mantra *Nyāsa*)

Sanskrit (Devanagri)	Sanskrit (IAST)	Description
ॐ अश्वपूर्वां हृदयाय नमः ।	oṃ aśvapūrvāṃ hradayāya namaḥ ।	Touch your heart region with your right-hand.
ॐ रथमध्यां शिरसे स्वाहा ।	oṃ rathamadhyāṃ śirase svāhā ।	Touch your forehead with your right-hand keeping the index finger away.

Sanskrit (Devanagri)	*Sanskrit (IAST)*	*Description*
हस्तिनादप्रबोधिनीम् शिखायै वषट् ।	hastinādaprabodhinīm śikhāyai vaṣaṭ ।	Make a fist with right-hand and extend your thumb. Now touch the crown of your head with your thumb.
श्रियं कवचाय हुं ।	śriyaṃ kavacāya huṃ ।	Touch your shoulders by crossing your hands.
देविमुपह्वये नेत्रत्रयाय वौषट् ।	devimupahvaye netratrayāya vauṣaṭ ।	Spread your right-hand and touch your right eye with your index finger, forehead with the middle finger and left eye with the ring finger simultaneously.
श्रीर्मा देविजूषताम् अस्त्राय फट् ।	śrīrmā devijūṣatām astrāya phaṭ ।	Take the right-hand over your head and then bring it back in front of you to clap softly.

Night 4

Chanting (Japa)	
Mantra Sanskrit (Devanagri)	ॐ आं ह्रीं श्रीं क्लीं ब्लूं सौं रं वं श्रीं ॐ श्रीं ह्रीं श्रीं नमः । कांसोस्मितां हिरण्यप्राकारामार्द्रां ज्वलन्तीं तृप्तां तर्पयन्तीम् । पद्मे स्थितां पद्मवर्णां तामिहोपह्वये श्रियम् ॥ नमो श्रीं ह्रीं श्रीं ॐ । ॐ आं ह्रीं श्रीं क्लीं ब्लूं सौं रं वं श्रीं ॐ ॥
Mantra Sanskrit (IAST)	oṃ āṃ hrīṃ śrīṃ klīṃ blūṃ sauṃ raṃ vaṃ śrīṃ oṃ śrīṃ hrīṃ śrīṃ namaḥ । kāṃsosmitāṃ hiraṇyaprākārāmārdrāṃ jvalantīṃ tṛptāṃ tarpayantīm । padme sthitāṃ padmavarṇāṃ tāmihopahvaye śriyam ॥ namo śrīṃ hrīṃ śrīṃ oṃ । oṃ āṃ hrīṃ śrīṃ klīṃ blūṃ sauṃ raṃ vaṃ śrīṃ oṃ ॥
Count	Chant this mantra 1000 times.
Fire offerings (Yajna)	
Mantra	Same as above. Just add '*Om Svaha*' (ॐ स्वाहा, oṃ svāhā) at the end of your mantra. Therefore, say the mantra, say '*Om Svaha*' and then make an offering in the fire pit.
Count	Make fire offerings 108 times.

Ingredients for fire-offerings	Ghee	200 grams
	Lotus seeds (*kamal gatta*)	100 count
	Havan samagri	1 packet
	Black sesame seeds	50 grams
	White sandalwood	One small piece
Instructions	Follow the standard procedure of fire offerings as stated in *How to Make Fire Offerings (Yajna).* 1. Mix lotus seeds, *havan samagri* and black sesame seeds. 2. Put five tablespoons of melted ghee in it. Mix it thoroughly. 3. After you have made 108 offerings (*ahuti*), offer the last one with the small piece of white sandalwood. Dip it in ghee or put a bit of ghee in it and offer it in the firepit. 4. Conclude by pouring any remaining ghee from the 200 grams you set aside for this *yajna.* If you feel the fire going off or dousing while you do *yajna*, feel free to pour more ghee on the fire. Keep the fire alive.	
Libations (Tarpana)		
Mantra	Same as the mantra above for chanting. Just add '*tarpyami*' (तर्प्यामि, tarpyāmi) at the end of your mantra.	
Instructions	Say the mantra, take a bit of water as per the instructions in step 32 in *Essential Steps in the Rites of Invocation (Puruscharana)*, and add '*tarpyami*' in the end when you put water back in the vessel.	
Count	Do libations 11 times.	

Coronation (*Marjana* or *Abhishekam*)

Mantra	Same as the mantra above for chanting. Just add '*marjyami*' (Skt: मार्जयामि, mārjayāmi) at the end of your mantra.
Instructions	Say the mantra, take a bit of water as per the instructions in step 33 in *Essential Steps in the Rites of Invocation (Puruscharana)*, and add '*marjyami*' in the end when you put water back in the vessel.
Count	Do coronation 11 times.

Follow the 36 steps of the rites of invocation but please note that vow — step 16 — is to be performed only on the first night. The rest of the steps remain the same. The *nyasa*, application (*viniyoga*) and mantra will change every night. The mantra has been already specified in the previous table; *viniyoga* and *nyasa* are as follows.

Application (*Viniyoga*)

Sanskrit (Devanagri)	*Sanskrit (IAST)*
ॐ अस्य श्री कांसोस्मिता इति श्रीसूक्त चतुर्थ मंत्रस्य श्री कर्दम चिक्लीत ऋषि, भगवती सर्व काम प्रदायै देवी, ह्रां बीज, चूडामणि शक्ति, महा शक्त्यै महाविद्या, ह्रां बीज, सर्व मंगल कारिण्यै भगवती लक्ष्मी प्रसाद सिद्धयर्थ चतुर्थ मंत्र जपे विनियोगः ।	oṃ asya śrī kāṃsosmitā iti śrīsūkta caturtha maṃtrasya śrī kardama ciklīta ṛṣi, bhagavatī sarva kāma pradāyai devī, hrāṃ bīja, cūḍāmaṇi śakti, mahā śaktyai mahāvidyā, hrāṃ bīja, sarva maṃgala kāriṇyai bhagavatī lakṣmī prasāda siddhayartha caturtha maṃtra jape viniyogaḥ ।

Follow the standard procedure of *viniyoga* by taking a bit of water in your palm (as explained in step 18 in *Essential Steps in the Rites of Invocation*).

Perform the *nyasa* as per the tables below, in that order, starting with *Nyasa* of the Sages (*Rishyadi nyasa*).

Nyasa of the Sages (_Rishyadi Nyasa_)

Sanskrit (Devanagri)	*Sanskrit (IAST)*	*Touch with your right-hand your...*
श्री कर्दम चिक्लीत ऋषये नमः सहस्त्रारे शिरसि ।	śrī kardama ciklīta ṛṣaye namaḥ sahastrāre śirasi ।	Crown of the head
भगवती सर्वकामप्रदायै देव्यै नमः द्वादशारे हृदि ।	bhagavatī sarvakāmapradāyai devyai namaḥ dvādaśāre hradi ।	Heart
चूडामणि शक्त्यै नमः दशारे नाभौ ।	cūḍāmaṇi śaktyai namaḥ daśāre nābhau ।	Navel
ह्रां बीजाय नमः षडारे योनौ ।	hrāṃ bījāya namaḥ ṣaḍāre yonau ।	Groin
महाशक्तयै महाविद्यायै नमः अंतरारे कंठे ।	mahāśaktayai mahāvidyāyai namaḥ aṃtarāre kaṃṭhe ।	Throat
सत्वगुणाय नमः अंतरारे मनसि ।	satvaguṇāya namaḥ aṃtarāre manasi ।	Heart (again)
नासिका ज्ञानेन्द्रियाय नमः ज्ञानेन्द्रिये ।	nāsikā jñāneindrāyāya namaḥ jñāneindraye ।	Nose
कर कर्मेन्द्रियाय नमः कर्मेन्द्रिये ।	kara karmendriyāya namaḥ karmendriye ।	Lips
मध्यम स्वराय नमः कंठमूले ।	madhyama svarāya namaḥ kaṃṭhamūle ।	Base of your throat (the soft area just below the Adam's apple)

Sanskrit (Devanagri)	*Sanskrit (IAST)*	*Touch with your right-hand your...*
भू तत्वाय नमः चतुरारे गुदे ।	bhū tatvāya namaḥ caturāre gude I	Lower back (near your anus but keep your clothes on and just touch your lower back symbolically)
प्रवृत्तिं कलायै नमः करतले ।	pravrṛttiṃ kalāyai namaḥ karatale I	The palm of your left-hand
श्रीं ह्रीं उत्कीलनाय नमः पादयोः ।	śrīṃ hrīṃ utkīlanāya namaḥ pādayoḥ I	Feet
मोहिनी मुद्रायै नमः सर्वांगे ।	mohinī mudrāyai namaḥ sarvāṃge I	Whole body (do this by rolling your right-hand over your upper body by bringing it around and then clapping gently)

Now perform *nyasa* of the hands (*kara nyasa*). The mudras are the same as in step 17 (purification of the hands) of this chapter. You can see the illustrations in that table. I am providing the description again.

Nyasa of the Hands (*Kara Nyasa*)

Sanskrit (Devanagri)	*Sanskrit (IAST)*	*Gesture with both hands*
ॐ कांसोस्मितां अंगुष्ठाभ्यां नमः ।	oṃ kāṃsosmitāṃ aṃguṣṭhābhyāṃ namaḥ I	Touch the tip of your thumb at the base of your index finger.

Sanskrit (Devanagri)	*Sanskrit (IAST)*	*Gesture with both hands*
हिरण्यप्राकारामार्द्रां तर्जनीभ्याम् स्वाहा ।	hiraṇyaprākārāmārdrāṃ tarjanībhyām svāhā I	Touch the tip of your thumb to the tip of your index finger.
ज्वलन्ती तृप्तां मध्यमाभ्यां वषट् ।	jvalantī tṛptāṃ madhyamābhyāṃ vaṣaṭ I	Touch the tip of your thumb to the tip of your middle finger.
तर्पयन्तीम् अनामिकाभ्यां हुं ।	tarpayantīm anāmikābhyāṃ huṃ I	Touch the tip of your thumb to the tip of your ring finger.
पद्मे स्थितां पद्मवर्णां कनिष्ठिकाभ्यां वौषट् ।	padme sthitāṃ padmavarṇāṃ kaniṣṭhikābhyāṃ vauṣaṭ I	Touch the tip of your thumb to the tip of your little finger.
तामिहोपह्वये श्रियम् करतलकरपृष्ठाभ्यां फट् ।	tāmihopahvaye śriyam karatalakarapṛṣṭhābhyāṃ phaṭ I	Touch the back of your left hand with the back of your right-hand and then clap softly.

Now do the final *nyasa* by performing six-limbed mantra *nyasa.* The mudras for this are the same as shown in Night 1. I'm giving the description again.

Six-Limbed Mantra *Nyasa* (*Shadanga* Mantra *Nyāsa*)

Sanskrit (Devanagri)	*Sanskrit (IAST)*	*Description*
ॐ कांसोस्मितां हृदयाय नमः ।	oṃ kāṃsosmitāṃ hradayāya namaḥ I	Touch your heart region with your right-hand.
हिरण्यप्राकारामार्द्रां शिरसे स्वाहा ।	hiraṇyaprākārā-mārdrāṃ śirase svāhā I	Touch your forehead with your right-hand keeping the index finger away.
ज्वलन्ती तृप्तां शिखायै वषट् ।	jvalantī tṛptāṃ śikhāyai vaṣaṭ I	Make a fist with right-hand and extend your thumb. Now touch the crown of your head with your thumb.
तर्पयन्तीम् कवचाय हुं ।	tarpayantīm kavacāya huṃ I	Touch your shoulders by crossing your hands.
पद्मे स्थितां पद्मवर्णां नेत्रत्रयाय वौषट् ।	padme sthitāṃ padmavarṇāṃ netratrayāya vauṣaṭ I	Spread your right-hand and touch your right eye with your index finger, forehead with the middle finger and left eye with the ring finger simultaneously.
तामिहोपह्वये श्रियम् अस्त्राय फट् ।	tāmihopahvaye śriyam astrāya phaṭ I	Take the right-hand over your head and then bring it back in front of you to clap softly.

Night 5

Chanting (Japa)	
Mantra Sanskrit (Devanagri)	ॐ आं ह्रीं श्रीं क्लीं ब्लूं सौं रं वं श्रीं ॐ श्रीं ह्रीं श्रीं नमः । चन्द्रां प्रभासां यशसा ज्वलन्तीं श्रियं लोके देवजुष्टामुदाराम् । तां पद्मिनीमीं शरणमहं प्रपद्ये'लक्ष्मीर्मे नश्यतां त्वां वृणे ॥ नमो श्रीं ह्रीं श्रीं ॐ । ॐ आं ह्रीं श्रीं क्लीं ब्लूं सौं रं वं श्रीं ॐ ।।
Mantra Sanskrit (IAST)	oṃ āṃ hrīṃ śrīṃ klīṃ blūṃ sauṃ raṃ vaṃ śrīṃ oṃ śrīṃ hrīṃ śrīṃ namaḥ । candrāṃ prabhāsāṃ yaśasā jvalantīṃ śriyaṃ loke devajuṣṭāmudārām । tāṃ padminīmīṃ śaraṇamahaṃ prapadye'lakṣmīrme naśyatāṃ tvāṃ vṛṇe ॥ namo śrīṃ hrīṃ śrīṃ oṃ । oṃ āṃ hrīṃ śrīṃ klīṃ blūṃ sauṃ raṃ vaṃ śrīṃ oṃ ।।
Count	Chant this mantra 1000 times.

Fire offerings (Yajna)		
Mantra	Same as above. Just add '*Om Svaha*' (ॐ स्वाहा, oṃ svāhā) at the end of your mantra. Therefore, say the mantra, say '*Om Svaha*' and then make an offering in the fire pit.	
Count	Make fire offerings 108 times.	
Ingredients for fire-offerings	Ghee	200 grams
	Grated dry coconut	100 grams

	Havan samagri	1 packet
	White sesame seeds	50 grams
	Red sandalwood	One small piece
Instructions	Follow the standard procedure of fire offerings as stated in *How to Make Fire Offerings (Yajna).* Mix grated dry coconut, *havan samagri* and sesame seeds. Put five tablespoons of melted ghee in it. Mix it thoroughly. After you have made 108 offerings (*ahuti*), offer the last one with the small piece of red sandalwood. Dip it in ghee and offer it in the fire pit. Conclude by pouring any remaining ghee from the 200 grams you set aside for this *yajna.* If you feel the fire going off or dousing while you do yajna, feel free to pour more ghee on the fire. Keep the fire alive.	

Libations (Tarpana)	
Mantra	Same as the mantra above for chanting. Just add '*tarpyami*' (तर्प्यामि, tarpyāmi) at the end of your mantra.
Instructions	Say the mantra, take a bit of water as per the instructions in step 32 in *Essential Steps in the Rites of Invocation (Puruscharana),* and add '*tarpyami*' in the end when you put water back in the vessel.
Count	Do libations 11 times.

Coronation (Marjana or Abhishekam)	
Mantra	Same as the mantra above for chanting. Just add '*marjyami*' (Skt: मार्जयामि, mārjayāmi) at the end of your mantra.
Instructions	Say the mantra, take a bit of water as per the instructions in step 33 in *Essential Steps in the Rites of Invocation (Puruscharana)*, and add 'marjyami' in the end when you put water back in the vessel.
Count	Do coronation 11 times.

Follow the 36 steps of the rites of invocation but please note that vow — step 16 — is to be performed only on the first night. The rest of the steps remain the same. The *nyasa*, application (*viniyoga*) and mantra will change every night. The mantra has been already specified in the previous table, *viniyoga* and *nyasa* are as follows.

Application (*Viniyoga*)

Sanskrit (Devanagri)	*Sanskrit (IAST)*
ॐ अस्य श्री चन्द्रां प्रभासां यशसा इति श्रीसूक्तपंचम मंत्रस्यश्री असित ऋषि, विष्णु देवता, वं बीज, माया शक्ति, कुमारी महाविद्या, ब्लौं उत्कीलन, सर्व मंगल कारिण्यै भगवती लक्ष्मी प्रसाद सिद्धयर्थ पंचम मंत्र जपे विनियोगः।	oṃ asya śrī candrāṃ prabhāsāṃ yaśasā iti śrīsūktapaṃcama maṃtrasyaśrī asita ṛṣi, viṣṇu devatā, vaṃ bīja, māyā śakti, kumārī mahāvidyā, blauṃ utkīlana, sarva maṃgala kāriṇyai bhagavatī lakṣmī prasāda siddhayartha paṃcama maṃtra jape viniyogaḥ।
Follow the standard procedure of *viniyoga* by taking a bit of water in your palm (as explained in step 18 in *Essential Steps in the Rites of Invocation*).	

Perform the *nyasa* as per the tables below, in that order, starting with *Nyasa* of the Sages (*Rishyadi nyasa*).

Nyasa of the Sages (Rishyadi Nyasa)

Sanskrit (Devanagri)	*Sanskrit (IAST)*	*Touch with your right-hand your...*
श्री असित ऋषये नमः सहस्त्रारे शिरसि ।	śrī asita ṛṣaye namaḥ sahastrāre śirasi ।	Crown of the head
श्री विष्णु देवताय नमः द्वादशारे ह्रदि ।	śrī viṣṇu devatāya namaḥ dvādaśāre hradi ।	Heart
माया शक्त्यै नमः दशारे नाभौ ।	māyā śaktyai namaḥ daśāre nābhau ।	Navel
वं बीजाय नमः षडारे योनौ ।	vaṃ bījāya namaḥ ṣaḍāre yonau ।	Groin
कुमारी महाविद्यायै नमः षोडशारे कंठे ।	kumārī mahāvidyāyai namaḥ ṣoḍaśāre kaṃṭhe ।	Throat
रजोगुणाय नमः अंतरारे मनसि।	rajoguṇāya namaḥ aṃtarāre manasi।	Heart (again)
श्रोत्र ज्ञानेन्द्रिय नमः ज्ञानेन्द्रिये ।	śrotra jñānenidraya namaḥ jñāneindraye ।	Ears
वाक् कर्मेन्द्रियाय नमः कर्मेन्द्रिये ।	vāk karmendriyāya namaḥ karmendriye ।	Lips
सौम्य स्वराय नमः कंठमूले ।	saumya svarāya namaḥ kaṃṭhamūle ।	Base of your throat (the soft area just below the Adam's apple)
आकाश तत्वाय नमः चतुरारे गुदे ।	ākāśa tatvāya namaḥ caturāre gude ।	Lower back (near your anus but keep your clothes on and just touch your lower back symbolically)

Sanskrit (Devanagri)	*Sanskrit (IAST)*	*Touch with your right-hand your...*
विघा कलायै नमः करतले ।	vighā kalāyai namaḥ karatale I	The palm of your left hand
ब्लौं उत्किलनाय नमः पादयोः ।	blauṃ utkilanāya namaḥ pādayoḥ I	Feet
द्राविणी मुद्रायै नमः सर्वांगे ।	drāviṇī mudrāyai namaḥ sarvāṃge I	Whole body (do this by rolling your right hand over your upper body by bringing it around and then clapping gently)

Now perform *nyasa* of the hands (*kara nyasa*). The mudras are the same as in step 17 (purification of the hands) of this chapter. You can see the illustrations in that table. I am providing the description again.

Nyasa of the Hands (Kara Nyasa)

Sanskrit (Devanagri)	*Sanskrit (IAST)*	*Gesture with both hands*
ॐ चन्द्रां प्रभासां अंगुष्ठाभ्यां नमः ।	oṃ candrāṃ prabhāsāṃ aṃguṣṭhābhyāṃ namaḥ I	Touch the tip of your thumb at the base of your index finger.
यशसा ज्वलन्तीं तर्जनीभ्याम् स्वाहा ।	yaśasā jvalantīṃ tarjanībhyām svāhā I	Touch the tip of your thumb to the tip of your index finger.

Sanskrit (Devanagri)	*Sanskrit (IAST)*	*Gesture with both hands*
श्रियं लोके मध्यमाभ्यां वषट् ।	śriyaṃ loke madhyamābhyāṃ vaṣaṭ I	Touch the tip of your thumb to the tip of your middle finger.
देवी जुष्टामुदाराम् अनामिकाभ्यां हुं ।	devī juṣṭāmudārām anāmikābhyāṃ huṃ I	Touch the tip of your thumb to the tip of your ring finger.
तां पद्मनेमिं शरणम् प्रपद्दे कनिष्ठिकाभ्यां वौषट् ।	tāṃ padmanemiṃ śaraṇam prapadde kaniṣṭhikābhyāṃ vauṣaṭ I	Touch the tip of your thumb to the tip of your little finger.
अलक्ष्मीर्मे नश्यतां त्वां वृणे करतलकरपृष्ठाभ्यां फट् ।	alakṣmīrme naśyatāṃ tvāṃ vṛṇe karatalakara-pṛṣṭhābhyāṃ phaṭ I	Touch the back of your left-hand with the back of your right-hand and then clap softly.

Now do the final *nyasa* by performing six-limbed mantra *nyasa*. The mudras for this are the same as shown in Night 1. I'm giving the description again.

Six-Limbed Mantra *Nyasa* (*Shadanga* Mantra *Nyāsa*)

Sanskrit (Devanagri)	*Sanskrit (IAST)*	*Description*
ॐ चन्द्रां प्रभासां हृदयाय नमः ।	oṃ candrāṃ prabhāsāṃ hradayāya namaḥ I	Touch your heart region with your right-hand.

Sanskrit (Devanagri)	*Sanskrit (IAST)*	*Description*
यशसा ज्वलन्तीं शिरसे स्वाहा ।	yaśasā jvalantīṃ śirase svāhā I	Touch your forehead with your right-hand keeping the index finger away.
श्रियं लोके शिखायै वषट् ।	śriyaṃ loke śikhāyai vaṣaṭ I	Make a fist with right-hand and extend your thumb. Now touch the crown of your head with your thumb.
देवी जुष्टामुदाराम् कवचाय हुं ।	devī juṣṭāmudārām kavacāya huṃ I	Touch your shoulders by crossing your hands.
तां पद्मनेमिं शरणम् प्रपद्दे नेत्रत्रयाय वौषट् ।	tāṃ padmanemiṃ śaraṇam prapadde netratrayāya vauṣaṭ I	Spread your right-hand and touch your right eye with your index finger, forehead with the middle finger and left eye with the ring finger simultaneously.
अलक्ष्मीर्मे नश्यतां त्वां वृणे अस्त्राय फट् ।	alakṣmīrme naśyatāṃ tvāṃ vṛṇe astrāya phaṭ I	Take the right-hand over your head and then bring it back in front of you to clap softly.

Night 6

Chanting (Japa)		
Mantra Sanskrit (Devanagri)	ॐ आं ह्रीं श्रीं क्लीं ब्लूं सौं रं वं श्रीं ॐ श्रीं ह्रीं श्रीं नमः । आदित्यवर्णे तपसो'धिजातो वनस्पतिस्तव वृक्षो'थ बिल्वः । तस्य फलानि तपसानुदन्तु मायान्तरायाश्च बाह्या अलक्ष्मीः ॥ नमो श्रीं ह्रीं श्रीं ॐ । ॐ आं ह्रीं श्रीं क्लीं ब्लूं सौं रं वं श्रीं ॐ ॥	
Mantra Sanskrit (IAST)	oṃ āṃ hrīṃ śrīṃ klīṃ blūṃ sauṃ raṃ vaṃ śrīṃ oṃ śrīṃ hrīṃ śrīṃ namaḥ । ādityavarṇe tapaso'dhijāto vanaspatistava vṛkṣo'tha bilvaḥ । tasya phalāni tapasānudantu māyāntarāyāśca bāhyā alakṣmīḥ ॥ namo śrīṃ hrīṃ śrīṃ oṃ । oṃ āṃ hrīṃ śrīṃ klīṃ blūṃ sauṃ raṃ vaṃ śrīṃ oṃ ॥	
Count	Chant this mantra 1000 times.	
Fire offerings (Yajna)		
Mantra	Same as above. Just add '*Om Svaha*' (ॐ स्वाहा, oṃ svāhā) at the end of your mantra. Therefore, say the mantra, say '*Om Svaha*' and then make an offering in the fire pit.	
Count	Make fire offerings 108 times.	
Ingredients for fire-offerings	Ghee	200 grams
	Raisins	50 grams
	Almonds	50 grams

	Havan samagri	1 packet
	Black sesame seeds	50 grams
	White sandalwood	One small piece
	Follow the standard procedure of fire offerings as stated in *How to Make Fire Offerings (Yajna).*	
Instructions	1. Mix raisins, almonds, *havan samagri* and sesame seeds. 2. Put five tablespoons of melted ghee in it. Mix it thoroughly. 3. After you have made 108 offerings (*ahuti*), offer the last one with the small piece of white sandalwood. Dip it in ghee or put a bit of ghee in it and offer it in the fire pit. 4. Conclude by pouring any remaining ghee from the 200 grams you set aside for this *yajna.*	
	If you feel the fire going off or dousing while you do *yajna*, feel free to pour more ghee on the fire. Keep the fire alive.	
Libations (Tarpana)		
Mantra	Same as the mantra above for chanting. Just add '*tarpyami*' (तर्प्यामि, tarpyāmi) at the end of your mantra.	
Instructions	Say the mantra, take a bit of water as per the instructions in step 32 in *Essential Steps in the Rites of Invocation (Puruscharana)*, and add '*tarpyami*' in the end when you put water back in the vessel.	
Count	Do libations 11 times.	

Coronation (*Marjana* or *Abhishekam*)	
Mantra	Same as the mantra above for chanting. Just add '*marjyami*' (Skt: मार्जयामि, mārjayāmi) at the end of your mantra.
Instructions	Say the mantra, take a bit of water as per the instructions in step 33 in *Essential Steps in the Rites of Invocation (Puruscharana)*, and add '*marjyami*' in the end when you put water back in the vessel.
Count	Do coronation 11 times.

Follow the 36 steps of the rites of invocation but please note that vow — step 16 — is to be performed only on the first night. The rest of the steps remain the same. The *nyasa*, application (*viniyoga*) and mantra will change every night. The mantra has been already specified in the previous table; *viniyoga* and *nyasa* are as follows.

Application (*Viniyoga*)

Sanskrit (Devanagri)	*Sanskrit (IAST)*
ॐ अस्य श्री आदित्यवर्णे तपसो'धिजातो इति श्री सूक्त षष्ठ मन्त्रस्य ब्रह्माऋषि, सूर्यो देवता, ॐ बीज, तेजसः शक्ति, मातंगी महाविद्या, ह्रीं उत्कीलन, सर्व मंगल कारिण्यै भगवती लक्ष्मी प्रसाद सिद्धयर्थ षष्ठ मंत्र जपे विनियोगः ।	oṃ asya śrī ādityavarṇe tapaso'dhijāto iti śrī sūkta ṣaṣṭha mantrasya brahmārṣi, sūryo devata, oṃ bīja, tejasaḥ śakti, mātaṃgī mahāvidyā, hrīṃ utkīlana, sarva maṃgala kāriṇyai bhagavatī lakṣmī prasāda siddhayartha ṣaṣṭha maṃtra jape viniyogaḥ ।
Follow the standard procedure of *viniyoga* by taking a bit of water in your palm (as explained in step 18 in *Essential Steps in the Rites of Invocation*).	

Perform the *nyasa* as per the tables below, in that order, starting with *Nyasa* of the Sages (*Rishyadi Nyasa*)

Nyasa of the Sages (Rishyadi Nyasa)

Sanskrit (Devanagri)	*Sanskrit (IAST)*	*Touch with your right-hand your...*
ॐ ब्रह्मा ऋषये नमः सहस्त्रारे शिरसि ।	oṃ brahmā ṛṣaye namaḥ sahastrāre śirasi I	Crown of the head
श्री सूर्योदेवताय नमः द्वादशारे हृदि ।	śrī sūryodevatāya namaḥ dvādaśāre hradi I	Heart
आं बीजाय नमः षडारे योनौ ।	āṃ bījāya namaḥ ṣaḍāre yonau I	Groin
तेजसः शक्त्यै नमः दशारे नाभौ ।	tejasaḥ śaktyai namaḥ daśāre nābhau I	Navel
मातंगी महाविद्यायै नमः षोडशारे कंठे ।	mātaṃgī mahāvidyāyai namaḥ ṣoḍaśāre kaṃṭhe I	Throat
तमोगुणाय नमः अंतरारे मनसि ।	tamoguṇāya namaḥ aṃtarāre manasi I	Heart (again)
चक्षु ज्ञानेन्द्रिय नमः ज्ञानेन्द्रिये ।	cakṣu jñānenidraya namaḥ jñāneindraye I	Ears

Sanskrit (Devanagri)	*Sanskrit (IAST)*	*Touch with your right-hand your...*
कर कर्मेन्द्रियाय नमः कर्मेन्द्रिये ।	kara karmendriyāya namaḥ karmendriye I	Lips
मृदुस्वराय नमः कंठमूले ।	mṛdusvarāya namaḥ kaṃṭhamūle I	Base of your throat (the soft area just below the Adam's apple)
खंस्तत्वायै नमः चतुरारे गुदे ।	khaṃstatvāyai namaḥ caturāre gude I	Lower back (near your anus but keep your clothes on and just touch your lower back symbolically)
शांतिकलायै नमः करतले ।	śāṃtikalāyai namaḥ karatale I	The palm of your left-hand
ह्रीं उत्किलनाय नमः पादयोः ।	hrīṃ utkilanāya namaḥ pādayoḥ I	Feet
सम्पुट मुद्रायै नमः सर्वांगे ।	sampuṭa mudrāyai namaḥ sarvāṃge I	Whole body (do this by rolling your right-hand over your upper body by bringing it around and then clapping gently)

Now perform *nyasa* of the hands (*kara nyasa*). The mudras are the same as in step 17 (purification of the hands) of this chapter. You can see the illustrations in that table. I am providing the description again.

Nyasa of the Hands (*Kara Nyasa*)

Sanskrit (Devanagri)	*Sanskrit (IAST)*	*Gesture with both hands*
ॐ आदित्यवर्णे तपसोऽधिजातो अंगुष्ठाभ्यां नमः ।	oṃ ādityavarṇe tapaso'dhijāto aṃguṣṭhābhyāṃ namaḥ I	Touch the tip of your thumb at the base of your index finger.
वनस्पतिस्तव वृक्षोथ तर्जनीभ्याम् स्वाहा ।	vanaspatistava vṛkṣotha tarjanībhyām svāhā I	Touch the tip of your thumb to the tip of your index finger.
बिल्व तस्य फलानि मध्यमाभ्यां वषट् ।	bilva tasya phalāni madhyamābhyāṃ vaṣaṭ I	Touch the tip of your thumb to the tip of your middle finger.
तपसा नुदन्तु अनामिकाभ्यां हुं ।	tapasā nudantu anāmikābhyāṃ huṃ I	Touch the tip of your thumb to the tip of your ring finger.
मायान्तरायाश्च कनिष्ठिकाभ्यां वौषट् ।	māyāntarāyāśca kaniṣṭhikābhyāṃ vauṣaṭ I	Touch the tip of your thumb to the tip of your little finger.
बाह्यालक्ष्मी करतलकरपृष्ठाभ्यां फट् ।	bāhrālakṣmī karatalakara-pṛṣṭhābhyāṃ phaṭ I	Touch the back of your left-hand with the back of your right-hand and then clap softly.

Now do the final *nyasa* by performing six-limbed mantra *nyasa*. The mudras for this are the same as shown in Night 1. I'm giving the description again.

Six-Limbed Mantra *Nyasa* (*Shadanga* Mantra *Nyāsa*)

Sanskrit (Devanagri)	*Sanskrit (IAST)*	*Description*
ॐ आदित्यवर्णे तपसो'धिजातो हृदयाय नमः ।	oṃ ādityavarṇe tapaso'dhijāto hradayāya namaḥ ।	Touch your heart region with your right-hand.
वनस्पतिस्तव वृक्षोथ शिरसे स्वाहा ।	vanaspatistava vṛkṣotha śirase svāhā ।	Touch your forehead with your right-hand keeping the index finger away.
बिल्व तस्य फलानि शिखायै वषट् ।	bilva tasya phalāni śikhāyai vaṣaṭ ।	Make a fist with your right-hand and extend your thumb. Now touch the crown of your head with your thumb.
तपसा नुदन्तु कवचाय हुं ।	tapasā nudantu kavacāya huṃ ।	Touch your shoulders by crossing your hands.
मायान्तरायाश्च नेत्रत्रयाय वौषट् ।	māyāntarāyāśca netratrayāya vauṣaṭ ।	Spread your right-hand and touch your right eye with your index finger, forehead with the middle finger and left eye with the ring finger simultaneously.
बाह्यलक्ष्मी अस्त्राय फट् ।	bāhrālakṣmī astrāya phaṭ ।	Take the right-hand over your head and then bring it back in front of you to clap softly.

Night 7

Chanting (*Japa*)	
Mantra Sanskrit (Devanagri)	ॐ आं ह्रीं श्रीं क्लीं ब्लूं सौं रं वं श्रीं ॐ श्रीं ह्रीं श्रीं नमः । उपैतु मां देवसखः कीर्तिश्च मणिना सह । प्रादुर्भूतो'स्मि राष्ट्रे'स्मिन् कीर्तिमृद्धिं ददातु मे ॥ नमो श्रीं ह्रीं श्रीं ॐ । ॐ आं ह्रीं श्रीं क्लीं ब्लूं सौं रं वं श्रीं ॐ ।।
Mantra Sanskrit (IAST)	oṃ āṃ hrīṃ śrīṃ klīṃ blūṃ sauṃ raṃ vaṃ śrīṃ oṃ śrīṃ hrīṃ śrīṃ namaḥ । upaitu māṃ devasakhaḥ kīrtiśca maṇinā saha । prādurbhūto'smi rāṣṭre'smin kīrtimṛddhiṃ dadātu me ॥ namo śrīṃ hrīṃ śrīṃ oṃ । oṃ āṃ hrīṃ śrīṃ klīṃ blūṃ sauṃ raṃ vaṃ śrīṃ oṃ ।।
Count	Chant this mantra 1000 times.

Fire offerings (*Yajna*)		
Mantra	Same as above. Just add '*Om Svaha*' (ॐ स्वाहा, oṃ svāhā) at the end of your mantra. Therefore, say the mantra, say '*Om Svaha*' and then make an offering in the fire pit.	
Count	Make fire-offerings 108 times.	
Ingredients for fire-offerings	Ghee	200 grams
	White rice	50 grams
	White sesame	50 grams
	Havan samagri	1 packet
	White sesame seeds	50 grams
	Red sandalwood	One small piece

Instructions	Follow the standard procedure of fire offerings as stated in *How to Make Fire Offerings (Yajna)*. 1. Mix rice, *havan samagri* and sesame seeds. 2. Put five tablespoons of melted ghee in it. Mix it thoroughly. 3. After you have made 108 offerings (*ahuti*), offer the last one with the small piece of red sandalwood. Dip it in ghee or put a bit of ghee in it and offer it in the fire pit. 4. Conclude by pouring any remaining ghee from the 200 grams you set aside for this *yajna*. If you feel the fire going off or dousing while you do *yajna*, feel free to pour more ghee on the fire. Keep the fire alive.

Libations (*Tarpana*)

Mantra	Same as the mantra above for chanting. Just add '*tarpyami*' (तर्प्यामि, tarpyāmi) at the end of your mantra.
Instructions	Say the mantra, take a bit of water as per the instructions in step 32 in *Essential Steps in the Rites of Invocation (Puruscharana)*, and add '*tarpyami*' in the end when you put water back in the vessel.
Count	Do libations 11 times.

Coronation (*Marjana* or *Abhishekam*)

Mantra	Same as the mantra above for chanting. Just add '*marjyami*' (Skt: मार्जयामि, mārjayāmi) at the end of your mantra.
Instructions	Say the mantra, take a bit of water as per the instructions in step 33 in *Essential Steps in the Rites of Invocation (Puruscharana)*, and add '*marjyami*' in the end when you put water back in the vessel.
Count	Do coronation 11 times.

Follow the 36 steps of the rites of invocation but please note that vow — step 16 — is to be performed only on the first night. The rest of the steps remain the same. The *nyasa*, application (*viniyoga*) and mantra will change every night. The mantra has been already specified in the previous table; *viniyoga* and *nyasa* are as follows.

Application (*Viniyoga*)

Sanskrit (Devanagri)	*Sanskrit (IAST)*
ॐ अस्य श्री उपैतु मां देवसखः इति श्री सूक्त सप्तम मन्त्रस्य मृकण्ड ऋषि, सर्व संपति पूरिण्यै देवता, सौं बीज, शिवा शक्ति, मातंगी महाविद्या, ऐं उत्कीलन, सर्व मंगल कारिण्यै भगवती लक्ष्मी प्रसाद सिद्धयर्थ सप्तम मंत्र जपे विनियोगः ।	oṃ asya śrī upaitu māṃ devasakhaḥ iti śrī sūkta saptama mantrasya mṛkaṇḍa ṛṣi, sarva saṃpati pūriṇyai devatā, sauṃ bīja, śivā śakti, mātaṃgī mahāvidyā, aiṃ utkīlana, sarva maṃgala kāriṇyai bhagavatī lakṣmī prasāda siddhayartha saptama maṃtra jape viniyogaḥ ।

Follow the standard procedure of *viniyoga* by taking a bit of water in your palm (as explained in step 18 in *Essential Steps in the Rites of Invocation*).

Perform the *nyasa* as per the tables below, in that order, starting with *Nyasa* of the Sages (*Rishyadi Nyasa*).

Nyasa of the Sages (*Rishyadi Nyasa*)

Sanskrit (Devanagri)	*Sanskrit (IAST)*	*Touch with your right-hand your...*
मृकण्ड ऋषये नमः सहस्त्रारे शिरसि ।	mṛkaṇḍa ṛṣaye namaḥ sahastrāre śirasi ।	Crown of the head
सर्व संपति पूरिण्यै' देवयै नमः द्वादशारे हृदि ।	sarva saṃpati pūriṇyai' devayai namaḥ dvādaśāre hradi ।	Heart

Sanskrit (Devanagri)	*Sanskrit (IAST)*	*Touch with your right-hand your...*
सौं बीजाय नमः षडारे योनौ ।	sauṃ bījāya namaḥ ṣaḍāre yonau I	Groin
शिवा शक्त्यै नमः दशारे नाभौ ।	śivā śaktyai namaḥ daśāre nābhau I	Navel
मातंगी महाविद्यायै नमः षोडशारे कंठे ।	mātaṃgī mahāvidyāyai namaḥ ṣoḍaśāre kaṃṭhe I	Throat
तमोगुणाय नमः अंतरारे मनसि ।	tamoguṇāya namaḥ aṃtarāre manasi I	Heart (again)
रसना ज्ञानेन्द्रिय नमः ज्ञानेन्द्रिये ।	rasanā jñānenidraya namaḥ jñāneindraye I	Mouth (keep your mouth just a bit open when you touch)
कर कर्मेन्द्रियाय नमः कर्मेन्द्रिये ।	kara karmendriyāya namaḥ karmendriye I	Lips
मध्यम स्वराय नमः कंठमूले ।	madhyama svarāya namaḥ kaṃṭhamūle I	Base of your throat (the soft area just below the Adam's apple)
जल तत्वाय नमः चतुरारे गुदे ।	jala tatvāya namaḥ caturāre gude I	Lower back (near your anus but keep your clothes on and just touch your lower back symbolically)
प्रतिष्ठा कलायै नमः करतले ।	pratiṣṭhā kalāyai namaḥ karatale I	The palm of your left-hand

Sanskrit (Devanagri)	*Sanskrit (IAST)*	*Touch with your right-hand your...*
ऐं उत्किलनाय नमः पादयोः ।	aiṃ utkilanāya namaḥ pādayoḥ ǀ	Feet
मत्स्य मुद्रायै नमः सर्वांगे ।	matsya mudrāyai namaḥ sarvāṃge ǀ	Whole body (do this by rolling your right hand over your upper body by bringing it around and then clapping gently)

Now perform *nyasa* of the hands (*kara nyasa*). The mudras are the same as in step 17 (purification of the hands) of this chapter. You can see the illustrations in that table. I am providing the description again.

Nyasa of the Hands (*Kara Nyasa*)

Sanskrit (Devanagri)	*Sanskrit (IAST)*	*Gesture with both hands*
ॐ उपैतु मां देवसखः अंगुष्ठाभ्यां नमः ।	oṃ upaitu māṃ devasakhaḥ aṃguṣṭhābhyāṃ namaḥ ǀ	Touch the tip of your thumb at the base of your index finger.
कीर्तिश्च तर्जनीभ्याम् स्वाहा ।	kīrtiśca tarjanībhyām svāhā ǀ	Touch the tip of your thumb to the tip of your index finger.
मणिना सह मध्यमाभ्यां वषट् ।	maṇinā saha madhyamābhyāṃ vaṣaṭ ǀ	Touch the tip of your thumb to the tip of your middle finger.

Sanskrit (Devanagri)	Sanskrit (IAST)	Gesture with both hands
प्रादुर्भूतो'स्मि अनामिकाभ्यां हुं ।	prādurbhūto'smi anāmikābhyāṃ huṃ I	Touch the tip of your thumb to the tip of your ring finger.
राष्ट्रे'स्मिन् कनिष्ठिकाभ्यां वौषट् ।	rāṣṭre'smin kaniṣṭhikābhyāṃ vauṣaṭ I	Touch the tip of your thumb to the tip of your little finger.
कीर्तिमृद्धिं ददातु मे करतलकरपृष्ठाभ्यां फट् ।	kīrtimṛddhiṃ dadātu me karatalakara-pṛṣṭhābhyāṃ phaṭ I	Touch the back of your left-hand with the back of your right-hand and then clap softly.

Now do the final *nyasa* by performing six-limbed mantra *nyasa*. The mudras for this are the same as shown in Night 1. I'm giving the description again.

Six-Limbed Mantra *Nyasa* (*Shadanga* Mantra *Nyāsa*)

Sanskrit (Devanagri)	Sanskrit (IAST)	Description
ॐ उपैतु मां देवसखः ह्रदयाय नमः ।	oṃ upaitu māṃ devasakhaḥ hradayāya namaḥ I	Touch your heart region with your right-hand.
कीर्तिश्च शिरसे स्वाहा ।	kīrtiśca śirase svāhā I	Touch your forehead with your right-hand keeping the index finger away.
मणिना सह शिखायै वषट् ।	maṇinā saha śikhāyai vaṣaṭ I	Make a fist with right-hand and extend your thumb. Now touch the crown of your head with your thumb.

Sanskrit (Devanagri)	*Sanskrit (IAST)*	*Description*
प्रादुर्भूतो'स्मि कवचाय हुं ।	prādurbhūto'smi kavacāya huṃ ।	Touch your shoulders by crossing your hands.
राष्ट्रे'स्मिन् नेत्रत्रयाय वौषट् ।	rāṣṭre'smin netratrayāya vauṣaṭ ।	Spread your right-hand and touch your right eye with your index finger, forehead with the middle finger and left eye with the ring finger simultaneously.
कीर्तिमृद्धिं ददातु मे अस्त्राय फट् ।	kīrtimṛddhiṃ dadātu me astrāya phaṭ ।	Take the right-hand over your head and then bring it back in front of you to clap softly.

Night 8

Chanting (*Japa*)	
Mantra Sanskrit (Devanagri)	ॐ आं ह्रीं श्रीं क्लीं ब्लूं सौं रं वं श्रीं ॐ श्रीं ह्रीं श्रीं नमः । क्षुत्पिपासामलां ज्येष्ठामलक्ष्मीं नाशयाम्यहम् । अभूतिमसमृद्धिं च सर्वां निर्णुद मे गृहात् ॥ नमो श्रीं ह्रीं श्रीं ॐ । ॐ आं ह्रीं श्रीं क्लीं ब्लूं सौं रं वं श्रीं ॐ ।।
Mantra Sanskrit (IAST)	oṃ āṃ hrīṃ śrīṃ klīṃ blūṃ sauṃ raṃ vaṃ śrīṃ oṃ śrīṃ hrīṃ śrīṃ namaḥ । kṣutpipāsāmalāṃ jyeṣṭhāmalakṣmīṃ nāśayāmyaham । abhūtimasamṛddhiṃ ca sarvāṃ nirṇuda me gṛhāt ॥ namo śrīṃ hrīṃ śrīṃ oṃ । oṃ āṃ hrīṃ śrīṃ klīṃ blūṃ sauṃ raṃ vaṃ śrīṃ oṃ ।।
Count	Chant this mantra 1000 times.

Fire offerings (*Yajna*)

Mantra	Same as above. Just add '*Om Svaha*' (ॐ स्वाहा, oṃ svāhā) at the end of your mantra. Therefore, say the mantra, say '*Om Svaha*' and then make an offering in the fire pit.
Count	Make fire offerings 108 times.
Ingredients for fire-offerings	Ghee — 200 grams Whole cashews — 50 grams Lotus seeds — 100 count *Havan samagri* — 1 packet Black sesame seeds — 50 grams White sandalwood — One small piece
Instructions	Follow the standard procedure of fire offerings as stated in *How to Make Fire Offerings (Yajna).* 1. Mix cashews, lotus seeds, *havan samagri* and sesame seeds. 2. Put five tablespoons of melted ghee in it. Mix it thoroughly. 3. After you have made 108 offerings (*ahuti*), offer the last one with the small piece of white sandalwood. Dip it in ghee or put a bit of ghee in it and offer it in the fire pit. 4. Conclude by pouring any remaining ghee from the 200 grams you set aside for this *yajna.* If you feel the fire going off or dousing while you do *yajna*, feel free to pour more ghee on the fire. Keep the fire alive.

Libations (*Tarpana*)

Mantra	Same as the mantra above for chanting. Just add '*tarpyami*' (तर्प्यामि, tarpyāmi) at the end of your mantra.

Instructions	Say the mantra, take a bit of water as per the instructions in step 32 in *Essential Steps in the Rites of Invocation (Puruscharana)*, and add '*tarpyami*' in the end when you put water back in the vessel.
Count	Do libations 11 times.
Coronation (*Marjana* or *Abhishekam*)	
Mantra	Same as the mantra above for chanting. Just add '*marjyami*' (Skt: मार्जयामि, mārjayāmi) at the end of your mantra.
Instructions	Say the mantra, take a bit of water as per the instructions in step 33 in *Essential Steps in the Rites of Invocation (Puruscharana)*, and add '*marjyami*' in the end when you put water back in the vessel.
Count	Do coronation 11 times.

Follow the 36 steps of the rites of invocation but please note that vow — step 16 — is to be performed only on the first night. The rest of the steps remain the same. The *nyasa*, application (*viniyoga*) and mantra will change every night. The *mantra* has been already specified in the previous table; *viniyoga* and *nyasa* are as follows.

Application (*Viniyoga*)

Sanskrit (Devanagri)	*Sanskrit (IAST)*
ॐ अस्य श्री क्षुत्पिपासामलां इति श्रीसूक्त अष्टम मंत्रस्य नारदो ऋषि, सर्व सौभाग्यदायिन देवी, सां बीज, ऐश्वर्यै शक्ति, लक्ष्मी महाविद्या, ह्रीं उत्कीलन, सर्व मंगल कारिण्यै भगवती लक्ष्मी प्रसाद सिद्धयर्थ अष्टम मंत्र जपे विनियोगः ।	oṃ asya śrī kṣutpipāsāmalāṃ iti śrīsūkta aṣṭama maṃtrasya nārado ṛṣi, sarva saubhāgyadāyina devī, sāṃ bīja, aiśvaryai śakti, lakṣmī mahāvidyā, hrīṃ utkīlana, sarva maṃgala kāriṇyai bhagavatī lakṣmī prasāda siddhayartha aṣṭama maṃtra jape viniyogaḥ ।

Follow the standard procedure of *viniyoga* by taking a bit of water in your palm (as explained in step 18 in *Essential Steps in the Rites of Invocation*).

Perform the *nyasa* as per the tables below, in that order, starting with *Nyasa* of the *Sages* (*Rishyadi Nyasa*).

Nyasa of the Sages (*Rishyadi Nyasa*)

Sanskrit (Devanagri)	*Sanskrit (IAST)*	*Touch with your right-hand your...*
नारद ऋषये नमः सहस्त्रारे शिरसि ।	nārada ṛṣaye namaḥ sahastrāre śirasi ।	Crown of the head
सर्वसौभाग्यदायिन्यै देव्यै नमः द्वादशारे हृदि ।	sarvasaubhāgyadāyinyai devyai namaḥ dvādaśāre hradi ।	Heart
सां बीजाय नमः षडारे योनौ ।	sāṃ bījāya namaḥ ṣaḍāre yonau ।	Groin
ऐश्वर्यै शक्त्यै नमः दशारे नाभौ ।	aiśvaryai śaktyai namaḥ daśāre nābhau ।	Navel
लक्ष्मी महाविद्यायै नमः षोडशारे कंठे ।	lakṣmī mahāvidyāyai namaḥ ṣoḍaśāre kaṃṭhe ।	Throat
रजोगुणाय नमः अंतरारे मनसि ।	rajoguṇāya namaḥ aṃtarāre manasi ।	Heart (again)
चक्षु ज्ञानेन्द्रियाय नमः ज्ञानेन्द्रिये ।	cakṣu jñāneindrayāya namaḥ jñāneindraye ।	Mouth (keep your mouth just a bit open when you touch)
भग कर्मेन्द्रियाय नमः कर्मेन्द्रिये ।	bhaga karmendriyāya namaḥ karmendriye ।	Groin (again)

Sanskrit (Devanagri)	*Sanskrit (IAST)*	*Touch with your right-hand your...*
सौम्य स्वराय नमः कंठमूले ।	saumya svarāya namaḥ kaṃṭhamūle I	Base of your throat (the soft area just below the Adam's apple)
भू तत्वाय नमः चतुरारे गुदे ।	bhū tatvāya namaḥ caturāre gude I	Lower back (near your anus but keep your clothes on and just touch your lower back symbolically)
प्रवृति कलायै नमः करतले ।	pravrṛti kalāyai namaḥ karatale I	The palm of your left-hand
ह्रीं उत्कीलनाय नमः पादयोः ।	hrīṃ utkīlanāya namaḥ pādayoḥ I	Feet
सम्पुट मुद्रायै नमः सर्वांगे ।	sampuṭa mudrāyai namaḥ sarvāṃge I	Whole body (do this by rolling your right-hand over your upper body by bringing it around and then clapping gently)

Now perform *nyasa* of the hands (*kara nyasa*). The mudras are the same as in step 17 (purification of the hands) of this chapter. You can see the illustrations in that table. I am providing the description again.

Nyasa of the Hands (_Kara- Nyasa_)

Sanskrit (Devanagri)	*Sanskrit (IAST)*	*Gesture with both hands*
ॐ क्षुत्पिपासामलां अंगुष्ठाभ्यां नमः ।	oṃ kṣutpipāsāmalāṃ aṃguṣṭhābhyāṃ namaḥ ।	Touch the tip of your thumb at the base of your index finger.
ॐ ज्येष्ठामलक्ष्मीं तर्जनीभ्याम् स्वाहा ।	oṃ jyeṣṭhāmalakṣmīṃ tarjanībhyām svāhā ।	Touch the tip of your thumb to the tip of your index finger.
नाशयाम्यहम् मध्यमाभ्यां वषट् ।	nāśayāmyaham madhyamābhyāṃ vaṣaṭ ।	Touch the tip of your thumb to the tip of your middle finger.
अभूतिमसमृद्धिं अनामिकाभ्यां हुं ।	abhūtimasamṛddhiṃ anāmikābhyāṃ huṃ ।	Touch the tip of your thumb to the tip of your ring finger.
च सर्वां निर्णुद कनिष्ठिकाभ्यां वौषट् ।	ca sarvāṃ nirṇuda kaniṣṭhikābhyāṃ vauṣaṭ ।	Touch the tip of your thumb to the tip of your little finger.
मे गृहात् करतलकरपृष्ठाभ्यां फट् ।	me gṛhāt karatalakara-pṛṣṭhābhyāṃ phaṭ ।	Touch the back of your left-hand with the back of your right-hand and then clap softly.

Now do the final *nyasa* by performing six-limbed mantra *nyasa*. The mudras for this are the same as shown in Night 1. I'm giving the description again.

Six-Limbed Mantra *Nyasa* (*Shadanga* Mantra *Nyāsa*)

Sanskrit (Devanagri)	*Sanskrit (IAST)*	*Description*
ॐ क्षुत्पिपासामलां हृदयाय नमः ।	oṃ kṣutpipāsāmalāṃ hradayāya namaḥ ।	Touch your heart region with your right-hand.
ज्येष्ठामलक्ष्मीं शिरसे स्वाहा ।	jyeṣṭhāmalakṣmīṃ śirase svāhā ।	Touch your forehead with your right-hand keeping the index finger away.
नाशयाम्यहम् शिखायै वषट् ।	nāśayāmyaham śikhāyai vaṣaṭ ।	Make a fist with right-hand and extend your thumb. Now touch the crown of your head with your thumb.
अभूतिमसमृद्धिं कवचाय हुं ।	abhūtimasamṛddhiṃ kavacāya huṃ ।	Touch your shoulders by crossing your hands.
च सर्वां निर्णुद नेत्रत्रयाय वौषट् ।	ca sarvāṃ nirṇuda netratrayāya vauṣaṭ ।	Spread your right-hand and touch your right eye with your index finger, forehead with the middle finger and left eye with the ring finger simultaneously.
मे गृहात् अस्त्राय फट् ।	me gṛhāt astrāya phaṭ ।	Take the right-hand over your head and then bring it back in front of you to clap softly.

Night 9

	Chanting (*Japa*)	
Mantra Sanskrit (Devanagri)	ॐ आं ह्रीं श्रीं क्लीं ब्लूं सौं रं वं श्रीं ॐ श्रीं ह्रीं श्रीं नमः । गन्धद्वारां दुराधर्षां नित्यपुष्टां करीषिणीम् । ईश्वरीं सर्वभूतानां तामिहोपह्वये श्रियम् ॥ नमो श्रीं ह्रीं श्रीं ॐ । ॐ आं ह्रीं श्रीं क्लीं ब्लूं सौं रं वं श्रीं ॐ ।।	
Mantra Sanskrit (IAST)	oṃ āṃ hrīṃ śrīṃ klīṃ blūṃ sauṃ raṃ vaṃ śrīṃ oṃ śrīṃ hrīṃ śrīṃ namaḥ । gandhadvārāṃ durādharṣāṃ nityapuṣṭāṃ karīṣiṇīm । īśvarīṃ sarvabhūtānāṃ tāmihopahvaye śriyam ॥ namo śrīṃ hrīṃ śrīṃ oṃ । oṃ āṃ hrīṃ śrīṃ klīṃ blūṃ sauṃ raṃ vaṃ śrīṃ oṃ ।।	
Count	Chant this mantra 1000 times.	
	Fire offerings (*Yajna*)	
Mantra	Same as above. Just add '*Om Svaha*' (ॐ स्वाहा, oṃ svāhā) at the end of your mantra. Therefore, say the mantra, say '*Om Svaha*' and then make an offering in the fire pit.	
Count	Make fire offerings 108 times.	
Ingredients for fire-offerings	Ghee	600 grams
	Red sandalwood	One small piece
Instructions	Follow the standard procedure of fire offerings as stated in *How to Make Fire Offerings (Yajna).*	

	1. Tonight's fire offerings are done only with ghee. 2. After you have made 108 offerings (*ahuti*) with ghee, offer the last one with the small piece of red sandalwood. Dip it in ghee or put a bit of ghee in it and offer it in the fire pit. 3. Conclude by pouring any remaining ghee from the 600 grams you set aside for this *yajna*. If you feel the fire going off or dousing while you do *yajna*, feel free to pour more ghee on the fire. Keep the fire alive.
Libations (*Tarpana*)	
Mantra	Same as the mantra above for chanting. Just add '*tarpyami*' (तर्प्यामि, tarpyāmi) at the end of your mantra.
Instructions	Say the mantra, take a bit of water as per the instructions in step 32 in *Essential Steps in the Rites of Invocation (Puruscharana)*, and add '*tarpyami*' in the end when you put water back in the vessel.
Count	Do libations 11 times.
Coronation (*Marjana* or *Abhishekam*)	
Mantra	Same as the mantra above for chanting. Just add '*marjyami*' (Skt: मार्जयामि, mārjayāmi) at the end of your mantra.
Instructions	Say the mantra, take a bit of water as per the instructions in step 33 in *Essential Steps in the Rites of Invocation (Puruscharana)*, and add '*marjyami*' in the end when you put water back in the vessel.
Count	Do coronation 11 times.

Follow the 36 steps of the rites of invocation but please note that vow — step 16 — is to be performed only on the first night. The rest of the steps remain the same. The *nyasa*, application (*viniyoga*) and mantra will change every night. The mantra has been already specified in the previous table; *viniyoga* and *nyasa* are as follows.

Application (*Viniyoga*)

Sanskrit (Devanagri)	*Sanskrit (IAST)*
ॐ अस्य श्री गन्धद्वारां दुराधर्षां इति श्रीसूक्त नवम मंत्रस्य मेधस ऋषि, श्री सर्वसिद्धि प्रदायै देवी ब्रीं बीज, भ्रामरी शक्ति, कमला महाविद्या, क्लीं उत्कीलन, सर्व मंगल कारिण्यै भगवती लक्ष्मी प्रसाद सिद्धयर्थ नवम मंत्र जपे विनियोगः ।	oṃ asya śrī gandhadvārāṃ durādharṣāṃ iti śrīsūkta navama maṃtrasya medhasa ṛṣi, śrī sarvasiddhi pradāyai devī brīṃ bīja, bhrāmarī śakti, kamalā mahāvidyā, klīṃ utkīlana, sarva maṃgala kāriṇyai bhagavatī lakṣmī prasāda siddhayartha navama maṃtra jape viniyogaḥ I
Follow the standard procedure of *viniyoga* by taking a bit of water in your palm (as explained in step 18 in *Essential Steps in the Rites of Invocation*).	

Perform the *nyasa* as per the tables below, in that order, starting with *Nyasa* of the Sages (*Rishyadi nyasa*).

Nyasa of the Sages (Rishyadi Nyasa)

Sanskrit (Devanagri)	*Sanskrit (IAST)*	*Touch with your right-hand your...*
मेधस ऋषये नमः सहस्त्रारे शिरसि ।	medhasa ṛṣaye namaḥ sahastrāre śirasi I	Crown of the head
श्री सर्वसिद्धि प्रदायै देवयै नमः द्वादशारे हृदि ।	śrī sarvasiddhi pradāyai devayai namaḥ dvādaśāre hradi I	Heart

Sanskrit (Devanagri)	*Sanskrit (IAST)*	*Touch with your right-hand your...*
'ब्रीं' बीजाय नमः षडारे योनौ ।	'brīṃ' bījāya namaḥ ṣaḍāre yonau ।	Groin
भ्रामरी शक्त्यै नमः दशारे नाभौ ।	bhrāmarī śaktyai namaḥ daśāre nābhau ।	Navel
कमला महाविद्यायै नमः षोडशारे कंठे ।	kamalā mahāvidyāyai namaḥ ṣoḍaśāre kaṃṭhe ।	Throat
रजो गुणाय नमः अंतरारे मनसि ।	rajo guṇāya namaḥ aṃtarāre manasi ।	Heart (again)
नासिका ज्ञानेन्द्रिय नमः ज्ञानेन्द्रिये ।	nāsikā jñānenidraya namaḥ jñāneindraye ।	Nose
पाणि कर्मेन्द्रियाय नमः कर्मेन्द्रिये ।	pāṇi karmendriyāya namaḥ karmendriye ।	Hands (bring your both hands together)
मृदु स्वराय नमः कंठमूले ।	mṛdu svarāya namaḥ kaṃṭhamūle ।	Base of your throat (the soft area just below the Adam's apple)
भू तत्वाय नमः चतुरारे गुदे ।	bhū tatvāya namaḥ caturāre gude ।	Lower back (near your anus but keep your clothes on and just touch your lower back symbolically)
मोहिनी कलायै नमः करतले ।	mohinī kalāyai namaḥ karatale ।	The palm of your left-hand
'क्लीं' उत्किलनाय नमः पादयोः ।	'klīṃ' utkilanāya namaḥ pādayoḥ ।	Feet

Sanskrit (Devanagri)	*Sanskrit (IAST)*	*Touch with your right-hand your...*
सम्पुट मुद्रायै नमः सर्वांगे ।	sampuṭa mudrāyai namaḥ sarvāṃge ।	Whole body (do this by rolling your right-hand over your upper body by bringing it around and then clapping gently)

Now perform *nyasa* of the hands (*kara nyasa*). The mudras are the same as in step 17 (purification of the hands) of this chapter. You can see the illustrations in that table. I am providing the description again.

Nyasa of the Hands (*Kara Nyasa*)

Sanskrit (Devanagri)	*Sanskrit (IAST)*	*Gesture with both hands*
ॐ गन्धद्वारां अंगुष्ठाभ्यां नमः ।	oṃ gandhadvārāṃ aṃguṣṭhābhyāṃ namaḥ ।	Touch the tip of your thumb at the base of your index finger.
दुराधर्षां तर्जनीभ्याम् स्वाहा ।	durādharṣāṃ tarjanībhyām svāhā ।	Touch the tip of your thumb to the tip of your index finger.
नित्यपुष्टां करीषिणीम् मध्यमाभ्यां वषट् ।	nityapuṣṭāṃ karīṣiṇīm madhyamābhyāṃ vaṣaṭ ।	Touch the tip of your thumb to the tip of your middle finger.
ईश्वरीं अनामिकाभ्यां हुं ।	īśvarīṃ anāmikābhyāṃ huṃ ।	Touch the tip of your thumb to the tip of your ring finger.

Sanskrit (Devanagri)	*Sanskrit (IAST)*	*Gesture with both hands*
सर्वभूतानां कनिष्ठिकाभ्यां वौषट् ।	sarvabhūtānāṃ kaniṣṭhikābhyāṃ vauṣaṭ ǀ	Touch the tip of your thumb to the tip of your little finger.
तामिहोपह्वये श्रियम् करतलकरपृष्ठाभ्यां फट् ।	tāmihopahvaye śriyam karatalakara-pṛṣṭhābhyāṃ phaṭ ǀ	Touch the back of your left-hand with the back of your right-hand and then clap softly.

Now do the final *nyasa* by performing six-limbed mantra *nyasa*. The mudras for this are the same as shown in Night 1. I'm giving the description again.

Six-Limbed Mantra *Nyasa* (*Shadanga* Mantra *Nyāsa*)

Sanskrit (Devanagri)	*Sanskrit (IAST)*	*Description*
ॐ गन्धद्वारां हृदयाय नमः ।	oṃ gandhadvārāṃ hradayāya namaḥ ǀ	Touch your heart region with your right-hand.
दुराधर्षां शिरसे स्वाहा ।	durādharṣāṃ śirase svāhā ǀ	Touch your forehead with your right-hand keeping the index finger away.
नित्यपुष्टां करीषिणीम् शिखायै वषट् ।	nityapuṣṭāṃ karīṣiṇīm śikhāyai vaṣaṭ ǀ	Make a fist with right-hand and extend your thumb. Now touch the crown of your head with your thumb.
ईश्वरीं कवचाय हुं ।	īśvarīṃ kavacāya huṃ ǀ	Touch your shoulders by crossing your hands.

Sanskrit (Devanagri)	*Sanskrit (IAST)*	*Description*
सर्वभूतानां नेत्रत्रयाय वौषट् ।	sarvabhūtānāṃ netratrayāya vauṣaṭ ।	Spread your right-hand and touch your right eye with your index finger, forehead with the middle finger and left eye with the ring finger simultaneously.
तामिहोपह्वये श्रियम् अस्त्राय फट् ।	tāmihopahvaye śriyam astrāya phaṭ ।	Take the right-hand over your head and then bring it back in front of you to clap softly.

Night 10

Chanting (*Japa*)	
Mantra Sanskrit (Devanagri)	ॐ आं ह्रीं श्रीं क्लीं ब्लूं सौं रं वं श्रीं ॐ श्रीं ह्रीं श्रीं नमः । मनसः काममाकूतिं वाचः सत्यमशीमहि । पशूनां रूपमन्नस्य मयि श्रीः श्रयतां यशः ॥ नमो श्रीं ह्रीं श्रीं ॐ । ॐ आं ह्रीं श्रीं क्लीं ब्लूं सौं रं वं श्रीं ॐ ।।
Mantra Sanskrit (IAST)	oṃ āṃ hrīṃ śrīṃ klīṃ blūṃ sauṃ raṃ vaṃ śrīṃ oṃ śrīṃ hrīṃ śrīṃ namaḥ । manasaḥ kāmamākūtiṃ vācaḥ satyamaśīmahi । paśūnāṃ rūpamannasya mayi śrīḥ śrayatāṃ yaśaḥ ॥ namo śrīṃ hrīṃ śrīṃ oṃ । oṃ āṃ hrīṃ śrīṃ klīṃ blūṃ sauṃ raṃ vaṃ śrīṃ oṃ ।।
Count	Chant this mantra 1000 times.

Fire offerings (*Yajna*)		
Mantra	Same as above. Just add '*Om Svaha*' (ॐ स्वाहा, oṃ svāhā) at the end of your mantra. Therefore, say the mantra, say '*Om Svaha*' and then make an offering in the fire pit.	
Count	Make fire-offerings 108 times.	
Ingredients for fire-offerings	Ghee	200 grams
	Jaggery	50 grams
	Raisins	50 grams
	Almonds	50 grams
	Havan samagri	1 packet
	Black sesame seeds	50 grams
	White sandalwood	One small piece
Instructions	Follow the standard procedure of fire offerings as stated in *How to Make Fire Offerings (Yajna)*. 1. Mix jaggery, raisins, almonds, *havan samagri* and sesame seeds. 2. Put five tablespoons of melted ghee in it. Mix it thoroughly. 3. After you have made 108 offerings (*ahuti*), offer the last one with the small piece of white sandalwood. Dip it in ghee or put a bit of ghee in it and offer it in the fire pit. 4. Conclude by pouring any remaining ghee from the 200 grams you set aside for this *yajna*. If you feel the fire going off or dousing while you do *yajna*, feel free to pour more ghee on the fire. Keep the fire alive.	

Libations (*Tarpana*)	
Mantra	Same as the mantra above for chanting. Just add '*tarpyami*' (तर्प्यामि, tarpyāmi) at the end of your mantra.
Instructions	Say the mantra, take a bit of water as per the instructions in step 32 in *Essential Steps in*

	the Rites of Invocation (Puruscharana), and add '*tarpyami*' in the end when you put water back in the vessel.
Count	Do libations 11 times.
Coronation (*Marjana or Abhishekam*)	
Mantra	Same as the mantra above for chanting. Just add '*marjyami*' (Skt: मार्जयामि, mārjayāmi) at the end of your mantra.
Instructions	Say the mantra, take a bit of water as per the instructions in step 33 in *Essential Steps in the Rites of Invocation (Puruscharana)*, and add '*marjyami*' in the end when you put water back in the vessel.
Count	Do coronation 11 times.

Follow the 36 steps of the rites of invocation but please note that vow — step 16 — is to be performed only on the first night. The rest of the steps remain the same. Th *nyasa*, application (*viniyoga*) and mantra will change every night. The mantra has been already specified in the previous table; *viniyoga* and *nyasa* are as follows.

Application (*Viniyoga*)

Sanskrit (Devanagri)	*Sanskrit (IAST)*
ॐ अस्य श्री मनसः काममाकूतिं इति श्रीसूक्त दशम मंत्रस्य श्री वेद व्यास ऋषि, श्री सर्व प्रियंकर्यै देवी, क्रों बीजं, शताक्षी शक्ति, श्री सुन्दरी महाविद्या, श्रीं उत्कीलन, सर्व मंगल कारिण्यै भगवती लक्ष्मी प्रसाद सिद्धयर्थ दशम मंत्र जपे विनियोगः ।	oṃ asya śrī manasaḥ kāmamākūtiṃ iti śrīsūkta daśama maṃtrasya śrī veda vyāsa ṛṣi, śrī sarva priyaṃkaryai devī, kroṃ bījaṃ, śatākṣī śakti, śrī sundarī mahāvidyā, śrīṃ utkīlana, sarva maṃgala kāriṇyai bhagavatī lakṣmī prasāda siddhayartha daśama maṃtra jape viniyogaḥ ।
Follow the standard procedure of *viniyoga* by taking a bit of water in your palm (as explained in step 18 in *Essential Steps in the Rites of Invocation*).	

Perform the *nyasa* as per the tables below, in that order, starting with *Nyasa* of the Sages (*Rishyadi nyasa*).

Nyasa of the Sages (_Rishyadi Nyasa_)

Sanskrit (Devanagri)	*Sanskrit (IAST)*	*Touch with your right-hand your*
श्री वेद व्यास ऋषये नमः सहस्त्रारे शिरसि ।	śrī veda vyāsa ṛṣaye namaḥ sahastrāre śirasi ।	Crown of the head
श्री सर्व प्रियं कर्यै देवयै नमः द्वादशारे हृदि ।	śrī sarva priyaṃ karyai devayai namaḥ dvādaśāre hradi ।	Heart
क्रों बीजाय नमः षडारे योनौ ।	kroṃ bījāya namaḥ ṣaḍāre yonau ।	Groin
शताक्षी शक्त्यै नमः दशारे नाभौ ।	śatākṣī śaktyai namaḥ daśāre nābhau ।	Navel
श्री सुन्दरी महाविद्यायै नमः षोडशारे कंठे ।	śrī sundarī mahāvidyāyai namaḥ ṣoḍaśāre kaṃṭhe ।	Throat
रजो गुणाय नमः अंतरारे मनसि ।	rajo guṇāya namaḥ aṃtarāre manasi ।	Heart (again)
श्रोत्र ज्ञानेन्द्रिय नमः ज्ञानेन्द्रिये ।	śrotra jñānenidraya namaḥ jñāneindraye ।	Ears
मन कर्मेन्द्रियाय नमः कर्मेन्द्रिये ।	mana karmendriyāya namaḥ karmendriye ।	Hands (bring your both hands together)
सौम्य स्वराय नमः कंठमूले ।	saumya svarāya namaḥ kaṃṭhamūle ।	Base of your throat (the soft area just below the Adam's apple)
जल तत्वाय नमः चतुरारे गुदे ।	jala tatvāya namaḥ caturāre gude ।	Lower back (near your anus but keep your clothes on and just touch your lower back symbolically)

Sanskrit (Devanagri)	*Sanskrit (IAST)*	*Touch with your right-hand your*
अविद्या कलायै नमः करतले ।	avidyā kalāyai namaḥ karatale I	The palm of your left-hand
श्रीं उत्किलनाय नमः पादयोः ।	śrīṃ utkilanāya namaḥ pādayoḥ I	Feet
योनि मुद्रायै नमः सर्वांगे ।	yoni mudrāyai namaḥ sarvāṃge I	Whole body (do this by rolling your right-hand over your upper body by bringing it around and then clapping gently)

Now perform *nyasa* of the hands (*kara nyasa*). The mudras are the same as in step 17 (purification of the hands) of this chapter. You can see the illustrations in that table. I am providing the description again.

Nyasa of the Hands (*Kara Nyasa*)

Sanskrit (Devanagri)	*Sanskrit (IAST)*	*Gesture with both hands*
ॐ मनसः अंगुष्ठाभ्यां नमः ।	oṃ manasaḥ aṃguṣṭhābhyāṃ namaḥ I	Touch the tip of your thumb at the base of your index finger.
काममाकूतिं तर्जनीभ्याम् स्वाहा ।	kāmamākūtiṃ tarjanībhyām svāhā I	Touch the tip of your thumb to the tip of your index finger.
वाचः सत्यमशीमहि मध्यमाभ्यां वषट् ।	vācaḥ satyamaśīmahi madhyamābhyāṃ vaṣaṭ I	Touch the tip of your thumb to the tip of your middle finger.
पशूनां रूपमन्नस्य अनामिकाभ्यां हुं ।	paśūnāṃ rūpamannasya anāmikābhyāṃ huṃ I	Touch the tip of your thumb to the tip of your ring finger.

Sanskrit (Devanagri)	*Sanskrit (IAST)*	*Gesture with both hands*
मयि श्रीः कनिष्किाभ्यां वौषट् ।	mayi śrīḥ kaniṣikābhyāṃ vauṣaṭ ǀ	Touch the tip of your thumb to the tip of your little finger.
श्रयतां यशः करतलकरपृष्ठाभ्यां फट् ।	śrayatāṃ yaśaḥ karatalakara-pṛṣṭhābhyāṃ phaṭ ǀ	Touch the back of your left-hand with the back of your right-hand and then clap softly.

Now do the final *nyasa* by performing six-limbed mantra *nyasa*. The mudras for this are the same as shown in Night 1. I'm giving the description again.

Six-Limbed Mantra *Nyasa* (*Shadanga* Mantra *Nyāsa*)

Sanskrit (Devanagri)	*Sanskrit (IAST)*	*Description*
ॐ मनसः ह्रदयाय नमः ।	oṃ manasaḥ hradayāya namaḥ ǀ	Touch your heart region with your right-hand.
काममाकूतिं शिरसे स्वाहा ।	kāmamākūtiṃ śirase svāhā ǀ	Touch your forehead with your right-hand keeping the index finger away.
वाचः सत्यमशीमहि शिखायै वषट् ।	vācaḥ satyamaśīmahi śikhāyai vaṣaṭ ǀ	Make a fist with right-hand and extend your thumb. Now touch the crown of your head with your thumb.
पशूनां रूपमन्नस्य कवचाय हुं ।	paśūnāṃ rūpamannasya kavacāya huṃ ǀ	Touch your shoulders by crossing your hands.

Sanskrit (Devanagri)	*Sanskrit (IAST)*	*Description*
मयि श्रीः नेत्र त्रयाय वौषट् ।	mayi śrīḥ netra trayāya vauṣaṭ ।	Spread your right-hand and touch your right eye with your index finger, forehead with the middle finger and left eye with the ring finger simultaneously.
श्रयतां यशः अस्त्राय फट् ।	śrayatāṃ yaśaḥ astrāya phaṭ ।	Take the right-hand over your head and then bring it back in front of you to clap softly.

Night 11

Chanting (*Japa*)	
Mantra Sanskrit (Devanagri)	ॐ आं ह्रीं श्रीं क्लीं ब्लूं सौं रं वं श्रीं ॐ श्रीं ह्रीं श्रीं नमः । मनसः काममाकूतिं वाचः सत्यमशीमहि । पशूनां रूपमन्नस्य मयि श्रीः श्रयतां यशः ॥ नमो श्रीं ह्रीं श्रीं ॐ । ॐ आं ह्रीं श्रीं क्लीं ब्लूं सौं रं वं श्रीं ॐ ।।
Mantra Sanskrit (IAST)	oṃ āṃ hrīṃ śrīṃ klīṃ blūṃ sauṃ raṃ vaṃ śrīṃ oṃ śrīṃ hrīṃ śrīṃ namaḥ । manasaḥ kāmamākūtiṃ vācaḥ satyamaśīmahi । paśūnāṃ rūpamannasya mayi śrīḥ śrayatāṃ yaśaḥ ॥ namo śrīṃ hrīṃ śrīṃ oṃ । oṃ āṃ hrīṃ śrīṃ klīṃ blūṃ sauṃ raṃ vaṃ śrīṃ oṃ ।।
Count	Chant this mantra 1000 times.

<table>
<tr><th colspan="3">Fire offerings (Yajna)</th></tr>
<tr><td>Mantra</td><td colspan="2">Same as above. Just add ‘Om Svaha’ (ॐ स्वाहा, oṃ svāhā) at the end of your mantra. Therefore, say the mantra, say ‘Om Svaha’ and then make an offering in the fire pit.</td></tr>
<tr><td>Count</td><td colspan="2">Make fire offerings 108 times.</td></tr>
<tr><td rowspan="7">Ingredients for fire offerings</td><td>Ghee</td><td>200 grams</td></tr>
<tr><td>Grated dry coconut</td><td>50 grams</td></tr>
<tr><td>Cardamons</td><td>50 grams</td></tr>
<tr><td>Cloves</td><td>20 grams</td></tr>
<tr><td>Havan samagri</td><td>1 packet</td></tr>
<tr><td>White sesame seeds</td><td>50 grams</td></tr>
<tr><td>Red sandalwood</td><td>One small piece</td></tr>
<tr><td>Instructions</td><td colspan="2">Follow the standard procedure of fire offerings as stated in How to Make Fire Offerings (Yajna).

1. Mix grated dry coconut, cardamoms, havan samagri and sesame seeds.
2. Put five tablespoons of melted ghee in it. Mix it thoroughly.
3. After you have made 108 offerings (ahuti), offer the last one with the small piece of red sandalwood. Dip it in ghee or put a bit of ghee in it and offer it in the fire pit.
4. Conclude by pouring any remaining ghee from the 200 grams you set aside for this yajna.

If you feel the fire going off or dousing while you do yajna, feel free to pour more ghee on the fire. Keep the fire alive.</td></tr>
<tr><th colspan="3">Libations (Tarpana)</th></tr>
<tr><td>Mantra</td><td colspan="2">Same as the mantra above for chanting. Just add ‘tarpyami’ (तर्प्यामि, tarpyāmi) at the end of your mantra.</td></tr>
</table>

Instructions	Say the mantra, take a bit of water as per the instructions in step 32 in *Essential Steps in the Rites of Invocation (Puruscharana)*, and add '*tarpyami*' in the end when you put water back in the vessel.
Count	Do libations 11 times.
Coronation (*Marjana or Abhishekam*)	
Mantra	Same as the mantra above for chanting. Just add '*marjyami*' (Skt: मार्जयामि, mārjayāmi) at the end of your mantra.
Instructions	Say the mantra, take a bit of water as per the instructions in step 33 in *Essential Steps in the Rites of Invocation (Puruscharana)*, and add '*marjyami*' in the end when you put water back in the vessel.
Count	Do coronation 11 times.

Follow the 36 steps of the rites of invocation but please note that vow — step 16 — is to be performed only on the first night. The rest of the steps remain the same. The *nyasa*, application (*viniyoga*) and mantra will change every night. The mantra has been already specified in the previous table; *viniyoga* and *nyasa* are as follows.

Application (*Viniyoga*)

Sanskrit (Devanagri)	*Sanskrit (IAST)*
ॐ अस्य श्री कर्दमेन प्रजाभूता इति श्रीसूक्त एकादश मंत्रस्य श्री विष्णु ऋषि, श्री सर्व व्याधि विनाशिन्यै देवी, ह्रां बीजं, श्री महा सरस्वती देवता, रूं बीजं, इन्द्राणी शक्ति, भुवनेश्वरी महाविद्या, ऐं उत्कीलन, सर्व मंगल कारिण्यै भगवती लक्ष्मी प्रसाद सिद्धयर्थ दशम मंत्र जपे विनियोगः ।	oṃ asya śrī kardamena prajābhūtā iti śrīsūkta ekādaśa maṃtrasya śrī viṣṇu ṛṣi, śrī sarva vyādhi vināśinyai devī, hrāṃ bījaṃ, śrī mahā sarasvatī devatā, rūṃ bījaṃ, indrāṇī śakti, bhuvaneśvarī mahāvidyā, aiṃ utkīlana, sarva maṃgala kāriṇyai bhagavatī lakṣmī prasāda siddhayartha daśama maṃtra jape viniyogaḥ I

Follow the standard procedure of *viniyoga* by taking a bit of water in your palm (as explained in step 18 in *Essential Steps in the Rites of Invocation*).

Perform the *nyasa* as per the tables below, in that order, starting with *Nyasa* of the Sages (*Rishyadi nyasa*).

Nyasa of the Sages (*Rishyadi Nyasa*)

Sanskrit (Devanagri)	*Sanskrit (IAST)*	*Touch with your right-hand your*
श्री विष्णु ऋषये नमः सहस्त्रारे शिरसि ।	śrī viṣṇu ṛṣaye namaḥ sahastrāre śirasi ।	Crown of the head
श्री सर्व व्याधि विनाशिन्यै देवयै नमः द्वादशारे ह्रदि ।	śrī sarva vyādhi vināśinyai devayai namaḥ dvādaśāre hradi ।	Heart
ह्रां बीजाय नमः षडारे योनौ ।	hrāṃ bījāya namaḥ ṣaḍāre yonau ।	Groin
इन्द्राणी शक्त्यै नमः दशारे नाभौ ।	indrāṇī śaktyai namaḥ daśāre nābhau ।	Navel
श्री भुवनेश्वरी महाविद्यायै नमः षोडशारे कंठे ।	śrī bhuvaneśvarī mahāvidyāyai namaḥ ṣoḍaśāre kaṃṭhe ।	Throat
सतो गुणाय नमः अंतरारे मनसि ।	sato guṇāya namaḥ aṃtarāre manasi ।	Heart (again)
त्वक् ज्ञानेन्द्रिय नमः ज्ञानेन्द्रिये ।	tvak jñānenidraya namaḥ jñāneindraye ।	Ears

Sanskrit (Devanagri)	*Sanskrit (IAST)*	*Touch with your right-hand your*
कर कर्मेन्द्रियाय नमः कर्मेन्द्रिये ।	kara karmendriyāya namaḥ karmendriye I	Hands (bring your both hands together)
मृदु स्वराय नमः कंठमूले ।	mṛdu svarāya namaḥ kaṃṭhamūle I	Base of your throat (the soft area just below the Adam's apple)
वायु स्तत्वाय नमः चतुरारे गुदे ।	vāyu statvāya namaḥ caturāre gude I	Lower back (near your anus but keep your clothes on and just touch your lower back symbolically)
शांति कलायै नमः करतले ।	śāṃti kalāyai namaḥ karatale I	The palm of your left-hand
'ऐं' उत्किलनाय नमः पादयोः ।	aiṃ utkilanāya namaḥ pādayoḥ I	Feet
सम्पुट मुद्रायै नमः सर्वांगे ।	sampuṭa mudrāyai namaḥ sarvāṃge I	Whole body (do this by rolling your right-hand over your upper body by bringing it around and then clapping gently).

Now perform *nyasa* of the hands (*kara nyasa*). The mudras are the same as in step 17 (purification of the hands) of this chapter. You can see the illustrations in that table. I am providing the description again.

Nyasa of the (Kara Nyasa)

Sanskrit (Devanagri)	*Sanskrit (IAST)*	*Gesture with both hands*
ॐ कर्दमेन प्रजाभूता अंगुष्ठाभ्यां नमः ।	oṃ kardamena prajābhūtā aṃguṣṭhābhyāṃ namaḥ ।	Touch the tip of your thumb at the base of your index finger.
मयि सम्भव तर्जनीभ्याम् स्वाहा ।	mayi sambhava tarjanībhyām svāhā ।	Touch the tip of your thumb to the tip of your index finger.
कर्दम मध्यमाभ्यां वषट् ।	kardama madhyamābhyāṃ vaṣaṭ ।	Touch the tip of your thumb to the tip of your middle finger.
श्रियं वासय अनामिकाभ्यां हुं ।	śriyaṃ vāsaya anāmikābhyāṃ huṃ ।	Touch the tip of your thumb to the tip of your ring finger.
मे कुले मातरं कनिष्किाभ्यां वौषट् ।	me kule mātaraṃ kaniṣikābhyāṃ vauṣaṭ ।	Touch the tip of your thumb to the tip of your little finger.
पद्ममालिनीम् करतलकरपृष्ठाभ्यां फट् ।	padmamālinīm karatalakara-pṛṣṭhābhyāṃ phaṭ ।	Touch the back of your left-hand with the back of your right-hand and then clap softly.

Now do the final *nyasa* by performing six-limbed mantra nyasa. The mudras for this are the same as shown in Night 1. I'm giving the description again.

Six-Limbed Mantra *Nyasa* (*Shadanga* Mantra *Nyāsa*)

Sanskrit (Devanagri)	*Sanskrit (IAST)*	*Description*
ॐ कर्दमेन प्रजाभूता हृदयाय नमः ।	oṃ kardamena prajābhūtā hradayāya namaḥ I	Touch your heart region with your right-hand.
मयि सम्भव शिरसे स्वाहा ।	mayi sambhava śirase svāhā I	Touch your forehead with your right-hand keeping the index finger away.
कर्दम शिखायै वषट् ।	kardama śikhāyai vaṣaṭ I	Make a fist with right-hand and extend your thumb. Now touch the crown of your head with your thumb.
श्रियं वासय कवचाय हुं ।	śriyaṃ vāsaya kavacāya huṃ I	Touch your shoulders by crossing your hands.
मे कुले मातरं नेत्र त्रयाय वौषट् ।	me kule mātaraṃ netra trayāya vauṣaṭ I	Spread your right-hand and touch your right eye with your index finger, forehead with the middle finger and left eye with the ring finger simultaneously.
पद्ममालिनीम् अस्त्राय फट् ।	padmamālinīm astrāya phaṭ I	Take the right-hand over your head and then bring it back in front of you to clap softly.

Night 12

Chanting (*Japa*)		
Mantra Sanskrit (Devanagri)	ॐ आं ह्रीं श्रीं क्लीं ब्लूं सौं रं वं श्रीं ॐ श्रीं ह्रीं श्रीं नमः । आपः सृजन्तु स्निग्धानि चिक्लीत वस मे गृहे । नि च देवीं मातरं श्रियं वासय मे कुले ॥ नमो श्रीं ह्रीं श्रीं ॐ । ॐ आं ह्रीं श्रीं क्लीं ब्लूं सौं रं वं श्रीं ॐ ।।	
Mantra Sanskrit (IAST)	oṃ āṃ hrīṃ śrīṃ klīṃ blūṃ sauṃ raṃ vaṃ śrīṃ oṃ śrīṃ hrīṃ śrīṃ namaḥ I āpaḥ sṛjantu snigdhāni ciklīta vasa me gṛhe I ni ca devīṃ mātaraṃ śriyaṃ vāsaya me kule II namo śrīṃ hrīṃ śrīṃ oṃ I oṃ āṃ hrīṃ śrīṃ klīṃ blūṃ sauṃ raṃ vaṃ śrīṃ oṃ II	
Count	Chant this mantra 1000 times.	
Fire offerings (*Yajna*)		
Mantra	Same as above. Just add '*Om Svaha*' (ॐ स्वाहा, oṃ svāhā) at the end of your mantra. Therefore, say the mantra, say '*Om Svaha*' and then make an offering in the fire pit.	
Count	Make fire offerings 108 times.	
Ingredients for fire offerings	Ghee	200 grams
	Grated dry coconut	50 grams
	Raisins	50 grams
	Almonds	50 grams
	Havan samagri	1 packet
	Black sesame seeds	50 grams
	White sandalwood	One small piece

Instructions	Follow the standard procedure of fire offerings as stated in *How to Make Fire Offerings (Yajna).* 1. Mix grated dry coconut, raisins, almonds, *havan samagri* and sesame seeds. 2. Put five tablespoons of melted ghee in it. Mix it thoroughly. 3. After you have made 108 offerings (*ahuti*), offer the last one with the small piece of white sandalwood. Dip it in ghee or put a bit of ghee in it and offer it in the fire pit. 4. Conclude by pouring any remaining ghee from the 200 grams you set aside for this *yajna*. If you feel the fire going off or dousing while you do *yajna*, feel free to pour more ghee on the fire. Keep the fire alive.
Libations (*Tarpana*)	
Mantra	Same as the mantra above for chanting. Just add '*tarpyami*' (तर्प्यामि, tarpyāmi) at the end of your mantra.
Instructions	Say the mantra, take a bit of water as per the instructions in step 32 in *Essential Steps in the Rites of Invocation (Puruscharana),* and add '*tarpyami*' in the end when you put water back in the vessel.
Count	Do libations 11 times.
Coronation (*Marjana* or *Abhishekam*)	
Mantra	Same as the mantra above for chanting. Just add '*marjyami*' (Skt: मार्जयामि, mārjayāmi) at the end of your mantra.

Instructions	Say the mantra, take a bit of water as per the instructions in step 33 in *Essential Steps in the Rites of Invocation (Puruscharana)*, and add '*marjyami*' in the end when you put water back in the vessel.
Count	Do coronation 11 times.

Follow the 36 steps of the rites of invocation but please note that vow — step 16 — is to be performed only on the first night. The rest of the steps remain the same. The *nyasa*, application (*viniyoga*) and mantra will change every night. The mantra has been already specified in the previous table; viniyoga and *nyasa* are as follows.

Application (*Viniyoga*)

Sanskrit (Devanagri)	*Sanskrit (IAST)*
ॐ अस्य श्री आपः सृजन्तु स्निग्धानि इति श्रीसूक्त द्वादश्य मंत्रस्य श्री अजस ऋषि, श्री महा लक्ष्मी देवता, ह्रां बीज, शूलधारिणी शक्ति, पीताम्बरा महाविद्या, ल्हीं उत्कीलन, सर्व मंगल कारिण्यै भगवती लक्ष्मी प्रसाद सिद्धयर्थ द्वादश मंत्र जपे विनियोगः ।	oṃ asya śrī āpaḥ sṛjantu snigdhāni iti śrīsūkta dvādaśya maṃtrasya śrī ajasa ṛṣi, śrī mahā lakṣmī devatā, hrāṃ bīja, śūladhāriṇī śakti, pītāmbarā mahāvidyā, lhīṃ utkīlana, sarva maṃgala kāriṇyai bhagavatī lakṣmī prasāda siddhayartha dvādaśa maṃtra jape viniyogaḥ ।

Follow the standard procedure of *viniyoga* by taking a bit of water in your palm (as explained in step 18 in *Essential Steps in the Rites of Invocation*).

Perform the *nyasa* as per the tables below, in that order, starting with *Nyasa* of the Sages (*Rishyadi nyasa*).

Nyasa of the Sages (*Rishyadi Nyasa*)

Sanskrit (Devanagri)	*Sanskrit (IAST)*	*Touch with your right hand your*
श्री अजस ऋषये नमः सहस्त्रारे शिरसि ।	śrī ajasa ṛṣaye namaḥ sahastrāre śirasi I	Crown of the head
श्री महालक्ष्मी देवयै नमः द्वादशारे ह्रदि ।	śrī mahālakṣmī devayai namaḥ dvādaśāre hradi I	Heart
ह्रां बीजाय नमः षडारे योनौ ।	hrāṃ bījāya namaḥ ṣaḍāre yonau I	Groin
शूलधारिणी शक्त्यै नमः दशारे नाभौ ।	śūladhāriṇī śaktyai namaḥ daśāre nābhau I	Navel
पीताम्बर महाविद्यायै नमः षोडशारे कंठे ।	pītāmbara mahāvidyāyai namaḥ ṣoḍaśāre kaṃṭhe I	Throat
रजो गुणाय नमः अंतरारे मनसि ।	rajo guṇāya namaḥ aṃtarāre manasi I	Heart (again)
त्वक् ज्ञानेन्द्रिय नमः ज्ञानेन्द्रिये ।	tvak jñānenidraya namaḥ jñāneindraye I	Neck (*tvak* is skin. You can touch anywhere on your body where there's bare skin)
गुदा कर्मेन्द्रियाय नमः कर्मेन्द्रिये ।	gudā karmendriyāya namaḥ karmendriye I	Lower back (near your anus but keep your clothes on and just touch your lower back symbolically)
गंभीर स्वराय नमः कंठमूले ।	gaṃbhīra svarāya namaḥ kaṃṭhamūle I	Base of your throat (the soft area just below the Adam's apple)

Sanskrit (Devanagri)	*Sanskrit (IAST)*	*Touch with your right hand your*
भू तत्वाय नमः चतुरारे गुदे ।	bhū tatvāya namaḥ caturāre gude I	Lower back (near your anus but keep your clothes on and just touch your lower back symbolically)
प्रवृतिं कलायै नमः करतले ।	pravṛtiṃ kalāyai namaḥ karatale I	The palm of your left-hand
ल्हीं उत्किलनाय नमः पादयोः ।	lhīṃ utkilanāya namaḥ pādayoḥ I	Feet
मत्स्य मुद्रायै नमः सर्वांगे ।	matsya mudrāyai namaḥ sarvāṃge I	Whole body (do this by rolling your right-hand over your upper body by bringing it around and then clapping gently)

Now perform nyasa of the hands (*kara nyasa*). The mudras are the same as in step 17 (purification of the hands) of this chapter. You can see the illustrations in that table. I am providing the description again.

Nyasa of the Hands (*Kara Nyasa*)

Sanskrit (Devanagri)	*Sanskrit (IAST)*	*Gesture with both hands*
ॐ आपः सृजन्तु अंगुष्ठाभ्यां नमः ।	oṃ āpaḥ sṛjantu aṃguṣṭhābhyāṃ namaḥ I	Touch the tip of your thumb at the base of your index finger.
स्निग्धानि चिक्लीत तर्जनीभ्याम् स्वाहा ।	snigdhāni ciklīta tarjanībhyām svāhā I	Touch the tip of your thumb to the tip of your index finger.

Sanskrit (Devanagri)	Sanskrit (IAST)	Gesture with both hands
वस मे गृहे मध्यमाभ्यां वषट् ।	vasa me gṛhe madhyamābhyāṃ vaṣaṭ ।	Touch the tip of your thumb to the tip of your middle finger.
नि च देवीं अनामिकाभ्यां हुं ।	ni ca devīṃ anāmikābhyāṃ huṃ ।	Touch the tip of your thumb to the tip of your ring finger.
मातरं श्रियं कनिष्किाभ्यां वौषट् ।	mātaraṃ śriyaṃ kaniṣikābhyāṃ vauṣaṭ ।	Touch the tip of your thumb to the tip of your little finger.
वासय मे कुले करतलकरपृष्ठाभ्यां फट् ।	vāsaya me kule karatalakara-pṛṣṭhābhyāṃ phaṭ ।	Touch the back of your left-hand with the back of your right-hand and then clap softly.

Now do the final *nyasa* by performing six-limbed mantra *nyasa*. The mudras for this are the same as shown in Night 1. I'm giving the description again.

Six-Limbed Mantra *Nyasa* (*Shadanga* Mantra *Nyāsa*)

Sanskrit (Devanagri)	Sanskrit (IAST)	Description
ॐ आपः सृजन्तु ह्रदयाय नमः ।	oṃ āpaḥ sṛjantu hradayāya namaḥ ।	Touch your heart region with your right-hand.
स्निग्धानि चिक्लीत शिरसे स्वाहा ।	snigdhāni ciklīta śirase svāhā ।	Touch your forehead with your right-hand keeping the index finger away.
वस मे गृहे शिखायै वषट् ।	vasa me gṛhe śikhāyai vaṣaṭ ।	Make a fist with right-hand and extend your thumb. Now touch the crown of your head with your thumb.

Sanskrit (Devanagri)	*Sanskrit (IAST)*	*Description*
नि च देवीं कवचाय हुं ।	ni ca devīṃ kavacāya huṃ I	Touch your shoulders by crossing your hands.
मातरं श्रियं नेत्र त्रयाय वौषट् ।	mātaraṃ śriyaṃ netra trayāya vauṣaṭ I	Spread your right-hand and touch your right eye with your index finger, forehead with the middle finger and left eye with the ring finger simultaneously.
वासय मे कुले अस्त्राय फट् ।	vāsaya me kule astrāya phaṭ I	Take the right-hand over your head and then bring it back in front of you to clap softly.

Night 13

Chanting (*Japa*)	
Mantra Sanskrit (Devanagri)	ॐ आं ह्रीं श्रीं क्लीं ब्लूं सौं रं वं श्रीं ॐ श्रीं ह्रीं श्रीं नमः । आर्द्रां पुष्करिणीं पुष्टिं पिङ्गलां पद्ममालिनीम् । चन्द्रां हिरण्मयीं लक्ष्मीं जातवेदो म आवह ॥ नमो श्रीं ह्रीं श्रीं ॐ । ॐ आं ह्रीं श्रीं क्लीं ब्लूं सौं रं वं श्रीं ॐ ।।
Mantra Sanskrit (IAST)	oṃ āṃ hrīṃ śrīṃ klīṃ blūṃ sauṃ raṃ vaṃ śrīṃ oṃ śrīṃ hrīṃ śrīṃ namaḥ I ārdrāṃ puṣkariṇīṃ puṣṭiṃ piṅgalāṃ padmamālinīm I

	candrāṃ hiraṇmayīṃ lakṣmīṃ jātavedo ma āvaha || namo śrīṃ hrīṃ śrīṃ oṃ | oṃ āṃ hrīṃ śrīṃ klīṃ blūṃ sauṃ raṃ vaṃ śrīṃ oṃ ||	
Count	Chant this mantra 1000 times.	
Fire offerings (*Yajna*)		
Mantra	Same as above. Just add 'Om *Svaha*' (ॐ स्वाहा, oṃ svāhā) at the end of your mantra. Therefore, say the mantra, say '*Om Svaha*' and then make an offering in the fire pit.	
Count	Make fire-offerings 108 times.	
Ingredients for fire offerings	Ghee	200 grams
	Jaggery	50 grams
	Honey	50 grams
	White rice	50 grams
	Havan samagri	1 packet
	White sesame seeds	50 grams
	Red sandalwood	One small piece
Instructions	Follow the standard procedure of fire offerings as stated in *How to Make Fire Offerings (Yajna)*. 1. Mix jaggery, honey, rice, *havan samagri* and sesame seeds. 2. Put five tablespoons of melted ghee in it. Mix it thoroughly. 3. After you have made 108 offerings (*ahuti*), offer the last one with the small piece of white sandalwood. Dip it in ghee or put a bit of ghee in it and offer it in the fire pit. 4. Conclude by pouring any remaining ghee from the 200 grams you set aside for this *yajna*.	

	If you feel the fire going off or dousing while you do *yajna*, feel free to pour more ghee on the fire. Keep the fire alive.
Libations (*Tarpana*)	
Mantra	Same as the mantra above for chanting. Just add '*tarpyami*' (तर्प्यामि, tarpyāmi) at the end of your mantra.
Instructions	Say the mantra, take a bit of water as per the instructions in step 32 in *Essential Steps in the Rites of Invocation (Puruscharana)*, and add '*tarpyami*' in the end when you put water back in the vessel.
Count	Do libations 11 times.
Coronation (*Marjana or Abhishekam*)	
Mantra	Same as the mantra above for chanting. Just add '*marjyami*' (Skt: मार्जयामि, mārjayāmi) at the end of your mantra.
Instructions	Say the mantra, take a bit of water as per the instructions in step 33 in *Essential Steps in the Rites of Invocation (Puruscharana)*, and add '*marjyami*' in the end when you put water back in the vessel.
Count	Do coronation 11 times.

Follow the 36 steps of the rites of invocation but please note that vow — step 16 — is to be performed only on the first night. The rest of the steps remain the same. The *nyasa*, application (*viniyoga*) and mantra will change every night. The mantra has been already specified in the previous table; *viniyoga* and *nyasa* are as follows.

Application (*Viniyoga*)

Sanskrit (Devanagri)	*Sanskrit (IAST)*
ॐ अस्य श्री आर्द्रां पुष्करिणीं पुष्टिं इति श्रीसूक्त त्रयोदश मंत्रस्य मेधस ऋषि, श्री सर्वसौभाग्यदायिन्यै देवी द्रां बीज, भीमा शक्ति, ज्येष्ठा महाविद्या, ऐं उत्कीलन, सर्व मंगल कारिण्यै भगवती लक्ष्मी प्रसाद सिद्धयर्थ त्रयोदश मंत्र जपे विनियोगः ।	oṃ asya śrī ārdrāṃ puṣkariṇīṃ puṣṭiṃ iti śrīsūkta trayodaśa maṃtrasya medhasa ṛṣi, śrī sarvasaubhāgyadāyinyai devī drāṃ bīja, bhīmā śakti, jyeṣṭhā mahāvidyā, aiṃ utkīlana, sarva maṃgala kāriṇyai bhagavatī lakṣmī prasāda siddhayartha trayodaśa maṃtra jape viniyogaḥ ।
Follow the standard procedure of *viniyoga* by taking a bit of water in your palm (as explained in step 18 in *Essential Steps in the Rites of Invocation*).	

Perform the *nyasa* as per the tables below, in that order, starting with *Nyasa* of the Sages (*Rishyadi nyasa*).

Nyasa of the Sages (*Rishyadi Nyasa*)

Sanskrit (Devanagri)	*Sanskrit (IAST)*	*Touch with your right-hand your...*
श्री मेधस ऋषये नमः सहस्त्रारे शिरसि ।	śrī medhasa ṛṣaye namaḥ sahastrāre śirasi ।	Crown of the head
श्री सर्वसौभाग्यदायिन्यै देवयै नमः द्वादशारे हृदि ।	śrī sarvasaubhāgya-dāyinyai devayai namaḥ dvādaśāre hradi ।	Heart
द्रां बीजाय नमः षडारे योनौ ।	drāṃ bījāya namaḥ ṣaḍāre yonau ।	Groin
भीमा शक्त्यै नमः दशारे नाभौ ।	bhīmā śaktyai namaḥ daśāre nābhau ।	Navel

Sanskrit (Devanagri)	*Sanskrit (IAST)*	*Touch with your right-hand your...*
ज्येष्ठा महाविद्यायै नमः षोडशारे कंठे ।	jyeṣṭhā mahāvidyāyai namaḥ ṣoḍaśāre kaṃṭhe I	Throat
रजो गुणाय नमः अंतरारे मनसि ।	rajo guṇāya namaḥ aṃtarāre manasi I	Heart (again)
घ्राणं ज्ञानेन्द्रिय नमः ज्ञानेन्द्रिये ।	ghrāṇaṃ jñānenidraya namaḥ jñāneindraye I	Nose
पाणिकर्मेन्द्रियाय नमः कर्मेन्द्रिये ।	pāṇikarmendriyāya namaḥ karmendriye I	Touch your left-hand with your right
दीन स्वराय नमः कंठमूले ।	dīna svarāya namaḥ kaṃṭhamūle I	Base of your throat (the soft area just below the Adam's apple)
वायुस्तत्वाय नमः चतुरारे गुदे ।	vāyustatvāya namaḥ caturāre gude I	Lower back (near your anus but keep your clothes on and just touch your lower back symbolically)
पराशांति कलायै नमः करतले ।	parāśāṃti kalāyai namaḥ karatale I	The palm of your left hand
ऐं उत्किलनाय नमः पादयोः ।	aiṃ utkilanāya namaḥ pādayoḥ I	Feet
धेनु मुद्रायै नमः सर्वांगे ।	dhenu mudrāyai namaḥ sarvāṃge I	Whole body (do this by rolling your right hand over your upper body by bringing it around and then clapping gently)

Now perform *nyasa* of the hands (*kara nyasa*). The mudras are the same as in step 17 (purification of the hands) of this chapter.

You can see the illustrations in that table. I am providing the description again.

Nyasa of the Hands (*Kara Nyasa*)

Sanskrit (Devanagri)	*Sanskrit (IAST)*	*Gesture with both hands*
ॐ आर्द्रां पुष्करिणीं अंगुष्ठाभ्यां नमः ।	oṃ ārdrāṃ puṣkariṇīṃ aṃguṣṭhābhyāṃ namaḥ ।	Touch the tip of your thumb at the base of your index finger.
पुष्टिं पिङ्गलां तर्जनीभ्याम् स्वाहा ।	puṣṭiṃ piṅgalāṃ tarjanībhyām svāhā ।	Touch the tip of your thumb to the tip of your index finger.
पद्ममालिनीम् मध्यमाभ्यां वषट् ।	padmamālinīm madhyamābhyāṃ vaṣaṭ ।	Touch the tip of your thumb to the tip of your middle finger.
चन्द्रां हिरण्मयीं अनामिकाभ्यां हुं ।	candrāṃ hiraṇmayīṃ anāmikābhyāṃ huṃ ।	Touch the tip of your thumb to the tip of your ring finger.
लक्ष्मीं जातवेदो कनिष्किाभ्यां वौषट् ।	lakṣmīṃ jātavedo kaniṣikābhyāṃ vauṣaṭ ।	Touch the tip of your thumb to the tip of your little finger.
म आवह करतलकरपृष्ठाभ्यां फट् ।	ma āvaha karatalakara-pṛṣṭhābhyāṃ phaṭ ।	Touch the back of your left-hand with the back of your right-hand and then clap softly.

Now do the final *nyasa* by performing six-limbed mantra *nyasa*. The mudras for this are the same as shown in Night 1. I'm giving the description again.

Six-Limbed Mantra *Nyasa* (*Shadanga* Mantra *Nyāsa*)

Sanskrit (Devanagri)	*Sanskrit (IAST)*	*Description*
ॐ आर्द्रां पुष्करिणीं हृदयाय नमः ।	oṃ ārdrāṃ puṣkariṇīṃ hradayāya namaḥ I	Touch your heart region with your right-hand.
पुष्टिं पिङ्गलां शिरसे स्वाहा ।	puṣṭiṃ piṅgalāṃ śirase svāhā I	Touch your forehead with your right-hand keeping the index finger away.
पद्ममालिनीम् शिखायै वषट् ।	padmamālinīm śikhāyai vaṣaṭ I	Make a fist with right-hand and extend your thumb. Now touch the crown of your head with your thumb.
चन्द्रां हिरण्मयीं कवचाय हुं ।	candrāṃ hiraṇmayīṃ kavacāya huṃ I	Touch your shoulders by crossing your hands.
लक्ष्मीं जातवेदो नेत्रत्रयाय वौषट् ।	lakṣmīṃ jātavedo netratrayāya vauṣaṭ I	Spread your right-hand and touch your right eye with your index finger, forehead with the middle finger and left eye with the ring finger simultaneously.
म आवह अस्त्राय फट् ।	ma āvaha astrāya phaṭ I	Take the right-hand over your head and then bring it back in front of you to clap softly.

Night 14

Chanting (*Japa*)	
Mantra Sanskrit (Devanagri)	ॐ आं ह्रीं श्रीं क्लीं ब्लूं सौं रं वं श्रीं ॐ श्रीं ह्रीं श्रीं नमः । आर्द्रां यः करिणीं यष्टिं सुवर्णां हेममालिनीम् । सूर्यां हिरण्मयीं लक्ष्मीं जातवेदो म आवह ॥ नमो श्रीं ह्रीं श्रीं ॐ । ॐ आं ह्रीं श्रीं क्लीं ब्लूं सौं रं वं श्रीं ॐ ।।
Mantra Sanskrit (IAST)	oṃ āṃ hrīṃ śrīṃ klīṃ blūṃ sauṃ raṃ vaṃ śrīṃ oṃ śrīṃ hrīṃ śrīṃ namaḥ । ārdrāṃ yaḥ kariṇīṃ yaṣṭiṃ suvarṇāṃ hemamālinīm । sūryāṃ hiraṇmayīṃ lakṣmīṃ jātavedo ma āvaha ॥ namo śrīṃ hrīṃ śrīṃ oṃ । oṃ āṃ hrīṃ śrīṃ klīṃ blūṃ sauṃ raṃ vaṃ śrīṃ oṃ ।।
Count	Chant this mantra 1000 times.
	Fire offerings (*Yajna*)
Mantra	Same as above. Just add '*Om Svaha*' (ॐ स्वाहा, oṃ svāhā) at the end of your mantra. Therefore, say the mantra, say '*Om Svaha*' and then make an offering in the fire pit.
Count	Make fire-offerings 108 times.
Ingredients for fire offerings	Ghee — 200 grams Almonds — 50 grams *Havan samagri* — 1 packet Black sesame seeds — 50 grams White sandalwood — One small piece
Instructions	Follow the standard procedure of fire offerings as stated in *How to Make Fire Offerings (Yajna).*

	1. Mix almonds, *havan samagri* and sesame seeds. 2. Put five tablespoons of melted ghee in it. Mix it thoroughly. 3. After you have made 108 offerings (*ahuti*), offer the last one with the small piece of white sandalwood. Dip it in ghee or put a bit of ghee in it and offer it in the firepit. 4. Conclude by pouring any remaining ghee from the 200 grams you set aside for this *yajna*. If you feel the fire going off or dousing while you do *yajna*, feel free to pour more ghee on the fire. Keep the fire alive.
Libations (*Tarpana*)	
Mantra	Same as the mantra above for chanting. Just add '*tarpyami*' (तर्प्यामि, tarpyāmi) at the end of your mantra.
Instructions	Say the mantra, take a bit of water as per the instructions in step 32 in *Essential Steps in the Rites of Invocation (Puruscharana),* and add '*tarpyami*' in the end when you put water back in the vessel.
Count	Do libations 11 times.
Coronation (*Marjana* or *Abhishekam*)	
Mantra	Same as the mantra above for chanting. Just add '*marjyami*' (Skt: मार्जयामि, mārjayāmi) at the end of your mantra.
Instructions	Say the mantra, take a bit of water as per the instructions in step 33 in *Essential Steps in the Rites of Invocation (Puruscharana)*, and add '*marjyami*' in the end when you put water back in the vessel.
Count	Do coronation 11 times.

Follow the 36 steps of the rites of invocation but please note that vow — step 16 — is to be performed only on the first night. The rest of the steps remain the same. The *nyasa*, application (*viniyoga*) and mantra will change every night. The mantra has been already specified in the previous table; *viniyoga* and *nyasa* are as follows.

Application (*Viniyoga*)

Sanskrit (Devanagri)	*Sanskrit (IAST)*
ॐ अस्य श्री आर्द्रां यः करिणीं यष्टिं इति श्रीसूक्त चतुर्दश मंत्रस्य श्री वेद व्यास ऋषि, श्री सर्वाहलादिन्यै देवी रूं बीज, वारुणी शक्ति, श्री तारा महाविद्या, क्रीं उत्कीलन, श्री सर्व मंगल कारिण्यै भगवती लक्ष्मी प्रसाद सिद्धयर्थ चतुर्दश मंत्र जपे विनियोगः ।	oṃ asya śrī ārdrāṃ yaḥ kariṇīṃ yaṣṭiṃ iti śrīsūkta caturdaśa maṃtrasya śrī veda vyāsa ṛṣi, śrī sarvāhlādinyai devī rūṃ bīja, vāruṇī śakti, śrī tārā mahāvidyā, krīṃ utkīlana, śrī sarva maṃgala kāriṇyai bhagavatī lakṣmī prasāda siddhayartha caturdaśa maṃtra jape viniyogaḥ ।
Follow the standard procedure of *viniyoga* by taking a bit of water in your palm (as explained in step 18 in *Essential Steps in the Rites of Invocation*).	

Perform the *nyasa* as per the tables below, in that order, starting with *Nyasa* of the Sages (*Rishyadi nyasa*).

Nyasa of the Sages (*Rishyadi Nyasa*)

Sanskrit (Devanagri)	*Sanskrit (IAST)*	*Touch with your right-hand your...*
श्री वेद व्यास ऋषये नमः सहस्त्रारे शिरसि ।	śrī veda vyāsa ṛṣaye namaḥ sahastrāre śirasi ।	Crown of the head
श्री सर्वाहलादिन्यै देवयै नमः द्वादशारे हृदि ।	śrī sarvāhlādinyai devayai namaḥ dvādaśāre hradi ।	Heart

Sanskrit (Devanagri)	*Sanskrit (IAST)*	*Touch with your right-hand your...*
रूं बीजाय नमः षडारे योनौ ।	rūṃ bījāya namaḥ ṣaḍāre yonau ।	Groin
वारुणी शक्त्यै नमः दशारे नाभौ ।	vāruṇī śaktyai namaḥ daśāre nābhau ।	Navel
तारा महाविद्यायै नमः षोडशारे कंठे ।	tārā mahāvidyāyai namaḥ ṣoḍaśāre kaṃṭhe ।	Throat
सतो गुणाय नमः अंतरारे मनसि ।	sato guṇāya namaḥ aṃtarāre manasi ।	Heart (again)
श्रोत्र ज्ञानेन्द्रिय नमः ज्ञानेन्द्रिये ।	śrotra jñānenidraya namaḥ jñāneindraye ।	Ears
पद कर्मेन्द्रियाय नमः कर्मेन्द्रिये ।	pada karmendriyāya namaḥ karmendriye ।	Touch your left-hand with your right
मध्यम स्वराय नमः कंठमूले ।	madhyama svarāya namaḥ kaṃṭhamūle ।	Base of your throat (the soft area just below the Adam's apple)
वायु स्तत्वाय नमः चतुरारे गुदे ।	vāyu statvāya namaḥ caturāre gude ।	Lower back (near your anus but keep your clothes on and just touch your lower back symbolically)
विघा कलायै नमः करतले ।	vighā kalāyai namaḥ karatale ।	The palm of your left-hand
क्रीं उत्किलनाय नमः पादयोः ।	krīṃ utkilanāya namaḥ pādayoḥ ।	Feet
आकर्षिणी मुद्रायै नमः सर्वांगे ।	ākarṣiṇī mudrāyai namaḥ sarvāṃge ।	Whole body (do this by rolling your right-hand over your upper body by bringing it around and then clapping gently)

Now perform *nyasa* of the hands (*kara nyasa*). The mudras are the same as in step 17 (purification of the hands) of this chapter. You can see the illustrations in that table. I am providing the description again.

Nyasa of the Hands (Kara Nyasa)

Sanskrit (Devanagri)	*Sanskrit (IAST)*	*Gesture with both hands*
ॐ आर्द्रां यः अंगुष्ठाभ्यां नमः ।	oṃ ārdrāṃ yaḥ aṃguṣṭhābhyāṃ namaḥ ।	Touch the tip of your thumb at the base of your index finger.
करिणीं यष्टिं तर्जनीभ्याम् स्वाहा ।	kariṇīṃ yaṣṭiṃ tarjanībhyām svāhā ।	Touch the tip of your thumb to the tip of your index finger.
सुवर्णां हेममालिनीम् मध्यमाभ्यां वषट् ।	suvarṇāṃ hemamālinīm madhyamābhyāṃ vaṣaṭ ।	Touch the tip of your thumb to the tip of your middle finger.
सूर्यां हिरण्मयीं अनामिकाभ्यां हुं ।	sūryāṃ hiraṇmayīṃ anāmikābhyāṃ huṃ ।	Touch the tip of your thumb to the tip of your ring finger.
लक्ष्मीं जातवेदो कनिष्किाभ्यां वौषट् ।	lakṣmīṃ jātavedo kaniṣikābhyāṃ vauṣaṭ ।	Touch the tip of your thumb to the tip of your little finger.
म आवह करतलकरपृष्ठाभ्यां फट् ।	ma āvaha karatalakara-pṛṣṭhābhyāṃ phaṭ ।	Touch the back of your left-hand with the back of your right-hand and then clap softly.

Now do the final *nyasa* by performing six-limbed mantra *nyasa*. The mudras for this are the same as shown in Night 1. I'm giving the description again.

Six-Limbed Mantra *Nyasa* (*Shadanga* Mantra *Nyāsa*)

Sanskrit (Devanagri)	*Sanskrit (IAST)*	*Description*
ॐ आर्द्रां यः हृदयाय नमः ।	oṃ ārdrāṃ yaḥ hradayāya namaḥ I	Touch your heart region with your right-hand.
करिणीं यष्टिं शिरसे स्वाहा ।	kariṇīṃ yaṣṭiṃ śirase svāhā I	Touch your forehead with your right hand keeping the index finger away.
सुवर्णां हेममालिनीम् शिखायै वषट् ।	suvarṇāṃ hemamālinīm śikhāyai vaṣaṭ I	Make a fist with right-hand and extend your thumb. Now touch the crown of your head with your thumb.
सूर्यां हिरण्मयीं कवचाय हुं ।	sūryāṃ hiraṇmayīṃ kavacāya huṃ I	Touch your shoulders by crossing your hands.
लक्ष्मीं जातवेदो नेत्रत्रयाय वौषट् ।	lakṣmīṃ jātavedo netratrayāya vauṣaṭ I	Spread your right-hand and touch your right eye with your index finger, forehead with the middle finger and left eye with the ring finger simultaneously.
म आवह अस्त्राय फट् ।	ma āvaha astrāya phaṭ I	Take the right-hand over your head and then bring it back in front of you to clap softly.

Night 15

Chanting (*Japa*)

Mantra Sanskrit (Devanagri)	ॐ आं ह्रीं श्रीं क्लीं ब्लूं सौं रं वं श्रीं ॐ श्रीं ह्रीं श्रीं नमः । तां म आवह जातवेदो लक्ष्मीमनपगामिनीम् । यस्यां हिरण्यं प्रभूतं गावो दास्यो'श्वान् विन्देयं पूरुषानहम् ॥ नमो श्रीं ह्रीं श्रीं ॐ । ॐ आं ह्रीं श्रीं क्लीं ब्लूं सौं रं वं श्रीं ॐ ।।
Mantra Sanskrit (IAST)	oṃ āṃ hrīṃ śrīṃ klīṃ blūṃ sauṃ raṃ vaṃ śrīṃ oṃ śrīṃ hrīṃ śrīṃ namaḥ । tāṃ ma āvaha jātavedo lakṣmīmanapagāminīm । yasyāṃ hiraṇyaṃ prabhūtaṃ gāvo dāsyo'śvān vindeyaṃ pūruṣānaham ॥ namo śrīṃ hrīṃ śrīṃ oṃ । oṃ āṃ hrīṃ śrīṃ klīṃ blūṃ sauṃ raṃ vaṃ śrīṃ oṃ ।।
Count	Chant this mantra 1000 times.

Fire offerings (*Yajna*)

Mantra	Same as above. Just add '*Om Svaha*' (ॐ स्वाहा, oṃ svāhā) at the end of your mantra. Therefore, say the mantra, say '*Om Svaha*' and then make an offering in the fire pit.	
Count	Make fire-offerings 108 times.	
Ingredients for fire offerings	Ghee	200 grams
	Grated dry coconut	100 grams
	Havan samagri	1 packet
	White sesame seeds	50 grams
	Red sandalwood	One small piece
Instructions	Follow the standard procedure of fire offerings as stated in *How to Make Fire Offerings (Yajna)*. 1. Mix grated coconut, *havan samagri* and sesame seeds.	

	2. Put five tablespoons of melted ghee in it. Mix it thoroughly. 3. After you have made 108 offerings (*ahuti*), offer the last one with the small piece of red sandalwood. Dip it in ghee or put a bit of ghee in it and offer it in the fire pit. 4. Conclude by pouring any remaining ghee from the 200 grams you set aside for this *yajna*. If you feel the fire going off or dousing while you do *yajna*, feel free to pour more ghee on the fire. Keep the fire alive.
Libations (*Tarpana*)	
Mantra	Same as the mantra above for chanting. Just add '*tarpyami*' (तर्प्यामि, tarpyāmi) at the end of your mantra.
Instructions	Say the mantra, take a bit of water as per the instructions in step 32 in *Essential Steps in the Rites of Invocation (Puruscharana)*, and add '*tarpyami*' in the end when you put water back in the vessel.
Count	Do libations 11 times.
Coronation (*Marjana* or *Abhishekam*)	
Mantra	Same as the mantra above for chanting. Just add '*marjyami*' (Skt: मार्जयामि, mārjayāmi) at the end of your mantra.
Instructions	Say the mantra, take a bit of water as per the instructions in step 33 in *Essential Steps in the Rites of Invocation (Puruscharana)*, and add '*marjyami*' in the end when you put water back in the vessel.
Count	Do coronation 11 times.

Follow the 36 steps of the rites of invocation but please note that vow — step 16 — is to be performed only on the first night. The rest of the steps remain the same. The nyasa, application (*viniyoga*) and mantra will change every night. The mantra has been already specified in the previous table; *viniyoga* and *nyasa* are as follows.

Application (*Viniyoga*)

Sanskrit (Devanagri)	*Sanskrit (IAST)*
ॐ अस्य श्री तां म आवह जातवेदो इति श्रीसूक्त पंचदश मंत्रस्य श्री ब्रह्मा ऋषि, श्री सर्व शक्तयै देवी ज्रां बीज, धनदा शक्ति, मातंगी महाविद्या, श्रीं उत्कीलन, सर्व मंगल कारिण्यै भगवती लक्ष्मी प्रसाद सिद्धयर्थ पंचदश मंत्र जपे विनियोगः ।	oṃ asya śrī tāṃ ma āvaha jātavedo iti śrīsūkta paṃcadaśa maṃtrasya śrī brahmā ṛṣi, śrī sarva śaktayai devī jrāṃ bīja, dhanadā śakti, mātaṃgī mahāvidyā, śrīṃ utkīlana, sarva maṃgala kāriṇyai bhagavatī lakṣmī prasāda siddhayartha paṃcadaśa maṃtra jape viniyogaḥ I

Follow the standard procedure of *viniyoga* by taking a bit of water in your palm (as explained in step 18 in *Essential Steps in the Rites of Invocation*).

Perform the nyasa as per the tables below, in that order, starting with *Nyasa* of the Sages (*Rishyadi nyasa*).

Nyasa of the Sages (*Rishyadi Nyasa*)

Sanskrit (Devanagri)	*Sanskrit (IAST)*	*Touch with your right-hand your...*
श्री ब्रह्मा ऋषये नमः सहस्त्रारे शिरसि ।	śrī brahmā ṛṣaye namaḥ sahastrāre śirasi I	Crown of the head
श्री सर्व शक्तयै देवयै नमः द्वादशारे ह्रदि ।	śrī sarva śaktayai devayai namaḥ dvādaśāre hradi I	Heart
ज्रां बीजाय नमः षडारे योनौ ।	jrāṃ bījāya namaḥ ṣaḍāre yonau I	Groin
धनदा शक्त्यै नमः दशारे नाभौ ।	dhanadā śaktyai namaḥ daśāre nābhau I	Navel

Sanskrit (Devanagri)	*Sanskrit (IAST)*	*Touch with your right-hand your...*
मातंगी महाविद्यायै नमः षोडशारे कंठे ।	mātaṃgī mahāvidyāyai namaḥ ṣoḍaśāre kaṃṭhe |	Throat
रजो गुणाय नमः अंतरारे मनसि ।	rajo guṇāya namaḥ aṃtarāre manasi |	Heart (again)
त्वक् ज्ञानेन्द्रिय नमः ज्ञानेन्द्रिये ।	tvak jñānenidraya namaḥ jñāneindraye |	Anywhere on your bare skin
पाद कर्मेन्द्रियाय नमः कर्मेन्द्रिये ।	pāda karmendriyāya namaḥ karmendriye |	Touch your left-hand with your right
मृदु स्वराय नमः कंठमूले ।	mṛdu svarāya namaḥ kaṃṭhamūle |	Base of your throat (the soft area just below the Adam's apple)
आकाश तत्वाय नमः चतुरारे गुदे ।	ākāśa tatvāya namaḥ caturāre gude |	Lower back (near your anus but keep your clothes on and just touch your lower back symbolically)
परा शांति कलायै नमः करतले ।	parā śāṃti kalāyai namaḥ karatale |	The palm of your left-hand
श्रीं उत्किलनाय नमः पादयोः ।	śrīṃ utkilanāya namaḥ pādayoḥ |	Feet
सम्पुट मुद्रायै नमः सर्वांगे ।	samputa mudrāyai namaḥ sarvāṃge |	Whole body (do this by rolling your right-hand over your upper body by bringing it around and then clapping gently)

Now perform *nyasa* of the hands (*kara nyasa*). The mudras are the same as in step 17 (purification of the hands) of this chapter. You can see the illustrations in that table. I am providing the description again.

Nyasa of the Hands (_Kara Nyasa_)

Sanskrit (Devanagri)	*Sanskrit (IAST)*	*Gesture with both hands*
ॐ तां म आवह अंगुष्ठाभ्यां नमः ।	oṃ tāṃ ma āvaha aṃguṣṭhābhyāṃ namaḥ ।	Touch the tip of your thumb at the base of your index finger.
जातवेदो तर्जनीभ्याम् स्वाहा ।	jātavedo tarjanībhyām svāhā ।	Touch the tip of your thumb to the tip of your index finger.
लक्ष्मीमनपगामिनीम् मध्यमाभ्यां वषट् ।	lakṣmīmanapa-gāminīm madhyamābhyāṃ vaṣaṭ ।	Touch the tip of your thumb to the tip of your middle finger.
यस्यां हिरण्यं अनामिकाभ्यां हुं ।	yasyāṃ hiraṇyaṃ anāmikābhyāṃ huṃ ।	Touch the tip of your thumb to the tip of your ring finger.
प्रभूतं गावो दास्यो'श्वान् कनिष्किाभ्यां वौषट् ।	prabhūtaṃ gāvo dāsyo'śvān kaniṣikābhyāṃ vauṣaṭ ।	Touch the tip of your thumb to the tip of your little finger.
विन्देयं पूरुषानहम् करतलकरपृष्ठाभ्यां फट् ।	vindeyaṃ pūruṣānaham karatalakara-pṛṣṭhābhyāṃ phaṭ ।	Touch the back of your left-hand with the back of your right-hand and then clap softly.

Now do the final *nyasa* by performing six-limbed mantra *nyasa*. The mudras for this are the same as shown in Night 1. I'm giving the description again.

Six-Limbed Mantra *Nyasa* (*Shadanga* Mantra *Nyāsa*)

Sanskrit (Devanagri)	*Sanskrit (IAST)*	*Description*
ॐ तां म आवह हृदयाय नमः ।	oṃ tāṃ ma āvaha hradayāya namaḥ I	Touch your heart region with your right-hand.
जातवेदो शिरसे स्वाहा ।	jātavedo śirase svāhā I	Touch your forehead with your right-hand keeping the index finger away.
लक्ष्मीमनपगामिनीम् शिखायै वषट् ।	lakṣmīmana-pagāminīm śikhāyai vaṣaṭ I	Make a fist with right-hand and extend your thumb. Now touch the crown of your head with your thumb.
यस्यां हिरण्यं कवचाय हुं ।	yasyāṃ hiraṇyaṃ kavacāya huṃ I	Touch your shoulders by crossing your hands.
प्रभूतं गावो दास्यो'श्वान् नेत्रत्रयाय वौषट् ।	prabhūtaṃ gāvo dāsyo'śvān netratrayāya vauṣaṭ I	Spread your right-hand and touch your right eye with your index finger, forehead with the middle finger and left eye with the ring finger simultaneously.
विन्देयं पूरुषानहम् अस्त्राय फट् ।	vindeyaṃ pūruṣānaham astrāya phaṭ I	Take the right-hand over your head and then bring it back in front of you to clap softly.

Night 16

Night 16 (Last Night)

Chanting (*Japa*)		
Mantra Sanskrit (Devanagri)	ॐ आं ह्रीं श्रीं क्लीं ब्लूं सौं रं वं श्रीं ॐ श्रीं ह्रीं श्रीं नमः । यः शुचिः प्रयतो भूत्वा जुहुयादाज्यमन्वहम् । सूक्तं पञ्चदशर्चं च श्रीकामः सततं जपेत् ॥ नमो श्रीं ह्रीं श्रीं ॐ । ॐ आं ह्रीं श्रीं क्लीं ब्लूं सौं रं वं श्रीं ॐ ॥	
Mantra Sanskrit (IAST)	oṃ āṃ hrīṃ śrīṃ klīṃ blūṃ sauṃ raṃ vaṃ śrīṃ oṃ śrīṃ hrīṃ śrīṃ namaḥ I yaḥ śuciḥ prayato bhūtvā juhuyādājyamanvaham I sūktaṃ pañcadaśarcaṃ ca śrīkāmaḥ satataṃ japet II namo śrīṃ hrīṃ śrīṃ oṃ I oṃ āṃ hrīṃ śrīṃ klīṃ blūṃ sauṃ raṃ vaṃ śrīṃ oṃ II	
Count	Chant this mantra 1000 times.	
Fire offerings (*Yajna*)		
Mantra	Same as above. Just add '*Om Svaha*' (ॐ स्वाहा, oṃ svāhā) at the end of your mantra. Therefore, say the mantra, say '*Om Svaha*' and then make an offering in the fire pit.	
Count	Make fire offerings 108 times.	
Ingredients for fire offerings	Ghee	500 grams
	Grated dry coconut	100 grams
	Lotus seeds	50 grams
	Jaggery	50 grams
	Almonds	50 grams

Cardamom	20 grams
White rice	50 grams
Havan samagri	2 packets
Black sesame seeds	50 grams
White sesame seeds	50 grams
White sandalwood	One small piece
Red sandalwood	One small piece
Full dry coconut	One piece

Instructions

Follow the standard procedure of fire offerings as stated in *How to Make Fire Offerings (Yajna)*.

1. Mix grated coconut, lotus seeds, jaggery, almonds, cardamom, rice, *havan samagri* and sesame seeds.
2. Put ten tablespoons of melted ghee in it. Mix it thoroughly.
3. Make 108 offerings (*ahuti*) with your mantra for the night.
4. Since this is the last night, make 108 more offerings with the following mantra:

ॐ महादेव्यै च विद्महे विष्णुपत्नी च धीमहि,
तन्नो लक्ष्मीः प्रचोदयात् ।

ōm mahādevyai ca vidmahe viṣṇupatnī ca dhīmahi,
tanno lakṣmīḥ pracodayāt ।

5. Once you are done making the offerings above, take both pieces of sandalwood (red and white) and dip them in ghee or pour a bit of ghee on them. Thereafter, offer both together with your mantra you used on the 16th night.
6. Draw a hole in your dry coconut and put some ghee in it alongwith a bit of the mixture of *havan samagri* above (where you mixed grated coconut and lotus seeds, etc.). Chant all the 16 verses of *Sri Suktam* and offer the coconut in the fire pit.

	7. Conclude by pouring any remaining ghee from the 500 grams you set aside for this *yajna*. If you feel the fire going off or dousing while you do *yajna*, feel free to pour more ghee on the fire. Keep the fire alive.
Libations (*Tarpana*)	
Mantra	Same as the mantra above for chanting. Just add '*tarpyami*' (तर्प्यामि, tarpyāmi) at the end of your mantra.
Instructions	Say the mantra, take a bit of water as per the instructions in step 32 in *Essential Steps in the Rites of Invocation (Puruscharana)*, and add '*tarpyami*' in the end when you put water back in the vessel.
Count	Do libations 11 times.
Coronation (*Marjana* or *Abhishekam*)	
Mantra	Same as the mantra above for chanting. Just add '*marjyami*' (Skt: मार्जयामि, mārjayāmi) at the end of your mantra.
Instructions	Say the mantra, take a bit of water as per the instructions in step 33 in *Essential Steps in the Rites of Invocation (Puruscharana)*, and add '*marjyami*' in the end when you put water back in the vessel.
Count	Do coronation 11 times.

Follow the 36 steps of the rites of invocation but please note that vow — step 16 — is to be performed only on the first night. The rest of the steps remain the same. The nyasa, application (*viniyoga*) and mantra will change every night. The mantra has been already specified in the previous table, *viniyoga* and *nyasa* are as follows.

Application (*Viniyoga*)

Sanskrit (Devanagri)	*Sanskrit (IAST)*
ॐ अस्य श्री यः शुचिः प्रयतो भूत्वा इति श्री सूक्त षोडश पंचदश मंत्रस्य श्री ब्रह्मा ऋषि, श्री महा सरस्वती देवता प्रूं बीज, सिद्धिदा शक्ति, श्री कमला महाविद्या, ह्रीं उत्कीलन, सर्व मंगल कारिण्यै भगवती लक्ष्मी प्रसाद सिद्धयर्थ षोडश मंत्र जपे विनियोगः।	oṃ asya śrī yaḥ śuciḥ prayato bhūtvā iti śrī sūkta ṣoḍaśa paṃcadaśa maṃtrasya śrī brahmā ṛṣi, śrī mahā sarasvatī devatā prūṃ bīja, siddhidā śakti, śrī kamalā mahāvidyā, hrīṃ utkīlana, sarva maṃgala kāriṇyai bhagavatī lakṣmī prasāda siddhayartha ṣoḍaśa maṃtra jape viniyogaḥ I

Follow the standard procedure of *viniyoga* by taking a bit of water in your palm (as explained in step 18 in *Essential Steps in the Rites of Invocation*).

Perform the *nyasa* as per the tables below, in that order, starting with Nyasa of the Sages (*Rishyadi nyasa*).

Nyasa of the Sages (*Rishyadi Nyasa*)

Sanskrit (Devanagri)	*Sanskrit (IAST)*	*Touch with your right-hand your...*
श्री ब्रह्मा ऋषये नमः सहस्त्रारे शिरसि ।	śrī brahmā ṛṣaye namaḥ sahastrāre śirasi I	Crown of the head
श्री महा सरस्वत्यै देव्यै नमः द्वादशारे हृदि ।	śrī mahā sarasvatyai devyai namaḥ dvādaśāre hradi I	Heart
'प्रूं' बीजाय नमः षडारे योनौ ।	'prūṃ' bījāya namaḥ ṣaḍāre yonau I	Groin
सिद्धिदा शक्त्यै नमः दशारे नाभौ ।	siddhidā śaktyai namaḥ daśāre nābhau I	Navel

Sanskrit (Devanagri)	*Sanskrit (IAST)*	*Touch with your right-hand your...*
श्री कमला महाविद्यायै नमः षोडशारे कंठे ।	śrī kamalā mahāvidyāyai namaḥ ṣoḍaśāre kaṃṭhe I	Throat
सतो गुणाय नमः अंतरारे मनसि ।	sato guṇāya namaḥ aṃtarāre manasi I	Heart (again)
घ्राणं ज्ञानेन्द्रिय नमः ज्ञानेन्द्रिये ।	ghrāṇaṃ jñānenidraya namaḥ jñāneindraye I	Anywhere on your bare skin
पाद कर्मेन्द्रियाय नमः कर्मेन्द्रिये ।	pāda karmendriyāya namaḥ karmendriye I	Touch your left-hand with your right.
मृदु स्वराय नमः कंठमूले ।	mṛdu svarāya namaḥ kaṃṭhamūle I	Base of your throat (the soft area just below the Adam's apple)
जल तत्वाय नमः चतुरारे गुदे ।	jala tatvāya namaḥ caturāre gude I	Lower back (near your anus but keep your clothes on and just touch your lower back symbolically)
शांति कलायै नमः करतले ।	śāṃti kalāyai namaḥ karatale I	The palm of your left-hand
ह्रीं उत्किलनाय नमः पादयोः ।	hrīṃ utkilanāya namaḥ pādayoḥ I	Feet
योनि मुद्रायै नमः सर्वांगे ।	yoni mudrāyai namaḥ sarvāṃge I	Whole body (Do this by rolling your right-hand over your upper body by bringing it around and then clapping gently)

Now perform *nyasa* of the hands (*kara nyasa*). The mudras are the same as in step no. 17 (purification of the hands) of this chapter. You can see the illustrations in that table. I am providing the description again.

Nyasa of the Hands (Kara Nyasa)

Sanskrit (Devanagri)	*Sanskrit (IAST)*	*Gesture with both hands*
ॐ यः शुचिः अंगुष्ठाभ्यां नमः ।	oṃ yaḥ śuciḥ aṃguṣṭhābhyāṃ namaḥ ।	Touch the tip of your thumb at the base of your index finger.
प्रयतो भूत्वा तर्जनीभ्याम् स्वाहा ।	prayato bhūtvā tarjanībhyām svāhā ।	Touch the tip of your thumb to the tip of your index finger.
जुहुयादाज्यमन्वहम् मध्यमाभ्यां वषट् ।	juhuyādājyamanvaham madhyamābhyāṃ vaṣaṭ ।	Touch the tip of your thumb to the tip of your middle finger.
सूक्तं पञ्चदशर्चं अनामिकाभ्यां हुं ।	sūktaṃ pañcadaśarcaṃ anāmikābhyāṃ huṃ ।	Touch the tip of your thumb to the tip of your ring finger.
च श्रीकामः कनिष्किाभ्यां वौषट् ।	ca śrīkāmaḥ kaniṣikābhyāṃ vauṣaṭ ।	Touch the tip of your thumb to the tip of your little finger.
सततं जपेत् करतलकरपृष्ठाभ्यां फट् ।	satataṃ japet karatalakara-pṛṣṭhābhyāṃ phaṭ ।	Touch the back of your left-hand with the back of your right-hand and then clap softly.

Now do the final *nyasa* by performing six-limbed mantra *nyasa*. The mudras for this are the same as shown in Night 1. I'm giving the description again.

Six-Limbed Mantra *Nyasa* (*Shadanga* Mantra *Nyāsa*)

Sanskrit (Devanagri)	*Sanskrit (IAST)*	*Description*
ॐ यः शुचिः हृदयाय नमः ।	oṃ yaḥ śuciḥ hradayāya namaḥ ǀ	Touch your heart region with your righthand.
प्रयतो भूत्वा शिरसे स्वाहा ।	prayato bhūtvā śirase svāhā ǀ	Touch your forehead with your right-hand keeping the index finger away.
जुहुयादाज्यमन्वहम् शिखायै वषट् ।	juhuyādājya-manvaham śikhāyai vaṣaṭ ǀ	Make a fist with right-hand and extend your thumb. Now touch the crown of your head with your thumb.
सूक्तं पञ्चदशर्चं कवचाय हुं ।	sūktaṃ pañcadaśarcaṃ kavacāya huṃ ǀ	Touch your shoulders by crossing your hands.
च श्रीकामः नेत्रत्रयाय वौषट् ।	ca śrīkāmaḥ netratrayāya vauṣaṭ ǀ	Spread your right-hand and touch your right eye with your index finger, forehead with the middle finger and left eye with the ring finger simultaneously.
सततं जपेत् अस्त्राय फट् ।	satataṃ japet astrāya phaṭ ǀ	Take the right-hand over your head and then bring it back in front of you to clap softly.

If you are someone who diligently followed the routine for a period of 960 days and have completed this *sadhana* with utmost devotion, I must tell you that you are a very special person. In the last 27 years, I have met so many *sadhakas* and less than .001% even try to go this right till the end. In fact, I've only met two people who have walked the path of this *sadhana* till the end.

If you have made this far and completed the *sadhana* of *Sri Suktam* as per the injunctions and instructions in this book, the grace of Devi now lives in you. I congratulate you and offer my deepest respects to you. I really do. Because you have accomplished that which is beyond the reach of an ordinary person. The goddess of prosperity and affluence blesses you.

RITES OF ATONEMENT (PRAYASHCHITTA)

न तदस्ति पृथिव्यां वा दिवि देवेषु वा पुनः।
सत्त्वं प्रकृतिजैर्मुक्तं यदेभिः स्यातित्रभिर्गुणैः।।

na tadasti pṛthivyāṃ vā divi deveṣu vā punaḥ।
sattvaṃ prakṛtijairmuktaṃ yadebhiḥ syātitrabhirguṇaiḥ।।

There is no one in this world or any other who is free from
the three modes of material nature
(sattva, rajas, tamas or goodness, passion and ignorance).
(Bhagavad Gita, 18.40. My own translation.)

It is not uncommon for an aspirant to make mistakes while treading the path. Such mistakes could be intentional or unintentional acts violating the principles of sadhana. Whether it is accidentally missing your japa or committing any other sin during the rites of invocation (*purushcharana*), it is important to understand various options available to you for expiation. In this chapter, I share with you the scriptural injunctions prescribed for the atonement of undesirable acts.

Immersed in a religious text, Rabbi Kagan, commonly known as the Chofetz Chaim, was traveling on a train. Three Jews, who sat alongside, invited him to play cards with them since they needed a fourth hand. The rabbi refused saying he preferred his reading over playing cards. The three travelers were clueless about the fact that the stranger they were soliciting was the famous Chofetz Chaim himself. They tried their luck a couple of times more and eventually becoming frustrated, got mad. One of them punched him in the face while the other two cheered. The rabbi grabbed his hanky to dab his wound but drops of blood had already leaked and fell on his book.

A few hours later, the train pulled into the station. Scores of people had gathered there to welcome the sage. He got off the train with a gashed face and the devotees demanded to know who hurt him. The rabbi whiffed aside the question and continued walking. The three culprits were plagued by guilt at the realization that they had not just beaten up some poor old fellow but the Chofetz Chaim.

They met him the next day at his home to seek his forgiveness. With remorse and shame, they begged him to absolve them. The rabbi, however, said no and refused them the gift of forgiveness. The rabbi's son, who was a witness to all this, was taken aback. It was a saint's job to forgive after all. The offenders pleaded again and yet again the rabbi said no. They left with a heavy heart.

"Father," his son said, "pardon me for saying this but I feel your behavior was a bit cruel. You are a spiritual icon, the whole community looks up to you. Why didn't you forgive them?"

"You are right, son," the rabbi said. "Denying them forgiveness was unbecoming of me, but the truth is it was not in my power to forgive them.

"Of course, I Rabbi Kagan, the Chofetz Chaim, forgive them," he continued, "but my forgiveness does not matter. The man they had beaten was the one they presumed to be a simple, unassuming poor person with no crowd of well-wishers waiting to greet him. He was the victim and only he can grant them forgiveness. Let them go find that person. I am incapable of releasing them from their guilt."

The Sanskrit word for atonement, repentance, expiation or penance is *prāyaścitta.* Of all the acts requiring expiation, the hardest is to seek forgiveness because sometimes there is no recourse. The other person may wish to forgive you but at times, it's just not possible. Therefore, before I share with you various ways to atone for your undesirable acts, I thought it was best to give you the greatest antidote at the outset. It is: mindfulness. The more mindful we are while thinking, speaking or acting, the less likely we are to make mistakes that harm ourselves and others or weaken us by making us feel guilty.

On the path of mantra yoga when you breach any of the rules of sadhana, you are required to perform rites of expiation (*prāyaścitta).* If there are any specific injunctions for the sadhanas listed in this book, I've stated them in the chapter on that sadhana. At any rate, the three core principles of mantra sadhana are non-violence, truthfulness and mantra chanting (*japa*). Living in the world, it is understandable that you may not always be able to speak the truth. Telling a lie does not mean that your sadhana is compromised, such acts do, however, weaken you somewhere within. All may be forgiven but an act of violence has no recourse. Still, no matter what you might have done, the rites of expiation will purify you and help you get past the guilt.

It is important to note that expiation does not mean that we keep committing mistakes and keep performing the rites to redeem ourselves. It only works when we are genuinely sorry for what we have done (consciously or otherwise) and have every intention of not repeating it. There are eleven ways to atone for your mistakes.

1. Fasting (*Vrata* or *Upavāsa*)

This is the most common act of repentance as per Puranas and other texts of *Sanatana Dharma.* In mantra sadhana, this is done by skipping all meals and surviving only on water for 24 hours. Or one wish to do it even harder, he or she can skip water as well. The lunar date of keeping this fast should be the same as when you started the sadhana. For example, you started your mantra sadhana on the night of full-moon. If you commit any act for which you need to atone, you must wait for the next full-moon for fasting. This is the simplest form of fasting. There are longer and harder fasts too (e.g. *Chandrayana vrata* etc.) that a guru may prescribe depending on the nature of your breach.

Fasting is not always done by way of dietary regulation. There are numerous other ways. For example, if you said hurtful words to anyone, you may observe complete silence for 24 hours and so on. In mantra yoga, however, fasting when done as atonement is often in the form of abstaining from food.

2. Penance (*Tapas*)

Though mantra sadhana is tapas in its own right, yet, for expiation purposes, you may choose to wear wet clothes till they dry on your body, or sleep on the ground, or any other practice that reminds you that you committed an act which you never wish to repeat.

3. Charity (*Dāna*)

Donating gold, silver, cows, milk, food grains, land or anything one can afford is another way. Ideally, charity should be given to a worthy recipient (*pātra*), the one who will make good use of your donation and use it for greater good. If you can't find a worthy recipient then charity may be given to anyone who is needy. Charity that is made to someone who is neither needy nor worthy, is worthless. Such philanthropy does not bring peace or inner strength.

4. Chanting (*Japa*)

You may double the amount of your mantra chanting for one, three or seven days during your sadhana. For example, if you have vowed to chant your mantra 1000 times every day for 40 days during the rites of invocation (*puruscharana*), on the day you wish to atone, chant the same mantra an additional 1000 times making it 2000 times all up.

5. Fire-offerings (*Yajna, Homa* or *Agnihotra*)

Simply do a yajna as mentioned in the chapter "How to Make Fire-Offerings". You may also engage a learned Vedic scholar to do a more elaborate yajna.

6. Repentance (*Anutāpa*)

You may go into solitude for a day or so and remind yourself of your evil action, mindfully firming your resolve to never repeat it.

7. Confession (*Abhiśasta*)

You go to a stranger's place, confess your act, seek forgiveness and beg them for a meal. You may also confess your sin in front of a living guru. If that is not possible, you may do so with utmost sincerity in front of a lamp, holy book or an idol. The best, under most (not all) circumstances, is to confess your crime in front of the victim and seek his or her forgiveness.

8. Pilgrimage (*Tirtha*)

You may undertake pilgrimage to a religious place. Traditionally, it was recommended to do that on foot so that every step on an arduous journey will make you more mindful about how you ought to live your life. Puranas define pilgrimage of three types:

a. Moving pilgrimage (*Jangama Tirtha*)

This is done by visiting a living guru, an accomplished saint or an ascetic. Their glimpse (darshan) relieves one of one's sins as per the scriptures. Goswami Tulasidas writes that just like the moon in winter takes away all the heat of the day, the darshan of a saint takes away the painful effects of our bad karma (*Sarda tapa Shashi nisi apaharahi, sant daras jimi pataka tarahi).*

b. Fixed pilgrimage (*Sthavara Tirtha*)

This is done by visiting a holy place like Kashi, Badrinath etc. or any of the numerous holy places around the world.

c. Mental Pilgrimage (*Manas Tirtha*)

When one is unable to visit his guru or any other holy place, it is said that he or she can simply make that visit in their mind. Self purification is also a mental pilgrimage. When you practice non-violence, truth, forgiveness and compassion, it's the equivalent of *manas tirtha.*

9. Bathing (*Snanam*)

Taking a dip in a holy river is also recommended in many religious texts for the atonement of one's sins.

10. Consuming concoction of cow products (*Panch gavya*)

Pancha gavya is made by mixing five products of a cow. They are cow-dung, urine, ghee, milk and yogurt. These are mixed in the following ratio:

20 units of yogurt
10 units of milk
5 units of ghee
2 units of urine
1 unit of cow-dung

Each unit is any measurement unit be it one milligram, gram, ounce or any other. Consumption of *panch gavya* is symbolic. I have stated it here for I wanted to share with you all the methods, though it is my personal belief that consumption of cow dung may lead to infection or other health problems. Particularly in this day and age when we have increasingly sensitive stomachs.

11. Word of the guru (*Guru vākyam*)

According to numerous religious texts, whatever act your guru prescribes for expiation takes precedence over all other methods of atonement. I would like to mention a word of caution here. Our world today is full of all kinds of gurus, many of whom are anything but genuine. Please be careful before you place your trust in someone's hands.

You may choose any, many or all of the above to atone your sins depending on the nature of your sin. If it's a major sin (*mahapātaka*) or a minor sin (*anupātaka*),expiation is a good way of becoming more mindful and reflecting on our actions that could have been avoided.

HOW TO MAKE FIRE OFFERINGS (YAJNA)

भूर्भुवःस्वस्तरुस्तारः सविता प्रपितामहः ।
यज्ञो यज्ञपतिर्यज्वा यज्ञाङ्गो यज्ञवाहनः ॥

यज्ञभृद् यज्ञकृद् यज्ञी यज्ञभुग् यज्ञसाधनः ।
यज्ञान्तकृद् यज्ञगुह्यमन्नमन्नाद एव च ॥

bhūrbhuvaḥsvastarustāraḥ savitā prapitāmahaḥ ।
yajño yajñapatiryajvā yajñāṅgo yajñavāhanaḥ ।

yajñabhṛd yajñakṛd yajñī yajñabhug yajñasādhanaḥ ।
yajñāntakṛd yajñaguhyamannamannāda eva ca ।

The one who is the essence of three lokas and three states of mind, nature and existence, that one who lights up our path and is the eternal father, his very nature is yajna. He alone is the enjoyer of all yajnas. He, the lord of yajnas, represents the Vedic injunctions of fire-offerings and all limbs of yajnas, he bestows the rewards of such yajna.

He, the ruler of yajnas, is the one performing fire-offerings (through me for, he's one without second, he alone exists). That sole enjoyer and the only recipient of all offerings made in that firepit. He, the final offering,

fulfils all yajnas and remains the greatest mystical realization of a yajna. He's all sustenance (food) and the enjoyer of such sustenance.
(Vishnu Sahasranamam, 104, 105. My own translation.)

If there's one thing without which no religious rite is ever performed in *sanatana dharma*, that will be the use of fire. Whether that fire is in the form of a lamp or offerings in a fire-pit or even libations (*arghyam*) to the greatest fire-ball, sun, often the presence of fire marks the beginning and end of life. The fire of passion is the seed of our body, the fire in a mother's womb sustains us, the fire of our desires propels us, the fire in our bellies digests our food, the fire in our bodies ages us and ultimately, it is to fire that we are given at the time of cremation.

Therefore, a *yajna* not only represents fire-offerings made in a fire-pit, but an expression of gratitude towards all things that govern our lives. In sanatana dharma (commonly known as the hindu religion), there are five types of yajna:

1. Offerings to all living beings (*bhuta-yajna*): This involves feeding birds and animals, planting trees, watering plants and mindful usage of natural resources.
2. Charity and mutual respect (*manushya-yajna*): To respectfully receive a guest, to respect other people's space, existence and freedom, to help others to the best of one's abilities is *manushya-yajna*.
3. Offerings to our ancestors (*pitr-yajna*): This involves donating food, money, clothes and so on in the memory of our ancestors to thank them. After all, even if they left no material legacy for someone, their seed is the reason why you are here.
4. Offerings to gods (*deva-yajna*): By making water and fire offerings, we perform deva-yajna. This type of yajna along with the one below is our primary focus presently.
5. Offering to the Universe (*brahma-yajna*): This is done by chanting Vedic mantras. Therefore, in mantra yoga, no fire

offerings are made without associating a mantra with them. For, on the path of mantra sadhana, sound (manifest or silence) is our first connection with the divine energy.

That which helps us realize the truth (*jna*) of now, the present moment, (*ya*) is *yajna*. Our life is a series of present-moments.

The yajna that has fire-offerings is also called *homam* or *agnihotra*. It can be as elaborate as easily lasting eight hours or more, or it can be concise enough to be wrapped up within 15-20 minutes. What kind of *yajna* you do depends entirely on the nature and purpose of your *sadhana*. In this chapter, as far as mantra-yoga is concerned, to make effective fire-offerings, I present to you the short but sufficient steps of a yajna.

Ingredients required for fire offerings

Bricks and sand if you are making your own elevated platform (vedi).

An oil lamp. Incense is optional.

Ghee (or any specific oil as prescribed in the sadhana).

Any Spoon or wooden spoons to make offerings of ghee.

A small water pot.

Yajna ingredients (they are different for various sadhanas. Once again, for the sadhanas listed in this book, I've specified the ingredients.)

Firewood (small sticks usually suffice unless you are doing a large yajna).

A dry coconut. This is used in the end to offer the last oblation (ahuti). The coconut is punctured (if it's with skin) or cut at the top (if it's without skin) and a bit of ghee and yajna ingredients are put in that (the lid is put back on the top if it's without skin).

A bucket of water (I've done thousands of yajnas in my life and never needed to douse the fire. But, if you are starting out, you may want to keep a bucket of water close by in case of any fire hazard.)

How to make a fire-pit (*yajna-kunda*)

The shape of a fire-pit can be a square, circle, rhombus, star, triangle, trapezium or undefined. The shape and size of a fire-pit is determined based on your mantra sadhana. For simplicity purposes and for the sadhanas contained in this book, you need the most commonly used fire-pit: a square.

You can buy them readymade from the market. They are portable and the most common ones are made from iron. Or you can dig a pit in the ground. Ideally, it should be as deep as wide and long. A fire-pit of 2 ft x 2 ft x 2 ft or even 1.5 ft x 1.5 ft x 1.5 ft is usually enough. If you can't dig a pit or source a fire-pit from the market, you can build your own platform, a slightly elevated piece of ground (*vedi*). Here's how to do it:

Fire-pit without boundary

This is suitable for small yajnas with no more than 108 fire offerings of the main (mula) mantra. You will need eight bricks to make the most basic one. Lay them horizontally on a clean surface in the following pattern as per the diagram below to make a fire-pit. Once done, make a thin layer of sand on it and sprinkle water. This is done to protect the surface (as it may have many small organisms) below the platform from the heat that's generated from the fire offerings.

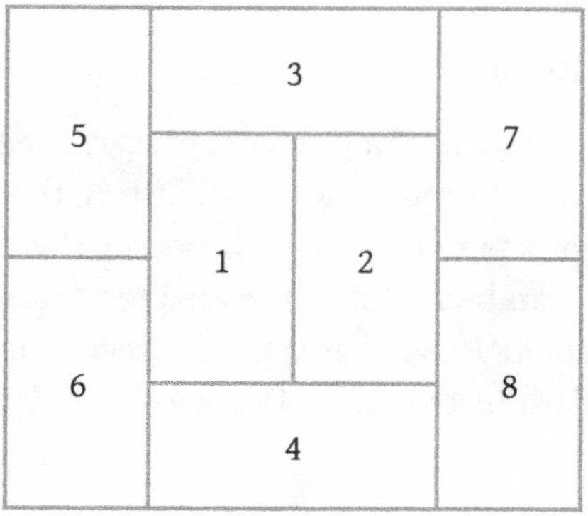

Fire-pit with boundary

You will need eighteen bricks to create this yajna-kunda. Make the exact same fire-pit as in the table above and then create a boundary by laying ten bricks vertically. This is suitable for up to 1000 fire offerings. As with the pit without the boundary, create a layer of sand and sprinkle water on it. It is important to filter the sand and to ensure that it is clean and that there are no insects in it that may lead to accidental harm to such tiny creatures. You can do this by leaving the sand out in the sun a day before and then washing it, drying it and sieving it.

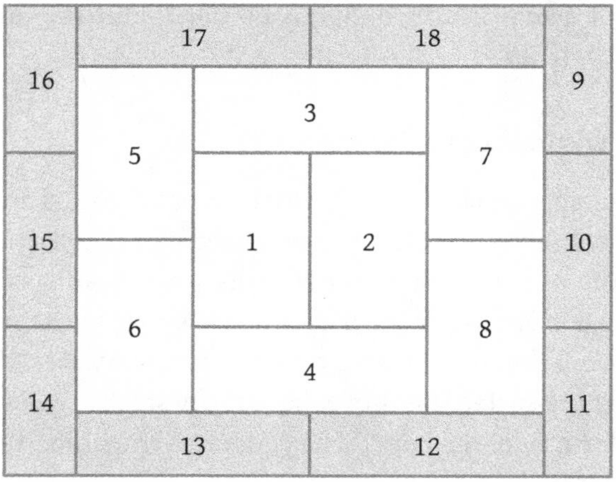

Performing the Yajna

Many preliminary steps of a yajna are exactly the same as the ones you do before you start your japa. I am listing those steps here but please note that the details of each one of this step and how to perform it etc. can be found in the chapter *Essential Steps in the Rites of Invocation (Puruscharana).* Wherever there is a deviation from the standard instructions, I've given the details next to that step.

Here are the thirty-six steps of Gayatri sadhana.

1. Bathe

   If you are performing your yajna immediately after your japa, you don't have to take bath. But, if you did japa in the morning but are doing yajna in the evening (or vice-versa) for example, you will have to bathe before making fire-offerings.
2. Put on fresh clothes

   Once again, if you are doing it immediately after your japa, you can wear the same clothes. Otherwise, put on fresh ones.
3. Keep a small pot of water in front of you (or on your right side) to do for purification.
4. A small container with ghee (clarified butter) will be required. You can use any spoon to make offering in the fire or if you want to do it the traditional way, use a wooden spoon. The two wooden spoons are called *sruka* and *sruva* that are used to make ghee-offerings in fire. Keep your pot of ghee to your right.
5. Keep the pot with the ingredients (charu) of fire-offerings in front of you. Ingredients for yajna vary from sadhana to sadhana. For all the sadhanas listed in this book, I've specified the ingredients next to them.
6. Purify the surroundings (pavitrikarana)

   Self purification (achamana)
7. Wash your hands (hasta prakshalana)
8. Light the lamp. (In addition, you can also light incense at this stage if you like, but it's optional).
9. Invoke Ganesha
10. Show three handlocks for Ganesha (Ganesh mudra)
11. Chant the Vedic hymn of auspiciousness (Svastivachana)
12. Meditate on your guru (Guru dhyana)
13. Chant your guru mantra (Guru mantra japa)
14. Offer obeisance to all siddhas
15. Meditate on your deity (Ishta dhyana)
16. Place your firewood in the fire-pit and light it. You can use the same mantra to light this as you do for lighting a lamp. You can

light camphor or a wick dipped in oil to ignite the fire. Simply place it on one of the wooden chips at the base and light it (camphor or wick in oil). Start arranging firewood around it keeping space for the air to flow.

17. Once the fire starts, you are ready to make fire-offerings. An important point to remember is that every offering made in the fire must end with the word "svahaa". The Sanskrit word svaha means to burn completely and it is used to burn all our afflictions. Svahaa in the Hindu tradition is the energy aspect of fire. It is responsible for taking the fire-offering to its destination. Make the following offerings with ghee alone. Every time, you say svahaa, pour ghee using your spoon (or wooden spoon). All offerings are made with your right hand only.

Sanskrit (Devanagri)	*Sanskrit (IAST)*
ॐ प्रजापतये स्वाहा ।	oṃ prajāpataye svāhā ।
इदं प्रजापतये इदन्न मम ।	idaṃ prajāpataye idanna mama ।
इति मनसा।	iti manasā।
ॐ इन्द्राय इदमिन्द्राय इदन्न मम ।	oṃ indrāya idamindrāya idanna mama ।
इत्याधारौ ।।	ityādhārau ।।
ॐ अग्नये स्वाहा ।	oṃ agnaye svāhā ।
इदमग्नेय इदन्न मम ।	idamagneya idanna mama ।
ॐ सोमाय स्वाहा ।	oṃ somāya svāhā ।
इंदसोमाय इदन्न मम ।	iṃdasomāya idanna mama ।
इत्याज्यभागौ ।	ityājyabhāgau ।
ॐ भूः स्वाहा ।	oṃ bhūḥ svāhā ।
इदमग्नेय इदन्न मम ।	idamagneya idanna mama ।

Sanskrit (Devanagri)	Sanskrit (IAST)
ॐ भुवः स्वाहा ।	oṃ bhuvaḥ svāhā I
इदं वायवे इदन्न मम ।	idaṃ vāyave idanna mama I
ॐ स्वः स्वाहा ।	oṃ svaḥ svāhā I
इदं सूर्याय इदन्न मम ।	idaṃ sūryāya idanna mama I
एता महाव्याहृतयः ।	etā mahāvyāhṛtayaḥ I
ॐ त्वन्नो अग्ने वरुणस्य विद्वान देवस्य हेडो अवयासिसीष्ठाः ।	oṃ tvanno agne varuṇasya vidvāna devasya heḍo avayāsisīṣṭhāḥ I
यजिष्ठोविह्नतमः शोशुचानो विश्वादेवाँ सिप्रमुग्ध्यस्मत् स्वाहा ।।	yajiṣṭhovihnatamaḥ śośucāno viśvādevām̐ sipramugdhyasmat svāhā II
इदमग्निवरुणाभ्याम् इदन्न मम ।	idamagnivaruṇābhyām idanna mama I
ॐ स त्वन्नो अग्नेवमो भवोती नेदिष्ठो वरुणँ	oṃ sa tvanno agnevamo bhavotī nediṣṭho varuṇam̐
रराणो वीहिमृडीकँ सुहवा न एधि स्वाहा ।	rarāṇo vīhimṛḍīkam̐ suhavā na edhi svāhā I

18. Make the following offerings (*ahuti*) with the ingredients (*charu*) of yajna. (Not ghee unless the sole ingredient being used in a yajna is ghee). All offerings are always made with your right hand in a yajna. The quantity in each offering ideally should be no more than a teaspoon. Hold it between your three fingers and thumb (keeping the index finger away). Any offering in the fire-pit should be made with a sense of reverence. Your palm should be facing up while making the offering.

Sanskrit (Devanagri)	Sanskrit (IAST)
ॐ प्रजापतये स्वाहा ।	oṃ prajāpataye svāhā ।
इदं प्रजापतये इदन्न मम ।	idaṃ prajāpataye idanna mama ।
इति मनसा प्राजापत्यम् ।।	iti manasā prājāpatyam ।।
ॐ अग्नये स्विष्टकृते ।	oṃ agnaye sviṣṭakṛte ।
ॐ गणपतये स्वाहा ।	oṃ gaṇapataye svāhā ।
इदं गणपतये ।	idaṃ gaṇapataye ।
ॐ ब्रह्म जज्ञानं प्रथमम्पुररस्ताद्विसीमतः स्वाहा ।	oṃ brahma jajñānaṃ prathamampurarastādvisīmataḥ svāhā ।
इदं ब्रह्मणे इदन्न मम ।	idaṃ brahmaṇe idanna mama ।
ॐ विष्णो रराट स्वाहा ।	oṃ viṣṇo rarāṭa svāhā ।
इदं विष्णवे इदन्न मम ।	idaṃ viṣṇave idanna mama ।
ॐ नमः शम्भवाय च स्वाहा ।	oṃ namaḥ śambhavāya ca svāhā ।
इदं शम्भवाय इदन्न म ।।	idaṃ śambhavāya idanna ma ।।
अधिदेवेभ्य स्वाहा ।	adhidevebhya svāhā ।
प्रत्यधिदेवेभ्यः स्वाहा ।	pratyadhidevebhyaḥ svāhā ।
पंचलोकपालेभ्यः स्वाहा ।	paṃcalokapālebhyaḥ svāhā ।
दशदिक्पालेभ्यः स्वाहा ।	daśadikpālebhyaḥ svāhā ।
वरुणदेवाय स्वाहा ।	varuṇadevāya svāhā ।
वास्तुकाय स्वाहा ।	vāstukāya svāhā ।
गौर्य्यादिषोडश मातृभ्यः स्वाहा ।	gauryyādiṣoḍaśa mātṛbhyaḥ svāhā ।
प्रधानदेवाय स्वाहा ।	pradhānadevāya svāhā ।
सर्वेभ्यो देवेभ्यः स्वाहा ।।	sarvebhyo devebhyaḥ svāhā ।।

19. Make five offerings with ghee alone:

Sanskrit (Devanagri)	*Sanskrit (IAST)*
ॐ प्राणाय स्वाहा ।	oṃ prāṇāya svāhā ।
ॐ अपानाय स्वाहा ।	oṃ apānāya svāhā ।
ॐ व्यानाय स्वाहा ।	oṃ vyānāya svāhā ।
ॐ उदानाय स्वाहा ।	oṃ udānāya svāhā ।
ॐ समानाय स्वाहा ।।	oṃ samānāya svāhā ।।

20. Now you are ready to make offerings with your main mantra (mula-mantra) of the sadhana. The ingredients prescribed and the number of offerings vary from one sadhana to another. For each one of the four sadhanas listed in this book, I've clearly specified the ingredients. An important practical aspect to mention here is counting. Since, now you are making offerings with your right hand, you may not be able to do the counting with beads. In that case, you have two options to choose from. You can choose whichever you are comfortable with.

a. Use counting beads. You can keep loose beads or pebbles on the side and move a pebble with your left hand every time you make an offering with your right one.

b. Simply see how long it takes you to chant your mantra using a timer. Add 20% time to it to cater for slow chanting at times. For example, let's say you have to make 100 offerings. If it takes you 10 seconds to chant your mantra, it'll take you 1000 seconds to chant it 100 times. Adding 20% will make it 1200 seconds or 20 minutes. When you come to this step, set aside 20 minutes to make fire offerings with your mantra. It is okay to offer bit more than required so don't be worried if you are overdoing it. The main thing is to not do it less than the minimum number required.

If at any time, you feel fire is ebbing in the pit, pour more ghee and/or place more firewood. Whenever you pour more ghee, do it with your main mantra and don't forget to add "om svaha" in the end.

21. Now make the following five offerings again with ghee.

Sanskrit (Devanagri)	Sanskrit (IAST)
ॐ प्राणाय स्वाहा ।	oṃ prāṇāya svāhā ।
ॐ अपानाय स्वाहा ।	oṃ apānāya svāhā ।
ॐ व्यानाय स्वाहा ।	oṃ vyānāya svāhā ।
ॐ उदानाय स्वाहा ।	oṃ udānāya svāhā ।
ॐ समानाय स्वाहा ।।	oṃ samānāya svāhā ।।

22. Make the last offering by placing the dry coconut (filled with yajna ingredients and a bit of ghee) in the middle of the fire pit. Do this carefully as there can be a fire hazard. Chant the following mantra while you do the final offering (*purna-ahuti*).

Sanskrit (Devanagri)	*Sanskrit (IAST)*
ॐ पूर्णमदः पूर्णमिदम् पूर्णात् पूर्णमुदच्यते । पूर्णस्य पूर्णमादाय पूर्णमेवावशिष्यते ॥ ॐ शान्तिः शान्तिः शान्तिः ॥	oṃ pūrṇamadaḥ pūrṇamidam pūrṇāt pūrṇamudacyate | pūrṇasya pūrṇamādāya pūrṇamevāvaśiṣyate || oṃ śāntiḥ śāntiḥ śāntiḥ ||
Translation	
May all sentient beings at peace, May no one suffer from illness, May all see what is auspicious, May no one suffer. Om peace, peace, peace.	

23. Fold your hands and circumambulate the fire-pit and chant the following mantra while doing so.

Sanskrit (Devanagri)	Sanskrit (IAST)
यानि कानि च पापानि जन्मान्तरकृतानि च । तानि तानि प्रणश्यन्ति प्रदक्षिणा पदे पदे ।।	yāni kāni ca pāpāni janmāntarakṛtāni ca I tāni tāni praṇaśyanti pradakṣiṇā pade pade II
Translation	
Whatever sins I may have committed in this lifetime or any other, may they be destroyed with each round of circumambulation.	

24. Chant the prayer of forgiveness. (It's the same as the one given in the rites of invocation. It's being given herein for ready reference).

Sanskrit (Devanagri)	Sanskrit (IAST)
अपराधसहस्त्राणि क्रियन्तेऽहर्निशं मया । दासोऽयमिति मां मत्वा क्षमस्व परमेश्र्वरि ॥ आवाहनं न जानामि न जानामि विसर्जनम् । पूजां चैव न जानामि क्षम्यतां परमेश्र्वरि ॥ मन्त्रहीनं क्रियाहीनं भक्तिहीनं सुरेश्र्वरि । यत्पूजितं मया देवि परिपूर्ण तदस्तु मे ॥	aparādhasahastrāṇi kriyantesharniśaṃ mayā I dāsosyamiti māṃ matvā kṣamasva parameśrvari āvāhanaṃ na jānāmi na jānāmi visarjanam I pūjāṃ caiva na jānāmi kṣamyatāṃ parameśrvari mantrahīnaṃ kriyāhīnaṃ bhaktihīnaṃ sureśrvari I yatpūjitaṃ mayā devi paripūrṇa tadastu me
Translation	
O Devi, I must have committed thousands of mistakes and errors in chanting your names. Please forgive me for my errors like a good master forgives his servant. I don't know how to invite you nor do I know how to see you off. I don't know how to pray to you, please forgive me for my ignorance. I am without the knowledge of mantras, actions or devotion, O Goddess. And yet, I dare to pray to you. Please grant me your grace.	

25. Close by praying for everyone's wellbeing. You can use the following mantra to do so:

Sanskrit (Devanagri)	*Sanskrit (IAST)*
ॐ सर्वे भवन्तु सुखिनः सर्वे सन्तु निरामयाः । सर्वे भद्राणि पश्यन्तु मा कश्चिद्दुःखभाग्भवेत् । ॐ शान्तिः शान्तिः शान्तिः ॥	oṃ sarve bhavantu sukhinaḥ sarve santu nirāmayāḥ । sarve bhadrāṇi paśyantu mā kaściddaḥkhabhāgbhavet । oṃ śāntiḥ śāntiḥ śāntiḥ
Translation	
May all sentient beings at peace, May no one suffer from illness, May all see what is auspicious, May no one suffer. Om peace, peace, peace.	

26. Have a hearty meal and sweets with your loved ones, or just by yourself if no one is around to partake.
27. Thank all the divine energies in whatever language you wish.

BOOK FOUR

DETAILED NOTES

TYPES OF MANTRAS

There are many ways in which mantras are classified. They can be masculine, feminine or neutral. All mantras ending with *swaha* are feminine mantras. Such mantras may belong to a male deity, of course, but they primarily strengthen the feminine and kinetic energies in the practitioner. All mantras ending with *phat, vaushta, vashat, hum* are masculine mantras. Once again, a female deity can have a masculine mantra because masculine mantra here means that its invocation will strengthen the masculine and potential energy in the adept. Neutral mantras are the ones that end with namah. When a mantra ends with neither namah, swaha, nor vaushta, vashat, hum or phat, such a mantra is also neutral. Neutral mantras strengthen both masculine and feminine energies in the adept.

Other than the classification mentioned above, mantra may also be classified in any of the six ways:

1. Pallava

When a mantra explicitly contains the name of the person it's targeted at, it is called Pallava. Specific tantric prayogas, especially those used with the intention to harm someone, are known as pallava.

2. Yojan Mantra

When a mantra contains the name of the person but is used to bring a positive change in the life of the beneficiary, it's called yojan mantra. It's used in the applications of peace and prosperity, and to bring calm.

3. Rodha Mantra

When a mantra is appended in the beginning, middle or at the end of the name of the beneficiary of a mantra, it's called rodha. It's used to pacify the planets, to appease fever and to rid the effects of poison.

4. Para Mantra

When a mantra is designed to be appended to every letter of the name of the beneficiary, it's called para mantra. It's generally exclusively used in shanti-karma.

5. Samputa mantra

When a name is enclosed within the confines of a mantra, it's called samputa. In samputa the mantra is prefixed and suffixed to the name of the beneficiary. Though I have used the term beneficiary, samputa is primarily used in krityas (negative karmas). Samputa mantra are often used with the ignoble intention to harm someone.

6. Vidarbha mantra

When you put two letters of your mantra followed by two letters of the name of the beneficiary and follow this sequence till the letters of the mantra or till the name gets exhausted, such a mantra is called vidarbha. If the letters in the name of the person are more than letters in the mantra, the mantra is repeated in that case. If the letters of the mantra are more than the letters in the person's name, the mantra is continued as usual once the letters in the name are over.

FLAWS IN A MANTRA

The six most common flaws are covered in the chapter 'Flaws in Mantras'. The remaining 44 are listed here.

1. **Shatru:** When you pick a mantra that is your enemy based on the *mitra-shatru* consideration.

2. **Baalaa:** While chanting your mantra, if you chant *harsva* (short) sound instead of *dhirga* (long), you change the nature of the mantra. The rishi, meter, etc., don't apply anymore because the original seer did not impart the mantra you are chanting, but the one with the long sound. Phonetic precision is a must. For example, in Gayatri chanting, I've seen countless practitioners pronouncing "*bhoo*" as "*bhu*". It's '*Om bhoor bhuva svaha...*' to chant it as '*Om bhur bhuva svaha...*' attaches the *baalaa* flaw.

3. **Nirjita:** When an aspirant has done excessive bad karma in his previous life, it can prevent him from attaining siddhi in this lifetime because the bulk of the chanting will go in cleaning his karmic field. The right kind of initiation can correct this flaw. Besides, if the aspirant already has an inkling towards spirituality, if he has a kind heart, he must have done enough good karma to be reading a book on mantra science and exploring it. Personally, it should not bother anyone whether they have done enough good karma in their past life. I've stated this flaw here so you have a complete understanding.

4. **Vridha:** *Vridha* is the exact opposite of *Baalaa*. When an aspirant elongates the sound, it changes the mantra itself and renders it flawed. When *dirgha* (long) sound is used instead of *harasva* (short) sound, the mantra attracts *vridha dosha*.

5. **Ahamsa:** If your mantra does not contain "*ha*" or "*sa*" sound, it attracts *ahamsa dosha*. The Vedic scriptures state that all living beings chant *hamsa* Gayatri all the time. With every breath in, they chant "*ham*", and every breath out, "sa". When the mantra you chant does not have "*ha*" or "*sa*", it's *ahamsa*. Having said that, this *dosha* does not apply to all the mantras, but only those that are designed for nirvana.

6. **Satvavijita:** A mantra that has no potency is called *satvavijita*. It is possible for a mantra to have no potency if no one has awakened or imparted it over the last few centuries. The phonetic potency of a mantra starts to diminish. It's like if you say something out very loud, your voice will only reach those who are closer to you. As it travels further, it'll become feebler. The energy of the mantra works in a similar fashion.

7. **Apoorna roopaa:** When a mantra is chanted incompletely, it's called *apporna roopa*. It is one of the most common flaws. Many aspirants, when pressed of time, or simply due to restlessness or impatience, speed up the chanting of their mantra completely distorting it, if not destroying, its phonetic lineage.

8. **Sanunaasikaa:** When chanting is done with excessive nasal sound, the flaw is called *sanunaasika*. It is quite common when pronouncing *anusvara* (dots above letters). Please carefully go through my chapter on how to pronounce *anusvara* to ensure your *japa* is pure and free from flaws.

9. **Supta:** This flaw only applies when performing the rites of *purushcharana* where chanting exceeds four hours at a stretch. During those four hours, at some point in time, one must

breath from one's right nostril. If your right nostril is blocked due to a medical condition, it's a different matter. Otherwise, if even after three hours into chanting your right breath hasn't started, you should briefly lie to your left side to activate the right nostril.

10. **Ruddha:** When a mantra is chanted without paying attention to joining or separating words (*sandhi vicheda*), it is said to have *ruddha dosha*. For example, in the chanting of the Gayatri Mantra, there's a pause between '*svaha*' and '*tata savitur*'. If you say it in one breath like, "*Om bhoor bhuva svahatatasavitur*", this will be *ruddha dosha*. It should be said like, "*Om bhoor bhuva svaha* (a tiny pause) *tata savitur varenayam...*"

11. **Kilita:** Most mantras are locked (*kilita*). To correct this flaw, either a mantra must be awakened with effort, grace and initiation or sometimes a mantra comes with *utakilana* (unlocking) process. Performing *utakilana* on a mantra rids it of this flaw.

12. **Praptadukha:** If the original seer of the mantra met with a misfortune immediately upon awakening the mantra, the mantra is said to be *praptadukha*. Anyone invoking the mantra after that seer will experience the same outcome. That is why there's no dearth of people who go online in search of mantras or pick them up from books and rather than benefitting or having reversal of fortune, they only meet with more misfortune. All four *sadhanas* mentioned in this book have been personally tested and awakened by me so as far as the mantras in this book are concerned, I can confirm that they are free of this flaw.

13. **Khandibhoota:** Every mantra *sadhana* comes with the procedure of *nyasa*. *Nyasa* is one of the most important elements of mantra *sadhana*. When an aspirant foregoes *nyasa* during their *sadhana*, the mantra suffers from the flaw of *khandibhoota*. The only way to correct this flaw is to begin your *sadhana* again, diligently following the procedure everyday.

14. **Heenaveerya:** A mantra that has not been imparted properly is not fit to be used for any *sadhana* as it's been rendered *heenaveerya* in the scriptures. *Heenaveerya* literally means lack of potency or creative energy. If the guru imparting the mantra is not an adept himself, the mantra is most likely to have this flaw. In the section on how to find an adept, I have shared the procedure you can follow to avoid this flaw in the *sadhanas* contained in this book.

15. **Kunthita:** When mantra *sadhana* is done without *viniyoga* (application of a verse or a mantra), the mantra is said to be *kunthita*. *Kunthita* literally means blunt or dull. A mantra where we don't specify what it's for is *kunthita*. It's only if we have clarity in our mind and speech that we can expect to benefit from the cosmic energy around us. Mantra *sadhana*, like meditation, requires a focused and clear effort. You cannot shoot one bullet in two directions at the same time. The aspirant must be clear for what purpose he is invoking the mantra by correctly chanting the *viniyoga*.

16. **Klishtta:** To delay the chanting of various letters in the mantra attaches the flaw *klishtta* to it. It's important to say the mantra with the same speed. The aspirant must maintain a sort of constancy. It's perfectly fine to slow down your chanting or to fasten (not rush) it a little (provided you still pronounce each letter clearly) to refresh your concentration. But, it is not okay to differ your speed in the same mantra. For example, if your mantra is '*Om Namaha Shivaaya*', it's okay to say '*Om—namaha—shivaaya*' or even '*Om—namaha—shivaaya*'. The sign '—' indicates the pause or rest between each word. But not '*Om-namaha—shivaaya*'. This flaw can be corrected by doing additional chanting.

17. **Rugna:** If you are chanting as if you are wailing, too loud or you are depressed while chanting, the mantra suffers from the

flaw of *rugna*. It's normal, even natural, that you can't always be happy. But to be depressed, thinking that chanting your mantra is a task you don't like or don't want to do, makes the mantra *rugna*. This is one of the reason why a certain degree of faith and devotion is required in mantra *sadhana* so you may maintain a pleasing and positive disposition. Like *klishtta*, *rugna* flaw can be corrected by additional chanting.

18. **Upeksha:** To forego parts of *sadhana* as per your convenience and not follow the instructions fully induces the flaw of *upeksha* in your mantra *sadhana*. If you inadvertently miss a step, your guru may help you, but if you consciously abandon certain steps thinking you don't need them, your mantra *sadhana* is compromised. The only way to handle this flaw is to restart your *sadhana* from the beginning, following every single step.

19. **Vaishamyta:** To have no reverence for the deity of the mantra and to treat mantras as merely empty sounds, or worse still, to actually dislike your deity, compromises your *sadhana*. There is no way to correct this flaw other than wait till you have a change of heart.

20. **Shaktiheena:** When a mantra does not have an associated shakti (devi or energy), it is said to be *shaktiheena*, devoid of shakti. There are some mantras that don't have a beeja (seed) or shakti (energy). Results from chanting those mantras come only if you are initiated into that mantra by a guru who's actually done enough *sadhana* to awaken the mantra himself. Generally, *shaktiheena* mantras are used for a one-off purpose. If your mantra has this flaw, you'll be better off selecting a different mantra for your *sadhana*. If, however, you are simply chanting a mantra because it gives you peace and strength, and not as part of some *sadhana*, you are welcome to continue chanting your mantra.

21. **Praanga mukha:** When a mantra is entirely comprised of the letters in *tvarga* and *tvarga* with no other consonants, the mantra is called *pranga mukha.* The literal meaning of *prang mukha* is drum like. Such mantra robs the practitioner of his peace and evokes the feelings of lust. Unless, you have selected this mantra or your guru has imparted it for a specific purpose (overcoming impotency, for example), you are better off not chanting such a mantra. There are other beautiful, peaceful and tranquil mantras to choose from.

22. **Badhir:** A mantra that has no *chanda* (meter) is called *badhir.* Unless, your mantra falls in the category of exceptions, a *badhir* mantra can not be used for others' benefit. A *sadhak* will still benefit from a *badhir* mantra, but the energy gained can't be passed on. If your guru imparted you the mantra, ask for the meter or if you are trying to awaken it yourself then refer to the *sadhana* notes. For the *sadhanas* mentioned in this book, I've specified the meter for each one of those.

23. **Netraheena:** A mantra missing its seer is called *netraheena.* Without knowing the seer, we don't know the authenticity or validity of the mantra. Once again, this rule only applies if you are trying to awaken the mantra in order to use it for a specific purpose. If you are chanting it for inner peace, the usual flaws of the mantras (including this one) doesn't apply. It's like this: you don't have to have a formal university degree to succeed in life but if you want a degree (which may increase your prospects of employment), you ought to follow the academic curriculum and score well within that framework.

24. **Bheeta:** Sometimes the energy of a mantra can frighten the aspirant. If you experience fear not on account of your external surroundings (for example, you may be chanting in the woods infested with wild animals or on the cremation grounds) but because of the sound of mantra, it is best to check with your

guru. If you don't have a guru and you have selected the mantra on your own, do thoroughly examine your *sadhana* notes to ensure you are not missing anything. If you stopped chanting due to fear, simply redo the entire round on your rosary. You don't have to start the whole *sadhana* from the beginning.

25. **Malin:** If you experience hatred, anger, jealousy towards anyone while chanting your mantra, the mantra becomes *malin*. The literal meaning of *malin* is soiled. In such an event, stop chanting for a moment. Seek forgiveness from the deity and restart that round of chanting from the beginning. You don't have to start the whole *sadhana* or even that day's *sadhana* from the beginning, do just that round. For example, let's say you sat down to chant 30 rounds of Gayatri Mantra and while chanting round 16, you discover that thoughts from your past have evoked emotions of anger or jealousy towards someone. Stop chanting, seek forgiveness and restart from round 16.

26. **Tiraskrit:** If you pass wind, sneeze, burp, pick your nose, intentionally touch your genitals (unless some *sadhana* explicitly requires it), the mantra becomes *tiraskrit*. It's considered obscene and is disrespectful to the deity. At that time, stop chanting, do *achamana* (a sip of water with mantra) and restart from where you left of. It's best to do that round from the beginning but even starting from exactly where you left is okay, too. In case you have to get up to attend to nature's call, you must do the entire purification ritual again. No need to do *nyasa* again, just the purification ritual will do.

27. **Bhedita:** When you disclose your mantra to anyone other than your guru, the mantra becomes *bhedita*. It's one of the worst and most common flaws. It completely compromises your *sadhana*. The only way out is to first confess in front of your guru. If you don't have a guru in a human form, then confess in front of your deity and start the *sadhana* from the beginning.

28. **Madonmata:** If the original seer or your guru awakened the mantra while consuming intoxicants like liquor, opium or anything else, the mantra suffers from the flaw of *madonmata.* Often it requires the practitioner to either abandon the guru and invoke the mantra afresh with his own efforts or to recreate the conditions and consciousness his guru was in at the time of the awakening. A large number of left-handed mantra *sadhanas* (in the tantric framework) require the practitioner to consume alcohol, opium, etc., while chanting. I have never awakened a mantra under the influence of any substance, so I'm not in a position to give any first-hand opinion on this. My only suggestion would be to pick a different mantra if you are in for the long haul.

29. **Moorchita:** A mantra is *moorchita* (unconscious) if the guru passed on the mantra without awakening it himself first. You can still invoke such mantra but it'll take much longer. When you invoke a moorchita mantra, you are entitled to impart it to others in the capacity of a guru.

30. **Shraapita:** It's quite common that some great sage or siddha in the past might have cursed the deity of the mantra. This makes the mantra *shraapit.* The famous Gayatri Mantra, for example, is *shraapit* by two sages (Vasishta, Vishvamitra) and Brahma himself. To awaken a *shraapit* mantra, the aspirant must do *shaap vimochana* for each curse. I've expounded on this process in the section under Gayatri *sadhana.*

31. **Nirbija:** A mantra that's missing its *bija* (seed) is called *nirbija.* Such a mantra is only good for a one-off use. It's like the seedless fruit, you can enjoy it once but you can't grow more fruits from it because it has no seed. Some mantras are *nirbija,* which means you have to awaken them repeatedly to benefit from them.

32. **Manda:** The literal meaning of *manda* is the scum of boiled rice or the thick part of milk, like cream. When a mantra is a

mouthful or tongue-twisting, it suffers from the flaw of *manda.* In chanting such a mantra, you are very likely to make mistakes of omission (omitting sounds inadvertently) and commission (adding sounds that are not part of the mantra or omitting sounds intentionally). It is best to select a different mantra but if you still want to persist with the mantra you have, the only way is to do it extremely mindfully and patiently. For that matter, all mantra *sadhana* should be done mindfully.

33. **Kekar:** The literal meaning of *kekar* is squint-eyed. When confusion prevails as to the seer of the mantra, the mantra is said to *kekar.* In such an event, you have no other option but to seek an adept who may have invoked that mantra to guide you further. You are better off selecting a different mantra (even of the same deity) if you don't have access to a guru.

34. **Dhumita:** When you ignore the direction you should be facing while chanting the mantra, it is said to have the *dhumita dosha.* The literal meaning of *dhumita* is obscured, darkened or the quarter towards which the sun turns first. To correct this *dosha,* an aspirant must start his *sadhana* from the beginning and face the right direction.

35. **Atidripta:** A mantra imparted by a guru who's angry, arrogant or proud is called *atidripta.* In other words, if your guru has none of the qualities mentioned in the section 'Signs of a Good Guru', chances are the mantra you are initiated into is suffering from the flaw of *atidripta.* If chanting of this mantra couldn't purify your guru, what hope do you have then? If you are still attached to this mantra for whatever reason, it's best to abandon that guru and start the *sadhana* afresh by first doing guru *sadhana* as mentioned under the *sadhana* section of this book.

36. **Angheena:** When a mantra is missing more than one limb (rishi, devata, *chand, bija,* shakti, *kilaka*), it is said to be *angheena.* It is normal and entirely possible for a mantra to not naturally

have one or two limbs if it's an exception to the norm or if the tradition you follow invoked the mantra without one of the limbs. Once again, usually mantras used for chanting and general peace, and not for awakening the energy in it, have missing limbs. Most mantras (more than 95 per cent) that follow the scriptures are intact with all the limbs.

37. **Atikrudha:** Like any fine piece of music, a mantra is a sophisticated arrangement of long sounds, short sounds and silence. Any mantra with no *dirgha* (long sound) suffers from the flaw of *atikrudha*. The literal meaning of *ati-krudha* is very angry. Such a mantra is like to make the practitioner aggressive. If you are chanting such a mantra, it could be that you are chanting it incorrectly. Either your guru can guide you or if you don't have a guru then pay close attention to the arrangement of letters. If you are following the phonetic guide as given in this book, you should be alright.

38. **Atikrura:** When all consonants in a mantra are taken from *Tvaraga* in the Brahmi or Devanagri alphabet (T, Th, D, Dh) the mantra is said to be *atikrura*. The literal meaning of *atikrura* is very cruel. Such a mantra makes the practitioner restless. Very few mantras (less than 1 per cent) are *atikrura*. It's best to invest your time, energy, faith and devotion in a different mantra. Some tantric mantras used for *kritya* (harming others) suffer from the flaws of *atikrudha* and *atikrura*. They may deliver a one-off impact but their use has a telling negative impact on the practitioner.

39. **Savrida:** This flaw is not as applicable today as it once used to be. Nevertheless, *savrida* means to shame. If the practitioner of a mantra, during the course of his sadhana, is part of a panel or panchayat that approves public shaming or mocking of any individual for any reason whatsoever, the flaw of *savrida* attaches to the mantra. It weakens the practitioner as well as

the mantra. The only way to correct this flaw is to apologize to the one you shamed and to begin your *sadhana* anew.

40. **Pidhita:** During the course of your *sadhana*, if you intentionally cause harm to any living being, it has a negative affect on your *sadhana*. *Pidhita* means to suffer. When you hurt or harm others while trying to awaken a mantra, both the practitioner and the mantra suffers. Corrective measure including an unconditional apology, a resolution to not harm again and starting your *sadhana* from the beginning must be taken if you want to awaken the mantra. An important word of caution here: by not harming other living creatures, I'm not suggesting that you drop pragmatism and discretion. If you are meditating in your home and it's getting infested with cockroaches, get rid of them.

41. **Danda:** During the course of *sadhana* if a practitioner punishes anyone by physically hurting them, the mantra attracts the *dosha* of *danda*. It should be avoided at all costs for mantra returns in multifold. Rather than benefitting, you will be punished in return in a way that fits the framework of nature. For example, if you slap someone while invoking the mantra, it's not that someone else will slap you too. Nature's slap may come in the form of a disease in your body.

42. **Vikala:** When you omit one or more consonants in a mantra either due to fast chanting or improper pronunciation, it's called *vikala*. The literal meaning of *vikala* is mutilated. You must do additional chanting as soon as you become aware. If you intentionally omit, the entire *sadhana* must be started from the beginning, but if you did so inadvertently, correct it as soon as you become aware and do additional chanting as much as you reasonably can.

43. **Koota:** A mantra imparted with wrong intentions or false statements, or a mantra gained by telling lies or trickery is called

koota. The only way to correct this flaw is to confess your actions, seek forgiveness and start afresh. If, however, a mantra suffers from *koota* because the guru made false statements, it's best to abandon that guru without soiling your own heart, For any emotional impurity will be an obstacle on your path.

44. **Aalingita:** Sometimes two mantras are joined to procreate a new kind of energy. For example, in *Maha-mrityunjaya* mantra: both Gayatri and *Mrityunja* mantras are combined along with a *samputa* of certain seed syllables. It's legit because the mantra was awakened by a seer and then passed on. And some mantras can be used as *samputa* (used as both prefix and suffix with another mantra) or *tara* (used either as the prefix or suffix) but when a practitioner enjoins two mantras as per his own convenience, such a mantra is called *aalingita*. To correct this flaw, the two mantras must be separated first. The aspirant should then choose one mantra and awaken that.

SIXTEEN SAMSKARAS OF SANATANA DHARMA

Santana Dharma, commonly known as Hinduism, states 16 *samskara* to mark the important event in the life of an individual. They are:

1. Garbhadan

The first coming together of the husband and wife for bringing about conception.

2. Pumsvan

Ceremony performed when the first signs of conception are seen, and is to be performed when someone desires a male child.

3. Seemantonayan

A ceremony of parting of the hair of the expectant mother to keep her spirits high and positive. Special music is arranged for her.

4. Jatakarma

After the birth of the child, the child is given a secret name, he is given a taste of honey and ghee, mother starts the first breast-feeding after chanting of a mantra.

5. Nama-karana

In this ceremony, the child is given a formal name. Performed on the 11th day.

6. Nishkramana

In this, the formal darshan of the sun and the moon is done for the child.

7. Annaprashana

This ceremony is performed when the child is given solid food (*anna*) for the first time.

8. Chudakarana

Cuda means the lock or tuft of hair kept after the remaining part is shaved off.

9. Karna-vedha

Piercing of the ears done in the 7th or 8th month.

10. Upanayan & Vedarambha

The thread ceremony. The child is thereafter authorized to perform all rituals. Studies of the Vedas begins with the guru.

11. Keshanta or Ritushuddhi

The first shave in the case of boys, *Keshanta,* is generally observed at the age of 16 or the celebration after the first period or coming of age in the case of girls, usually done at the age of 13 or on any auspicious day after the completion of their first menstrual cycle - *ritushuddhi.*

12. Samavartan

Returning to the house after completing the education. Graduation ceremony indicates end of formal education and a celibate or single way of life. Generally observed at the age of 25-*samavartana.*

13. Vivaha

Marriage ceremony.

14. Vanprastha

As old age approaches, the person retires for a life of tapas and studies.

15. Sannyasa

Before leaving the body, a Hindu sheds all sense of responsibility and relationships to awake and revel in the timeless truth.

16. Antyeshthi

The last rites or the cremation rituals.

SIXTEEN SIGNIFICANT ASPECTS OF MANTRA SADHANA

There are 16 aspects of mantra *sadhana*. They are:

1. Bhakti (devotion)

Devotion and reverence towards the deity of the mantra is called bhakti. Compassion for all living beings is an important aspect of devotion because if you really believe in God, by definition, you then also believe that God lives in all living entities. And, compassion towards others is an expression of devotion.

2. Shudhi (purification)

There are four types of purification in mantra yoga. They are *kaya-shudhi* (purifying your body), *chitta-shuddhi* (purifying your mind), *dika-shuddhi* (purifying the energies in all directions around you) and *sthana-shuddhi* (purifying the place of worship).

3. Asana (seat)

Different mantras require different kinds of *asana* (seats). Please refer to the section on *sadhana* to understand what kind of seat you require.

4. Panchang sevan (five types of food)

When it comes to mantra yoga, the five types of food that feed your mantra are the *Bhagavad Gita*, *Sahasranama*, *Stava*, *Kavach* and *Hridaya*. The *Bhagavad Gita* can be the popular *Bhagavad Gita* or it can be any of the 24 *Gitas* found in the *Mahabharata*. Depending on which lineage you are initiated into, it could also be any other *Gita* your guru may have assigned you. In the absence of any physical guru or one-on-initiation, just adopt *Srimad Bhagavad Gita* (where Krishna instructed Arjuna). *Sahasranama* literally means 1000 names. It can be any like *Vishnu Sahasranama*, *Lalita Sahasranama*, *Durga Sahasranama*, *Shiva Sahasranama*, etc. *Stava* is a hymn dedicated to the deity of your mantra. *Kavacha* is the protective mantra, an energy shield, of your deity. *Hridaya* is eulogizing your deity with devotion and mindfulness and is often a type of hymn (generally one-tenth the size of *Sahasranama*). *Aditya Hridayam*, *Devi Hridayam*, etc., are examples of *Hridayam stotras*.

5. Achara (conduct)

A mantra can be invoked by following any of the three types of *acahara*. *Dakishnachara* (the right-handed path), *Vamachara* (the left-handed path) and *Divyachara* (the divine path of moderation). Each *achara* represents a school of thought. All *sadhanas* in this book are as per *Dakishnachara* — the right-handed path.

6. Dharana (concentration)

With dedication and practice alone can anyone champion the art of concentration. Concentration is one of the most important factors of mindfulness. Without single-pointed concentration, any mantra chanting is of little use.

7. Divyadesh sevan (self-identification)

Divya desh literally means a divine region. There are 16 divine regions where mantra invocation becomes easier. Depending on whether a *sadhak* is performing inner or outer worship, an appropriate *divya desha* can be selected. Broadly, they are:

> *Vahni* (fire): Refers to worshipping in your manipura chakra (solar plexus) or lighting an *akhanda jyoti* (a constant lamp) throughout the duration of your *sadhana*. It also means to do your entire *sadhana* with *yajna* alone. So, there's no *japa* in this *sadhana*. Instead, with each mantra you chant, you make a fire offering.
>
> *Ambu* (water): It refers to worshipping in your *muladhara* chakra (root plexus) or doing your entire *sadhana* next to a water source like river, stream, lake or an ocean.
> *Linga*: It refers to meditating on *Shivalinga* or in some mantra *sadhanas*, *linga* refers to meditating on your *svadhishthana* chakra (sacral plexus).

8. Prana-kriya (breath regulation)

This refers to doing pranayama with your mantra.

9. Mudra (hand locks)

In mantra yoga, mudras refer to hand locks. Mudras are gestures performed to invoke the divine energy in you and to become one with your deity.

10. Tarpana (libations)

Tarpana are water offerings to your deity, ancestors, living beings around you and the subtle energies we are made of.

11. Havan (fire offerings)

Havan refers to fire offerings. Most mantra *sadhanas* require the *sadhaka* to perform *yajna* in the form of *havan* (fire offerings). I've listed the process of *havan* in relevant *sadhana* chapters in this book.

12. Bali (sacrifice)

To offer food that your deity demands is called *bali*. Various mantra *sadhanas* require different kinds of sacrifice. No matter what the nature of your *sadhana* or deity, *dakishnachara* (the right-handed path) and *divyachara* (the divine path) abiding by the principle of *ahimsa* strictly prohibit sacrifice of any living entity. Animal sacrifice of any nature is never done in mantra *sadhana*. Such sacrifices are done only in certain tantric rituals of the left-handed path. Even there, depending on your guru, initiation or the lineage, often, rather than sacrificing animals, flowers, fruits and other ingredients (like garlic, black beans, etc.) are offered. In mantra *sadhanas* that require inner worship, sacrifice refers to practicing certain austerities or never compromising on your principles. So, you may drop the urge to retaliate (sacrifice of ego) when provoked, for example.

13. Yaag (contemplation and inner worship)

Even if you are doing an external worship of the mantra, contemplation and inner worship remain an integral part of mantra *sadhana*. The more you meditate on your mantra or on the form of your deity, the more you identify with them. And, more identification invariably leads to acquiring the power of your object of worship.

14. Japa (chanting)

No mantra *sadhana* is complete without chanting. Chanting refers to repeated recall of your mantra.

15. Dhyana (meditation)

Meditation refers to meditating on the sound of your mantra (by recalling it mindfully) or meditating on the form of your deity (by repeated recollection of the form in your mind). It's important to know that merely chanting your mantra loud or staring at a picture or idol of your deity is not meditation but an act of concentration.

16. Samadhi (absorption)

True and correct mantra *sadhana* does lead to periods of deep absorption (*samadhi*). This has been my unfailing experience. The more intense your sadhana, the deeper and more long-lasting will be your *samadhi.*

VEDIC METERS (CHANDA)

All Vedic mantras that can be invoked will always have a meter. Here's a list of all the 26 Vedic meters.

1. Ukkatha
2. Atyukatha
3. Madhya
4. Pratishta
5. Supratistha
6. Gayatri
7. Ushnik
8. Anushtubh
9. Brihati
10. Pankit
11. Trishtubh
12. Jagati
13. Atijagati
14. Sharkari
15. Atisharkari
16. Ashti
17. Atyashti
18. Dhriti
19. Atidhriti
20. Kriti

21. Prakriti
22. Akriti
23. Vikrati
24. Satkriti
25. Atikriti and
26. Utkriti.

ARRANGEMENT OF POTS (PATRASADANA)

Patra means a vessel or a receptacle and *asadana* means to lay out. *Patrasadana* is the precise process of laying out various pots or vessels used in your pooja. Together, they are called *pancha patra* – five vessels used for various things and sixth is a saucer like small plate you use to put aside your offerings. These are usually small pots each one containing no more than 100 ml of water. In addition to this, a spoon (*achamani*) is used to take water from these pots and to put them in the saucer or your hand depending on the ritual you are performing.

The five pots (patras) are:

1. Water for purification (*Achamana*)

This vessel contains the water you use for your consumption throughout the pooja. When performing *achmana*, a bit of water is taken in your right palm using the spoon. Generally, *achmana* is done for purification and can be different for different *sadhanas*. For the four *sadhanas* listed in this book, I've clearly written wherever you need to take *achamana*. Other than drinking, in the beginning of any pooja, a bit of water is taken from this pot and sprinkled in the air to purify the environment and energies around you.

2. Plain water for offering (*arghya*)

From this vessel, you offer water to the deity of the mantra and his/her companion energies. When offering *arghya*, you take a bit of water from the *arghya* pot and put it in the small saucer/plate to collect this water. You can use the same spoon to offer water that you used to offer *achmana* or you can keep a separate spoon for this.

3. Fragrant water for offering (*Sugandhita arghaya*)

As part of the five, ten or sixteen offerings, fragrant water may be offered to the deity. If any particular *sadhana* requires a special kind of fragrance, I've listed it there. If nothing is specified, you can make the water fragrant by keeping a few petals of rose in it. Or by mixing it with sandalwood paste. You can also put a drop of any all-natural extract of any fragrant substance like flowers, etc. To understand the various types of offerings, you can refer to *Types of Offering (Upacharas)* in Detailed Notes.

4. Water for libations (*Tarpana*)

Water from this pot is used for offering libations to the deity, other energies and ancestors. There are many ways to do libations depending on the nature of the libation and your *sadhana*, but the simplest way is to chant the mantra for libation, take a bit of water using the spoon (you can use the same spoon as *achamana*) and put it back in the libation pot.

5. Water for washing (*Padyam*)

Every time an aspirant does *achamana* (drink water for purification), he's supposed to wash his hands. This is done using water from this pot, usually using a different spoon and not the same one as for *achamana*. A bit of water is taken in your right hand and the spoon is put back in the pot. Both hands are then rubbed on your left side using this little water for purification. Water from this pot is also used to offer *padyam* to the deity while making 10 or 16 offerings. Take a bit of water from this pot using a spoon and put it in the plate next to you.

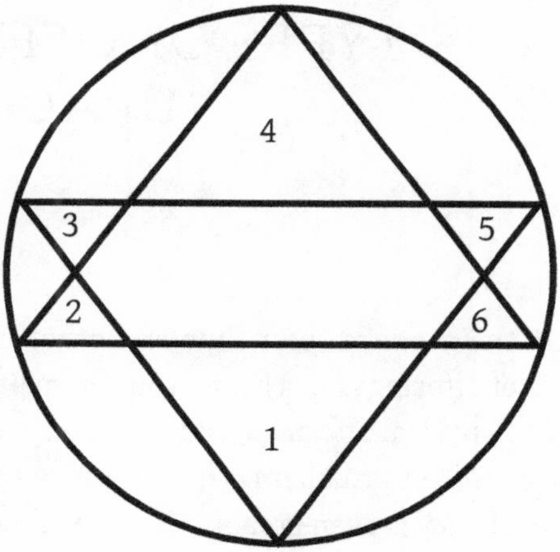

The sixth is a saucer. It's a little plate used to collect water. Please see the diagram above to understand the scriptural injunctions on how to lay out these pots in front of you.

TYPES OF OFFERINGS (UPACHARAS)

Depending on the availability of time and other resources there are many types of offerings (*upacharas*) you can make to your deity. In the absence of physical offerings, you can make mental offerings. Mental offering involves visualizing the substance and offering it to your deity. The efficacy is even great in the case of mental offerings. Regardless, whether you make mental or physical offerings, there are three different types of *upacharas* as follows:

Shodoshopchara

Shodosha means 16. *Shodoshopchara* involves making 16 different types of offerings. They are:

i. **Asanam** is to offer a seat to your deity. The literal meaning of *asana* is seat.
Mantra: *Om Asanam Samarpyami.*

ii. **Swagata Prashna** is to welcome the deity and enquire about their well-being.
Mantra: *Om Swagatam Karomi.*

iii. **Padyam** is to wash the feet of your deity out of reverence.
Mantra: *Om Padyam Samarpyami.*

iv. **Arghyam** is to offer respects befitting a guest. It can be in the form of doing full-length prostration or an equivalent gesture mentally.
Mantra: *Om Arghyam Samarpyami.*

v. **Achmanam** is to offer water to the deity.
Mantra: *Om Achamanam Samarpyami.*

vi. **Madhuparka** is a mixture of honey and milk or sometimes honey and clarified butter (ghee). After offering water to the deity, *madhuparka* is offered.
Mantra: *Om Madhuparkam Samarpyami.*

vii. **Achmanam.** Fresh water is offered again to the deity.
Mantra: *Om Achmanam Samarpyami.*

viii. **Snanam.** Once again water is offered to deity for purification. *Snanam* literally means bathing. In *shodoshopchara*, it means offering water for cleansing. For example, visualizing that your deity just had something sweet and then water afterwards, he/she may want to wash their hands or take a bath to freshen up altogether.
Mantra: *Om Snanam Samarpyami.*

ix. **Vastram** refers to offering clothing. Generally, it's done by offering a red sacred thread (*mauli*) that's usually tied on the wrist, at your altar, or even the white sacred thread (*yajnopaveet* or *janeyu*) that's worn around the shoulder touching the waist. In more elaborate rituals, you may offer an actual piece of cloth or saree at your altar. At the end of the pooja, usually it's taken home by the Brahmin or the priest conducting the rituals. Or, if you are performing them yourself, you can offer it to anyone you deem fit. Ideally, that person should be of noble conduct or at least, believe in your deity as much as you do.
Mantra: *Om Vastram Samarpyami.*

x. **Alamkara** refers to jewelry or accessories. You may offer anything made from silver, gold or any of the stones like

diamond, emerald, red coral, opal, etc. This is done as per your financial capacity. Once again, at the end of the pooja, you may offer it to anyone you deem fit or if a priest conducted your pooja, he may take it with him.
Mantra: *Om Alamkaram Samarpyami.*

xi. **Gandham** is to offer a fragrant substance to the deity. It could be in the form of sandalwood paste, perfume (concentrated or mixed with water) or any other fragrant substance. In South India, *gandham* also means sectarial mark on the forehead. In the context of mantra *sadhana*, though, *gandham* means fragrant substance. There are 10 types of fragrant substances that can be offered.

1. **Ishta** (इष्ट): When the fragrance of a substance is desirable and evokes pleasant emotions, it's called *ishta.* Any substance particularly pleasing to the deity is also called *ishta.* The scent of Jasmine or Mogra is *ishta gandham* in Devi pooja, while the scent of sandalwood is particularly *ishta* in Deva pooja.
2. **Anishta** (अनिष्ट)*: Anishta* is the opposite of ishta. It means undesirable, unpleasant or displeasing to the deity. It can change from *sadhana* to *sadhana*, but broadly, smells from all stale or rotting substances are classified as *anishta gandham.* When a *gandham* has already been offered in another pooja, it becomes unfit for offering again.
3. **Madhur** (मधुर): *Madhur* means sweet. A substance offering sweet smell is *madhur gandham.* Rose, for example, has a sweet smell.
4. **Katu**(कटु): The literal meaning of *katu* is bitter. *Katu gandham* is when the offering has a bitter smell. It is used in many tantric *sadhanas.*
5. **Nirharin** (निर्हारिन्): *Nirharin* means diffusively fragrant. The scent of camphor is *nirharin.*

6. **Samhata (संहत):** *Samhat* means complex or compound. Any offering whose smell is difficult to classify or is an amalgamation of many types of smells, it is known to be *samhata gandham*. In my experience, many lotuses, most notably, Brahma kamal and Neel kamal (found in the high regions of the Himalayas) have *samhata* fragrance.
7. **Snigdha (स्नग्धि):** *Snigdha* means tender, soft, agreeable. Nargis flower, a kind of daffodil, has *snigdha* fragrance.
8. **Ruksha (रूक्ष):** *Ruksha* means rough, dry, arid and dreary. *Gandham* offered with cowdung or *guggal* is called *ruksha gandham*.
9. **Vishad (विशद):** *Vishad* means spelndid, beautiful, soft and brilliant. The smell of musk will be *vishad gandham*.
10. **Amla (अम्ल):** *Amla* means sour or acidic. Any fragrance made by fermenting fruits is *amla gandham*. Any offering containing alcohol, wine or other fermented drinks will be called *amla gandham*.

Mantra: *Om Gandham Samarpyami*

xi. **Pushpam** means flower. *Pushpan* is an offering of fresh flowers to your deity. You may offer only petals, a complete flower or many flowers.
Mantra: *Om Pushpam Samarpyami.*

xii. **Dhoopam** means incense. After *pushpam*, incense is offered to the deity.
Mantra: *Om Dhoopam Samarpyami.*

xiii. **Deepam** is lamp. The light of a lamp is shown to the deity. What kind of lamp is lit in your *sadhana* depends on the nature of the *sadhana*. I've covered this in greater detail in the chapter on direction and lamps.
Mantra: *Om Deepam Samarpyami.*

xiv. **Naivadyam** means an offering of eatables presented to a deity. You can offer a plateful of assorted items or just fruits, dry fruits or anything edible at all that you can afford. Even a grain of rice or natural sugar is good enough.
Mantra: *Om Naivadyam Samarpyami.*

xv. **Namaskaram** is paying your respects. You can fold your hands as in 'Namaste' gesture.
Mantra: *Om Namaskaram Karomi.*

Dashopchara (Ten Offerings)

i. Padyam (Washing of the feet)
ii. Arghyam (Water offering for washing hands and all)
iii. Achamanam (Fresh water for drinking)
iv. Madhuparka (Honey and milk offering)
v. Snanam (Bathing)
vi. Gandham (Perfume or scented water)
vii. Pushpam (Flower or flowers)
viii. Dhoopam (Incense)
ix. Deepam (Lamp)
x. Naivadyam (Meal offering)

Panchopchara (Five Offerings)

i. Gandham (Perfume or scented water)
ii. Pushpam (Flower or flowers)
iii. Dhoopam (Incense)
iv. Deepam (Lamp)
v. Naivadyam (Meal offering)

The mantra to be chanted in the case of five or ten offerings are the same as in 16 offerings. I've specified the mantra you can chant after explaining each offering. Please note that chanting of the mantra is optional after making an offering. You can simply just offer. Chanting that mantra brings about better mindfulness though.

In some sects or lineages, these sixteen, ten or five offerings may differ. Some offer, *tambula* (paan or betel leaves) and *poongi-phala* (*supari*) in *panchopchara*, for example.

If your guru has instructed you to make certain offerings, stick to that. If you don't have a guru but the *sadhana* you are doing is clear about what offerings to make, follow that. If, however, they both are quiet about it, you can make standard offerings as stated above in this chapter.

MANTRA COMPATIBILITY

In the chapter, 'Correcting Flaws in Your Mantra', I shared the most important and common method. There are many more available. Out of those, here are the top two. You don't have to use all three methods (one covered in the chapter and four here). You can use just any one of these.

Zodiac Compatibility

In zodiac compatibility, the efficacy of the mantra is tested based on the 12 signs in the zodiac. If the mantra is compatible with the zodiac sign of the aspirant, invoking such a mantra will be beneficial to the *sadhak*. To check zodiac compatibility, please see the table below:

	Sign	*Assigned Letters of the Alphabet*
1	Aries (Mesha)	a, ā, i, I
2	Tauras (Vrisha)	u, U, hR
3	Gemini (Mithuna)	hR, lr
4	Cancer (Karka)	e, ai
5	Leo (Simha)	o, ou
6	Virgo (Kanya)	am, ah, sh, Sh, sa, ha, Ksha
7	Libra (Tula)	ka, kha, ga, gha, ṅa
8	Scorpio (Vrishchik)	ca, cha, ja, jha, ña

	Sign	Assigned Letters of the Alphabet
9	Sagitarius (Dhanu)	ṭa, ṭha, ḍa, ḍha, ṇa
10	Capricorn (Makara)	ta, tha, da, dha, na
11	Aquarius (Kumbha)	pa, pha, ba, bha, ma
12	Piesces (Meena)	ya, ra, la, va

How to ascertain compatibility

1. From the table above, ascertain your sign based on first letter of your name.
2. Now, ascertain the sign of your mantra based on the first letter of the mantra.
3. If the mantra sign is the same as your sign, you'll receive great benefit from chanting this mantra.
4. If it falls on the 5th or 9th then the mantra is still beneficial.
5. When mantra sign is 2nd, 6th or 10th from your sign, the mantra is going to benefit you by creating favorable circumstances.
6. When mantra falls 3rd, 7th or 11th from your sign, it'll bestow inner strength upon you.
7. If the mantra sign is 6th from your sign, the mantra is not going to be beneficial to you.
8. If it falls on the 8th or the 12th position from your sign, this mantra should be avoided at all costs as it will only create more difficulties on the path.

   To calculate the position of the mantra sign from your sign, you must begin counting from your sign. For example, if your sign is Aries and you want to calculate 6th sign from Aries, it'll be Virgo, from Libra the 8th sign will be Tauras and so on.

TABLE – 1

Zodiac sign		Assigned Letters
Aries (Mesha)	अ, ल, ई	a, la, ī
Tauras (Vrisha)	ब, व, ऊ	ba, va, ū

Zodiac sign	Assigned Letters	
Gemini (Mithuna)	क, छ, घ	ka, cha, gha
Cancer (Karka)	ड, ह	ḍa, ha
Leo (Simha)	म, ट	ma, ṭa
Virgo (Kanya)	प, ठ, ण	pa, ṭha, ṇa
Libra (Tula)	र, त	ra, ta
Scorpio (Vrishchik)	न, य	na, ya
Sagitarius (Dhanu)	भ, ध, फ, ढ	bha, dha, pha, ḍha
Capricorn (Makara)	ख, ज	kha, ja
Aquarius (Kumbha)	ग, स, श, ष	ga, sa, śa, ṣa
Piesces (Meena)	द, च, थ, झ	da, ca, tha, jha

It is important to note that the zodiac table given above is not the standard way of ascertaining signs in astrology. While you don't require it on the path of mantra yoga, for your reference and knowledge, I'm also sharing with you the two standard ways of ascertaining your moon sign based on your name. While sun sign is based on the placement of the sun, moon sign, as the name implies, is based on the movement of the moon in the zodiac. The letters assigned to each moon sign vary from region to region in India, but broadly they are done in two different ways. As follows:

TABLE – 2

Zodiac sign	Assigned Letters	
Aries (Mesha)	चू , चे , चो , ला , ली , लू , लो , अ	cū , ce , co , lā , lī , lū , lo , a
Tauras (Vrisha)	इ, उ , ए , ओ , वा , वी , वू , वे , वो	i, u , e , o , vā , vī , vū , ve , vo
Gemini (Mithuna)	का, की, कु , के, को, घ , ड़ , छ , हा	kā, kī, ku , ke, ko, gha , ḍa , cha , hā

Zodiac sign	*Assigned Letters*	
Cancer (Karka)	ही, हू , हे , हो, डा,डी , डू , डे , डो	hī, hū , he , ho, ḍā,ḍī , ḍū , ḍe , ḍo
Leo (Simha)	मा , मी, मू , में, मो, टा , टी, टू , टे	mā , mī, ma ū , meṃ, mo, ṭā , ṭī, ṭū , ṭe
Virgo (Kanya)	टो , पा , पी, पू , पे, पो, ष , ण , ठ	ṭo , pā , pī, pū , pe, po, ṣa , ṇa , ṭha
Libra (Tula)	रा , री, रू, रे, रो, ता, ती , तू , ते	rā , rī, rū, re, ro, tā, tī , tū , te
Scorpio (Vrishchik)	तो, ना, नी, नू, ने, नो, या यी, यू	to, nā, nī, nū, ne, no, yā yī, yū
Sagitarius (Dhanu)	ये, यो , भा , भी , भू, भे, फा , ढा , ध	ye, yo , bhā , bhī , bhū, bhe, phā , ḍhā , dha
Capricorn (Makara)	भो, जा, जी , खा, खी, खू , खो, गा, गी	bho, jā, jī , khā, khī, khū , kho, gā, gī
Aquarius (Kumbha)	गू , गे, गो , दा, सा , सी , सू , से, सो	gū , ge, go , dā, sā , sī , sū , se, so
Piesces (Meena)	दी, दू , दे, दो, चा, ची, थ, झ, त्र	dee, doo, de, do, cha, chee, tha, jha, tra

If you ever need to ascertain your zodiac sign based on your name, you could use either of the two charts above. Personally, throughout my years of practice in astrology, I used the second table. Western astrology predominantly focuses on sun signs. That is a sign based on the movement of the sun in the zodiac. For example, anyone born between Mar 21 – Apr 19 will have the sign Aries; between Apr 20 – May 20, Tauras; between May 21 – Jun 20, Gemini and so on.

Indian system of astrology, however, also places a great deal of emphasis on moon signs. That is a sign based on the first letter of your name. Astrology recommends that a person should be named based on the placement of moon in their horoscope for maximum compatibility with the cosmic energy around.

There are 27 asterisms (*nakshatras*). Roughly 2.25 asterisms make up one sign. Each asterism has certain letters assigned to them. At the time a person is born, the position of moon in a certain asterism determines the zodiac sign the moon is in. That becomes the moon sign which further becomes the basis of finding out what the first letter of your name should be. The second table above is more popular among astrologers (particularly in North India).

Creditor-Debtor Method (Rinni-dhani chakra)

The path of mantra yoga believes that our relationship with mantra is not just from one lifetime but many. If you have accumulated the energy of a mantra from your previous life and not used it, the mantra is said to be your debtor. The mantra owes you. Chanting a debtor mantra is more beneficial because you already start with a base. It brings quicker results. If you got initiated into a mantra in your past life and utilized its power without accumulating it by chanting or invoking it then the mantra is your creditor. You owe the mantra. Therefore, in this lifetime when you chant that mantra, the first major chunk will not yield any results because a debt is owed.

You may wonder how you can use the energy of a mantra without accumulating it first. Well, that's the power of initiation. Initiation is like a credit card. You have a certain privilege to draw upon something you haven't earned yet but you have to pay it back.

When even after sincere performance of the rites of invocation, you still don't get results from your mantra, your guru may recommend that the mantra be checked for debtor-creditor compatibility. If you don't have a guru, or have a guru who is not an expert in the science of mantras, you may then ascertain your debtor-creditor relationship with the mantra using the following method.

DEBTOR-CREDITOR TABLE

Vowels (*matrika* or swara)										
6	6	6	0	3	4	4	0	0	0	3
a ā	i I	u U	hr hR	lr lR	e	ai	o	ou	am	ah
Consonants (*vyanjana*)										
2	2	5	0	0	2	1	0	4	4	1
ka	kha	ga	gha	ṅa	Ca	cha	ja	jha	ña	ṭa
ṭh	ḍa	ḍha	ṇa	Ta	tha	da	dha	na	pa	pha
ba	bha	ma	ya	Ra	La	va	sh	Sh	sa	ha

The table above is divided into two parts: vowels and consonants. Each vowel or a consonant has a score. Please note that in vowels, you have hr, hR, lr and lR. They don't sound like traditional vowels as in the English language but in Sanskrit they are called swara or matrika. For the purposes of this exercises, consider them as vowels. Here's how to calculate if the mantra is your debtor or creditor.

1. Add the score of the vowels and consonants in your name.
2. Divide the total by 8 and note down the remainder. (If the divisor is less than 8 then simply take that number)
3. Now, add the score of the vowels and consonants of the mantra.
4. Divide the total by 8 and note down the remainder.

If the mantra scores more than your name, it means that the mantra is your debtor. Chanting such a mantra has heightened your chances of success. If the score of the mantra is the same as your name's score, the mantra is still beneficial as whatever you'll chant will get accumulated in your energy account. If, however, the score of the mantra is lower than your name's score, it means the mantra is your creditor. You owe the mantra from an earlier time. It may take long before you'll see any benefits from such mantra.

For example, a person by the name of Jay Sharma wants to chant the mantra *Om gam gaṇapatayae namah*. This is how to calculate:

Name score will be J + a + y + Sh + a + r + m + a which according to the table above becomes 0 + 6 + 0 + 0 + 6 + 0 + 5 + 6 = 23. Dividing it by 8 gives us the remainder 7.

Mantra score will be O + m + G + am + ga + ṇa + pa + ta + y + e + na + ma + ah which according to the table above becomes 0 + 5 + 5 + 5 + 0 + 4 + 0 + 0 + 4 + 4 + 5 + 3 = 35. Dividing it by 8 leaves a remainder of 3.

The mantra score of 3 is less than the name score of 7. This means that this mantra won't be beneficial to the practitioner or it may take a long time before the aspirant will attain mantra siddhi.

I would like to remind you here that none of these compatibility considerations are necessary when a mantra falls under exceptions (as per the chapter on exceptions) or if you are initiated into a mantra and your guru foregoes compatibility calculations.

Other less frequently used methods are a-ka-da-ma method, a-ka-tha-ha method and asterism compatibility. In a-ka-da-ma method, the letters of the mantra and your name are matched for compatibility. It's called a-ka-da-ma because the arrangement of the letters begins with the letters a, ka, da and ma. The same goes for a-ka-tha-ha method, the only difference is that the letters are arranged beginning with a-ka-tha-ha.

FURTHER READING

Much of this book is based on my personal experiences. Theoretical exposition is mostly my own but majority of the base concepts are traditional and time-honored views of remarkable sages who existed before me. Therefore, if you wish to read more on the mantra sadhana, you can check out the following texts that I grew up reading. With a bit of research, you should be able to get your hands on good translations. I know that Hindi translations must be available for most of these books and English translation only for some. This is not your standard bibliography with publishers and translators, for I don't have much of that information. Nevertheless, I'm sharing with you the names of various books you can read to know more about mantra yoga. In particular, I would like to acknowledge the translation of *Mantra Maharnava* by Ram Kumar Rai, *Mantra Rahasya* by Narayandutt Shrimali, and most importantly the excellent transation of *Lakshmi Tantra* by Sanjukta Gupta. Here's the list. With a bit of research, you should be able to get your hands on these. Translated or other texts.

1. *Mantra Maharnava*, Devata Khand.
2. *Mantra Maharnava*, Devi Khand
3. *Mantra Maharnava*, Mishra Khand.
4. *Mantra Mahodhadhi*
5. *Narada Panchratra*

6. *Lakshmi Tantra* (Original Sanskrit text + Sanjukta Gupta translation)
7. *Mantra Yoga Samhita* (Omprakash Khushwaha Translation)
8. *Mantra Rahasya by Narayan Dutt Shrimali*
9. *Tantra Raj Tantra* (Kapildev Narayan Translation)
10. *Mudra Vigyana*
11. *Rudrayamalam*
12. *Vigyan Bhairava Tantra*
13. *Nandikeshvara Tantra*
14. *Srividya Tantra, Charya khand*

CPSIA information can be obtained
at www.ICGtesting.com
Printed in the USA
LVHW111307130123
736976LV00003B/89

9 789386 34871